NAG HAMMADI,
GNOSTICISM,
& EARLY CHRISTIANITY

NAG HAMMADI, GNOSTICISM, & EARLY CHRISTIANITY

Contributors

Harold W. Attridge
Stephen Gero
Charles W. Hedrick
Helmut Koester
Bentley Layton
George W. MacRae †
Elaine H. Pagels

Douglas M. Parrott
Birger A. Pearson
Pheme Perkins
James M. Robinson
Hans-Martin Schenke
John D. Turner
Frederik Wisse

Edited by

Charles W. Hedrick and Robert Hodgson, Jr.

HENDRICKSON
PUBLISHERS
PEABODY, MASSACHUSETTS 01961-3473

Excerpts in chapter 7 from: *Soziologie des Urchristentums* by G. Theis-sen. Copyright © 1979 by J. C. B. Mohr. *Trajectories through Early Chris-tianity* by J. M. Robinson and H. Koester, Copyright © 1968 by Fortress. *The Gospel of Thomas and Christian Wisdom* by S. L. Davies. Copyright © 1983 by Seabury. *Sayings of the Risen Jesus: Christian Prophecy in the Synoptic Tradition* by M. E. Boring. Copyright © 1982 by Cambridge University Press. *The Other Gospels: Non-Canonical Gospel Texts* by R. Cameron ed. Copyright © 1982 by Westminster. *Le Origini dello Gnos-ticismo: Colloquio di Messina 13–18 Aprile 1966* by U. Bianchi, ed. Copyright © 1970 by E. J. Brill. *Studies in Gnosticism and Hellenistic Religions Presented to Gilles Quispel on the Occasion of his 65th Birth-day* by R. van den Broek and M. J. Vermaseren eds. Copyright © 1981 by E. J. Brill. Used by permission.

The cover reproduces page 84 of Nag Hammadi Codex VII, showing the colophon of the *Apocalypse of Peter* (NHC VII, 3) and the prescript title of the *Teachings of Silvanus* (NHC VII, 4). Silvanus is also mentioned in the New Testament as a companion of Paul (2 Cor 1:19; 1 Thess 1:1) and the scribe of Peter (1 Pet 5:12).

George W. MacRae, S. J.
1928–1985
In Memoriam

TABLE OF CONTENTS

ABOUT THE EDITORS

Charles W. Hedrick was awarded the Ph.D. from Claremont Graduate School in 1977. His dissertation under James M. Robinson, a literary and source analysis of the *Apocalypse of Adam*, was published by Scholars Press in 1980. Since receiving his degree, his academic interests have led him to Southwest Missouri State University, where he has served as an Associate Professor of Religious Studies since 1983.

Dr. Hedrick's publications include articles in the *Journal of Biblical Literature, New Testament Studies,* and *Novum Testamentum.* A major contributor to the understanding of gnosticism, Dr. Hedrick is the volume editor of Nag Hammadi Codices XI, XII, and XIII, and is currently working on NHC VIII. Other projects range from a translation of a 16th century French commentary on the Gospel of Mark to involvement in professional societies such as the Society of Biblical Literature, Studiorum Novi Testamenti Societas, and the International Association for Coptic Studies.

Outside of academic circles Dr. Hedrick has been a minister, a deputy probation officer (for Los Angeles county), and he is currently serving as a chaplain in the Army Reserve.

Robert Hodgson, Jr. graduated with honors from Heidelberg University in 1976. He holds an undergraduate degree in philosophy from Gonzaga University (1965) and a master's degree in theology from Marquette University (1970).

From 1977 to 1980 he served as an appointed missionary to St. Andrew's Theological Seminary and the Southeast Asian Graduate School of Theology in Manila, Republic of the Philippines. During this period he was executive secretary to the Anglican-Roman Catholic Dialogue of the Philippines.

His doctoral dissertation, entitled "Die Quellen der paulinischen Ethik," was written under Erich Dinkler. He has contributed articles to the *Anchor Bible Dictionary,* the *Journal of Biblical Literature, Zeitschrift für die neutestamentliche Wissenschaft,* and *Biblica.*

PREFACE

This book includes thirteen papers circulated and discussed at the 1983 Springfield, Missouri Working Seminar on Gnosticism and Early Christianity. The Springfield Seminar, in session from March 30 to April 2, 1983, followed in the tradition of conferences held at Messina, Italy; New Haven, Connecticut; Stockholm, Sweden; and Montreal, Canada. It differed from these earlier conferences because it was the first to concentrate exclusively on the relationship between gnosticism and early Christianity.

Each contributor is an internationally recognized scholar in the disciplines of gnosticism, New Testament studies, and early church history. Each received the general charge from the editors to prepare a paper that would represent the cutting edge of current research and would stimulate further exploration of the literary, historical, and theological bonds between gnosticism and early Christianity. The choice of the specific topic fell to the individual scholar. The reader will note, however, that a common thread runs through all the papers: the investigation of the recently discovered (1945) Nag Hammadi Library with its fifty-one tractates. By gathering the papers under three headings (Non-Christian Gnosticism; Gnosticism, the New Testament, and Early Christianity; Gnosticism and the Early Church) the editors have identified for the reader the scope of the Working Seminar and the general direction of ongoing research as well.

The book acquaints the beginner with the topic of gnosticism and early Christianity and presents to the specialist some of the new frontiers their colleagues are exploring. For the beginner there is a concise introduction to gnosticism. It covers the issues of origin, literature, leading ideas, and possible links with early Christianity. Each contributor has prepared a preface to his or her paper that points to its salient features and explains how the essay fits into the overall subject of the book.

The editors have prepared an Abbreviations and Short Titles List for the bibliographical entries in the footnotes to each paper. The List can also serve the reader as a basic bibliography for the subject of gnosticism and early Christianity. The editors have also provided the selective indices to ancient texts and modern authors.

The editors have held to the original text and spirit of the working papers as far as possible. They have standardized grammar, spelling, and style in each paper but not among papers. Thus, for example, one author may capitalize "gnosticism," while another does not. A desire for clarity and correct usage has guided all editorial changes. Although each contributor has verified the accuracy of footnotes and bibliographical entries, readers are encouraged to communicate lapses to the editors.

Heartfelt thanks are due to a long list of individuals and institutions for the success of the Working Seminar and the publication of the book: The National Endowment for the Humanities; Hendrickson Publishers; the former President and Provost of Southwest Missouri State University, Drs. Duane Meyer and Robert Gilmore, respectively; the former Dean of the College of Arts and Humanities, Dr. Holt Spicer; Media Productions at Southwest Missouri State University, particularly Pat Gosley and Gary Ellis; The Chamber of Commerce and the Hilton Inn of Springfield, Missouri.

Thanks also go to Drs. Gerit J. tenZythoff and Stanley Burgess for help in drafting the original grant proposal to the National Endowment for the Humanities. JoAnne Brown provided efficient and cheerful logistical support. Patrick H. Alexander of Hendrickson Publishers copyedited the manuscript and drew up the biographical sketches.

Finally, the editors and contributors wish to temper the loss of their friend and colleague, George W. MacRae, S. J. by dedicating this book to his memory. His sudden death on September 6, 1985 robbed the academy and the church of a genial scholar whose life's work indeed redounded *ad maiorem Dei gloriam*.

Robert Hodgson, Jr.

ABBREVIATIONS AND SHORT TITLES

I. Abbreviations of Biblical Books and Related Texts

a. OLD TESTAMENT

Gen	Genesis	Ps	Psalms
Exod	Exodus	Prov	Proverbs
Num	Numbers	Isa	Isaiah
Deut	Deuteronomy	Jer	Jeremiah
1 Kgs	1 Kings	Ezek	Ezekiel

b. NEW TESTAMENT

Matt	Matthew	1 Thess	1 Thessalonians
Rom	Romans	2 Thess	2 Thessalonians
1 Cor	1 Corinthians	1 Tim	1 Timothy
2 Cor	2 Corinthians	2 Tim	2 Timothy
Gal	Galatians	1 Pet	1 Peter
Eph	Ephesians	2 Pet	2 Peter
Phil	Philippians	Rev	Revelation
Col	Colossians		

c. APOCRYPHA, PSEUDEPIGRAPHA, QUMRAN TEXTS, MISHNA, TARGUMIC MATERIAL AND EARLY PATRISTIC WRITINGS

Adam and Eve	Books of Adam and Eve	1QSb	Appendix B (Blessings) to 1QS
Apoc. Mos.	Apocalypse of Moses		
CD	Cairo Damascus Document	4 QTestim	Testimonia text from Qumran Cave 4
2 Clem.	2 Clement		
Did.	Didache	m. Sanh.	Mishna Sanhedrin
2 Enoch	Slavonic Enoch	Sir	Sirach
2 Esdr	2 Esdras	Test. Adam	Testament of Adam
Jub.	Jubilees	Tg. Ps.-J	Targum Pseudo-Jonathan
Mid. Gen. Rab.	Midrash Genesis Rabbah		
Odes Sol.	Odes of Solomon	T. Judah	Testament of Judah
1QM	War Scroll	T. Levi	Testament of Levi
1QS	Manual of Discipline	T. Reub.	Testament of Reuben
		Wis	Wisdom of Solomon

d. Coptic Gnostic Tractates

I,1	The Prayer of the Apostle Paul	Pr. Paul
I,2	The Apocryphon of James	Ap. Jas.
I,3	The Gospel of Truth	Gos. Truth
I,4	The Treatise on the Resurrection	Treat. Res.
I,5	The Tripartite Tractate	Tri. Trac.
II,1	The Apocryphon of John	Ap. John
II,2	The Gospel of Thomas	Gos. Thom.
II,3	The Gospel of Philip	Gos. Phil.
II,4	The Hypostasis of the Archons	Hyp. Arch.
II,5	On the Origin of the World	Orig. World
II,6	The Exegesis on the Soul	Exeg. Soul
II,7	The Book of Thomas the Contender	Thom. Cont.
III,1	The Apocryphon of John	Ap. John
III,2	The Gospel of the Egyptians	Gos. Eg.
III,3	Eugnostos	Eugnostos
III,4	The Sophia of Jesus Christ	Soph. Jes. Chr.
III,5	The Dialogue of the Savior	Dial. Sav.
IV,1	The Apocryphon of John	Ap. John
IV,2	The Gospel of the Egyptians	Gos. Eg.
V,1	Eugnostos	Eugnostos
V,2	The Apocalypse of Paul	Apoc. Paul
V,3	The (First) Apocalypse of James	1 Apoc. Jas
V,4	The (Second) Apocalypse of James	2 Apoc. Jas.
V,5	The Apocalypse of Adam	Apoc. Adam
VI,1	The Acts of Peter and the Twelve Apostles	Acts Pet. 12 Apost.
VI,2	The Thunder: Perfect Mind	Thund.
VI,3	Authoritative Teaching	Auth. Teach.
VI,4	The Concept of our Great Power	Great Pow.
VI,5	Plato, Republic 588b–589b	Plato Rep.
VI,6	The Discourse on the Eighth and Ninth	Disc. 8–9
VI,7	The Prayer of Thanksgiving	Pr. Thanks.
VI,8	Asclepius 21–29	Asclepius
VII,1	The Paraphrase of Shem	Paraph. Shem
VII,2	The Second Treatise of the Great Seth	Treat. Seth
VII,3	The Apocalypse of Peter	Apoc. Pet.
VII,4	The Teachings of Silvanus	Teach. Silv.
VII,5	The Three Steles of Seth	Steles Seth
VIII,1	Zostrianos	Zost.
VIII,2	The Letter of Peter to Philip	Ep. Pet. Phil.
IX,1	Melchizedek	Melch.
IX,2	The Thought of Norea	Norea
IX,3	The Testimony of Truth	Testim. Truth
X	Marsanes	Marsanes
XI,1	The Interpretation of Knowledge	Interp. Know.
XI,2	A Valentinian Exposition	Val. Exp.
XI,2a	On the Anointing	On Anoint.
XI,2b	On Baptism A	On Bap. A
XI,2c	On Baptism B	On Bap. B

XI,2d	On the Eucharist A	On Euch. A
XI,2e	On the Eucharist B	On Euch. B
XI,3	Allogenes	Allogenes
XI,4	Hypsiphrone	Hypsiph.
XII,1	The Sentences of Sextus	Sent. Sextus
XII,2	The Gospel of Truth	Gos. Truth
XII,3	Fragments	Frm.
XIII,1	Trimorphic Protennoia	Trim. Prot.
XIII,2	On the Origin of the World	Orig. World
BG,1	The Gospel of Mary	Gos. Mary
BG,2	The Apocryphon of John	Ap. John
BG,3	The Sophia of Jesus Christ	Soph. Jes. Chr.
BG,4	The Act of Peter	Act Pet.

e. OTHER ABBREVIATIONS

ad loc.	ad locum, at the place	LXX	Septuagint
B.C.E.	Before the Common Era (=B.C.)	MS	manuscript
BG	Papyrus Berolinensis Gnosticus	MT	Masoretic Text
ca.	circa, around	n.	note
C.E.	Common Era (=A.D.)	NT	New Testament
cf.	confer, compare	OT	Old Testament
ch(s).	chapter(s)	par.	parallel(s)
col(s).	column(s)	pl.	plate(s)
cont.	continued	plu.	plural
e.g.	exempli gratia, for example	P. Oxy.	Papyrus Oxyrhynchus
esp.	especially	p(p).	page(s)
ET	English translation	sc.	scilicet, namely
et al.	et alii, and others	seq.	et sequentia,
f(f).	and following		and following
fem.	feminine	sg.	singular
ibid.	ibidem, in the same place	s.v.	sub verbo, under
id.	idem, the same		the word
i.e.	id est, that is	vol(s).	volume(s)
no(s).	number(s)	vs.	versus, contrary to
		vs(s)	verse(s)

II. Short Titles

AB   Anchor Bible

Abbeloos-Lamy, Chronicon   Abbeloos, J. B. and Lamy, Th. J., eds. Gregorii Barhebraei chronicon ecclesiasticum. 3 vols. Louvain: Peeters, 1872–77.

Abramowski, "Eunomios"   Abramowski, L. "Eunomios," RAC 6 (1966) cols. 936–47.

Abu al-Barakât, Lampe des ténèbres   Abu al-Barakât ibn Kabar. Livre de la lampe des ténèbres, et de l'exposition lumineuse du service de l'église. Edited and translated by L. Villecourt. PO 20. Paris: Firmin-Didot, 1929, 579–733.

AcOr   *Acta Orientalia*

AKG   Arbeiten zur Kirchengeschichte

Akinian, *Kanones*   Akinian, P. N., ed. *Die Kanones der Synode von Schahapiwan*. Wien: Mechitharisten-Drückerei, 1953.

Akinian, *Koriwn*   Akinian, P. N., ed. *Koriwn, Biographie des hl. Maštoç*. 2nd ed. Wien: Mechitharisten-Drückerei, 1952.

Aland, *Gnosis*   Aland, B., ed. *Gnosis: Festschrift für Hans Jonas*. Göttingen: Vandenhoeck & Ruprecht, 1978.

Aland, "Herakleon"   Aland, B. "Erwählungstheologie und Menschenklassenlehre. Die Theologie des Herakleon als Schlüssel zum Verständnis der christlichen Gnosis?" in M. Krause, ed. *Seventh Conference on Patristic Studies*, 148–81.

Albinus, *Did.*   *Didaskalikos*

Altaner-Stuiber, *Patrologie*   Altaner, B. and Stuiber, A. *Patrologie*. 7th ed. Freiburg: Herder, 1966.

Altheim-Stiehl, *Araber*   Altheim, Fr. and Stiehl, R., eds, *Die Araber in der Alten Welt*. 7 vols. Berlin: de Gruyter, 1965.

AnBib   Analecta biblica

ANET   J. B. Pritchard (ed.), *Ancient Near Eastern Texts*.

ANF   The Ante-Nicene Fathers

ANRW   Aufstieg und Niedergang der römischen Welt

AP   *Anthologia Palatina*

APl   Planudean Appendix

Arai, *Christologie*   Arai, S. *Die Christologie des Evangelium Veritatis: Eine religionsgeschichtliche Untersuchung*. Leiden: Brill, 1964.

Arai, "Christologie"   Arai, S. "Zur Christologie des Apokryphons des Johannes." *NTS* 15 (1969) 302–18.

Aristot. *Metaph.*   Aristotle, *Metaphysica*

Aristotle, Po   Aristotle, *Poetica*

Armstrong, "Gnosis"   Armstrong, A. H. "Gnosis and Greek Philosophy" in Aland, *Gnosis*, 87–124.

Asatir   Gaster, M. *The Asatir. The Samaritan Book of the Secrets of Moses*. Oriental Translation Fund, New Series 26. London: Royal Asiatic Society, 1927.

Athenaeus, *Deipnosophistai*

Attridge-MacRae, "Gospel of Truth"   Attridge, H. W. and MacRae, G. W. "The Gospel of Truth" in Attridge, *Nag Hammadi Codex I*, 55–81.

Attridge, *Nag Hammadi Codex I*   Attridge, H. W., ed. *Nag Hammadi Codex I (The Jung Codex)*. 2 vols. NHS 22–23. Leiden: Brill, 1985.

Attridge-Oden, *Philo*   Attridge, H. W. and Oden, R. A. *Philo of Byblos: The Phoenician History*. CBQMS 9. Washington: CBA, 1981.

Attridge-Pagels, "Tripartite Tractate"   Attridge, H. W. and Pagels, E. "The Tripartite Tractate" in Attridge, *Nag Hammadi Codex I*, 159–90.

Augustine, *De haeresibus*   Augustine. *De haeresibus*. CC, series latina 46. Turnhout: Brepols, 1969.

Bammel, "Q"   Bammel, E. "Das Ende von Q" in Böcher-Haacker, *Verborum Veritas*, 39–50.

Barc, *Colloque*   Barc, B., ed. *Colloque International sur les Textes de Nag Hammadi*. Québec: Université Laval, 1981.

Barc, *L'Hypostase*   Barc, B., ed. *L'Hypostase des Archontes: Traité gnostique sur l'origine de l'homme, du monde et des archontes NH II.4*. BCNH, Section Études 1. Québec: Université Laval; Louvain: Peeters, 1981.

Barc, "Samaèl"   Barc, B. "Samaèl-Saklas-Yaldabaôth: Recherche sur la genèse d'un mythe gnostique" in Barc, *Colloque*, 123–50.
Bardy, "Borboriens"   Bardy, G. "Borboriens." *DHGE* 9 (1937) 1778–79.
Barnes-Browne-Shelton, *Cartonnage*   Barnes, J. W. B.; Browne, G. M.; and Shelton, J. C., eds. *Nag Hammadi Codices: Greek and Coptic Papyri from the Cartonnage of the Covers.* NHS 16. Leiden: Brill, 1981.
Bauer, *Orthodoxy*   Bauer, W. *Orthodoxy and Heresy in Earliest Christianity.* Translation of German 2nd ed. Edited by R. A. Kraft and G. Krodel. Philadelphia: Fortress, 1971.
Bauer, *Rechtgläubigkeit*   Bauer, W. *Rechtgläubigkeit und Ketzerei im ältesten Christentum.* BHT 10. Tübingen: Mohr (Siebeck), 1934; 2nd ed. Tübingen: Mohr, 1964.
BCNH   Bibliothèque copte de Nag Hammadi.
Beardslee, *Literary Criticism*   Beardslee, W. A. *Literary Criticism of the New Testament.* Philadelphia: Fortress, 1970.
Beardslee, "Proverb"   Beardslee, W. A. "Uses of the Proverb in the Synoptic Gospels." *Int* 24 (1970) 61–73.
Beardslee, "Wisdom Tradition"   Beardslee, W. A. "The Wisdom Tradition and the Synoptic Gospels." *JAAR* 35 (1967) 231–40.
Beck, "Ephraem"   Beck, E. "Ephraem Syrus." *RAC* 5 (1962) cols. 520–31.
Becker, "Abschiedsreden"   Becker, J. "Die Abschiedsreden Jesu im Johannesevangelium." *ZNW* 61 (1970) 215–46.
Becker, "Aufbau"   Becker, J. "Aufbau, Schichtung und theologiegeschichtliche Stellung des Gebetes in Johannes 17." *ZNW* 60 (1969) 56–83.
Becker, *Reden*   Becker, H. *Die Reden des Johannesevangeliums und der Stil der gnostischen Offenbarungsrede.* FRLANT 68. Göttingen: Vandenhoeck & Ruprecht, 1956.
Bedjan, *Acta*   Bedjan, P., ed. *Acta martyrium et sanctorum.* 7 vols. Paris/Leipzig: Harrassowitz, 1891.
Bedjan, *Histoire*   Bedjan, P., ed. *Histoire de Mar-Jabalaha, de trois autres patriarches, d'un prêtre et de deux laïques, nestoriens.* Paris/Leipzig: Harrassowitz, 1895.
Bell-Skeat, *Unknown Gospel*   Bell, H. I. and Skeat, T. C. *Fragments of an Unknown Gospel and Other Early Christian Papyri.* London: British Museum, 1935.
Beltz, *Adamapokalypse*   Beltz, W. *Die Adamapokalypse aus Codex V von Nag Hammadi: Jüdische Bausteine in gnostischen Systemen.* Dr. Theol. diss.; Humboldt-Universität, 1970.
Beltz, "Samaritanertum"   Beltz, W. "Samaritanertum und Gnosis" in Tröger, *Gnosis*, 89–95.
Benko, "Phibionites"   Benko, S. "The Libertine Gnostic Sect of the Phibionites according to Epiphanius." *VC* 21 (1967) 103–19.
Bergman, *Ex Orbe Religionum*   Bergman, J. et al., eds. *Ex Orbe Religionum: Studia Geo. Widengren oblata.* 2 vols. Leiden: Brill, 1972.
Bergman, *Isis*   Bergman, J. *Ich bin Isis.* Acta Universitatis Upsalliensis, Historia Religionum 3; Uppsala: Almqvist & Wiksell, 1968.
BETH   Beiträge zur Evangelischen Theologie
Bethge, "Nebront"   Bethge, H.-G., et al. "'Nebront'; Die zweite Schrift aus Nag-Hammadi-Codex VI: Eingeleitet und übersetzt vom Berliner Arbeitskreis für koptisch-gnostische Schriften." *ThLZ* 98 (1973) 97–104.

Bethge, "Petrus an Philipus"   Bethge, H.-G. "Der sogenannte 'Brief des Petrus an Philipus': Die zweite 'Schrift' aus Nag-Hammadi-Codex VIII eingeleitet und übersetzt vom Berliner Arbeitskreis für koptisch-gnostische Schriften." ThLZ 103 (1978) 161–70.

BETL   Bibliotheca ephemeridum theologicarum lovaniensium

BHT   Beiträge zur historischen Theologie

Bianchi, "Colloque"   Bianchi, U. "Le colloque international sur les origines du Gnosticisme. Messine, avril 1966." Numen 13 (1966) 156–59.

Bianchi, Origini   Bianchi, U., ed. Le Origini dello Gnosticismo: Colloquio di Messina 13–18 Aprile 1966. Numen Supplement 12. Leiden: Brill, 1970.

Bianchi, "Problème"   Bianchi, U. "Le problème des origines du gnosticisme" in Bianchi, Origini, 1–27.

Bianchi, "Proposal"   Bianchi, U., ed. "Proposal for a terminological and conceptual agreement with regard to the theme of the Colloquium" in Bianchi, Origini, xxvi–xxix.

Bidez, Philostorgius   Bidez, J., ed. Philostorgius. Kirchengeschichte. GCS 21; Leipzig: Hinrichs, 1913.

BKV   Bibliothek der Kirchenväter

Blum, Rabbula   Blum, G. Rabbula von Edessa. Der Christ, der Bischof, der Theologe. CSCO 300; Louvain: Secrétariat CSCO, 1969.

Böcher-Haacker, Verborum Veritas   Böcher, O. and Haacker, K., eds. Verborum Veritas. Festschrift für Gustav Stählin zum 70. Geburtstag. Wuppertal: Brockhaus, 1970.

Böhlig, "Adamapokalypse"   Böhlig, A. "Jüdisches und Iranisches in der Adampokalypse des Codex V von Nag Hammadi" in Böhlig, Mysterion, 149–61.

Böhlig, "Antimimon"   Böhlig, A. "Zum Antimimon Pneuma in den koptisch-gnostischen Texten" in Böhlig, Mysterion, 162–74.

Böhlig-Labib, Apokalypsen   Böhlig, A. and Labib, P. Koptisch-gnostische Apokalypsen aus Codex V von Nag Hammadi im Koptischen Museum zu Alt Kairo. Halle-Wittenberg: Wissenschaftliche Zeitschrift der Martin-Luther-Universität, 1963.

Böhlig, Gnosis   Böhlig, A., ed. Die Gnosis. 3 vols.; Zürich/München: Artemis, 1980.

Böhlig-Wisse, Gospel of the Egyptians   Böhlig, A. and Wisse, F., eds. Nag Hammadi Codices III, 2 and IV, 2: The Gospel of the Egyptians. NHS 4. Leiden: Brill, 1975.

Böhlig, "Hintergrund"   Böhlig, A. "Der jüdische Hintergrund in gnostischen Texten von Nag Hammadi" in Böhlig, Mysterion, 80–101.

Böhlig, "Manichäismus"   Böhlig, A. "Der Manichäismus im Lichte der neueren Gnosisforschung" in Böhlig, Mysterion, 188–201.

Böhlig, Mysterion   Böhlig, A. Mysterion und Wahrheit: Gesammelte Beiträge zur spätantiken Religionsgeschichte. Leiden: Brill, 1968.

Böhlig-Labib, Schrift ohne Titel   Böhlig, A. and Labib, P. Die koptisch-gnostische Schrift ohne Titel aus Codex II von Nag Hammadi. Deutsche Akademie der Wissenschaften zu Berlin, Institut für Orientforschung. Veröffentlichung 58. Berlin: Akademie, 1962.

Böhlig, "Triade"   Böhlig, A. "Triade und Trinität in den Schriften von Nag Hammadi" in Layton, Rediscovery, 2.617–34.

Böhlig, "Ursprache"   Böhlig, A. "Ursprache des Evangelium Veritatis." Le Muséon 76 (1966) 317–33.

Boring, Sayings of the Risen Jesus   Boring, M. E. Sayings of the Risen Jesus: Christian Prophecy in the Synoptic Tradition. SNTSMS 46. Cambridge: University Press, 1982.

Borsch, Son of Man   Borsch, F. H. The Son of Man in Myth and History. NTL. Philadelphia: Westminster, 1967.

Bousset, Kyrios Christos   Bousset, W. Kyrios Christos: A History of the Belief in Christ from the Beginnings of Christianity to Irenaeus. Translated by J. E. Steely; Nashville/New York: Abingdon, 1970.

Bowersock, Greek Sophists   Bowersock, G. W. Greek Sophists in the Roman Empire. Oxford: Clarendon, 1969.

Brandt, Mandäische Religion   Brandt, W. Die mandäische Religion. Leipzig: Hinrichs, 1889.

Braun, Märtyrer   Braun, O. Ausgewählte Akten persischer Märtyrer. BKV 22. München: Kösel, 1915.

Braun, Nicaena   Braun, O. De sancta Nicaena synodo. Münster: Schöningh, 1898.

Brock, "Christians"   Brock, S. P. "Christians in the Sasanian Empire: A Case of Divided Loyalties." Studies in Church History 18 (1982) 1–19.

Brock, "Greek Words in Syriac"   Brock, S. P. "Some Aspects of Greek Words in Syriac" in Dietrich, Synkretismus, 80–108.

Brockelmann, Lexicon   Brockelmann, C. Lexicon syriacum. Halle: Niemeyer, 1928.

van den Broek, "Autogenes"   Broek, R. van den. "Autogenes and Adamas: The Mythological Structure of the Apocryphon of John" in Krause, Eighth Conference on Patristic Studies, 16–25.

van den Broek-Vermaseren, Studies   Broek, R. van den and Vermaseren, M. J., eds. Studies in Gnosticism and Hellenistic Religions. Presented to Gilles Quispel on the Occasion of his 65th Birthday. Études préliminaires aux religions orientales dans l'Empire romain 91. Leiden: Brill, 1981.

Brown, Community of the Beloved Disciple   Brown, R. E. The Community of the Beloved Disciple. New York: Paulist, 1979.

Brown, "Gospel of Thomas"   Brown, R. E. "The Gospel of Thomas and the Fourth Gospel." NTS 9 (1962/63) 155–77.

Brown, Johannine Epistles   Brown, R. E. The Johannine Epistles. AB 30. Garden City, N.Y.: Doubleday, 1982.

Brown, John   Brown, R. E. The Gospel according to John. 2 vols. AB 28–29. Garden City, N.Y.: Doubleday, 1966–1970.

Brown, "Sheep"   Brown, R. E. "'Other Sheep not of this Fold': The Johannine Perspective on Christian Diversity in the Late First Century." JBL 97 (1978) 5–22.

Brown-Griggs, "Apocalypse of Peter"   Brown, S. K. and Griggs, C. W. "The Apocalypse of Peter: Introduction and Translation." Brigham Young University Studies 15 (1975) 131–45.

Brox, "Nikolaos und Nikolaiten"   Brox, N. "Nikolaos und Nikolaiten." VC 19 (1965) 23–30.

Budge, Book of Governors   Budge, E. A. W., ed. The Book of Governors. The Historia Monastica of Thomas of Marga A. D. 840. 2 vols. London: Kegan Paul, 1893.

Budge, Coptic Apocrypha   Budge, E. A. W. Coptic Apocrypha in the Dialect of Upper Egypt. London: British Museum, 1913.

Bullard, Hypostasis of the Archons   Bullard, R. A. The Hypostasis of the Archons. Berlin: de Gruyter, 1970.

Bultmann, *Johannes*   Bultmann, R. *Das Evangelium des Johannes.* Meyer/K. 2;
  18th ed. Göttingen: Vandenhoeck & Ruprecht, 1964.
Bultmann, *John*   Bultmann, R. *The Gospel of John: A Commentary.* Translated by
  G. R. Beasley-Murray, et al. Philadelphia: Westminster, 1971.
Bultmann, *Primitive Christianity*   Bultmann, R. *Primitive Christianity in its
  Contemporary Setting.* Translated by R. H. Fuller. New York: Meridian, 1956.
Bultmann, *Theologie des NT*   Bultmann, R. *Theologie des Neuen Testaments.*
  Tübingen: Mohr, 1948 (1st ed.), 1958 (3rd ed.).
Bultmann, *Theology*   Bultmann, R. *Theology of the New Testament.* Translated
  by K. Grobel. 2 vols. New York: Scribners, 1951–55.
Burkert, "Craft versus Sect"   Burkert, W. "Craft versus Sect: The Problem of
  Orphics and Pythagoreans" in Meyer-Sanders, *Self-Definition,* 183–89.
Burkitt, *Church and Gnosis*   Burkitt, F. C. *Church and Gnosis: A Study of
  Christian Thought and Speculation in the Second Century.* Cambridge:
  University Press, 1932.
BZ   *Biblische Zeitschrift*
BZNW   Beihefte zur ZNW
Cameron-Dewey, *Mani Codex*   Cameron, R. and Dewey, A. *The Cologne Mani
  Codex* (P. Colon. inv. nr. 4780) "*Concerning the Origin of His Body.*" SBLTT 15.
  Missoula, Mont.: Scholars, 1979.
Cameron, *The Other Gospels*   Cameron, R., ed. *The Other Gospels: Non-
  Canonical Gospel Texts.* Philadelphia: Westminster, 1982.
von Campenhausen, *Bible*   Campenhausen, H. von. *The Formation of the
  Christian Bible.* Translated by J. A. Baker. Philadelphia: Fortress, 1972.
Carr, *Angels and Principalities*   Carr, W. *Angels and Principalities. The
  Background, Meaning and Development of the Pauline Phrase hai archai kai
  hai exousiai.* Cambridge: University Press, 1981.
CBQ   *Catholic Biblical Quarterly*
CBQMS   Catholic Biblical Quarterly—Monograph Series
CC   Corpus Christianorum
CG   Cairenensis Gnosticus (cf. NHC)
Chabot, *Chronique*   Chabot, J.-B., ed. *Chronique de Michel le Syrien.* 1899–1910.
  Reprint. 4 vols. Bruxelles: Culture et Civilization, 1963.
Chabot, *Synodicon*   Chabot, J.-B. *Synodicon orientale.* Notices et extraits des
  manuscrits de la Bibliothèque Nationale 37. Paris: Imprimerie Nationale, 1902.
Chadwick, "Enkrateia"   Chadwick, H. "Enkrateia." *RAC* 5 (1962) cols. 349–51.
Charles, *APOT*   Charles, R. H. *The Apocrypha and Pseudepigrapha of the Old
  Testament.* 2 vols. 1913. Reprint. Oxford: Clarendon, 1977.
Chaumont, "L'inscription"   Chaumont, M.-L., ed. "L'inscription de Kartīr à la
  'Ka῾bah de Zoroastre' (Texte, Traduction, Commentaire)." *JA* 258 (1960) 339–80.
Chérix, *Le Concept*   Chérix, P., ed. *Le Concept de Notre Grande Puissance (CG
  VI, 4).* Fribourg: Éditions Universitaires, 1982.
Cherniss, *Moralia*   Cherniss, H., ed. *Plutarch's Moralia.* LCL 13.2. Cambridge,
  Mass.: Harvard, 1976.
Cherniss-Helmbold, *Plutarch's Moralia*   Cherniss, H. and Helmbold, W., eds.
  Plutarch's Moralia. LCL 12. Cambridge, Mass.: Harvard, 1968.
Cicero, *Nat. Deor.*   Cicero, *De Natura Deorum*
Cicero, *Or.*   Cicero, *De Oratore*
Clem. Alex., *Strom.*   Clement of Alexandria, *Stromata*
Collins, *Morphology*   Collins, J. J., ed. *Apocalypse: The Morphology of a Genre.*
  Semeia 14. Missoula, Mont.: Scholars, 1979.

Colpe, "Messina Kongress"   Colpe, C. "Vorschläge des Messina Kongresses von 1966 zur Gnosisforschung" in Eltester, *Christentum*, 129–32.

Colpe, "Sethian Ages"   Colpe, C. "Sethian and Zoroastrian Ages of the World" in Layton, *Rediscovery*, 2.540–52.

Colpe, "Überlieferung"   Colpe, C. "Heidnische, jüdische, und christliche Überlieferung in den Schriften aus Nag Hammadi III." *JAC* 17 (1974) 125–46.

Conzelmann, "Literaturbericht"   Conzelmann, H. "Literaturbericht zu den synoptischen Evangelien." *ThR* 37 (1972) 220–72.

Cornford, *Cosmology*   Cornford, F. *Plato's Cosmology*. LLA. Indianapolis: Bobbs Merrill, n.d.

CRAIBL   Comptes rendus de l'Academie des inscriptions et de belles lettres.

Cross, *The Jung Codex*   Cross, F. L., ed. *The Jung Codex: A Newly Discovered Gnostic Papyrus*. London: Mowbray, 1955.

Crossan, *In Fragments*   Crossan, J. D. *In Fragments: The Aphorisms of Jesus*. San Francisco: Harper and Row, 1983.

CSCO   Corpus scriptorum christianorum orientalium

CSEL   Corpus scriptorum ecclesiasticorum latinorum

Dahl, "Archon"   Dahl, N. A. "The Arrogant Archon and the Lewd Sophia: Jewish Traditions in Gnostic Revolt" in Layton, *Rediscovery*, 2.689–712.

Dan-Talmage, *Jewish Mysticism*   Dan, J. and Talmage, F., eds. *Studies in Jewish Mysticism. Proceedings of Regional Conferences Held at the University of California, Los Angeles, and McGill University in April 1978*. Cambridge: Association for Jewish Studies, 1981.

Daniélou, *Gospel*   Daniélou, J. *Gospel Message and Hellenistic Culture*. Translated by J. A. Baker. Philadelphia: Westminster, 1973.

Dauer, *Passionsgeschichte*   Dauer, A. *Die Passionsgeschichte im Johannesevangelium*. SANT 30. München: Kösel, 1972.

Dauer, "Wort des Gekreuzigten"   Dauer, A. "Das Wort des Gekreuzigten an seine Mutter und den 'Jünger, den er liebte.'" *BZ* 11 (1967) 222–39; 12 (1968) 80–93.

Davies, *Thomas and Wisdom*   Davies, S. L. *The Gospel of Thomas and Christian Wisdom*. New York: Seabury, 1983.

DCB   *Dictionary of Christian Biography*.

Dehandschutter, "L'Évangile de Thomas"   Dehandschutter, B. "L'Évangile de Thomas comme collection de paroles de Jésus" in Delobel, *Logia*, 507–15.

Dehandschutter, "Thomasevangelie"   Dehandschutter, B. "Het Thomasevangelie: Overzicht van het onderzoek," Dissertation, Leuven, 1975.

Delobel, *Logia*   Delobel, J., ed. *Logia: Les paroles de Jésus - The Sayings of Jesus*. BETL 59. Leuven: Peeters & Leuven University, 1982.

Demke, "Logos-Hymnus"   Demke, C. "Der sogennante Logos-Hymnus im johanneischen Prolog." *ZNW* 58 (1967) 45–68.

DHGE   Dictionnaire d'histoire et de géographie ecclésiastiques

Dietrich, *Synkretismus*   Dietrich, A., ed. *Synkretismus im syrisch-persischen Kulturgebiet*. Abhandlungen der Akademie der Wissenschaften, Göttingen, phil.-hist. Klasse, 3. Folge 96. Göttingen: Vandenhoeck & Ruprecht, 1975.

Dillon, *Middle Platonists*   Dillon, J. *The Middle Platonists. A Study of Platonism 80 B.C. to A.D. 220*. London: Duckworth, 1977.

Disdier, "Atticus"   Disdier, M. "Atticus, patriarche de Constantinople." *DHGE* 5 (1931) 161–66.

Dodd, *Historical Tradition*   Dodd, C. H. *Historical Tradition in the Fourth Gospel*. Cambridge: University Press, 1963.

Dodds, "The Parmenides of Plato"   Dodds, E. R. "The Parmenides of Plato and the Origin of the Neoplatonic One." Classical Quarterly 22 (1928) 129–42.
Dodds, Proclus   Dodds, E. R. Proclus: The Elements of Theology. 2nd ed. Oxford: Clarendon, 1963.
Doresse, "Livres gnostiques"   Doresse, J. "Trois livres gnostiques inédits." VC 2 (1948) 137–60.
Doresse, Livres secrets   Doresse, J. Les livres secrets des gnostiques d'Égypte. 2 vols. Paris: Plon, 1958–59.
Dörrie, "Cosmologie"   Dörrie, H. "Divers aspects de la cosmologie de 70 avant J.-C. à 20 après J.-C." RThPh 3.22 (1972) 400–5.
Douglas, Symbols   Douglas, M. Natural Symbols: Explorations in Cosmology. New York: Random House, 1973.
Drijvers, Bardaişan   Drijvers, H. J. W. Bardaişan of Edessa. Assen: van Gorcum, 1966.
Drijvers, "Bardaişan, Repräsentant des syrischen Synkretismus"   Drijvers, H. J. W. "Bardaişan von Edessa als Repräsentant des syrischen Synkretismus im 2. Jahrhundert n. Chr." in Dietrich, Synkretismus, 109–22.
Drijvers, "Christentum"   Drijvers, H. J. W. "Edessa und das jüdische Christentum." VC 24 (1970) 4–33.
Drijvers, "Edessa"   Drijvers, H. J. W. "Edessa." ThRE 9 (1982) 277–88.
Drijvers, "Odes"   Drijvers, H. J. W. "Odes of Solomon and Psalms of Mani: Christians and Manichaeans in Third-Century Syria" in van den Broek-Vermaseren, Studies, 117–30.
Drijvers, "Quq"   Drijvers, H. J. W. "Quq and the Quqites. An Unknown Sect in Edessa in the Second Century A. D." Numen 14 (1967) 104–29.
Drijvers, "Rechtgläubigkeit"   Drijvers, H. J. W. "Rechtgläubigkeit und Ketzerei im ältesten syrischen Christentum." OrChrA 197 (1974) 291–370.
Drijvers, "Syriac-Speaking Christianity"   Drijvers, H. J. W. "Facts and Problems in Early Syriac-Speaking Christianity." The Second Century 2 (1982) 157–75.
Drower-Macuch, Mandaic Dictionary   Drower, E. S. and Macuch, R. A Mandaic Dictionary. Oxford: Clarendon, 1963.
Dubois, "Contexte"   Dubois, J.-D. "Le contexte judaïque du 'nom' dans l'Évangile de Vérité." RThPh 24 (1974) 198–216.
Dümmer, "Angaben"   Dümmer, J. "Die Angaben über die gnostische Literatur bei Epiphanius, Pan. haer. 26" in Koptologische Studien in der DDR. Halle-Wittenberg: Wissenschaftliche Zeitschrift der Martin-Luther-Universität, 1965, 191–219.
Dümmer, "Sprachkenntnisse"   Dümmer, J. "Die Sprachkenntnisse des Epiphanius" in Altheim-Stiehl, Die Araber, 5.1. 428–30.
EEF   Egypt Exploration Fund
EKK   Evangelisch-Katholischer Kommentar zum Neuen Testament
Eltester, Apophoreta   Eltester, W. Apophoreta: Festschrift für Ernst Haenchen zu seinem siebzigsten Geburtstag am 10. Dezember 1964. BZNW 30. Berlin: Töpelmann, 1964.
Eltester, Christentum   Eltester, W. Christentum und Gnosis. BZNW 37. Berlin: Töpelmann, 1969.
Ephrem, Contra haereses   Ephrem. Hymnen contra haereses. Edited by E. Beck. CSCO 169. Louvain, Secrétariat CSCO, 1957.
Ephrem, De paradiso   Beck, E., ed. Des heiligen Ephraem des Syrers Hymnen de Paradiso und Contra Julianum. CSCO 174. Louvain: Secréteriat CSCO, 1957.
Epiph. Pan.   Epiphanius, Panarion

van Ess, *Häresiographie*   Ess, J. van, ed. *Frühe muʿtazilitische Häresiographie.*
  Beirut: Orient-Institut, 1971.
Eusebius, *Eccl. Hist.*   Eusebius. *The Ecclesiastical History.* Edited by K. Lake and
  J. E. L. Oulton. 2 vols. Cambridge and London: Heinemann, 1964–65.
Eutychius, *Annales*   Eutychius of Alexandria. *Eutychii patriarchae Alexandrini
  annales pars 2.* Edited by L. Cheikho, et al. CSCO 50–51. Louvain: Imprimerie
  Orientaliste, 1954.
EvTh   *Evangelische Theologie*
Fallon, "Apocalypses"   Fallon, F. T. "The Gnostic Apocalypses" in Collins,
  Morphology, 123–58.
Fallon, *Enthronement*   Fallon, F. T. *The Enthronement of Sabaoth. Jewish
  Elements in Gnostic Creation Myths.* NHS 10. Leiden: Brill, 1978.
Farmer, *Jesus*   Farmer, W. R. *Jesus and the Gospel.* Philadelphia: Fortress, 1982.
de Faye, *Gnostiques*   Faye, E. de. *Gnostiques et gnosticisme.* 2nd ed. Paris:
  Geuthner, 1925.
Fecht, "Der erste 'Teil'"   Fecht, G. "Der erste 'Teil' des sogennanten Evangelium
  Veritatis (s. 16, 31–22, 2)." *Or* 30 (1961) 371–90.
Fendt, "Borborianer"   Fendt, L. "Borborianer." *RAC* 2 (1954) 510–13.
Fendt, *Mysterien*   Fendt, L. *Gnostische Mysterien.* München: Kaiser, 1922.
Fiey, *Jalons*   Fiey, J. M. *Jalons pour une histoire de l'Église en Iraq.* CSCO 310.
  Louvain: Secréteriat CSCO, 1970.
Fiey, "Marcionites"   Fiey, J. M. "Les Marcionites dans les textes historiques de
  l'Église de Perse." *Le Muséon* 73 (1970) 183–87.
Filastrius, *Haer.*   Filastrius of Brescia. *Diversarum haereseon liber.* Edited by F.
  Heylen. CC, series latina 9. Turnhout: Brepols, 1959.
Fineman, "Piety"   Fineman, J. "Gnosis and the Piety of Metaphor: *The Gospel of
  Truth*" in Layton, *Rediscovery,* 1.289–318.
Finnestad, "Fall"   Finnestad, R. B. "The Cosmogonic Fall in the Evangelium
  Veritatis." *Temenos* 7 (1971) 38–49.
Fischer, "Christus"   Fischer, K. M. "Der johanneische Christus und der gnostische
  Erlöser" in Tröger, *Gnosis und Neues Testament,* 245–66.
Fitzmyer, "Gnostic Gospels"   Fitzmyer, J. A. "The Gnostic Gospels according to
  Pagels." *America* 123 (16 February, 1980) 122–24.
Fitzmyer, *Luke*   Fitzmyer, J. A. "*The Gospel According to Luke I–IX.* AB 28.
  Garden City, N.Y.: Doubleday, 1981.
Foerster, *Die Gnosis*   Foerster, W., ed. *Die Gnosis.* 3 vols. Zürich: Artemis, 1969–
  80.
Foerster, *Gnosis*   Foerster, W., ed. *Gnosis: A Selection of Gnostic Texts.*
  Translated and edited by R. McL. Wilson. 2 vols. Oxford: Clarendon, 1972–74.
Forestell, *Word*   Forestell, J. T. *The Word of the Cross: Salvation as Revelation in
  the Fourth Gospel.* AnBib 57. Rome: Pontifical Biblical Institute, 1974.
Francis-Meeks, *Conflict at Colossae*   Francis, F. O. and Meeks, W. A., eds. and
  trans. *Conflict at Colossae: A Problem in the Interpretation of Early Christianity
  Illustrated by Selected Modern Studies.* Sources for Biblical Study 4. Missoula,
  Mont.: Scholars Press, 1975 rev.
Fredouille, *Tertullien*   Fredouille, J.-C. *Tertullien, Contra les Valentiniens.* SC
  280. Paris: Cerf, 1980.
Friedländer, *Gnosticismus*   Friedländer, M. *Der vorchristliche jüdische
  Gnosticismus.* Göttingen: Vandenhoek & Ruprecht, 1898; Farnborough: Gregg
  International, 1972.

FRLANT   Forschungen zur Religion und Literatur des Alten und Neuen
    Testaments.
Garsoïan, Heresy   Garsoïan, N. G. The Paulician Heresy. The Hague: Mouton,
    1967.
GCS   Die griechischen christlichen Schriftsteller der ersten Jahrhunderte
Geerard, Clavis   Geerard, M. Clavis patrum graecorum. 4 vols. Turnhout: Brepols,
    1974–83.
Gero, Barṣauma   Gero, S. Barṣauma of Nisibis and Persian Christianity in the
    Fifth Century. CSCO 426. Louvain: Peeters, 1981.
Gero, "Kirche"   Gero, S. "Die Kirche des Ostens. Zum Christentum in Persien in
    der Spätantike." OSt 30 (1981) 22–27.
Gero, "See of Peter"   Gero, S. "The See of Peter in Babylon: Western Influences
    on the Ecclesiology of Early Persian Christianity" in N. Garsoïan et al., eds. East
    of Byzantium: Syria and Armenia in the Formative Period. Washington:
    Dumbarton Oaks, 1982, 45–51.
Gignoux, "L'inscription"   Gignoux, Ph., ed. "L'inscription de Kartir à Sar Mašhad."
    JA 256 (1968) 387–418.
Giversen, Apocryphon   Giverson, S. Apocryphon Johannis. Copenhagen:
    Munksgaard, 1963.
GOF   Göttinger Orientforschungen
Goguel, Introduction   Goguel, M. Introduction au Nouveau Testament. 4 vols.
    Paris: Leroux, 1923–26.
Graf, Geschichte   Graf, G. Geschichte der christlichen arabischen Literatur. 5
    vols. Vatican: Biblioteca Apostolica, 1944–53.
Grant, Gnosticism: A Source Book   Grant, R. M. Gnosticism: A Source Book of
    Heretical Writings from the Early Christian Period. New York: Harper, 1961.
Grant, Gnosticism   Grant, R. M. Gnosticism and Early Christianity. 2nd ed. rev.
    New York: Harper and Row, 1966.
Grant, "Manichees and Christians"   Grant, R. M. "Manichees and Christians in
    the Third and Fourth Centuries" in Bergman, Ex Orbe Religionum, 430–39.
Grenfell-Hunt, LOGIA   Grenfell, B. P. and Hunt, A. S. LOGIA IESOU: Sayings of
    Our Lord from an Early Greek Papyrus. London: Frowde, 1897.
Grenfell-Hunt, Papyri I   Grenfell, B. P. and Hunt, A. S. The Oxyrhynchus Papyri,
    Part I. London: EEF, 1898.
Grenfell-Hunt, Papyri IV   Grenfell, B. P. and Hunt, A. S. The Oxyrhynchus
    Papyri, Part IV. London: EEF, 1904.
Grobel, Gospel of Truth   Grobel, K. The Gospel of Truth: A Valentinian
    Meditation on the Gospel. New York: Abingdon, 1960.
Grobel, "Thomas"   Grobel, K. "How Gnostic is the Gospel of Thomas?" NTS 8
    (1961/1962) 367–73.
Gruenwald, Apocalyptic and Merkavah Mysticism   Grunewald, I. Apocalyptic
    and Merkavah Mysticism. Leiden: Brill, 1980.
Gruenwald, "Controversy"   Gruenwald, I. "Aspects of the Jewish-Gnostic
    Controversy" in Layton, Rediscovery, 2.713–23.
Gruenwald, "Merkavah"   Gruenwald, I. "Jewish Merkavah Mysticism and
    Gnosticism" in Dan-Talmage, Jewish Mysticism, 41–55.
Guidi, Chronica   Guidi, I., ed. Chronica Minora I. CSCO 1. 1903. Reprint.
    Louvain: Secréteriat CSCO, 1960.
Guillaumont, "Sémitismes"   Guillaumont, A. "Les sémitismes dans l'Évangile
    selon Thomas: Essai de classement" in van den Broek-Vermaseren, Studies, 190–
    204.

Guillaumont, *Thomas*   Guillaumont, A.; Puech, H.-Ch.; Quispel, G.; Till, W. and
ʿAbd al Masîḥ, Y., eds. *The Gospel According to Thomas. Coptic Text
Established and Translated*. Leiden: Brill, 1959.
Haardt, *Gnosis*   Haardt, R. *Die Gnosis: Wesen und Zeugnisse*. Salzburg: Müller,
1967.
Haardt, *Gnosis: Character*   Haardt, R. *Gnosis: Character and Testimony*.
Translated by J. F. Hendry. Leiden: Brill, 1971.
Haardt, "Struktur"   Haardt, R. "Zur Struktur des Plane-Mythos im Evangelium
Veritatis des Codex Jung." *WZKM* 58 (1962) 24–38.
Hadot, *Porphyre*   Hadot, P. *Porphyre et Victorinus*. 2 vols. Paris: Études
Augustiniennes, 1968.
Haenchen, *Acts*   Haenchen, E. *The Acts of the Apostles*. Translated by B. Noble
and G. Shinn. Philadelphia: Westminster, 1971.
Haenchen, *Johannesevangelium*   Haenchen, E. *Das Johannesevangelium*. Edited
by U. Busse. Tübingen: Mohr, 1980.
Haenchen, "Literatur"   Haenchen, E. "Literatur zum Codex Jung." *ThR* 30 (1964)
39–82.
Hamman, *Patrologiae*   Hamman, A., ed. *Patrologiae cursus completus.
Supplementum*. Series latina. 5 vols. Paris: Garnier, 1963–74.
Harder, "Schrift Plotins"   Harder, R. "Eine neue Schrift Plotins." *Hermes* 71
(1936) 1–10.
von Harnack, *Altchristlichen Literatur*   Harnack, A. von. *Geschichte der
altchristlichen Literatur bis Eusebius*. 2 vols. Leipzig: Hinrichs, 1893.
von Harnack, *Dogma*   Harnack, A. von. *History of Dogma*. Translated by N.
Buchanan. 3rd German ed. 7 vols. New York: Russell and Russell, 1958.
von Harnack, *Ketzer-Katalog*   Harnack, A. von. *Der Ketzer-Katalog des Bischofs
Maruta von Maipherkat*. TU Neue Serie 19:4.3. Leipzig: Hinrichs, 1899.
von Harnack, "Nicolaitans"   Harnack, A. von. "The Sect of the Nicolaitans and
Nicolaus, the Deacon of Jerusalem." *JR* 3 (1923) 413–22.
von Harnack, *Studien*   Harnack A. von. *Studien zur Geschichte des Neuen
Testaments und der Alten Kirche*. AKG 19. Berlin/Leipzig: de Gruyter, 1931.
Hartmann, "Vorlage"   Hartmann, G. "Die Vorlage der Osterberichte in Joh 20."
ZNW 55 (1964) 197–220.
Hauschild, *Geist*   Hauschild, W.-D. *Gottes Geist und der Mensch: Studien zur
frühchristlichen Pneumatologie*. München: Kaiser, 1972.
Hawkin, "Beloved Disciple"   Hawkin, D. J. "The Function of the Beloved Disciple
Motif in the Johannine Redaction." *LThPh* 33 (1977) 135–50.
Hedrick, "Adam"   Hedrick, C. W. "The Apocalypse of Adam: A Literary and
Source Analysis" in L. C. McGaughy, ed. *The Society of Biblical Literature One
Hundred Eighth Annual Meeting Book of Seminar Papers Friday-Tuesday, 1–5
September 1972 Century Plaza Hotel-Los Angeles, CA*. 2 vols. Los Angeles: SBL,
1972, 1. 581–90.
Hedrick, *Apocalypse*   Hedrick, C. W. *The Apocalypse of Adam: A Literary and
Source Analysis*. SBLDS 46. Chico, Calif.: Scholars, 1980.
Hedrick, "Gnostic Proclivities"   Hedrick, C. W. "Gnostic Proclivities in the Greek
Life of Pachomius and the *Sitz im Leben* of the Nag Hammadi Library." *NovT*
22 (1980) 78–94.
Hedrick, "Kingdom Sayings and Parables"   Hedrick, C. W. "Kingdom Sayings and
Parables of Jesus in the *Apocryphon of James*: Tradition and Redaction." *NTS*
29 (1983) 1–24.

Heldermann, "Isis"   Heldermann, J. "Isis as Plane in the *Gospel of Truth*" in
  Krause, *Eighth Conference on Patristic Studies*, 21–46.
Heldermann, "Zelten"   Heldermann, J. "'In ihrer Zelten . . .': Bemerkungen zu
  Codex XIII von Nag Hammadi, p. 47: 14–18 in Hinblick auf Joh. 1:14" in T.
  Baarda, et al., eds. *Miscellanea Neotestamentica*. NovTSup 47–48. 2 vols.
  Leiden: Brill, 1978, 1.181–211.
Hennecke-Schneemelcher, *NT Apocrypha*   Hennecke, E. W. and
  Schneemelcher, W. *New Testament Apocrypha*. Edited by R. McL. Wilson. 2
  vols. Philadelphia: Westminster, 1963.
Henrichs, "Mani Codex"   Henrichs, A. "Literary Criticism of the Cologne Mani
  Codex" in Layton, *Rediscovery*, 2.724–33.
Henrichs-Koenen, "Mani-Kodex"   Henrichs, A. and Koenen, L. "Der Kölner
  Mani-Kodex (P. Colon. inv. nr. 4780)." *ZPE* 19 (1975) 1–85.
HThKNT   Herders Theologischer Kommentar zum Neuen Testament
Hilgenfeld, *Ketzergeschichte*   Hilgenfeld, A. *Die Ketzergeschichte des
  Urchristentums*. Leipzig: Fues (R. Reisland), 1884.
Hinz, "Inschrift"   Hinz, W., ed. "Die Inschrift des Hohenpriesters Karder am
  Turm von Naqsh-e Rostam." *Archäologische Mitteilungen aus Iran* 3 (1970) 251–
  65.
Hipp. *Ref.*   Hippolytus, *Refutatio omnium haeresium*
Hodgson, "Dialogue with James M. Robinson"   Hodgson, R. "On the Gattung of Q:
  A Dialogue with James M. Robinson." *Biblica* 66 (1985) 73–95.
Hodgson, "Testimony Hypothesis"   Hodgson, R. "The Testimony Hypothesis." *JBL*
  98 (1979) 361–78.
Hoffmann, *Auszüge*   Hoffmann, G. *Auszüge aus syrischen Akten persischer
  Märtyrer*. Leipzig: Hinrichs, 1880.
Hoffman, *Theologie der Logienquelle*   Hoffman, P. *Studien zur Theologie der
  Logienquelle*. NTAbh NF 8. Münster: Aschendorff, 1972.
Holl, *Anakephalaiosis*   See Holl, *Epiphanius*
Holl, *Epiphanius*   Holl, K. *Epiphanius: Ancoratus und Panarion*. GCS 25, 31, 37. 3
  vols. Leipzig: Henrichs, 1915–33.
Hörig, *Dea Syria*   Hörig, M. *Dea Syria. Studien zur religiösen Tradition der
  Fruchtbarkeitsgöttin in Vorderasien*. Neukirchen-Vluyn: Neukirchener Verlag,
  1979.
Hort-Mayor, *Clement*   Hort, F. J. A. and Mayor, J. B., eds. *Clement of Alexandria:
  Miscellanies Book VII*. London: Macmillan, 1902.
HR   *History of Religions*
HTR   *Harvard Theological Review*
Hübschmann, *Grammatik*   Hübschmann, H. *Armenische Grammatik*. 2 vols.
  Leipzig: Harrassowitz, 1897.
Hussey, *Socrates*   Hussey, P., ed. *Socratis scholastici historia ecclesiastica*.
  Oxford: Clarendon, 1853.
IDBSup   Supplementary volume to the *Interpreter's Dictionary of the Bible*.
Inglisian, "Leben"   Inglisian, V. "Leben des heiligen Maschtotz von seinem
  Schüler Koriun" in W. Schamoni, ed. *Ausbreiter des Glaubens im Altertum
  zusammengestellt und eingeleitet von Wilhelm Schamoni*. Düsseldorf: Patmos,
  1963, 119–46.
Int   *Interpretation*
Iren. *Haer.*   Irenaeus, *Adversus haereses*
JA   *Journal asiatique*

JAAR   *Journal of the American Academy of Religion*
JAC   *Jarhbuch für Antique und Christentum*
Jaeger, *Paideia*   Jaeger, W. *Paideia: The Ideals of Greek Culture.* Translated by G. Highet. 2nd German ed. New York: Oxford, 1945.
Jansen, "Spuren"   Jansen, H. L. "Spuren sakramentaler Handlungen im Evangelium Veritatis?" *AcOr* 28 (1964) 215–19.
Janssens, *Trimorphe*   Janssens, Y. *La Protennoia Trimorphe (NH XIII, 1)*: Texte établi et présenté. BCNH, Textes 4. Québec: Université Laval, 1978.
JBL   *Journal of Biblical Literature*
Jer. Ep.   Jerome, *Epistolae*
Jeremias, "Schicht"   Jeremias, J. "Die älteste Schicht der Menschensohn-Logien." *ZNW* 58 (1967) 159–72.
Jeremias, *Sprache*   Jeremias, J. *Die Sprache des Lukasevangeliums: Redaktion und Tradition im Nicht-Markusstoff des dritten Evangeliums.* MeyerK. Göttingen: Vandenhoeck & Ruprecht, 1980.
Jonas, "Evangelium Veritatis"   Jonas, H. "Evangelium Veritatis and the Valentinian Speculation" in F. L. Cross ed. *Studia Patristica* 6. TU 81. Berlin: Akademie, 1962, 96–111.
Jonas, *Gnosis*   Jonas, H. *Gnosis und spätantiker Geist.* 2 vols. 3rd ed. Göttingen: Vandenhoeck & Ruprecht, 1964.
Jonas, *Gnostic Religion*   Jonas, H. *The Gnostic Religion: The Message of the Alien God and the Beginnings of Christianity.* 2nd ed. rev. Boston: Beacon, 1958.
Jonas, "Gnostic Syndrome"   Jonas, H. "The Gnostic Syndrome: Typology of its Thought, Imagination, and Mood" in Jonas, *Philosophical Essays*, 263–76.
Jonas, "Hymn of the Pearl"   Jonas H. "The Hymn of the Pearl: Case Study of a Symbol, and the Claims for a Jewish Origin of Gnosticism" in Jonas, *Philosophical Essays*, 277–90.
Jonas, *Philosophical Essays*   Jonas, H. *Philosophical Essays: From Ancient Creed to Technological Man.* Englewood Cliffs, N.J.: Prentice-Hall, 1974.
Jonas, "Review of Malinine"   Jonas, H. "Review of Malinine, *Evangelium Veritatis.*" *Gnomon* 32 (1960) 327–35.
de Jonge, *L'Évangile de Jean*   Jonge, M. de, ed. *L'Évangile de Jean: Sources, rédaction, théologie.* BETL 44. Gembloux: Duculot, 1977.
Jos. Ant.   Josephus, *Antiquities of the Jews*
Jos. Ap.   Josephus, *Contra Apionem*
JR   *Journal of Religion*
JTS   *Journal of Theological Studies*
Justin, 1 Apol.   Justin, *First Apology*
Kaestli, "Valentinianisme"   Kaestli, J.-D. "Valentinianisme italien et valentinianisme orientale: leurs divergences à propos de la nature du corps de Jésus" in Layton, *Rediscovery*, 1.391–403.
Käsemann, *Testament*   Käsemann, *The Testament of Jesus.* Translated by G. Krodel. Philadelphia: Fortress, 1968.
Kee, "Christology"   Kee, H. C. "Christology and Ecclesiology: Titles of Christ and Models of Community" in K. H. Richards, ed. *SBL Seminar Papers.* Chico, Calif.: Scholars, 1982.
Kelber, *Oral and Written Gospel*   Kelber, W. *The Oral and Written Gospel.* Philadelphia: Fortress, 1983.
El-Khoury, *Interpretation*   El-Khoury, N. *Die Interpretation der Welt bei Ephraem dem Syrer.* Mainz: Grünewald, 1976.

Klijn, *Seth*   Klijn, A. F. J. *Seth in Jewish, Christian and Gnostic Literature.*
Leiden: Brill, 1977.
Kloppenborg, "Synoptic Sayings Source"   Kloppenborg, J. S. "The Literary Genre
of the Synoptic Sayings Source." Unpublished Ph.D. Dissertation, University of
St. Michael's College, Toronto, 1984.
Kloppenborg, *Formation of Q*   Kloppenborg, J. S. *The Formation of Q:*
Trajectories in Ancient Wisdom Collections. Studies in Antiquity and
Christianity 2, forthcoming.
Koenen, "Baptism"   Koenen, L. "From Baptism to the Gnosis of Manichaeism" in
Layton, *Rediscovery*, 2.734–56.
Koep, *Buch*   Koep, L. *Das himmlische Buch in Antike und Urchristentum.* Bonn:
Hanstein, 1952.
Koester, "Apocryphal and Canonical Gospels"   Koester, H. "Apocryphal and
Canonical Gospels." *HTR* 73 (1980) 105–30.
Koester, "Dialog und Sprachüberlieferung"   Koester, H. "Dialog und Sprachüber-
lieferung in den gnostischen Texten von Nag Hammadi." *EvTh* 39 (1979) 544–56.
Koester, *Einführung*   Koester, H. *Einführung in das Neue Testament.* Berlin: de
Gruyter, 1980 (ET = Koester, *Introduction*).
Koester, "Gnomai"   Koester, H. "Gnomai Diaphoroi: the Origin and Nature of
Diversification in the History of Early Christianity" in Robinson-Koester, *Trajec-*
tories, 114–57.
Koester, "Gnostic Writings"   Koester, H. "Gnostic Writings as Witnesses for the
Development of the Sayings Tradition" in Layton, *Rediscovery*, 1.238–61.
Koester, *Introduction*   Koester, H. *Introduction to the New Testament.* Translated
by H. Koester. 2 vols. Philadelphia: Fortress, 1982 (German = Koester,
Einführung).
Koester, "Thomas"   Koester, H. "Introduction to the Gospel of Thomas" in Layton,
Nag Hammadi Codex II.
Koester, "Tradition and History"   Koester, H. "Tradition and History of the Early
Christian Gospel Literature." Shaffer Lectures, Yale University, 1980.
Koester, "Überlieferung und Geschichte"   Koester, H. "Überlieferung und
Geschichte der frühchristlichen Evangelienliteratur." ANRW 2 (*Principat*). 25.2,
1463-1542.
Koschorke, "Patristische Materialien"   Koschorke, K. "Patristische Materialien zur
Spätgeschichte der valentinianischen Gnosis" in Krause, *Eighth Conference on*
Patristic Studies, 120–39.
Koschorke, *Polemik*   Koschorke, K. *Die Polemik der Gnostiker gegen das*
kirchliche Christentum. NHS 12. Leiden: Brill, 1978.
Kotter, *Schriften*   Kotter, B., ed. *Die Schriften des Johannes von Damaskos.* 4
vols. Berlin: de Gruyter, 1981.
Kragerud, "Apocryphon Johannis"   Kragerud, A. "Apocryphon Johannis: En
formanalyse." *NTT* 66 (1965) 15–38.
Kragerud, *Lieblingsjünger*   Kragerud, A. *Der Lieblingsjünger im*
Johannesevangelium. Oslo: Universitätsverlag; Hamburg: Wegner, 1959.
Krämer, *Ursprung*   Krämer, H. J. *Der Ursprung der Geistmetaphysik:*
Untersuchung zur Geschichte des Platonismus zwischen Platon und Plotin.
Amsterdam: Schippers, 1964.
Krause, *Drei Versionen*   Krause, M. *Die drei Versionen des Apokryphon des*
Johannes im koptischen Museum zu Alt-Kairo. Wiesbaden: Harrassowitz, 1962.

Krause, *Eighth Conference on Patristic Studies*   Krause, M., ed. *Gnosis and Gnosticism: Papers Read at the Eighth International Conference on Patristic Studies. Oxford, September 3rd–8th, 1979.* NHS 17. Leiden: Brill, 1981.

Krause, *Essays*   Krause, M., ed. *Essays on the Nag Hammadi Texts in Honour of Alexander Böhlig.* NHS 3. Leiden: Brill, 1972.

Krause, "Eugnostosbriefes"   Krause, M. "Das literarische Verhältnis des Eugnostosbriefes zur Sophia Jesu Christi: Zur Auseinandersetzung der Gnosis mit dem Christentum" in S. Stuiber and A. Hermann, eds. *Mullus: Festschrift Theodor Klauser.* JAC Ergänzungsband 1. Münster, Westfalen: Aschendorff, 1964, 215–23.

Krause, *Seventh Conference on Patristic Studies*   Krause, M., ed. *Gnosis and Gnosticism: Papers Read at the Seventh International Conference on Patristic Studies (Oxford, September 8th–13th 1975).* NHS 8. Leiden: Brill, 1977.

Krause-Labib, *Codex II und Codex VI*   Krause, M. and Labib, P. *Gnostische und hermetische Schriften aus Codex II und Codex VI.* Glückstadt: Augustin, 1971.

Kropp, *Zaubertexte*   Kropp, A. M. *Ausgewählte koptische Zaubertexte.* 3 vols. Bruxelles: Fondation Egyptologique Reine Elisabeth, 1930–31.

Krüger, *Corpus*   Krüger, P., ed. *Corpus iuris civilis.* 3 vols. 2nd ed. Berlin: Weidmann, 1887–95.

Kümmel, *Einleitung*   Kümmel, W. G., et al. *Einleitung in das Neue Testament.* 12th ed. Heidelberg: Quelle and Meyer, 1963.

Kümmel, *Introduction*   Kümmel, W. G. *Introduction to the New Testament.* Translated by A. J. Mattill, Jr. Nashville: Abingdon, 1966.

Kümmel, *Investigation*   Kümmel, W. G. *The New Testament: The History of the Investigation of its Problems.* Translated by S. M. Gilmour and H. C. Kee. Nashville and New York: Abingdon, 1970.

Labourt, *Christianisme*   Labourt, J. *Le Christianisme dans l'empire perse sous la dynastie sassanide 224–632.* Paris: Firmin-Didot, 1904.

Langbrandtner, *Weltferner Gott*   Langbrandtner, W. *Weltferner Gott oder Gott der Liebe.* Beiträge zur biblischen Exegese und Theologie 6. Frankfurt a.M.: Peter Lang, 1977.

Layton, "Hypostasis"   Layton, B. "The Hypostasis of the Archons, or the Reality of the Rulers." *HTR* 67 (1974) 351–426; 69 (1976) 31–102.

Layton, *Nag Hammadi Codex II*   Layton, B., ed. *Nag Hammadi Codex II, 2–7, together with XIII, 2*, Brit. Lib. Or. 4926 (1) and P. Oxy. 1, 654, 655:* Volume 1: *Gospel According to Thomas, Gospel According to Philip, Hypostasis of the Archons, Indexes.* Coptic Gnostic Library; NHS 20. Leiden: Brill, forthcoming.

Layton, *Rediscovery*   Layton, B., ed. *The Rediscovery of Gnosticism; Proceedings of the International Conference on Gnosticism at Yale, New Haven, Connecticut March 28–31, 1978.* Supplement to Numen 41. Studies in the History of Religions 41. 2 vols. Leiden: Brill, 1980–81.

Layton, "Resurrection"   Layton, B. "Vision and Revision: A Gnostic View of Resurrection" in Barc, *Colloque*, 190–217.

Layton, "Riddle"   Layton, B. "The Riddle of the Thunder, (NHC VI, 2)." Paper presented and discussed at the NEH Working Seminar on Gnosticism and Early Christianity, March 30–April 2, 1983, at Springfield, Missouri.

LCC   Library of Christian Classics

LCL   Loeb Classical Library

Leisegang, *Gnosis*   Leisegang, H. *Die Gnosis.* Stuttgart: Kroner, 1941 (3rd ed.); 1955 (4th ed.).

Liboron, Gnosis   Liboron, H. Die karpokratianische Gnosis. Leipzig: Vogel, 1938.
Lidzbarski, Ginza   Lidzbarski, M., ed. Ginza. Der Schatz oder das grosse Buch
der Mandäer. Göttingen: Vandenhoeck & Ruprecht, 1925.
LLA   Library of Liberal Arts
Logan-Wedderburn, New Testament and Gnosis   Logan, H. B. and Wedderburn,
A. J. M., eds. The New Testament and Gnosis: Essays in Honour of Robert McL.
Wilson. Edinburgh: T. & T. Clark, 1983.
Lorenzen, Lieblingsjünger   Lorenzen, T. Der Lieblingsjünger im
Johannesevangelium. SBS 55. Stuttgart: Katholisches Bibelwerk, 1971.
LSJ   Liddell-Scott-Jones, Greek-English Lexicon
LThPh   Laval théologique et philosophique
Ludin, "Spuren"   Ludin, J. H. "Spuren sakramentaler Handlungen im Evangelium
Veritatis?" AcOr 28 (1964) 215–19.
Lührmann, "Liebet eure Feinde"   Lührmann, D. "Liebet eure Feinde (Lk 6, 27–
36/Mt 5, 39–48)." ZThK 69 (1972) 412–58.
Luttikhuizen, "Peter to Philip"   Luttikhuizen, G. P. "The Letter of Peter to Philip
and the New Testament" in Wilson, Nag Hammadi, 96–102.
MacDonald, "Male and Female"   MacDonald, D. R. "There Is No Male and
Female: Galatians 3:26–28." Unpublished Ph.D Dissertation, Harvard University;
Cambridge, Massachusetts, 1978.
MacRae, "Apocalypse of Adam"   MacRae, G. "The Apocalypse of Adam V,5:64,1–
85,32" in Parrott, Codices V and VI, 151–95.
MacRae, "Nag Hammadi"   MacRae, G. "Nag Hammadi." IDBSup, 613–19.
MacRae, "Nag Hammadi and the New Testament"   MacRae, G. "Nag Hammadi
and the New Testament" in Aland, Gnosis, 144–57.
MacRae, "Sophia Myth"   MacRae, G. "The Jewish Background of the Gnostic
Sophia Myth." NTS 12 (1970) 82–101.
MacRae, Thunder   MacRae, G. W. The Thunder, Perfect Mind: Protocol of the
5th Colloquy of the Center for Hermeneutical Studies in Hellenistic and Modern
Culture, 11 March 1973. Berkeley: Center for Hermeneutical Studies, 1975.
Malinine, Evangelium Veritatis   Malinine, M.; Puech, H.-Ch.; Quispel, G.
[Zacharias, G. P.; Wall, H.]. Evangelium Veritatis: Codex Jung f. VIIIv–XVIv (p.
16–32)/f. XIXr–XXIIr (p. 37–43). Studien aus dem C. G. Jung-Institute 6. Zürich:
Rascher, 1956.
Malinine, Evangelium Veritatis Supplementum   Malinine, M.; Puech, H.-Ch.;
Quispel, G.; Till, W.[Wilson, R. McL.]. Evangelium Veritatis: [Supplementum]
Codex Jung F. XVIIr–F. XVIIIv (p. 33–36). Studien aus dem C. G. Jung-Institute
6. Zürich and Stuttgart: Rascher, 1961.
Malinine-Puech, Epistula Iacobi   Malinine, M.; Puech, H.-Ch.; Quispel, G.; Till,
W.; Kasser, R.; Wilson, R. McL.; and Zandee, J., eds. Epistula Iacobi Apocrypha.
Codex Jung F. Ir–F. VIIIv (p. 1–16). Zürich and Stuttgart: Rascher, 1968.
Marcovich, "Naasene Psalm"   Marcovich, M. "The Naasene Psalm in Hippolytus
(Haer. 5.10.2)" in Layton, Rediscovery, 2.770–78.
Marrou, "Diffusion"   Marrou, H. "L'Évangile de Vérité et la diffusion du comput
digital dans l'antiquité." VC 12 (1958) 98–103.
Martin, "Homélie"   Martin, F., ed. "Homélie de Narsès sur les trois docteurs
nestoriens." JA 14 (1899) 446–92.
Martyn, Fourth Gospel   Martyn, J. L. History and Theology in the Fourth Gospel.
2nd ed. Nashville: Abingdon, 1979.
McCue, "Valentinianism"   McCue, J. F. "Conflicting Versions of Valentinianism?
Irenaeus and the Excerpta ex Theodoto" in Layton, Rediscovery, 1.404–16.

Ménard, "Datation"   Ménard, J.-É. "La datation des manuscrits." *Histoire et archéologie* 70 (1983) 12–13.

Ménard, "Élucubrations"   Ménard, J.-É. "Les élucubrations de l'*Evangelium Veritatis* sur le 'Nom.'" *Studia Montis Regii* 5 (1962) 185–214.

Ménard, *L'Évangile de Vérité*   Ménard, J.-É. *L'Évangile de Vérité: Traduction française, introduction et commentaire.* NHS 2. Leiden: Brill, 1972.

Ménard, *L'Évangile selon Thomas*   Ménard, J.-É. *L'Évangile selon Thomas.* NHS 5. Leiden: Brill, 1975.

Ménard, *Pierre à Philippe*   Ménard, J.-É. *La Lettre de Pierre à Philippe.* Québec: L'Université Laval, 1977.

Ménard, "*Plane*"   Ménard, J.-É. "La *plane* dans l'Évangile de Vérité." *Studia Montis Regii* 7 (1964) 3–36.

Ménard, "Structure"   Ménard, J.-É. "La structure et la langue originale de l'Évangile de Vérité." *RevScRel* 44 (1970) 128–37.

Merlan, "Plato to Plotinus"   Merlan, P. "Greek Philosophy from Plato to Plotinus" in A. H. Armstrong, ed. *The Cambridge History of Later Greek and Early Medieval Philosophy.* Cambridge: University Press, 1967, 14–132.

Meyer K   H. A. W. Meyer, Kritisch-exegetischer Kommentar über das Neue Testament

Meyer, *Peter to Philip*   Meyer, M. W. *The Letter of Peter to Philip. Text, Translation, and Commentary.* SBLDS 53. Chico, Calif.: Scholars, 1981.

Meyer-Mommsen, *Leges*   Meyer, P. M. and Mommsen, Th., eds. *Leges novellae ad Theodosianum pertinentes.* Berlin: Weidmann, 1905 (=Mommsen, *Theodosiani*, vol. 2).

Meyer-Sanders, *Self-Definition*   Meyer, B. F. and Sanders, E. P. *Jewish and Christian Self-Definition.* 3 vols. London: SCM, 1982.

Millar, *Empire*   Millar, F., ed. *The Roman Empire and Its Neighbours.* New York: Delacorte, 1967.

Mommsen, *Theodosiani*   Mommsen, Th., ed. *Theodosiani libri XVI cum Constitutionibus Sirmondianis.* 2 vols. Berlin: Weidmann, 1905. (=Meyer-Mommsen, *Leges*).

Montgomery, *Samaritans*   Montgomery, J. *The Samaritans.* 1907. Reprint. New York: KTAV, 1968.

Morard, "Adam-interprétation"   Morard, F. "L'Apocalypse d'Adam de Nag Hammadi: un essai d'interprétation" in Krause, *Eighth Conference on Patristic Studies*, 35–42.

Morard, "Adam-polémique"   Morard, F. "L'Apocalypse d'Adam du Codex V de Nag Hammadi et sa polémique anti-baptismale." *RevScRel* 51 (1977) 214–33.

Moses Khorenaçi   Moses Khorenaçi, *Patmut' iwn Hayots'* (History of the Armenians). Tiflis, 1913. Reprint. R. W. Thompson, ed. Delmar: Caravan, 1981.

Mühlenberg, "Erlösungen"   Mühlenberg, E. "Wieviel Erlösungen kennt der Gnostiker Herakleon?" *ZNW* 66 (1975) 170–93.

Müller, *Engellehre*   Müller, C. D. G. *Die Engellehre der koptischen Kirche.* Wiesbaden: Harrassowitz, 1959.

Müller, "Parakletenvorstellung"   Müller, U. B. "Die Parakletenvorstellung im Johannesevangelium." *ZThK* 71 (1974) 31–77.

Murray, "Ephraem"   Murray, R. "Ephraem Syrus." *ThRE* 9 (1982) 755–62.

Murray, "Exhortation"   Murray, R. "The Exhortation to Candidates for Ascetical Vows at Baptism." *NTS* 21 (1974/1975) 59–80.

al-Nadim, *Fihrist*   al-Nadim. *The Fihrist of al-Nadim.* Translated by B. Dodge. 2 vols. New York and London: Columbia University, 1970.

Nagel, "Auslegung"   Nagel, P. "Die Auslegung der Paradieserzählung in der Gnosis" in Tröger, *Altes Testament*, 49–70.

Nagel, "Codex II"   Nagel, P. "Grammatische Untersuchungen zu Nag Hammadi Codex II" in Altheim, *Araber*, 5.2. 393–469.

Nagel, "Herkunft"   Nagel, P. "Die Herkunft des Evangelium Veritatis in sprachlicher Sicht." *OLZ* 61 (1966) 5–14.

Nagel, *Studia*   Nagel, P., ed. *Studia Coptica*. Berliner Byzantinische Arbeiten 45. Berlin: Akademie, 1974.

Nagel, "Thomas"   Nagel, P. "Thomas der Mitstreiter (zu NHC II, 7: p. 138,8)" in *Mélanges offerts à M. Werner Vycichl*. Bulletin de la Société d' Egyptologie Genève 4. Genève: Société d'Egyptologie, 1980, 65–71.

Nau, *Barḥadbešabbā*   Nau, F., ed. *La seconde partie de l'histoire de Barḥadbešabbā Arbaya*. PO 9, 5. Paris: Firmin-Didot, 1913.

Nau, *La lettre à Cosme*   Nau, F., ed. *Histoire de Nestorius, d'après la lettre à Cosme et l'hymne de Ṣliba de Manṣourya*. PO 13,2. Paris: Firmin-Didot, 1916.

NEH   National Endowment for the Humanities

Neirynck, "Q"   Neirynck, F. "Q" in *IDBSup*, 715–6.

NH(C)   Nag Hammadi (Codex)

NF   Neue Folge

NHLE   *Nag Hammadi Library in English*

NHS   Nag Hammadi Studies

NTAbh   Neutestamentliche Abhandlungen

NTL   New Testament Library

NTS   *New Testament Studies*

NTT   *Norsk Teologisk Tidsskrift*

Nickelsburg, "Apocalyptic and Myth"   Nickelsburg, G. W. E. "Apocalyptic and Myth in 1 Enoch 6–11." *JBL* 96 (1977) 383–405.

Nickelsburg, *Jewish Literature*   Nickelsburg, G. W. E. *Jewish Literature Between the Bible and the Mishnah*. Philadelphia: Fortress, 1981.

Nickelsburg, "Related Traditions"   Nickelsburg, G. W. E. "Some Related Traditions in the Apocalypse of Adam, the Books of Adam and Eve and 1 Enoch" in Layton, *Rediscovery*, 2.515–39.

Nickelsburg, *Resurrection*   Nickelsburg, G. W. E. *Resurrection, Immortality, and Eternal Life in Intertestamental Judaism*. Cambridge, Mass.: Harvard University, 1972.

Nock-Festugière, *Hermès*   Nock, A. D. and A.-J. Festugière. *Hermès Trismégistes*. 4 vols. Paris: Société d'Édition "Les Belles Lettres," 1946–54.

Nock, "Library"   Nock, A. D. "A Coptic Library of Gnostic Writings." *JTS* 9 (1950) 314–24.

Nöldeke, *Chronik*   Nöldeke, Th. *Die von Guidi herausgegebene syrische Chronik*. Sitzungsberichte der phil.-hist. Klasse der kaiserlichen Akademie der Wissenschaften 128, 9. Wien: Tempsky, 1893.

Nöldeke, *Grammatik*   Nöldeke, Th. *Kurzgefasste syrische Grammatik*. 2nd ed. Darmstadt: Wissenschaftliche Buchgesellschaft, 1977.

NovT   *Novum Testamentum*

NovTSup   Novum Testamentum, Supplements

Oehler, *Corporis haereseologici*   Oehler, F. *Corporis haereseologici continens scriptores haereseologicos minores latinos*. 5 vols. Berlin: Ascher, 1856–61.

Ohlert, *Rätsel*   Ohlert, K. *Rätsel und Rätselspiele der alten Griechen*. 2nd ed. Berlin: Mayer & Müller, 1912.

OLZ   Orientalische Literaturzeitung
Or   Orientalia (Rome)
Orbe, Procesión del Verbo   Orbe, A. Hacia la primera theología de la procesión del verbo. Estudios Valentinianos-Volume 1.1. Analecta Gregoriana 99. Series Facultatis Theologicae, Sectio A (n. 17). Rome: Aedes Universitatis Gregorianae, 1958.
OrChrA   Orientalia Christiana Analecta
Orlandi, "Catechesis"   Orlandi, T. "A Catechesis against Apocryphal Texts by Shenute and the Gnostic Texts of Nag Hammadi." HTR 75 (1982) 85–95.
Origen, Cels.   Origen, Contra Celsum
Origen, Comm. in Mt.   Origen, Commentarii in Matthaeum
Ost   Ostkirchliche Studien
Oulton-Chadwick, Alexandrian Christianity   Oulton, J. E. L. and Chadwick, H. Alexandrian Christianity. LCC 2. Philadelphia: Westminster, 1954.
Outtier, "Ephrèm"   Outtier, B. "Saint Ephrèm d'après ses biographes et ses oeuvres." Parole de l'Orient 4 (1973) 11–33.
Overbeck, Ephraemi   Overbeck, J. J. S. Ephraemi Syri Rabbulae episcopi Edesseni Balaei aliorumque opera selecta. Oxford: Clarendon, 1865.
Pagels, "Controversies concerning Marriage"   Pagels, E. "Adam and Eve, Christ and the Church: A Survey of Second Century Controversies concerning Marriage" in Logan-Wedderburn, New Testament and Gnosis, 146–75.
Pagels, Gnostic Gospels   Pagels, E. The Gnostic Gospels. New York: Random, 1979.
Pagels, Gnostic Paul   Pagels, E. The Gnostic Paul: Gnostic Exegesis of Pauline Letters. Philadelphia: Fortress, 1975.
Pagels, "Gnosticism"   Pagels, E. "Gnosticism." IDBSup, 364–68.
Pagels, "Valentinian Eschatology"   Pagels, E. "Conflicting Versions of Valentinian Eschatology: Irenaeus' Treatise vs. the Excerpts from Theodotus." HTR 67 (1974) 35–53.
Parmentier, Theodoret   Parmentier, L. Theodoret, Kirchengeschichte. GCS 44. 2nd ed. Berlin: Akademie, 1954.
Parrott, Codices V and VI   Parrott, D. M., ed. Nag Hammadi Codices V, 2–5 and VI with Papyrus Berolinensis 8502, 1 and 4. NHS 11. Leiden: Brill, 1979.
Parrott, "Relation between Gnosticism and Christianity"   Parrott, D. M. "The Significance of the Letter of Eugnostos and the Sophia of Jesus Christ for the Understanding of the Relation between Gnosticism and Christianity" in The Society of Biblical Literature One Hundred Seventh Annual Meeting Seminar Papers—28–31 October 1971 Regency Hyatt House—Atlanta, Ga. 2 vols. SBL, 1971, 2. 397–416.
Parrott, "Religious Syncretism"   Parrott, D. M. "Evidence of Religious Syncretism in Gnostic Texts from Nag Hammadi" in Pearson, Syncretism, 173–89.
Pearson, Codices IX and X   Pearson, B., ed. Nag Hammadi Codices IX and X. NHS 15. Leiden: Brill, 1981.
Pearson, "Exegesis"   Pearson, B. A. "Biblical Exegesis in Gnostic Literature" in M. Stone, ed. Armenian and Biblical Studies. Jerusalem: St. James, 1976, 70–80.
Pearson, "Gnostic Self-Definition"   Pearson, B. A. "Jewish Elements in Gnosticism and the Development of Gnostic Self-Definition" in Sanders, Christianity, 151–60.
Pearson, "Haggadic Traditions"   Pearson, B. A. "Jewish Haggadic Traditions in the Testimony of Truth from Nag Hammadi (CG IX, 3)" in Bergman, Ex Orbe Religionum 1.457–70.

Pearson, "Judaism and Gnostic Origins"   Pearson, B. A. "Friedländer Revisited: Alexandrian Judaism and Gnostic Origins." *Studia Philonica* 2 (1973), 23–39.

Pearson, *Man and Salvation*   Pearson, B. A. *Philo and the Gnostics on Man and Salvation.* Berkeley: Center for Hermeneutical Studies in Hellenistic and Modern Culture, 1977.

Pearson, "Marsanes"   Pearson, B. A. "The Tractate Marsanes (NHC X) and the Platonic Tradition" in Aland, *Gnosis*, 373–84.

Pearson, "Norea"   Pearson, B. A. "The Figure of Norea in Gnostic Literature" in Widengren, *Proceedings*, 143–52.

Pearson, "Review"   Pearson, B. A. "Review of B. Barc, *L'Hypostase des Archontes.*" *The Second Century* 2 (1982) 183–85.

Pearson, "Seth"   Pearson, B. A. "The Figure of Seth in Gnostic Literature" in Layton, *Rediscovery*, 2.472–504.

Pearson, "Sources"   Pearson, B. A. "Jewish Sources in Gnostic Literature" in Stone, *Jewish Writings*, 443–81.

Pearson, *Syncretism*   Pearson, B. A., ed. *Religious Syncretism in Antiquity.* Missoula, Mont.: Scholars, 1975.

Pearson, *Terminology*   Pearson, B. A. *The Pneumatikos-Psychikos Terminology.* SBLDS 12. Missoula, Mont.: Scholars, 1973.

Pearson, "Tree"   Pearson, B. A. "'She Became a Tree'—A Note to CG II, 4:89, 25–26." *HTR* 69 (1976) 413–15.

Peeters, "Observations"   Peeters, P. "Observations sur la vie syriaque de Mar Aba catholicos de l'église de Perse (540–552)" in Peeters, *Recherches*, 1.117–63.

Peeters, "Pour l'histoire"   Peeters, P. "Pour l'histoire des origines de l'alphabet arménien" in Peeters, *Recherches*, 1.171–207.

Peeters, *Recherches*   Peeters, P. *Recherches d'histoire et de philologie orientales.* 2 vols. Brussels: Sociétés Bollandi, 1951.

Perkins, "Genre and Function"   Perkins, P. "Apocalypse of Adam: The Genre and Function of a Gnostic Apocalypse." *CBQ* 39 (1977) 382–95.

Perkins, *Gnostic Dialogue*   Perkins, P. *The Gnostic Dialogue.* New York: Paulist, 1980.

Perkins, "Irenaeus and the Gnostics"   Perkins, P. "Irenaeus and the Gnostics: Rhetoric and Composition in *Adversus Haereses* Book One." *VC* 30 (1976) 193–200.

Perkins, *Johannine Epistles*   Perkins, P. *The Johannine Epistles.* New Testament Message 21. Wilmington, Del.: Glazier, 1979.

Perkins, "Soteriology"   Perkins, P. "The Soteriology of Sophia of Jesus Christ" in *The Society of Biblical Literature One Hundred Seventh Annual Meeting Seminar Papers—28–31 October 1971 Regency Hyatt House—Atlanta, Ga.* 2 vols. SBL, 1971, 2.165–81.

Petermann, *Thesaurus*   Petermann, H., ed. *Thesaurus s[ive] Liber magnus.* 2 vols. Leipzig: Pietz, 1967–.

PG   J. Migne, *Patrologia Graeca*

Philo, *Abr.*   Philo, *De Abrahamo*

Philo, *Aet. Mund.*   Philo, *De Aeternitate Mundi*

Philo, *Conf.*   Philo, *De Confusione Linguarum*

Philo, *Fug.*   Philo, *De Fuga et Inventione*

Philo, *Her.*   Philo, *Quis rerum divinarum heres sit*

Philo, *L.A.*   Philo, *Legum Allegoriarum*

Philo, *Mig.*   Philo, *De Migratione Abrahami*

Philo, *Op. Mund.*   Philo, *De Opificio Mundi*
Philo, *Post.*   Philo, *De Posteritate Caini*
Philo, *Prob.*   Philo, *Quod omnis probus liber*
Philo, *Quaest. in Exod.*   Philo, *Quaestiones et Solutiones in Exodum*
Philo, *Quod Deus*   Philo, *Quod deus sit immutabilis*
Philo, *Somn.*   Philo, *De Somniis*
Philo, *Virt.*   Philo, *De Virtutibus*
Philo, *Vit. Mos.*   Philo, *De Vita Mosis*
PL   J. Migne, *Patrologia Latina*
Plato, *Cra.*   Plato, *Cratylus*
Plato, *Laws*   Plato, *The Laws*
Plato, *Tim.*   Plato, *Timaeus*
Plutarch, *Com. Not.*   *De communibus notitiis adversus Stoicos*
Plutarch, *De Fac. Lun.*   *De facie quae in orbe lunae apparet*
Plutarch, *Def. Or.*   *De defectu oraculorum*
Plutarch, *Is. Osir.*   *De Iside Osiride*
Plutarch, *Plat. Qu.*   *Platonicae quaestiones*
Plutarch, *Stoic. Repug.*   *De Stoicorum repugnantiis*
PO   Patrologia orientalis
Poirier, "L'Évangile de Vérité"   Poirier, P.-H. "L'Évangile de Vérité, Ephrem la Syrien et le comput digital." *Revue des Études Augustiniennes* 25 (1979) 27–34.
Polag, *Christologie der Logienquelle*   Polag, A. *Die Christologie der Logienquelle*. WMANT 45. Neukirchen-Vluyn: Neukirchener Verlag, 1977.
Polotsky, *Kephalaia*   Polotsky, H. J., ed. *Kephalaia*. Stuttgart: Kohlhammer, 1940.
Porph. *Vit. Plot.*   Porphyry, *Vita Plotini*
Prigent, "L'hérésie asiate"   Prigent, P. "L'hérésie asiate et l'église confessante de l'Apocalypse à Ignace." *VC* 31 (1977) 1–22.
Priscillian, *Tractatus I*   Priscillian, *Tractatus I*. CSEL 18. Edited by G. Schepps. Wien: Tempsky, 1899.
Przybylski, "Calendrical Data"   Przybylski, B. "The Role of Calendrical Data in Gnostic Literature." *VC* 34 (1980) 56–70.
Ps.-Clem. Hom.   *Pseudo-Clementine Homilies*
Ps.-Clem. Rec.   *Pseudo-Clementine Recognitions*
Ps.-Ephrem, *Testament*   Pseudo-Ephrem. *Testament des heiligen Ephrem des Syrers Sermones IV*. CSCO 334. Edited by E. Beck. Louvain: Secréteriat CSCO, 1973.
Ps.-Tertullian, *Haer.*   Pseudo-Tertullian, *Adversus omnes haereses*. Edited by E. Kroymann. Vol. 2. in Tertullian, *Opera*. 2 vols.; CC series latina 1–2. Turnhout: Brepols, 1953–54. 2.1401–10.
Puech, "Allogène"   Puech, H.-Ch. "Fragments retrouvés de l'Apocalypse d'Allogène" in *En quête de la gnose*. 2 vols. Paris: Gallimard, 1978, 1.271–300.
Puech, "Archontiker"   Puech, H.-C. "Archontiker." *RAC* (1960) 1.634–35.
Puech, "Gospel of Truth"   Puech, H.-Ch. "The Gospel of Truth" in Hennecke-Schneemelcher, *NT Apocrypha*, 1.233–40.
Puech, "Review of Drower"   Puech, H.-Ch. "Reveiw of E. S. Drower, The Mandaeans of Iraq and Iran." *RHR* 124 (1941) 63–74.
PW   Pauly-Wissowa, Real-Encyclopädie der klassischen Altertumswissenschaft
Quasten, *Patrology*   Quasten, J. *Patrology*. 3 vols. Utrecht-Antwerp: Spectrum, 1966.

Quispel, "Borborianer"   Quispel, G. "Borborianer (Borboriten)." *RGG* (1957) 1.1365.

Quispel, "Ezekiel"   Quispel, G. "Ezekiel 1:26 in Jewish Mysticism and Gnosis." *VC* 34 (1980) 1–13.

Quispel, "Gnosis"   Quispel, G. "Gnosis" in Vermaseren, *Die orientalischen Religionen*, 413–35.

Quispel, "Gnostic Demiurge"   Quispel, G. "The Origins of the Gnostic Demiurge" in *Gnostic Studies*. 2 vols. Istanbul: Nederlands Historisch-Archaeologisch Instituut, 1974–75, 1.213–20.

Quispel, "Jung Codex"   Quispel, G. "The Jung Codex and its Significance" in Cross, *The Jung Codex*, 35–78.

Quispel, "Valentinian Gnosis"   Quispel, G. "Valentinian Gnosis and the Apocryphon of John" in Layton, *Rediscovery*, 1.118–27.

RAC   *Reallexikon für Antike und Christentum*

Reinink, "Problem"   Reinink, G. "Das Problem des Ursprungs des Testaments Adams." *OrChrA* 197 (1972) 387–99.

Rensberger, "Apostle"   Rensberger, D. K. "As the Apostle Teaches: The Development of the Use of Paul's Letters in Second Century Christianity," Unpublished Ph.D. Dissertation, Yale University, New Haven, 1981.

RevScRel   *Revue des sciences religieuses*

RGG   *Religion in Geschichte und Gegenwart*

RHR   *Revue de l'histoire des religions*

Roberge, *Norea*   Roberge, M. *Norea*. BCNH, Texte 5. Québec: Université Laval, 1980.

Robinson, "Collections"   Robinson, J. M. "Early Collections of Jesus' Sayings" in Delobel, *Logia*, 389–94.

Robinson, *Facsimile Edition*   Robinson, J. M. ed. *The Facsimile Edition of the Nag Hammadi Codices*. 12 vols. Leiden: Brill, 1972–84.

Robinson, *Future of Our Religious Past*   Robinson, J. M., ed. *The Future of Our Religious Past: Essays in Honour of Rudolf Bultmann*. Translated by C. E. Carlston and R. P. Scharlemann. London: SCM, 1971.

Robinson, "*Gattung* of Mark"   Robinson, J. M. "On the *Gattung* of Mark (and John)" in *Jesus and Man's Hope*. 2 vols. Pittsburgh, Penn.: Pittsburgh Theological Seminary, 1970, 1.99–129.

Robinson, "Gnosticism and the New Testament"   Robinson, J. M. "Gnosticism and the New Testament" in Aland, *Gnosis*, 125–43.

Robinson, "Jesus from Easter to Valentinus"   Robinson, J. M. "Jesus from Easter to Valentinus (or to the Apostles' Creed)." *JBL* 101 (1982) 5–37.

Robinson, "Jung Codex"   Robinson, J. M. "The Jung Codex: The Rise and Fall of a Monopoly." *Religious Studies Review* 3 (1977) 17–30.

Robinson, "LOGOI SOPHŌN"   Robinson, J. M. "*LOGOI SOPHŌN*: On the *Gattung* of Q" in Robinson, *Future of our Religious Past*, 84–130.

Robinson, "LOGOI SOPHŌN"   Robinson, J. M. "LOGOI SOPHŌN: Zur Gattung der Spruchquelle Q" in E. Dinkler, ed. *Zeit und Geschichte*. Tübingen: Mohr, 1964, 77–96.

Robinson, *Nag Hammadi Codices*   Robinson, J. M. *The Nag Hammadi Codices*. 2nd ed. rev. Claremont, Calif.: Institute for Antiquity and Christianity, 1977.

Robinson, "Narrative"   Robinson, J. M. "The Gospels as Narrative" in F. McConnell, ed. *The Bible and the Narrative Tradition*. New York: Oxford University, forthcoming.

Robinson, *NHLE*   Robinson, J. M., gen. ed. *The Nag Hammadi Library in English*. New York: Harper and Row, 1977.

Robinson, "Sethians"   Robinson, J. M. "Sethians and Johannine Thought: The *Trimorphic Protennoia* and the Prologue of the Gospel of John" in Layton, *Rediscovery*, 2.643–62.

Robinson, "Steles"   Robinson, J. M. "The Three Steles of Seth and the Gnostics of Plotinus" in Widengren, *Proceedings*, 132–42.

Robinson-Koester, *Entwicklungslinien*   Robinson, J. M. and Koester, H. *Entwicklungslinien durch die Welt des frühen Christentums*. Tübingen: Mohr, 1971.

Robinson-Koester, *Trajectories*   Robinson, J. M. and Koester, H. *Trajectories through Early Christianity*. Philadelphia: Fortress, 1968.

Robinson, S., *Adam*   Robinson, S. E. *The Testament of Adam: An Examination of the Syriac and Greek Traditions*. SBLDS 52. Chico, Calif.: Scholars, 1982.

Roloff, "Lieblingsjünger"   Roloff, J. "Der johanneische 'Lieblingsjünger' und der Lehrer der Gerechtigkeit." *NTS* 15 (1968/1969) 129–51.

Rousseau-Doutreleau, *Haereses*   Rousseau, A. and Doutreleau, L., eds. *Irénée de Lyon: Contre les hérésies*. Paris: Cerf, 1979.

RThPh   *Revue de théologie et de philosophie*

Rudolph, *Baptisten*   Rudolph, K. *Antike Baptisten: Zu den Überlieferungen über frühjüdische und christliche Taufsekten*. Sitzungsberichte der sächsischen Akademie der Wissenschaften zu Leipzig. Phil.-hist. Klasse Bd. 121, Heft 4. Berlin: Akademie, 1981.

Rudolph, "Christentum"   Rudolph, K. "Das Christentum in der Sicht der mandäischen Religion." *Wissenschaftliche Zeitschrift der Karl-Marx-Universität Leipzig*. Gesellschaftliche und sprachwissenschaftliche Reihe 7 (1957–1958) 651–59.

Rudolph, "Gnosis, ein Forschungsbericht"   Rudolph, K. "Gnosis und Gnostizismus: Ein Forschungsbericht." *ThR* 34 (1969) 121–75, 181–231, 358–61; 36 (1971) 1–61, 89–124; 37 (1972)289–360 and 38 (1973) 1–25.

Rudolph, *Gnosis: Nature and History*   Rudolph, K. *Gnosis: The Nature and History of Gnosticism*. Translated by R. McL. Wilson. San Francisco: Harper and Row, 1983 (=*Gnosis: Wesen und Geschichte*).

Rudolph, *Gnosis: Wesen und Geschichte*   Rudolph, K. *Die Gnosis: Wesen und Geschichte einer spätantiken Religion*. Göttingen: Vandenhoeck & Ruprecht, 1977 (=*Gnosis: Nature and History*).

Rudolph, *Gnostizismus*   Rudolph, K., ed. *Gnosis und Gnostizismus*. Wege der Forschung 262. Darmstadt: Wissenschaftliche Buchgesellschaft, 1975.

Rudolph, "Weltreligion"   Rudolph, K. "Gnosis–Weltreligion oder Sekte (Zur Problematik sachgemässer Terminologie in der Religionswissenschaft)." *Kairos* 21 (1979) 255–63.

Rudolph, *Mandäer*   Rudolph, K. *Die Mandäer*. 2 vols. Göttingen: Vandenhoeck & Ruprecht, 1960–61.

Runia, "Philo"   Runia, D. T. "Philo's *Aeternitate Mundi*: The Problem of its Interpretation." *VC* 35 (1981) 105–51.

Sachau, *Chronology*   Sachau, E., ed. *The Chronology of Ancient Nations*. London: Allen, 1879.

Sachau, *Klosterbuch*   Sachau, E. *Vom Klosterbuch des Šabušti*. Abhandlungen der preussischen Akademie der Wissenschaften. Phil.-hist. Klasse 10. Berlin: de Gruyter, 1919.

Sanders, E., *Christianity*   Sanders, E. *The Shaping of Christianity in the Second and Third Centuries.* London: SCM; Philadelphia: Fortress, 1980.

SANT   Studien zum Alten und Neuen Testament

SBL   Society of Biblical Literature

SBLDS   Society of Biblical Literature Dissertation Series

SBLSP   Society of Biblical Literature Seminar Papers

SBLTT   SBL Texts and Translations

SBS   Stuttgarter Bibelstudien

SC   Sources chrétiennes

Schelkle, "Zeugnis"   Schelkle, K. H. "Das Evangelium Veritatis als kanongeschichtliches Zeugnis." *BZ* 5 (1961) 90–91.

Schenke, G., "'Dreigestaltige Protennoia'"   Schenke, G. "'Die dreigestaltige Protennoia': Eine gnostische Offenbarungsrede in koptischer Sprache aus dem Fund von Nag Hammadi eingeleitet und übersetzt vom Berliner Arbeitskreis für koptisch-gnostische Schriften." *ThLZ* 99 (1974) 731–46.

Schenke, G., "Protennoia"   Schenke, G. "Die dreigestaltige Protennoia (Nag-Hammadi-Codex XIII) herausgegeben und kommentiert," Dr. Theol. Dissertation, Rostock, 1977.

Schenke, H.-M., "Book of Thomas"   Schenke, H.-M. "The Book of Thomas (NHC II. 7): A Revision of a Pseudepigraphical Epistle of Jacob the Contender" in LoganWedderburn, *New Testament and Gnosis*, 213–28.

Schenke, H.-M., "Christologie"   Schenke, H.-M. "Die neutestamentliche Christologie und der gnostische Erlöser" in Tröger, *Gnosis*, 205–29.

Schenke, H.-M., "Gnosis"   Schenke, H.-M. "Die Gnosis" in J. Leipoldt and W. Grundmann, eds. *Umwelt des Christentums.* 3 vols. 6th ed. Berlin: Evangelische Verlagsanstalt, 1982, 1.371–415.

Schenke, H.-M., *Gott "Mensch"*   Schenke, H.-M. *Der Gott "Mensch" in der Gnosis.* Göttingen: Vandenhoeck & Ruprecht, 1962.

Schenke, H.-M., *Herkunft*   Schenke, H.-M. *Die Herkunft des sogennanten Evangelium Veritatis.* Berlin: Evangelischer Verlag, 1958; Göttingen: Vandenhoeck & Ruprecht, 1959.

Schenke, H.-M., "Jakobusbrief"   Schenke, H.-M. "Der Jakobusbrief aus dem Codex Jung." *OLZ* 66 (1971) 117–30.

Schenke, H.-M., Melchisedek"   Schenke, H.-M. "Die jüdische Melchisedek-Gestalt als Thema der Gnosis" in Tröger, *Altes Testament*, 111–36.

Schenke, H.-M., "Review"   Schenke, H.-M. "Review of Le Origini dello Gnosticismo." *ThLZ* 93 (1968) 903–5.

Schenke, H.-M., "Review of Ménard"   Schenke, H.-M. "Review of Ménard, L'Évangile selon Thomas." *OLZ* 77 (1982) cols. 262–64.

Schenke, H.-M., "Sethianism"   Schenke, H.-M. "The Phenomenon and Significance of Gnostic Sethianism" in Layton, *Rediscovery*, 2.588–616.

Schenke, H.-M., "Studien I"   Schenke, H.-M. "Nag Hammadi Studien I: Das literarische Problem des Apokryphon Johannis." *ZRGG* 14 (1962) 57–63.

Schenke, H.-M., "Studien II"   Schenke, H.-M. "Nag Hammadi Studien II: Das System der Sophia Jesu Christi." *ZRGG* 14 (1962) 263–78.

Schenke, H.-M. "System"   Schenke, H.-M., "Das sethianische System nach Nag-Hammadi-Handschriften" in Nagel, *Studia*, 165–73.

Schenke-Fischer, *Einleitung*   Schenke, H.-M. and Fischer, K. M. *Einleitung in die Schriften des Neuen Testaments.* 2 vols. Berlin: Evangelische Verlagsanstalt, 1978.

Scher, *Theodorus bar Koni*   Scher, A., ed. *Theodorus bar Koni, Liber Scholiorum.*
CSCO 65-6. 2 vols. Parisiis. E Typographeo Reipublicae, 1910. Reprint. Louvain:
CSCO, 1954.
Schmidt, "Borborianer (Borboriten)"   Schmidt, C. "Borborianer (Borboriten)."
RGG² (1927) 1.1200.
Schmidt, "Irenaeus"   Schmidt, C. "Irenaeus und seine Quelle in adv. haer. I. 29"
in A. Harnack, et al., eds. *Philotesia. Paul Kleinert zum LXX. Geburtstag.* Berlin:
Trowizsch, 1907, 315-36.
Schmidt, *Schriften*   Schmidt, C. *Gnostische Schriften in koptischer Sprache aus
dem Codex Brucianus.* TU 8. Leipzig: Hinrichs, 1892.
Schmidt-MacDermot, *Bruce Codex*   Schmidt, C. and MacDermot, V., eds. *The
Books of Jeu and the Untitled Text in the Bruce Codex.* NHS 13. Leiden: Brill,
1978.
Schmidt-MacDermot, *Pistis Sophia*   Schmidt, C. and MacDermot, V., eds. *Pistis
Sophia.* NHS 9. Leiden: Brill, 1978.
Schmidt-Till, *Schriften*   Schmidt, C. *Koptisch-gnostische Schriften. Erster Band.
Die Pistis Sophia. Die beiden Bücher des Jeû, Unbekanntes altgnostisches Werk.*
Edited by W. Till. CGS 45. 3rd ed. Berlin: Akademie, 1962.
Schmithals, *Paul and the Gnostics*   Schmithals, W. *Paul and the Gnostics.*
Translated by J. E. Steely. Nashville/New York: Abingdon, 1972 (German 1965).
Schnackenburg, *Johannesevangelium*   Schnackenburg, R. *Das
Johannesevangelium.* HThKNT 4. 3 vols. Freiburg: Herder, 1965-1975.
Schnackenburg, "Jünger"   Schnackenburg, R. "Der Jünger, den Jesus liebte." *EKK*
2 (1970) 97-117.
Schoedel, "Monism"   Schoedel, W. R. "Gnostic Monism and the *Gospel of Truth*"
in Layton, *Rediscovery*, 1.379-90.
Schoedel, "Theology"   Schoedel, W. R. "Topological Theology and Some Monistic
Tendencies in Gnosticism" in Krause, *Essays*, 88-108.
Schoeps, *Zeit*   Schoeps, H. J. *Aus frühchristlicher Zeit.* Tübingen: Mohr, 1950.
Scholem, *Traditions*   Scholem, G. *Jewish Gnosticism, Merkabah Mysticism, and
Talmudic Traditions.* New York: Jewish Theological Seminary of America, 1965.
Scholar, *Nag Hammadi Bibliography*   Scholer, D. M. *Nag Hammadi
Bibliography 1948-1969.* Leiden: Brill, 1971.
Schottroff, "Animae"   Schottroff, L. "Animae naturaliter salvandae" in Eltester,
Christentum, 65-97.
Schottroff-Stegemann, *Jesus*   Schottroff, L. and Stegemann, W. *Jesus von
Nazareth: Hoffnung der Armen.* Stuttgart: Kohlhammer, 1978.
Schrage, "Evangelienzitate"   Schrage, W. "Evangelienzitate in Oxyrhynchus-
Logien und im koptischen Thomas-Evangelium" in Eltester, *Apophoreta*, 251-68.
Schrage, *Verhältnis*   Schrage, W. *Das Verhältnis des ThEv zur synoptischen
Tradition und zu den koptischen Bibelübersetzungen.* BZNW 29. Berlin:
Töpelmann, 1965.
Schulz, *Q*   Schulz, S. *Q: Die Spruchquelle der Evangelisten.* Zürich:
Theologischer Verlag, 1972.
Schultz, "Rätsel"   Schultz, W. "Rätsel." *PW* 1A/1 (1914) 62-125.
Schultz, *Rätsel aus dem hellenischen Kulturkreise*   Schultz, W. *Rätsel aus dem
hellenischen Kulturkreise.* 2 vols. Mythologische Bibliotek III/1, V/1. Leipzig:
Henrichs, 1909, 1912.
Scobie, *John the Baptist*   Scobie, C. *John the Baptist.* Philadelphia: Fortress, 1964.

Scopello, "Youel et Barbelo"   Scopello, M. "Youel et Barbelo dans le traité de l'Allogène" in Barc, *Colloque*, 86–98.

Segel, *Two Powers in Heaven*   Segel, A. F. *Two Powers in Heaven: Early Rabbinic Reports about Christianity and Gnosticism.* Leiden: Brill, 1977.

Segelberg, "Confirmation Homily"   Segelberg, E. "Evangelium Veritatis: A Confirmation Homily and its Relation to the Odes of Solomon." *Orientalia Suecana* 8 (1959) 3–42.

Seneca, *Ep.*   Seneca, *Epistulae morales*

Shellrude, "Adam"   Shellrude, G. M. "The Apocalypse of Adam: Evidence for a Christian-Gnostic Provenance" in Krause, *Eighth Conference on Patristic Studies*, 82–91.

Shibata, "Character"   Shibata, Y. "Non-Docetic Character of the Evangelium Veritatis." *Annual of the Japanese Bible Institute* 1 (1975) 127–34.

Sieber, "Barbelo Aeon"   Sieber, J. "The Barbelo Aeon as Sophia in *Zostrianos* and Related Tractates" in Layton, *Rediscovery*, 2.788–95.

Sieber, "Zostrianos"   Sieber, J. "An Introduction to the Tractate Zostrianos from Nag Hammadi." *NovT* 15 (1973) 233–40.

Siegert, *Register*   Siegert, F. *Nag-Hammadi-Register.* Tübingen: Mohr, 1982.

Siegert, "Selbstbezeichnungen"   Siegert, F. "Selbstbezeichnungen der Gnostiker in den Nag-Hammadi-Texten." *ZNW* 71 (1980) 129–32.

Smart, *Worldviews*   Smart, N. *Worldviews: Crosscultural Explorations of Human Beliefs.* New York: Scribners, 1983.

Smith, "Garments"   Smith, J. Z. "Garments of Shame." *HR* 5 (1965/1966) 217–38.

Smith, "Gnostikos"   Smith, M. "History of the Term Gnostikos" in Layton, *Rediscovery*, 2.796–807.

Smith, *Secret Gospel: Discovery*   Smith, M. *The Secret Gospel: The Discovery and Interpretation of the Secret Gospel according to Mark.* New York: Harper and Row, 1973.

Smith, *Secret Gospel of Mark*   Smith, M. *Clement of Alexandria and a Secret Gospel of Mark.* Cambridge, Mass.: Harvard, 1973.

Smith, *Thesaurus*   Smith, R. P. *Thesaurus syriacus.* 2 vols. Oxford: Clarendon, 1879–1901.

Socrates, *Hist. eccl.*   Socrates, *Historia ecclesiastica*

SNTSMS   Society for New Testament Studies Monograph Series

Speyer, "Vorwürfen"   Speyer, W. "Zu den Vorwürfen der Heiden gegen die Christen." *JAC* 6 (1963) 129–35.

Stählin-Früchtel, *Clem. Alex., Stromata*   Stählin, O. and Früchtel, L., eds. *Clemens Alexandrinus. 2. Band. Stromata Buch I–VI.* CGS 52. 3rd ed. Berlin: Akademie, 1960.

Standaert, "L'Évangile de Vérité"   Standaert, B. "L'Évangile de Vérité: critique et lecture." *NTS* 22 (1975) 243–75.

Standaert, "Titre"   Standaert, B. "'Evangelium Veritatis' et 'veritas evangelium': La question du titre et les témoins patristiques." *VC* 30 (1976) 138–50.

Stegemann, *Das Evangelium und die Armen*   Stegemann, W. *Das Evangelium und die Armen: über den Ursprung der Theologie der Armen im Neuen Testament.* München: Kaiser, 1981.

Stone, *Jewish Writings*   Stone, M. E., ed. *Jewish Writings of the Second Temple Period: Apocrypha, Pseudepigrapha, Qumran Sectarian Writings, Philo, Josephus.* Compendia Rerum Iudaicarum ad Novum Testamentum 2.2. Assen: Van Gorcum; Philadelphia: Fortress, 1984.

Stone, *Profile of Judaism*   Stone, M. *Scriptures, Sects, and Visions: A Profile of Judaism from Ezra to the Jewish Revolts.* Philadelphia: Fortress Press, 1980.

Story, *Truth*   Story, C. I. K. *The Nature of Truth in the "Gospel of Truth" and in the Writings of Justin Martyr.* NovTSup 25. Leiden: Brill, 1970.

Strecker, "Bergpredigt"   Strecker, G. "Die Antithesen der Bergpredigt (Mt 5 21–48 par)." *ZNW* 69 (1978) 36–71.

Stroumsa, *Another Seed*   Stroumsa, G. *Another Seed: Studies in Gnostic Mythology.* NHS 24. Leiden: Brill, 1984.

Tardieu, "Epiphane contre les gnostiques"   Tardieu, M. "Epiphane contre les gnostiques." *Tel Quel* 88 (1981) 64–91.

Tardieu, "Les livres de Seth"   Tardieu, M. "Les livres mis sous le nom de Seth, et les Séthiens de l'hérésiologie" in Krause, *Seventh Conference on Patristic Studies, 204–10.*

Tardieu, "Mythes"   Tardieu, M. *Trois Mythes Gnostiques: Adam, Eros et les animaux d'Egypte, dans un écrit de Nag Hammadi (II, 5).* Études Augustiniennes: Paris, 1974.

Tate, "Allegory"   Tate, J. "Allegory, Greek" and "Allegory, Latin." *Oxford Classical Dictionary.* 2nd ed. Clarendon, 1970, 45–46.

Theissen, "Itinerant Radicalism"   Theissen, G. "Itinerant Radicalism." *Radical Religion* 2 (1975) 84–93.

Theissen, *Sociology*   Theissen, G. *Sociology of Early Palestinian Christianity.* Translated by J. Bowden. Philadelphia: Fortress, 1978.

Theissen, *Soziologie*   Theissen, G. *Soziologie der Jesusbewegung.* München: Kaiser, 1977.

Theissen, *Studien*   Theissen, G. *Studien zur Soziologie des Urchristentums.* WUNT 19. Tübingen: Mohr, 1979.

Theissen, *Followers*   Theissen, G. *The First Followers of Jesus.* Translated by J. Bowden. London: SCM, 1978.

Theissen, "Wanderradikalismus"   Theissen, G. "Wanderradikalismus." *ZThK* 70 (1973) 249–71.

Theissen, "Nachfolge und soziale Entwürzelung"   Theissen, G. "Wir haben alles verlassen (Mc 10:28): Nachfolge und soziale Entwürzelung in der jüdisch-palästinischen Gesellschaft des 1. Jahrhunderts n. Chr." *NovT* 19 (1977) 161–96.

Theod. *Hist. eccl.*   Theodoret, *Historia ecclesiastica*

ThLZ   *Theologische Literaturzeitung*

Thomas, *Mouvement baptiste*   Thomas, J. *Le mouvement baptiste en Palestine et Syrie (150 av J.-C – 300 ap. J.-C).* Gembloux: Duculot, 1935.

Thomson, *Moses*   Thomson, R. W. *Moses Khorenaçi, History of the Armenians.* Cambridge, Mass.: Harvard, 1978.

ThR   *Theologische Rundschau*

ThRE   *Theologische Realenzyklopädie*

Thyen, "Entwicklungen"   Thyen, H. "Entwicklungen innerhalb der johanneischen Theologie und Kirche im Spiegel von Joh 21 und der Lieblingsjüngertexte des Evangeliums" in de Jonge, *L'Évangile de Jean,* 259–99.

Thyen, "Johannes 13"   Thyen, H. "Johannes 13 und die 'kirchliche Redaktion' des vierten Evangeliums" in G. Jeremias, et al., eds. *Tradition und Glaube: Festgabe für Karl-Georg Kuhn.* Göttingen: Vandenhoeck & Ruprecht, 1971, 343–56.

Thyen, "Johannesevangelium"   Thyen, H. "Aus der Literatur zum Johannesevangelium (3.Fortsetzung)." *ThR* 42 (1977) 213–61.

Till, "Bemerkungen"   Till, W. C. "Bemerkungen zur Erstausgabe des 'Evangelium veritatis.'" *Or* 27 (1958) 269–86.

Till-Schenke, *Papyrus Berolinensis 8502*   Till, W. C. and Schenke, H.-M. *Die gnostischen Schriften des koptischen Papyrus Berolinensis 8502.* TU 60. 2nd ed. Berlin: Akademie, 1972.

von Tischendorf, *Apocalypses Apocryphae*   Tischendorf, K. von. *Apocalypses Apocryphae.* 1866. Reprint. Hildesheim: Olms, 1966.

Trenchard, *Ben Sira*   Trenchard, W. C. *Ben Sira's View of Women: A Literary Analysis.* Brown Judaic Series 28. Chico, Calif.: Scholars, 1982.

Tröger, *Altes Testament*   Tröger, K.-W., ed. *Altes Testament-Frühjudentum-Gnosis: Neue Studien zu "Gnosis und Bibel."* Berlin: Evangelische Verlagsanstalt, 1980.

Tröger, *Gnosis*   Tröger, K.-W., ed. *Gnosis und Neues Testament: Studien aus Religionswissenschaft und Theologie.* Berlin: Evangelische Verlagsanstalt, 1973.

Tröger, "Spekulativ-esoterische Ansätze"   Tröger, K.-W. "Spekulativ-esoterische Ansätze (Frühjudentum und Gnosis)" in J. Maier and J. Schreiner, eds. *Literatur und Religion des Frühjudentums.* Würzburg: Echter, 1973, 310–19.

Tröger, "Attitude"   Tröger, K.-W. "The Attitude of the Gnostic Religion towards Judaism as Viewed in a Variety of Perspectives" in Barc, *Colloque,* 86–98.

TU   Texte und Untersuchungen

Turner, "Threefold Path"   Turner, J. "The Gnostic Threefold Path to Enlightenment: The Ascent of Mind and the Descent of Wisdom." *NovT* 22 (1980) 324–51.

van Unnik, "Document"   Unnik, W. C. van. "A Document of Second Century Theological Discussion (Irenaeus, *A. H.* I. 10.3)." *VC* 31 (1977) 205–26.

van Unnik, "Neid"   Unnik, W. C. van. "Der Neid in der Paradiesgeschichte nach einigen gnostischen Texten" in Krause, *Essays,* 120–32.

van Unnik, "*Komponente*"   Unnik, W. C. van. "Die jüdischen Komponente in der Entstehung der Gnosis" in Rudolph, *Gnostizismus,* 65–82.

van Unnik, "Gospel of Truth"   Unnik, W. C. van. "The Gospel of Truth and the New Testament" in Cross, *The Jung Codex,* 79–129.

van Unnik, "Origin"   Unnik, W. C. van. "The Origin of the Recently Discovered 'Apocryphon Jacobi.'" *VC* 10 (1956) 149–56.

VC   *Vigiliae christianae*

Venables, "Aetius"   Venables, E. "Aetius." *DCB,* 1.50–53.

Vermaseren, *Die Orientalischen Religionen*   Vermaseren, M. J. ed. *Die Orientalischen Religionen im Römerreich.* Études préliminaires aux religions orientales dans l'Empire romain 93. Leiden: Brill, 1981.

Vielhauer, *Aufsätze*   Vielhauer, Ph. *Aufsätze zum Neuen Testament.* Theologische Bücherei 31. München: Kaiser, 1965.

Vielhauer, "Gottesreich und Menschensohn"   Vielhauer, Ph. "Gottesreich und Menschensohn in der Verkündigung Jesu" in W. Schneemelcher, ed. *Festschrift für Günther Dehn zum 75. Geburtstag am 18. April 1957 dargebracht von der Evangelisch-Theologischen Fakultät der Rheinischen Friedrich Wilhelms-Universität zu Bonn.* Neukirchen Kreis Moers: Erziehungsverein, 1957, 51–79.

Vielhauer, "Jesus und der Menschensohn"   Vielhauer, Ph. "Jesus und der Menschensohn: Zur Diskussion mit Heinz Eduard Tödt und Eduard Schweizer." *ZThK* 60 (1963) 133–77.

Vilmar, *Abulfathi annales*   Vilmar, E., ed. *Abulfathi annales samaritani quos ad fidem codicum manuscriptorum Berolinensium, Bodlejani, Parisini edidit et prolegomenis instruxit.* Gotha: no publisher, 1865.

Vööbus, *Asceticism*   Vööbus, A. *History of Asceticism in the Syrian Orient.* CSCO 184. Louvain: Secrétariat CSCO, 1958.

Vööbus, *Canons*   Vööbus, A., ed. *The Canons Ascribed to Maruta of Maipherkat and Related Sources.* CSCO 439. Louvain: Peeters, 1982.

Vööbus, *Celibacy*   Vööbus, A. *Celibacy, a Requirement for Admission to Baptism in the Early Syrian Church.* Stockholm: Almqvist, 1954.

Vosté, *Theodori Mopsuestensi*   Vosté, J. M., ed. *Theodori Mopsuestensi commentarius in Evangelium Johannis.* CSCO 115. Louvain: Peeters, 1940.

Wegner, "Image of Woman"   Wegner, J. R. "The Image of Woman in Philo" in K. H. Richards, ed. *Society of Biblical Literature 1982 Seminar Papers.* SBLSP 21. Chico, Calif.: Scholars, 1982, 551–63.

Welburn, "Identity"   Welburn, A. J. "The Identity of the Archons in the 'Apocryphon Johannes.'" *VC* 32 (1978) 241–54.

Whittaker, "Self-Generating Principles"   Whittaker, J. "Self-Generating Principles in Second Century Gnostic Systems" in Layton, *Rediscovery,* 1.176–89.

Widengren, *Proceedings*   Widengren, G. *Proceedings of the International Colloquium on Gnosticism, Stockholm August 20–25, 1973.* Kungl. Vitterhets Historie och Anikvitets Akademiens. Handlingaar, Filologisk–filosofiska serien 17. Stockholm: Almqvist & Wiksell; Leiden: Brill, 1977.

Williams, "Stability"   Williams, M. A. "Stability as a Soteriological Theme in Gnosticism" in Layton, *Rediscovery,* 2.819–29.

Wilson, *Gnosis*   Wilson, R. McL. *Gnosis and the New Testament.* Philadelphia: Fortress, 1968.

Wilson, *Nag Hammadi*   Wilson, R. McL., ed. *Nag Hammadi and Gnosis: Papers at the First International Congress of Coptology (Cairo, December 1976).* NHS 14. Leiden: Brill, 1978.

Wilson, "Valentinianism"   Wilson, R. McL. "Valentinianism and the Gospel of Truth" in Layton, *Rediscovery,* 1.333–45.

Winston, *Philo*   Winston, D., ed. *Philo of Alexandria: The Contemplative Life, the Giants, and Selections.* New York: Paulist, 1981.

Winston, *Wisdom of Solomon*   Winston, D. *The Wisdom of Solomon: A New Translation with Introduction and Commentary.* AB 43. Garden City, N.Y.: Doubleday, 1979.

Wisse, "Monasticism in Egypt"   Wisse, F. "Gnosticism and Early Monasticism in Egypt" in Aland, *Gnosis,* 431–40.

Wisse, "Prolegomena"   Wisse, F. "Prolegomena to the Study of the New Testament and Gnosis" in Logan-Wedderburn, *New Testament and Gnosis,* 138–45.

Wisse, "Epistle of Jude"   Wisse, F. "The Epistle of Jude in the History of Heresiology" in Krause, *Essays,* 133–43.

Wisse, "Heresiologists"   Wisse, F. "The Nag Hammadi Library and the Heresiologists." *VC* 25 (1971) 205–23.

Wisse, "Redeemer Figure"   Wisse, F. "The Redeemer Figure in the Paraphrase of Shem." *NovT* 12 (1970) 130–40.

Wisse, "Die Sextus-Sprüche"   Wisse, F. "Die Sextus-Sprüche und das Problem der gnostischen Ethik" in A. Böhlig and F. Wisse, eds. *Zum Hellenismus in den Schriften von Nag Hammadi.* GOF 6.2. Wiesbaden: Harrassowitz, 1975, 55–86.

WMANT   Wissenschaftliche Monographien zum Alten und Neuen Testament.

Wright, *Julian*   Wright, W. C., ed. *The Works of the Emperor Julian.* 2 vols. Cambridge, Mass.: Harvard; London: Heinemann, 1913–23.

WUNT   Wissenschaftliche Untersuchungen zum Neuen Testament

Wutz, *Onomastica*   Wutz, F. *Onomastica Sacra*. TU 41. Leipzig: Hinrichs, 1914–
    1915.

WZKM   *Weiner Zeitschrift für die Kunde des Morgenlandes.*

Yamauchi, "Jewish Gnosticism?"   Yamauchi, E. M. "Jewish Gnosticism? The
    Prologue of John, Mandaean Parallels, and the Trimorphic Protennoia" in van
    den Broek-Vermaseren, *Studies*, 467–97.

Yamauchi, *Gnosticism*   Yamauchi, E. M. *Pre-Christian Gnosticism: A Survey of*
    the Proposed Evidences. Grand Rapids: Eerdmans, 1973.

ZNW   *Zeitschrift für die neutestamentliche Wissenschaft*

ZPE   *Zeitschrift für Papyrologie und Epigraphik*

ZRGG   *Zeitschrift für Religions-und Geistesgeschichte*

ZThK   *Zeitschrift für Theologie und Kirche*

INTRODUCTION: NAG HAMMADI, GNOSTICISM, AND EARLY CHRISTIANITY —A BEGINNER'S GUIDE

Charles W. Hedrick

I. The Problem of Definitions

Bianchi, *Origini*, xx–xxii, 1–60; Jonas, *Gnostic Religion*; Pagels, "Gnosticism"; Wilson, *Gnosis*; Yamauchi, *Gnosticism*, 13–26.

The term "gnosticism" is a noun that derives from a Greek word (γνῶσις) meaning "knowledge." In general, the term "gnosticism" is applied to a series of widespread and rather diverse religio-philosophical movements in late antiquity that nevertheless are understood to have some similarities. Although a precise definition of gnosticism and a clear dating for its emergence in the Hellenistic world are still matters of scholarly debate, working definitions have generally included certain elements. It is understood to have an anti-cosmic or world-rejecting stance. In the religio-philosophical systems the highest spiritual order of reality is diametrically opposed to the created order of things. Indeed, the highest spiritual reality has nothing to do with the origins of cosmic or created reality. The material realm does, however, hold trapped within it elements from the spiritual realm. The ignorant or slumbering spiritual elements reside in the material, in humankind, like dying embers in a cold fire-pit. While these elements possess the full potential of the spiritual realm, their current situation is hopeless. They may only be awakened, informed, and reclaimed for the highest spiritual order by the activity of an emissary sent from the highest levels of the spiritual order; he enters the material realm and brings a special knowledge, which alone can ignite the spark and cast off the chains of the great ignorance that enslave the spiritual element. Of course, the movements

1

and their systems differ. And the student may expect to find a bewild-
ering array of actors participating in the various mythological narratives
describing this divine drama.

All can agree that the term "gnosticism" and the common elements to
the above working description apply to those clearly developed gnostic
systems of the second century C.E. as they are described and refuted by
such church fathers as Irenaeus, Justin Martyr, Hippolytus, and Epiphanius. Not all are agreed, however, that gnosticism existed earlier
than the second century C.E. Some argue that gnosticism is strictly a
second-century phenomenon and propose other ways to describe gnostic motifs and features found in the pre-second-century literature, such
as the Pauline correspondence, the Deutero-Paulines, the Pastorals, the
Gospel of John, and the Dead Sea Scrolls. During the first international
conference on gnosticism held in 1966 at Messina in Italy, it was
proposed, for example, that the term "gnosticism" be reserved for the
developed gnostic systems of the second century C.E. and that one
should use the term "gnosis" when referring to similar phenomena prior
to the second century C.E. This distinction, however, has not generally
been followed.

Other scholars argue that these rather sophisticated second-century
religio-philosophical systems did not get that way overnight, since it
would appear that a certain amount of lead time is required for their
development. Indeed, such syncretistic and widespread systems must
have had a pre-history that extended into the first century C.E. It is
further argued that there is no reason to think that the church fathers,
who were primarily concerned with combating heresy and diversity
within Christianity, would have been interested in non-Christian gnostic
movements. They would simply have ignored the non-Christian roots of
the second-century systems until their influence began to affect Christianity. Since there is evidence of a non-Christian substratum to some of
these developed gnostic systems of the second century C.E., it seems
reasonable to assume that their matrix in the first century was a type of
non-Christian "gnosticism" existing side by side with early Christianity.

II. The Problem of Sources

Foerster, *Gnosis*; Haardt, *Gnosis*; Robinson, *NHLE*; Schmidt-MacDermot,
Bruce Codex; Schmidt-MacDermot, *Pistis Sophia* (Askew Codex); Till-
Schenke, *Papyrus Berolinensis 8502*.

The debate over definitions is largely due to a lack of primary source
material datable into the first century C.E. Until the middle of the twentieth century, students of gnosticism were limited primarily to the

second-century descriptions of gnostic-Christian heretics found in the writings of the church fathers who opposed and refuted them. These church writers focused their refutations on those movements within Christianity that posed a threat to the church. Included among these extensive apologetical refutations one finds only short quotations from gnostic teachers along with brief descriptions of gnostic systems.

In addition to these secondhand reports, scholars did have access to three ancient Coptic manuscripts of primary source material, none of which were dated into the first century: Codex Brucianus, Codex Askewianus, Codex Berolinensis Gnosticus 8502. These manuscripts contain only seven individual gnostic writings, and reflect a type of speculative Christian gnosticism. Because the primary source material is later than the first century C.E. and reflects a type of Christian gnosticism, the conclusion that gnosticism was a second-century C.E., post-Christian phenomenon appeared inevitable.

III. The Problem of Origins

Grant, Gnosticism; von Harnack, Dogma, 1.222–364; Jonas, Gnostic Religion, 3–27; Segel, Two Powers in Heaven; Wisse, "Heresiologists"; Yamauchi, Gnosticism.

The debate over where and when gnosticism originated has continued for some time. Until the end of the nineteenth century, gnosticism was thought to have begun as a Christian heresy. The church fathers, for example, traced the origins of gnosticism to Simon Magus (cf. Acts 8:10), whom they considered "the father of all heresies." Its rapid growth in the ancient world was fueled and fostered by an early Christian fascination with Greek philosophy and mythology. The classic statement of this position was made by Adolph von Harnack, the great church historian of the nineteenth century, who described gnosticism as the "acute Hellenization of Christianity." Rejecting their Old Testament and Jewish roots and embracing Platonic dualism (the philosophical distinction between a real [visible] and ideal [unseen] world), radical Christians attempted to fuse Christianity with Greek culture and philosophy. The result was gnosticism.

Near the beginning of the twentieth century, a few history of religions scholars (scholars who studied Christian origins in the context of its cultural setting) challenged this monolithic view of gnostic origins that had persisted since the second century C.E. Working with the meager and mostly secondary evidence in the reports of the church fathers, early scholars such as F. C. Baur, R. Reitzenstein, and W. Bousset succeeded in uncovering evidence that pointed to an origin in the East, specifically in Iranian, Mandaean, and Persian thought. More recently, Hans Jonas, has described gnosticism as a syncretistic phenomenon, a widespread mood of late antiquity which may be described as a wave of latent Eastern mysticism (astrological fatalism and magic) expressed in the logical categories of Greek thought. Hence, according to Jonas, gnosticism had no one single point of beginning but was an attitude of late antiquity that simultaneously emerged throughout the ancient world with the blending of Eastern and Greek ways of thinking.

Others have sought the origins of gnosticism in the context of radical Judaism, either in the frustration of Jewish apocalyptic movements to realize the immediate appearing of God's kingdom, or in the challenge to God's character because of the presence of evil in the world. By definition, a righteous and benevolent God could not be the source of evil and disorder in the universe. And since the creator God of the Old Testament can be understood to have acted in capricious and questionable ways (as for example in Job), it would naturally follow that he is not the righteous and benevolent father; rather, he proves to be merely a blind and ignorant fashioner of worlds.

The lack of primary source material simply would not permit a definitive answer to the issue of origins that satisfied everyone. The discussion seemed to have reached an impasse, with scholars divided over the significance of the evidence for gnosticism in the first century C.E.

IV. The Nag Hammadi Library

Attridge, *Nag Hammadi Codex I*; Barnes-Browne-Shelton, *Cartonnage*; MacRae, "Nag Hammadi"; Parrott, *Codices V and VI*; Pearson, *Codices IX and X*; Robinson, *Nag Hammadi Codices*; Robinson, *NHLE*, particularly, 1–25.

In 1945 in Upper Egypt near the large modern village of Nag Hammadi a peasant accidentally discovered a collection of twelve leather-bound papyrus books and one individual tractate. The texts contain some fifty-one individual writings, the bulk of which were unknown to scholarship prior to their discovery. In general, they may be described as heretical Christian-gnostic writings, although they are really more diverse than that general designation implies. The collection contains a number of texts that were not composed in a Christian-gnostic context but derive, for example, from Greek wisdom literature, Sethianism, Hermeticism, and Judaism. Other texts reflect a type of non-Christian gnosticism having a superficial Christianizing "veneer" added sometime after the original composition of the text. While the books were manufactured in the middle of the fourth century C.E., some of the texts they contain date from within the first or early second centuries C.E. The discovery of the

Nag Hammadi Library casts new light on the questions of definition and gnostic origins. Indeed, while the library presents new source material, it also raises new questions at almost every level of research into the relationship between gnosticism and early Christianity. In the light of this phenomenal archaeological discovery, an entire generation of scholarship will have to be rethought.

A Facsimile Edition of the library was completed in 1977, and translations of all the manuscripts appeared in English only as recently as 1977. To date, critical editions containing transcription, translation, introduction and notes of Codices I; III,2 and IV,2; III,5; Codices V and VI; IX and X; and a cartonnage volume have appeared. Critical editions of Codices XI, XII and XIII; and Codex II are to appear in 1987. The remainder (about twenty percent of the library) is expected to appear in the near future.

There are three major centers throughout the world where team research is being conducted on the manuscripts: The Institute for Antiquity and Christianity in Claremont, California (U.S.A.), under the direction of Professor James M. Robinson; Humboldt University in East Berlin (The People's Democratic Republic of Germany) by the *Berliner Arbeitskreis* under the direction of Professor Hans-Martin Schenke; the University of Laval (Quebec, Canada), a French language team under the leadership of Professor Paul-Hubert Poirier.

V. Early Christianity and Gnostic Influence

Bauer, *Orthodoxy*; Bousset, *Kyrios Christos*; Bultmann, *Primitive Christianity*; Bultmann, *Theology*, 1.164–83; Francis-Meeks, *Conflict at Colossae*; Schmithals, *Paul and the Gnostics*; Yamauchi, *Gnosticism*.

Working backwards from the apologetical reports of the church fathers, many scholars did find indirect evidence of gnostic influence on early Christianity within the New Testament itself. Certain New Testament passages, it was argued, reflected evidence of gnostic influence on the development of early Christianity in the first century. For example, some argued that the opponents with whom Paul debated in certain of his letters were gnostic, or had fallen under the influence of gnosticism. If this was the case, then one could reconstruct their theological position on the basis of Paul's own statements. Like reconstructing the unheard half of a telephone conversation, one asks: What is it that the opponent must have said to have prompted such a response by Paul. (Many find a continuum between such reconstructions and the second-century systems.) Sometimes in the debate Paul will use the language of his opponents. For example, in 1 Cor 2:14–3:1, Paul uses the expressions "the spiritual man," "the natural man," and "the fleshly man." These terms appear in gnostic systems of the second century as technical ways of sorting out classes of humanity. Another example is the "Christ hymn" in Phil 2:5–11. Since the nineteenth century, scholars have thought it to be an early, independent composition whose concepts derive ultimately from gnosticism and general Hellenistic cosmology. Paul, it is argued, borrowed and preserved the hymn (a stylized and well-balanced literary unit consisting of two strophes having three stanzas with three lines each) just as he had used confessional statements from the pre-Pauline Hellenistic churches, in which he learned the Christian "basics" (cf. 1 Cor 15:3–5). In this way, in spite of the lack of gnostic texts from the first century C.E., many scholars are able to reconstruct points of contact between early Christianity and gnostic-like groups contemporary with the New Testament.

Gnostic influence has been detected at many points in the New Testament literature. For example, some have argued that the purpose of Luke–Acts is to counter a gnostic polemic against history. The prologue to the Gospel of John has been seen as a Johannine adaptation of a gnostic hymn or poem; the emphasis in the Gospel of John upon a realized existential eschatology, as opposed to a futuristic cosmic eschatology, also reflects a gnostic concern. Colossians, Ephesians, 2 Thessalonians, the Epistles of John, the Pastorals and the General Epistles, it is argued, reflect traces of the first-century debate between Christianity and its gnostic opponents.

Those who see gnostic influence on early Christianity find that from the very beginning Christianity developed diverse theological and sociological patterns. Only later, when one of the many diverse strands achieved an ascendancy over the others, is there a standardizing, and a developing of an "orthodox" tradition. This diversity in the early period is clearly reflected in the New Testament. For example, the Hellenistic Christian confession that Paul used in Rom 1:2–5 says that Jesus was "designated" Son of God by his resurrection, rather than having pre-existed in that role. The "Christ hymn" in Phil 2:5–11 describes Jesus as a totally divine figure who was not truly human. He had merely temporarily adopted human form as a guise.

The standards for "orthodox" Christianity that one finds articulated in the Pastorals, 1 John and the Apostolic Fathers constitute attempts to standardize and domesticate the great varieties of early Christian movements in the formative period. The second-century gnostic systems should also be understood as a part of those diverse early Christian traditions that fell victim to standardization and institutionalization in

Christianity. The end of this development from diversity to uniformity is reached with the emergence of the early Roman Catholic Church.

Of course, it has continued to be objected that the lack of evidence for gnosticism in the form of primary source material datable within the first century C.E. puts such studies on a hypothetical footing. Hence, the discovery of new source material in the Nag Hammadi Library has begun an entirely new chapter in the discussion of these issues.

VI. The Nag Hammadi Library:
Problems and Possibilities

Hedrick, *Apocalypse*; Hedrick, "Kingdom Sayings and Parables"; Koester, "Apocryphal and Canonical Gospels"; MacRae, "Nag Hammadi and the New Testament"; Robinson, "Gnosticism and the New Testament"; Robinson, "Sethians"; Robinson, "Jung Codex"; Wisse, "Heresiologists."

The discovery of the Nag Hammadi Library, as with most modern archaeological discoveries, initially presented more problems than solutions. There were political monopolies that had to be broken in order to get the material into the public domain. The papyrus originals had to be reconstructed, conserved, and photographed prior to the publication of the Facsimile Edition, whose completion in 1977 made the materials available to all Coptic scholars around the world, simultaneously giving free and open access to the texts. This was followed by the time-consuming task of producing translations and critical editions of the texts. Hence, the assessment of these materials for understanding the origins of gnosticism and its interaction with early Christianity has only just begun. The Yale Conference on Gnosticism in 1978, the Quebec Conference on the Nag Hammadi Codices in 1978, and the Springfield Working Seminar on Gnosticism and Early Christianity in 1983 are the first three conferences on gnosticism to be conducted since the publication in 1977 of the Nag Hammadi Library in facsimile and English translation. The Springfield Conference was the first to focus specifically on the relationship between gnosticism and early Christianity since the publication of the Nag Hammadi Library, and the only Working Seminar in the history of the discussion.

One problem that has emerged in the discussion is the present inability of scholarship to harmonize satisfactorily the texts in the Nag Hammadi Library with the categories under which the church fathers discussed their gnostic opponents. Some of the Nag Hammadi texts can be identified with certain of those groups opposed by the church fathers in the second century and later. For example, the second tractate of

Codex XI, lacking an ancient title, has been given the modern title *A Valentinian Exposition*, because of its affinities with the second-century gnostic teacher Valentinus. Likewise the *Gospel of Truth* in Codex I and Codex XII, the *Tripartite Tractate* in Codex I and the *Gospel of Philip* in Codex II have also been identified as Valentinian documents. Others have been identified with the Hermetic literature: the *Discourse on the 8th and 9th*, the *Prayer of Thanksgiving*, and *Asclepius*. Certain other texts belong to a cycle of documents associated with Sethianism: the *Apocryphon of John*, the *Hypostasis of the Archons*, the *Gospel of the Egyptians*, the *Apocalypse of Adam*, *Three Steles of Seth*, *Zostrianos*, *Melchizedek*, the *Thought of Norea*, *Marsanes*, *Allogenes*, and *Trimorphic Protennoia*. Excluding certain other previously known texts, such as the *Sentences of Sextus* and the excerpt from Plato's *Republic*, the bulk of the library does not fit easily into any of the gnostic systems described by the church fathers, although there are abundant parallel motifs.

The lack of a common thread of theology or mythology that joins the library together is another difficulty. The texts do not appear to be a collection of religious writings composed for one particular community, although even radically different writings could have been widely collected and used by a single community. Nor has a communal center for the users of the texts yet been identified, as in the case of Qumran for the Dead Sea Scrolls. A series of excavations at Faw Qibli near the site of the discovery has succeeded in clarifying the historical period (ca. 350 C.E.) in which the manuscripts were buried and their place of manufacture (ancient Bau), but not yet the group or groups that used them.

Nevertheless, the diversity of these texts and the lack of archaeological evidence for a particular user community does not exclude the collecting and use of the library by a particular gnostic-Christian group in antiquity. The Bible itself is a quite diverse collection of texts sacred to two ancient religions (Judaism and Christianity) spanning some two thousand years, and yet both collections are used as the holy literature of diverse Christian groups in the twentieth century.

The discovery of the Nag Hammadi Library clearly solves one of those problems faced by scholars in previous generations. What they lacked in primary source materials is supplied in the Nag Hammadi corpus. It is a massive amount of material that must be carefully analyzed and studied in relationship to other ancient literature. In a sense the very wealth and abundance of the discovery is a hurdle that will not be completely overcome by the present generation of scholars.

There is as yet no consensus in the dating of individual texts. Scholarship agrees that the papyrus manuscripts themselves date from the middle of the fourth century C.E., and it concurs that their composition occurred at an earlier period. But how much earlier is unclear, and debated. At least two of the texts have been dated as early as the first century: The *Apocalypse of Adam* and the *Gospel of Thomas*. The former appears to reflect a type of Jewish gnosticism that has emerged out of Jewish apocalypticism. The latter is a collection of the traditional words of Jesus; some of which are identical to sayings in the canonical Synoptic Gospels. Other sayings are not found in the canonical Gospels, but nevertheless are very much at home in that setting. Most of the sayings in the collection are quite different in character and spirit from the synoptic tradition.

That late manuscripts contain narratives composed at a much earlier time should not be surprising. Research into the canonical Jesus traditions proceeds on the basic assumption that the canonical Gospels, although dating from 70 C.E. and later, contain traditions that come from a much earlier period of time. And an accepted canon of textual criticism holds that late manuscripts do contain earlier readings.

The Nag Hammadi Library may prove to be a key that will help to unlock the secret of the origins of gnosticism. Because the library does contain several gnostic texts that show no evidence of having been influenced by Christianity (the *Apocalypse of Adam*, the *Paraphrase of Shem*, the *Three Steles of Seth*, and *Eugnostos*), it demonstrates beyond question that gnosticism was not simply a Christian heresy. For further support one may also point to other originally non-Christian texts that were later appropriated for Christian gnosticism through a sometimes extremely thin veneer of Christianizing: the *Gospel of the Egyptians*, the *Apocryphon of John*, the *Hypostasis of the Archons* and the *Trimorphic Protennoia*. While there may be no extant gnostic manuscripts from the early first century C.E. to show that there existed a pre-Christian gnosticism in a *chronological* sense, these texts clearly demonstrate the existence of pre-Christian gnosticism in an *ideological* sense. Such hard evidence presents a previously unavailable avenue for investigating the interaction between Christianity and its gnostic opponents. They provide concrete sources not only for studying a gnosticism uninfluenced by Christianity but they also give us an insight into the influence of Christianity upon gnosticism, and gnosticism upon Christianity.

Because it presents new primary source material, it is likely that the Nag Hammadi Library may also open up new possibilities for examining the social worlds of gnosticism and early Christianity. Where, for example, would one expect to find "gnostics" in the ancient world? Were there gnostic monastic communities or churches? Would we expect to find schools of gnostic teachers and students? Could the "schools"

reflected in the Johannine correspondence, and the clearly defined
parties at Corinth (1 Corinthians 1–4) with their heroes, claims to
wisdom, and exclusiveness parallel or be related to the kind of social
matrix in which gnosticism may have flourished into the developed
schools of the second century?

All of these issues and more may be clarified in future research. The
nature of the new materials clearly reflects worshipping communities in
competition both with early Christianity and other gnostic groups. Such
texts as Zostrianos, the Three Steles of Seth, the Gospel of Philip, A
Valentinian Exposition and Trimorphic Protennoia present the raw
material requisite to a worshipping community: hymns, prayers, creeds,
liturgy and sacraments. The gnostic attempt to evangelize Christian
communities appears in gnostic tracts such as the Sophia of Jesus Christ
and the Tripartite Tractate. The partial success of their evangelistic
efforts may be seen in the Christianizing of the Gospel of the Egyptians.
A Valentinian Exposition gives us a much clearer view of the schools in
Valentinianism. Compared to early Christianity the role of women
seems to be improved in gnosticism, where women appear as revealers
of the arcane gnosis. In the canonical Gospels, on the other hand,
women play a subordinate role in receiving and giving revelation (e.g.,
cf. Mark 16:8; Luke 24:10–11, and John 21:14 where Mary does not
appear to be counted as receiving a revelation). In the gnostic revelation
material, however, they are given equal status with males as revealer
figures; Mary even has a gospel under her name.

VII. The Discussion Continues

Foerster, Gnosis, 365–67; Haardt, Gnosis, 398–416; Jonas, Gnostic Religion, 342–
52; Rudolf, "Gnosis, ein Forschungsbericht"; Scholer, Nag Hammadi Bibliography, updated annually in Novum Testamentum beginning with volume
thirteen (1971).

Essays presented in this volume are a part of the continuing discussion.
They were prepared for criticism and evaluation at the first international Working Seminar on Gnosticism and Early Christianity held in
Springfield, Missouri 29 March through 1 April 1983 and modified after
discussion for publication in this volume. Each essay provides the
reader with new insights into Christian and gnostic origins; each suggests new approaches to the old problems and sets the discussion of
gnosticism and early Christianity in new directions. Professor Pearson's
essay argues "that the earliest Gnostic literature was produced by Jewish
intellectuals, as a product of their revolt against the Jewish God and his
capacity as World-Creator and Lawgiver." Professor Robinson's paper

compares and contrasts two early collections of the sayings of Jesus, Q (a hypothetical early Christian sayings collection) and the *Gospel of Thomas* (a collection of sayings influenced in part by gnosticism). He assesses their significance for reciprocal understanding, and pulls together the various strands in the debate over the dating of the *Gospel of Thomas*. Drawing upon Nag Hammadi texts and related documents, Professor Schenke's essay aims at solving the puzzle of the function and background of the Beloved Disciple in the Gospel of John. Professor Perkins focuses upon the debate between Irenaeus, the second-century C.E. Christian apologist, and his gnostic opponents over the issue of creation. Professor Attridge proposes that the *Gospel of Truth* is a Valentinian document written as a missionary tract for circulation among ordinary Christians, an open invitation to Christians to become followers of Valentinus. Professor Pagels argues that certain Nag Hammadi texts drew upon Genesis chapters 1–3 and the writings of Paul to develop their ethical and cosmological arguments. Professor Parrott investigates the role of named and unnamed disciples in gnosticism and early Christianity. Professor Layton's essay identifies the paradoxical *Thunder* as a "riddle," whose solution will surprise the reader. Professor Turner's contribution clarifies the characteristics of Sethianism as an independent religious movement in antiquity and discusses its inter-action with early Christianity. Professor Gero's paper traces references to certain groups in early Mesopotamian Christianity that may be iden-tified with the gnostic sect, the "Borborites," found in Epiphanius. Professor MacRae discusses the background of the Gospel of John and points out seven points of contact between John and gnosticism that need further discussion. Drawing on parallels in the *Gospel of Thomas*, the *Apocryphon of James*, the *Dialogue of the Saviour*, and Papyrus Egerton 2, Professor Koester identifies traditional sayings of Jesus lying behind the speeches in John chapter 8. Professor Wisse contends that the conflict between "orthodoxy" and "heresy" in the third and fourth centuries C.E. should not be applied to an earlier period. This obser-vation has significant implications for the study of early Christianity and gnosticism.

PART I
NON-CHRISTIAN GNOSTICISM

1

THE PROBLEM
OF "JEWISH GNOSTIC" LITERATURE

Birger A. Pearson

Birger Pearson is Professor of Religious Studies at the University of California, Santa Barbara. Gnostic studies have been his main research activity since 1968. As a member of the Coptic Gnostic Project of the Institute for Antiquity and Christianity (Claremont), Professor Pearson has helped in the translation and preparation of several Nag Hammadi Codices.

Professional services include being a former officer, section chairperson, and series editor for the Society of Biblical Literature. He also is a member of the American Society for the Study of Religion, Studiorum Novi Testamenti Societas, The International Association for Coptic Studies, and The American Schools of Oriental Research, as well as several others.

His more recent publications have been in the area of gnostic studies and his monograph on *Pneumatikos-Psychikos Terminology in 1 Corinthians*, first published in 1973 (Scholars) remains a standard in Pauline studies. He has contributed to such publications as the *Harvard Theological Review*, the *Encyclopaedia Judaica*, and the *Journal of Biblical Literature*.

Preface

The problem of Jewish Gnostic literature is part of the larger issue of the relationship among Gnosticism, Judaism, and Christianity. The Nag Hammadi discoveries have decisively put to rest the old idea that Gnosticism is a Christian heresy in its origins. The massive array of Jewish traditions found in many Nag Hammadi texts have brought the issue of the relationship between Gnosticism and Judaism to the foreground of the discussion, even if most (but not all!) of the Nag Hammadi texts in question appear in Christian dress. In this paper two Nag Hammadi documents are taken up for special consideration: the *Apocryphon of John* and the *Apocalypse of Adam*. Both are treated as examples of "Jewish Gnostic" literature; the *Apocryphon of John* has been subjected to Christian redaction whereas the *Apocalypse of Adam* shows no Christian traits at all. The form and content of these documents are analyzed with special attention to their use of Jewish literary genres, Jewish literature, and Jewish exegetical traditions. It is argued that the earliest Gnostic literature was produced by Jewish intellectuals, as a product of their revolt against the Jewish God in his capacity as World-Creator and Lawgiver. The *Apocalypse of Adam* is illustrative of the development of non-Christian forms of Gnosticism, of which Mandaeism emerges as the most important enduring example. The *Apocryphon of John* illustrates the appropriation by Gnostics of the Christian message about Christ and the widespread tendency to attribute the Gnostic revelation to Jesus Christ. During the second century C.E. the Christian forms of the new Gnostic religion tend to predominate, while at the same time the Jewish elements in the Gnostic religion begin to recede into the background. The two documents treated here, therefore, exemplify the complicated relationships among Judaism, Christianity, and Gnosticism in the second century of our era.

I. Introduction

As implied in the title of this paper, to speak of Jewish Gnostic literature involves a larger problem of considerable proportions, one which is crucial to an understanding of the genesis and development of Gnosticism itself. This larger problem is the historical relationship between Gnosticism and Judaism. To be sure, it can no longer be doubted that Gnosticism, especially in its earliest forms, displays a fundamental indebtedness to Jewish concepts and traditions. The Nag Hammadi discovery has provided much new material of relevance here. Nevertheless, the precise historical relationship between Gnosticism and Judaism is still a very controversial issue. Some scholars, the present author included, have argued that Gnosticism originated from within Judaism.[1] Other scholars contend that such a circumstance is improb-

---

[1] An early proponent of this view was Friedländer, *Gnosticismus*; cf. Pearson, "Judaism and Gnostic Origins." For some recent treatments see e.g., Quispel, "Gnostic Demiurge," and "Gnosis"; MacRae, "Sophia Myth"; Dahl, "Archon"; Pearson, "Haggadic Traditions," esp. 469–70, and "Gnostic Self-Definition," esp. 159–60. For other studies see Rudolph's discussion in "Gnosis, ein Forschungsbericht," esp. *ThR* 36 (1971) 89–119; cf. also Rudolph, *Gnosis: Wesen und Geschichte*, 291–99 (ET=*Gnosis: Nature and History*, 275–82).

able, if not impossible.[2] Still others adopt a broader view of Gnosticism, and speak of various forms of the Gnostic religion: Jewish, Christian, and pagan. In this view, one which I share, one can legitimately speak of Jewish Gnosticism,[3] as well as Christian and other forms of Gnosticism. Such a Jewish Gnosticism should, of course, be differentiated from the kind of Jewish Gnosticism described by G. Scholem in one of his famous books;[4] this is more appropriately designated as Jewish mysticism.[5]

Gnosticism should really be understood as a religion, or worldview, in its own right.[6] There are very good reasons for using such a designation as the Gnostic religion instead of Gnosticism or Gnosis, terms which have been used with a notable lack of precision in scholarly discourse.[7] When one begins to assess the relationship between the Gnostic religion and Judaism one runs into the difficulty that the former seems to be essentially *anti-Jewish*, especially so in its earliest forms. The Gnostic spirit is radically *anti-cosmic*, whereas Judaism is the clearest example in late antiquity of a religion which affirms the cosmos, with its doctrine of the one and only God, Creator of heaven and earth.[8] The anti-Jewish character of the Gnostic religion is tied to its anti-cosmicism, in that it adopts a hostile stance vis-à-vis the Jewish Creator God.[9] To speak of a Jewish Gnosticism, therefore, appears, at first glance, to imply a contradiction in terms. But history, especially religious history, is not the same thing as logic!

It is one of the curious facts of the religious history of late antiquity that certain Jewish intellectuals could, and did, use the materials of their

---

[2] See e.g., Jonas, "Hymn of the Pearl," and "Gnostic Syndrome," esp. 274; and van Unnik, "Komponente." More recent studies in which the Jewish factor is minimized are nevertheless more ambiguous on the question. See e.g., Yamauchi, "Jewish Gnosticism?"; Gruenwald, "Controversy," and "Merkavah." In the last-named article, for example, Gruenwald takes issue with my contention that Gnosticism "originates *in a Jewish environment*" (p. 44, italics his), yet eight pages later he expresses his agreement with K. Rudolph that "Gnosticism emerged from a Jewish matrix" (p. 52)!

[3] See e.g., Stone, *Profile of Judaism*, 99–103.

[4] Scholem, *Traditions*.

[5] See e.g., Jonas, "Hymn of the Pearl," 288; Gruenwald, "Merkavah," 41–42. Cf. also Gruenwald, *Apocalyptic and Merkavah Mysticism*, esp. 110.

[6] I take "religion" and "worldview" here to be functional equivalents, though one could also say that the Gnostic "worldview" develops into various Gnostic "religions," such as Manichaeism and Mandaeism. On "worldviews" and their analysis as "religions" see Smart, *Worldviews*. The best full-length study of the Gnostic religion is indubitably Rudolph, *Gnosis: Nature and History*.

[7] Cf. the attempt at defining Gnosticism set forth at the Messina Colloquium on the Origins of Gnosticism, published in Bianchi, *Origini*, xxvi–xxix. Cf. Rudolph's criticisms in "Gnosis, ein Forschungsbericht," *ThR* 36 (1971) 13–22.

[8] These issues are treated with extraordinary insight by Tröger, "Attitude." Cf. also his article, "Spekulativ-esoterische Ansätze," esp. 318.

[9] This important point is stressed by Dahl, "Archon."

ancient religion, the Bible and various extra-biblical sources and traditions, in giving expression to a new, anti-cosmic religion of transcendental gnōsis "knowledge." Such a step involved a fundamental
religious protest against the older traditions, an apostasy from Judaism as
normatively defined. The religious movement thus conceived expressed
itself in literature. It is against this historical background (reconstructed,
to be sure) that one can speak of Jewish Gnostic literature. This Jewish
Gnostic literature adopted and adapted the forms of the (non-Gnostic)
Jewish literature of the Second Temple period (apocalypse, testament,
scriptural commentary, midrash, and epistle).[10] The Gnostic documents
were also frequently attributed pseudonymously to important patriarchs
and other personages of the Bible (e.g., Adam, Seth, Enosh, Enoch,
Shem, Ham, Moses, Abraham, Melchizedek, Solomon),[11] as was the case
with so much of the Jewish pseudepigraphic and apocryphal literature
of the period. We must assume that the vast bulk of this Gnostic
literature is irretrievably lost.

As it happens, it is the Christian forms of the Gnostic religion which
are the best known, and whose materials and testimonies are the most
abundant. Indeed, one can hardly speak of the problem of Jewish
Gnostic literature without addressing the central theme of this Working
Seminar: "Gnosticism and Early Christianity." The theme itself involves
the crucial clash of religions, Gnosticism and Christianity, which looms
so large in second-century C.E. religious history. We have to do with two
religions, each of them (I would argue) rooted in a third (Judaism) and
one of them (Christianity) threatened with being engulfed and swal-
lowed up by the other (Gnosticism). The importance of this for our
special topic is that much (but not all!) of the relevant Gnostic material
now extant appears in Christian dress, i.e., in Christianized versions.

I cannot take up the full range of the evidence for discussion here.[12]
What I intend to do, instead, is to examine two examples of what I take
to be Jewish Gnostic literature, look at them as Jewish Gnostic texts, and
then examine their relationship to Christianity. Admittedly, what I will

[10] For a good treatment of Jewish literature of the Second Temple period see Nickelsburg, *Jewish Literature*. See now also Stone, *Jewish Writings*.
[11] Adam: see below. Seth: NHC III,2; VII,2 and 5; XI,1; plus numerous patristic and
other references (See Pearson, "Seth," 491–96). Enosh: *Mani Codex* (Cameron-Dewey)
48.16–60.12 (apocalypses of Adam, Seth, Enosh, Shem, and Enoch, perhaps not Gnostic).
Enoch: *Mani Codex*; *Pistis Sophia* 99,134. Shem: *Mani Codex*; NHC VII,1. Ham:
Basilidians according to Clem. Alex. *Strom.* 6.6.53.5. Moses: Cf. *Orig. World* II,5: 102,
8–9. Abraham: Sethians according to Epiph. *Pan.* 39.5.1; Audians according to Theodore
Bar Konai (on which see Puech, "Allogène," 273). Melchizedek: NHC IX,1. Solomon: Cf.
Orig. World II,5:107,3. Cf. also Norea, wife-sister of Seth: NHC IX,2; cf. *Orig. World* II,5:
102,10–11.24–25; and numerous patristic references (see Pearson, "Norea").
[12] See my article, "Sources," 443–81.

be doing is "rushing in" (like the proverbial fool) to an area of controversy where more timid souls (like the proverbial angels) may perhaps fear to tread. One of the examples I have chosen, I will argue, is not in any sense a Christian document: the *Apocalypse of Adam*.[13] The other one, in my view, has undergone secondary Christianization: the *Apocryphon of John*.[14] This material having been examined, some general conclusions may then be extrapolated pertaining to Jewish Gnostic literature on the one hand, and the relationship of Jewish Gnosticism to Christian forms of the Gnostic religion on the other.

II. The Apocryphon of John

This document is extant in two basic recensions, a shorter one and a longer one.[15] While there are some minor differences to be observed among all four versions, two of them[16] are very fragmentary and can safely be ignored for our present purposes. The *Apocryphon of John* is surely one of the most important of all Gnostic texts known, for it contains a basic Gnostic myth which was widely used and elaborated. For example, this myth probably served as the basis for the Gnostic mythology of the Christian Gnostic teacher Valentinus, and was further elaborated by Valentinus' disciples.[17] The *Apocryphon of John* is widely (and correctly) taken to be a key text of *Sethian* Gnosticism.[18]

In its extant form, the *Apocryphon of John* is an apocalypse, containing a revelation given by the risen Christ to his disciple John.[19] Within the apocalypse frame at the beginning and end of the document there are two main sections, a revelation discourse and a commentary on Genesis 1-6. The commentary has been editorially modified, in a rather clumsy manner, into a dialogue between Jesus and his interlocutor John. A number of sources seem to be reflected in the document as a whole, and considerable internal confusion is evident. The basic structure, nevertheless, is quite clear.

The following outline represents my analysis of the structure and

---

[13] NHC V,5.

[14] NHC II,1; III,1; IV,1; BG,2.

[15] For the texts see Till-Schenke, *Papyrus Berolinensis 8502*; Krause, *Drei Versionen* (NHC II,1; III,1; IV,1); and Giversen, *Apocryphon* (NHC II,1). The shorter recension is represented by BG,2 and NHC III,1; the longer by NHC II,1 and IV,1.

[16] NHC III,1; IV,1. For ET of NHC II,1, by F. Wisse, see NHLE, 98–116; for that of BG,2, by M. Krause and R. McL. Wilson, see Foerster, *Gnosis*, 1. 105–20.

[17] See esp. Quispel, "Valentinian Gnosis."

[18] For ground-breaking studies of the Sethian Gnostic system see H.-M. Schenke, "System," and "Sethianism." See also Stroumsa's important monograph, *Another Seed*.

[19] An especially useful discussion of the structure and form of the *Apocryphon of John* is that of Kragerud, "Apocryphon Johannis."

content of the *Apocryphon of John*. I use as a basis the version in NH Codex II, and show the corresponding sections in BG in parentheses:

Preamble and apocalyptic frame	1,1–2,26 (19,6–22,17)
I. Revelation discourse	2,26–13,13 (22,17–44,18)
A. Theosophy	
1. Negative theology; the unknown God	2,26–4,10 (22,17–26,6)
2. The heavenly world	4,10–9,24 (26,6–36,15)
B. Cosmogony	
1. Fall of Sophia	9,25–10,23 (36,15–39,4)
2. The cosmic world of darkness	10,23–13,5 (39,4–44,9)
3. Blasphemy of the demiurge	13,5–13 (44,9–18)
II. Dialogue: soteriology	13,13–31,25 (44,19–75,15)
1. Repentance of Sophia	13,13–14,13 (44,19–47,18)
2. Anthropogony[20]	14,13–21,16 (47,18–55,18)
3. Adam in Paradise	21,16–24,8 (55,18–62,3)
4. Seduction of Eve; Cain and Abel	24,8–34 (62,3–63,12)
5. Seth and his seed	24,35–25,16 (63,12–64,12)
6. Two spirits; classes of men	25,16–27,30 (64,12–71,2)
7. Production of *Heimarmenē* "Fate"	27,31–28,32 (71,2–72,12)
8. Noah and the Flood	28,32–29,15 (72,12–73,18)
9. The angels and the daughters of men	29,16–30,11 (73,18–75,10)
10. The triple descent of *Pronoia* "Foreknowledge"[21]	30,11–31,25 (75,10–13)
Apocalyptic frame and title	31,25–32,9 (75,14–77,5)

I have already stated my view that the *Apocryphon of John* is a document whose present form represents a secondary Christianization of previously non-Christian material.[22] Its literary structure suggests such a conclusion: when we remove from the *Apocryphon of John* the apocalyptic framework at the beginning and the end, together with the dialogue features involving the ten questions put to Christ by his interlocutor John, we are left with material in which nothing Christian remains, except for some easily removed glosses. The revelation discourse (I in our outline), containing the theosophical and cosmogonical teaching, may originally have been a separate unit. Indeed it is this

---

[20] The longer recension has a lengthy section devoted to the work of 365 cosmic angels: II,1:15,29–19,2. Cf. the reference to 360 angels in BG,2:50,8–51,1.

[21] The hymn of the triple descent of *Pronoia* is absent from BG.

[22] The classic example of such a Christianizing redaction of non-Christian material is *Sophia of Jesus Christ* (NHC III,4; BG,3) in relation to *Eugnostos* (NHC III,3; V,1). The latter is an "epistle" containing a discussion of the unknown God and the heavenly world, reflecting a sophisticated Gnostic exegesis of key texts in Genesis. It has no obvious Christian elements in it. *Sophia of Jesus Christ* is a composite document in which the text of *Eugnostos* has been taken over and opened up into a revelation dialogue between Christ and his disciples. See esp. Krause, "Eugnostosbriefes," and Parrott, "Religious Syncretism."

material which is parallel to Irenaeus' description of the doctrine of the "Barbelognostics."[23] Apparently this is all that Irenaeus had; he certainly gives no indication that he is excerpting a section from an "Apocryphon of John."[24] The dialogue (II in our outline) consists essentially of a commentary on Genesis 1–6, expanded by means of questions 1–3 + 10 of the dialogue between Christ and John. The material treated in questions 4–9 on the destiny of the soul (II,6 in our outline) is extraneous material which has been interpolated into the commentary.[25]

As for the aforementioned Christianizing glosses, these vary in extent from one version to another. For example, the heavenly aeon Autogenes is identified by means of glosses with the pre-existent Christ in the first part of the revelation discourse; this identification is made initially in the BG version at 30,14–17, but it is absent from the parallel passage in Codex II.[26] Sophia in Codex II is called "our sister Sophia" in the BG version.[27] On the other hand, whereas the BG version has *Epinoia* "Thought" (a manifestation of Sophia) teach Adam and Eve knowledge from the forbidden tree, in the other version it is Christ who does this.[28] Such examples could be multiplied, but the main point here is that the various versions of the *Apocryphon of John*, taken together, show that the Christian elements in it are altogether secondary.[29] We have essentially to do with a Jewish Gnostic body of literature, as can be seen from its content.

A survey of the content of the *Apocryphon of John* will show that its various sections, especially the basic myth, are based upon the Jewish Bible and Jewish traditions of biblical interpretation, as well as Jewish apocryphal writings. The Jewish traditions in question are not only those of Greek-speaking diaspora Judaism but there are also some from Aramaic-speaking Palestinian Judaism. Now to specifics.

The theology of the "unknown God" in the *Apocryphon of John* (I,A,1 in our outline) is based upon a Platonizing Jewish theology of divine transcendence, such as is richly documented in first-century Judaism. To be sure, the Platonic ingredient here is important. As is well known,

[23] *Haer.* I.29.
[24] Cf. H.-M. Schenke, "Studien I," and Krause's discussion in Foerster, *Gnosis*, 1.100–103.
[25] So Kragerud, "Apocryphon Johannis," 31, 34–35; cf. Krause in Foerster, *Gnosis*, 1. 100–101. Krause suggests that this material was already in dialogue form before being woven together with the commentary material.
[26] 6,23–25.
[27] Cf. NHC II,1:9,25 and BG,2:36,16. Both versions, however, have "our sister Sophia" in a later passage: II,1:23,21 and BG,2:54,1 (restored in a lacuna).
[28] Cf. BG,2:60,16–61,2 and II,1:23,26–28.
[29] This has been shown conclusively by Arai, "Christologie." Cf. also Perkins, *Gnostic Dialogue*, 91–92; and H.-M. Schenke, "Sethianism," 611.

doctrines of divine transcendence were developing in Platonic schools
of the period, and the *via negativa* of the sort found here in the
Apocryphon of John could be accounted for without recourse to
Judaism. But, in my view, the Platonic elements have been mediated
through Hellenistic Judaism. Philo of Alexandria provides numerous
examples of the sort of *Jewish*-Platonic theology I would posit as a
theological background for the *Apocryphon of John's* doctrine of divine
transcendence.[30] Josephus is also an interesting witness to a first-century
C.E. Jewish theology of transcendence. According to him, Moses represented the biblical Creator as "One, uncreated, and immutable to all
eternity; in beauty surpassing all mortal thought, made known to us by
His power, although the nature of His real being passes knowledge."[31]
What the Gnostics do, of course, is split the transcendent God of the
Bible into a supreme ineffable being (I,A,1) and a lower creator respon-
sible for the material world (I,B). It is precisely this radical dualism
which marks the decisive step *out* of (normative) Judaism taken by the
Gnostic thinkers.

The heavenly world as presented in the *Apocryphon of John* (I,A,2) is
populated by a number of emanations from the supreme God; chief
among them are the "thought" (*ennoia*) of God, called "Barbelo," and her
product "Autogenes" ("self-begotten"). Dependent upon the latter are the
four luminaries (Armozel, Oriel, Daveithai, and Eleleth). Heavenly
prototypes of Adam and his son Seth are also given prominence. While
much of this is presumably based upon theological speculations of
contemporary philosophy,[32] the key figures have their origin in Jewish
biblical exegesis and incipient Jewish mysticism. The supreme God is
given the esoteric name "Man," obviously read out of Gen 1:26f.,[33] and
possibly Ezek 1:26 as well.[34] The figures of Autogenes and (Piger)-
adamas may have been spun out of an earlier Jewish Gnostic *Anthropos*

---

[30] See e.g., *Somn.* 1.67: God is "unnameable (ἀκατονόμαστος), "ineffable" (ἄρρητος), and
"incomprehensible" (ἀκατάληπτος). All three of these terms are reflected in the Coptic
text of a single passage in *Ap. John* BG,2:24,2–6. Cf. also *Quod Deus* 62; *Quaest. in Exod.*
2.45; *Post.* 168–69. On the basis of such passages as these H. Jonas has argued that Philo
was really a Gnostic! See Jonas, *Gnosis*, 2.1, 70–121. Philo is more appropriately
considered as standing within the tradition of Middle Platonism. See e.g., Dillon, *Middle
Platonists*, 139–83.

[31] *Ap.* 2.167 (Thackeray's translation in the LCL edition). Note especially the phrase
ὁποῖος δὲ κατ'οὐσία ἐστὶν ἄγνωστον. The term ἄγνωστος "unknown," as applied to the
transcendent God, is widely regarded as a favorite term of the Gnostics. It does not occur
in the *Apocryphon of John*, however. On "the Unknown God in Neoplatonism" see
Dodds, *Proclus*, Appendix I, 310–13.

[32] See e.g., Whittaker, "Self-Generating Principles."

[33] See H.-M. Schenke's ground-breaking study, *Gott "Mensch."*

[34] Quispel, "Ezekiel."

myth.[35] The esoteric name for the first divine emanation, "Barbelo," is probably based on a wordplay on the divine tetragrammaton.[36] The four luminaries have their biblical prototypes in the four angelic beings beneath the throne of God in Ezekiel's vision.[37] The heavenly Adam and Seth are Platonic projections into the divine realm of the biblical patriarchs,[38] and recall the Platonizing exegesis of the double creation story in Genesis 1 and 2 such as is found, for example, in Philo.[39] Adam and Seth also play key roles in the development of Gnostic *Heilsgeschichte*.[40]

The Gnostic figure of Sophia—her fall, repentance, and subsequent role in salvation-history are central features of Gnostic mythology[41]—is clearly derived from the Wisdom theology of Judaism. What is said of Sophia in the Gnostic sources cannot be understood without attention to her pre-history in Jewish tradition, even if (or because) the Gnostics turn much of this tradition upside down.[42]

The myth of the origin of the Gnostic demiurge[43] as an "abortion"[44] of Sophia (I,B,1; II,1) reflects a sophisticated reworking of the biblical traditions of the fall of Eve, the birth of Cain, and the fall of the "sons of God," together with extra-biblical Jewish traditions of interpretation.[45] The use of the word "abortion" in this connection reflects a Hebrew wordplay documented in rabbinic haggadah.[46]

The description of the world of darkness (I,B,2), with its demonization of the seven planets and the twelve zodiacal signs, is based upon contemporary astrological speculation enriched by specifically Jewish lore.[47]

The tradition of the "blasphemy of the demiurge," found in a number

[35] Van den Broek, "Autogenes."
[36] *barba"ēlo*, "in four, God." This etymology, first proposed by W. Harvey in his 1857 edition of Irenaeus (vol. 1, 221, n. 2) but not widely accepted, has been more convincingly stated by Scopello, "Youel et Barbelo"; see esp. 378–79.
[37] Ezek 1:4–21. See Böhlig, "Hintergrund," 84. Cf. also the four archangels of 1 Enoch 9–10, suggested by Stroumsa, *Another Seed*, 55. On the use of 1 Enoch in the *Apocryphon of John* see below.
[38] Gen 5:1–3.
[39] *Op. Mund.* 66–135. Cf. Pearson, *Man and Salvation*, 3–8.
[40] These roles are especially important in the *Apocalypse of Adam*; see below.
[41] See I,B,1; II,1–8, 10, in our outline.
[42] See esp. MacRae, "Sophia Myth."
[43] On the names "Yaldabaoth," "Saklas," and "Samael," as applied to the demiurge, see Pearson, "Haggadic Traditions," 466–68; and Barc, "Samaèl."
[44] *houhe* "abortion," BG,2:46,10.
[45] Gen 3:4–6; 4:1; 6:1. This is admirably treated in Stroumsa, *Another Seed*.
[46] *nepilim*, "fallen ones"—*nepalim*, "abortions"; see *Midr. Gen. Rab.* 26.7, and Stroumsa, *Another Seed*, 106; cf. 65–70. Dahl ("Archon," 703) traces the concept of the demiurge as an "abortion" to Jewish interpretations of Isa 14:19.
[47] See esp. Welburn, "Identity."

of other Gnostic sources as well,[48] reflects the end-product of a discussion in Judaism concerning "two powers in heaven," in which a
number of biblical texts appear both in the background and in the
foreground. Here in the *Apocryphon of John*, Exod 20:5 and Isa 46:9 are
combined. This tradition is a succinct reflection of the "revolution" on
the part of Jewish Gnostics against the biblical Creator-Lawgiver.[49]

The anthropogony which follows the blasphemy of the demiurge and
the repentance of Sophia (II,2 in our outline) is organized around
several key texts in Genesis: 1:2; 1:26–27; 2:7; and 2:18. The Gnostic
commentary is based upon Jewish traditions of exegesis, both Alexandrian and Palestinian. For example, one can see in it both the Alexandrian Jewish tradition that God relegated the creation of man's mortal
nature to the angels[50] and the Palestinian tradition that God created man
as a *golem* ("formless mass").[51] I have treated these and other details in
the text elsewhere.[52]

The rest of the material in the second main section of the *Apocryphon
of John* (except II,6 and 10)[53] continues an elaborate commentary on
Genesis 1–6, much of which has parallels in other Gnostic texts.[54]
Especially important is the section on the birth of Seth (II,5 in our
outline), built upon the key texts Gen 4:25 and 5:3. Seth is the prototype
of the Gnostic; indeed his "seed" or "race" constitutes the totality of the
Gnostic elect.[55] In contrast to some other "Sethian" Gnostic texts, here in
the *Apocryphon of John* Seth (with his seed) assumes a passive role in
salvation. That is, there does not seem to be explicit here the notion of
Seth as "savior." It is the Mother (Sophia in her various manifestations)
who initiates salvation for the race of Seth, by sending down her
"spirit."[56]

---

[48] E.g., *Hypostasis of the Archons* NHC II,4, *On the Origin of the World* NHC II,5;
Gospel of the Egyptians NHC III,2 and IV,2; Iren. *Haer.* I.29 and 30.

[49] See Dahl's seminal study, "Archon."

[50] E.g., Philo, *Fug.* 68–70; cf. Plato, *Tim.* 41A–42B.

[51] E.g., *Midr. Gen. Rab.* 14.8; cf. Ps 139:16.

[52] Pearson, "Exegesis"; cf. *Man and Salvation*, 9–15.

[53] The hymn of the triple descent of *Pronoia* (II,10), absent from BG, may be regarded
as a re-interpretation of, or alternative to, the triple appearance of the redeemer Seth in
other Gnostic texts, such as the *Apocalypse of Adam* and *Gospel of the Egyptians* (see
below). The *Pronoia* hymn constitutes the basis for the structure and content of
Trimorphic Protennoia NHC XIII,1. See Turner, "Threefold Path," 326–28, and his
contribution to this volume. On II,6 see below.

[54] See esp. *Hypostasis of the Archons* NHC II,4 and Barc's edition with introduction
and commentary, *L'Hypostase*.

[55] Numerous studies have appeared on the role of the Gnostic Seth and his seed, and
the Jewish traditions reflected in the Gnostic material. See e.g., Klijn, *Seth*; Pearson,
"Seth"; Stroumsa, *Another Seed*.

[56] II,1:25,2–16. Cf. Pearson, "Seth," 481.

The section corresponding to the account in Gen 6:1–4 of the descent of the "sons of God" (II,9 in our outline) is undoubtedly dependent upon 1 *Enoch* 6–8, which itself is part of a commentary on Gen 6:1–4.[57] It also shows influence from other Jewish apocryphal texts dealing with that crucial passage in Genesis 6, which in Second Temple Judaism was a *locus classicus* for the explanation of the origins of evil on earth.[58] For example, the *Apocryphon of John* has the angels assume the likenesses of the husbands of the daughters of men in order to accomplish their purpose. This detail is found in *T. Reub.* 5:5–7, but not in 1 *Enoch*.[59] The occurrence of the "Imitation Spirit"[60] also represents a deviation from 1 *Enoch*, and ties this section with the passage on the "two spirits" and the classes of men found earlier (II,6). The editor who interpolated that passage into the *Apocryphon of John* may also be responsible for working the "Imitation Spirit" into the material taken from 1 *Enoch*.

The interpolated passage on the two spirits and classes of men has been referred to as a Jewish "catechism," in which the ultimate fate of the human soul is tied to the operation of two spirits: the "Spirit of Life" and the "Imitation Spirit."[61] The resemblance of this doctrine to that of the Rule Scroll from Qumran[62] has also been noted, and it can hardly be doubted that it has been Gnosticized here in the *Apocryphon of John*. "The immoveable race" on whom the "Spirit of Life" descends is, of course, the "race" of Gnostics. The interpolated passage now stands in the text of the *Apocryphon of John* as an anthropological excursus, elaborating upon the previous section in the text dealing with Seth and his seed.[63]

In summary, it must be seen that the basic content of the *Apocryphon of John* is Jewish Gnostic, in that its various elements have been drawn from *Jewish* traditions. The Christian veneer applied in its final redaction is a thin one indeed!

---

[57] I have discussed the use of 1 *Enoch* in the *Apocryphon of John* and other Gnostic texts in my study, "Sources."

[58] See Nickelsburg, "Apocalyptic and Myth."

[59] Cf. Stroumsa, *Another Seed*, 37–38.

[60] I prefer this translation of *pepneuma etšēs* (II,1:27,32–33 and elsewhere) to "despicable spirit," the rendering in *NHLE*. Cf. BG,2:71,4–5: *antimimon pneuma*. See Böhlig, "Antimimon." Presumably the Coptic *etšēs* is a misreading of *antimimon* as *atimon* ("despicable").

[61] See Hauschild, *Geist*, 225–47.

[62] 1QS 3,13–26.

[63] So Kragerud, "Apocryphon Johannis," 35.

III. The Apocalypse of Adam

This document consists essentially of a testamentary revelation mediated by Adam to his son Seth, setting forth the subsequent history of the
world and the salvation of the elect (i.e., the Gnostics). Its first editor, A.
Böhlig,[64] regards this text as a document of pre-Christian Sethian Gnosticism, originating in a Jewish Gnostic baptismal sect in Palestine or
Syria. Its most recent editor, G. MacRae, takes cognizance of the
document's dependence upon Jewish apocalyptic traditions, and suggests that it represents a "transitional stage in an evolution from Jewish
to gnostic apocalyptic."[65] To be sure, the Jewish-Gnostic background of
the document has not gone unchallenged in recent scholarly discussions,
and some scholars argue for a comparatively late date for the document.[66] In my view, however, it is still possible to regard the Apocalypse
of Adam as an example of "Jewish Gnostic" literature, a point which will
be elaborated in what follows.

A complicating factor in the discussion is the question of the literary
history of the Apocalypse of Adam. C. Hedrick has recently argued, for
example, that the document as it now stands is the product of the
amalgamation of two distinct sources, edited with additions by a final
redactor at around the end of the first century C.E. The starting point for
this source-analysis is the presence of what are taken to be two introductions and two conclusions. The first introduction (64,6–65,23 + 66,12–
67,12) is assigned to source A, the second (65,24–66,12 + 67,12–67,21) to
source B. The first conclusion (85,19–22a) is assigned to source A, and the
second (85,22b–31) to the redactor.[67] These observations are more cogent
than the division of the main body of the text, i.e., the apocalypse
proper, into sources and redaction, for Hedrick's analysis breaks up the
tripartite structure of the Gnostic history of salvation, organized around
the three critical events of flood, fire, and end-time struggle. This
structure is integral to the document as a whole.[68] An alternative way of
understanding the obvious seams dividing up the two "introductions"
would be to posit the redactional weaving-together of materials which
might have occurred previously in sequence, i.e., to posit that the
material in Hedrick's second introduction followed upon that of his first

---

[64] Böhlig-Labib, Apokalypsen.

[65] MacRae, "Apocalypse of Adam," 152; cf. Hedrick, Apocalypse, 85–87.

[66] For discussion of the literature on the Apocalypse of Adam see Hedrick, Apocalypse, 9–17.

[67] Hedrick, Apocalypse, esp. 21–28.

[68] See Perkins, "Genre and Function," 387–89; but cf. Hedrick, Apocalypse, 31 and 48
n.46.

introduction. To be sure, such a suggestion implies the activity of an editor, who might also be responsible for additions to his source.

As an example of additional editorial activity, I would cite the passage concerning the thirteen kingdoms plus the "kingless generation." I subscribe to the argument of those who see in this passage a later interpolation into the text,[69] presumably by the document's final redactor. The second conclusion may also be assigned to the redactor, as Hedrick has suggested.

My understanding of the structure and content of the *Apocalypse of Adam* may be set forth in the following outline:

<table>
<tr><td>Introduction</td><td>64,1–5</td></tr>
<tr><td>I. The Setting: Adam's testamentary speech to Seth</td><td>64,5–67,21</td></tr>
<tr><td> A. Adam relates his and Eve's experiences with their Creator</td><td>64,5–65,23</td></tr>
<tr><td> B. Adam's dream vision: three heavenly men address him in a revelation</td><td>65,24–66,8</td></tr>
<tr><td> C. Adam and Eve's experiences (continued)</td><td>66,9–67,14</td></tr>
<tr><td> D. Adam intends to transmit the heavenly revelations to Seth</td><td>67,14–21</td></tr>
<tr><td>II. The Revelation</td><td>67,22–85,18</td></tr>
<tr><td> A. The end of Adam's generation[70]</td><td>67,22–28+</td></tr>
<tr><td> B. The Flood, first deliverance</td><td>69,2–73,29</td></tr>
<tr><td> C. Destruction by fire, second deliverance</td><td>73,30–76,7</td></tr>
<tr><td> D. Third episode: end-time threat and redemption</td><td>76,8–85,18</td></tr>
<tr><td>   1. Coming of the Illuminator</td><td>76,8–77,3</td></tr>
<tr><td>   2. The Powers' wrath against the Illuminator</td><td>77,4–18</td></tr>
<tr><td>   3. Interpolation: competing views about the Illuminator</td><td>77,18–83,4</td></tr>
<tr><td>   a. The Powers' quandary</td><td>77,18–27</td></tr>
<tr><td>   b. The thirteen kingdoms</td><td>77,27–82,19</td></tr>
<tr><td>   c. The generation without a king</td><td>82,19–83,4</td></tr>
<tr><td>   4. Final struggle, repentance of the peoples</td><td>83,4–84,3</td></tr>
<tr><td>   5. Condemnation of the peoples</td><td>84,4–28</td></tr>
<tr><td>   6. Final salvation of the seed of Seth</td><td>85,1–6</td></tr>
<tr><td> E. Revelations put on a high rock</td><td>85,7–18</td></tr>
<tr><td>First conclusion</td><td>85,19–22</td></tr>
<tr><td>Second conclusion and title</td><td>85,22–32</td></tr>
</table>

[69] 77,18–83,4. See e.g., MacRae, "Apocalypse of Adam," 152. For a contrary view see Stroumsa, *Another Seed*, 82–103. Böhlig-Labib refer to this passage as an "excursus" (*Apokalypsen* 87, 91–93, 109). Hedrick includes the passage in his source B, yet sees it as originally a separate unit (*Apocalypse*, 115–19).

[70] The death of Adam is implied in the phrase, "after I have completed the times of this generation" (67,22–24). Noah is probably to be supplied in the lacuna in line 28. Cf. Hedrick's translation (*Apocalypse*, 233): "[then Noah], a servant [of God...]." Cf. also the translation, by Krause and Wilson, in Foerster, *Gnosis*, 2.17. Note also that p. 68 in the MS is blank.

Formally, the *Apocalypse of Adam* is both an "apocalypse" and a
"testament." It is an apocalypse in that it contains a revelation given by
heavenly informants to Adam, who mediates the revelation to his son
Seth. It adheres closely to the "apocalypse" genre.[71] It is also a
"testament," with close formal connections with the Jewish testamentary
literature, in that it is presented as a speech given by Adam to his son
just before his death, "in the seven hundredth year."[72]

The close parallels between the *Apocalypse of Adam* and the Jewish
Adam literature, especially the *Life of Adam and Eve* and the *Apocalypse of Moses*, have often been noted.[73] G. Nickelsburg, for example,
posits the existence of an apocalyptic testament of Adam as a common
source utilized by the *Apocalypse of Adam* and *Adam and Eve*.[74]
Another Adam book has also recently been brought into purview,
namely the Syriac *Testament of Adam*.[75] The prophetic section of this
work (ch. 3) consists of a prophecy given by Adam to Seth of future
catastrophes of flood and fire, and the coming of a savior who will
deliver the elect posterity of Adam. G. Reinink has noted the close
correspondences between the *Apocalypse of Adam* and the Syriac
Testament, and has plausibly posited the existence of an early document
upon which both are based.[76]

We should also take note here of the Adam apocalypses referred to in
the *Mani Codex*. Indeed an Adam "apocalypse" is quoted in that
important document, in which a radiant angel says to Adam, "I am
Balsamos,[77] the greatest angel of light. Wherefore take and write these

---

[71] See Fallon, "Apocalypses," 126–27; and Perkins, "Genre and Function."

[72] 64,4. See MacRae, "Apocalypse of Adam," 152; Perkins, "Genre and Function," 384–
86; Hedrick, *Apocalypse*, 243. The figure of 700 follows the LXX of Gen 5:3, setting Adam's
age at the birth of Seth at 230 rather than 130, as in the MT. Adam's death at the age of
930 years (Gen 5:4) would then account for the figure of 700. Cf. also Jos. *Ant.* 1.67, where
the same figures are used.

[73] See Perkins, "Genre and Function"; Pearson, "Seth," 492–94; Nickelsburg, "Related
Traditions."

[74] Nickelsburg, "Related Traditions," esp. 537.

[75] See now S. Robinson, *Adam*. Robinson has published the Syriac text, with English
translations, of three recensions of this important work, with a very useful discussion of
its place in the Adam cycle of traditions. Unfortunately he omits any consideration of the
apocalypses of Adam mentioned in the *Mani Codex*, on which see below.

[76] Reinink, "Problem," esp. 397–98.

[77] The name is originally that of the Phoenician "Lord of Heaven" (*Ba'al Šamēm*); cf.
Beelsamēn in the *Phoenician History* of Philo of Byblos (see Attridge-Oden, *Philo*, 40–1,
81). "Balsamos" is the name of an angel in the Coptic *Apocalypse of Bartholomew* (Rec.
A) in a hymn sung by angels to Adam in Paradise. See Kropp, *Zaubertexte*, 1.80.
Balsamos' name is in a lacuna in the MS used by Budge, *Coptic Apocrypha*; see pl. XXIII
and p. 23 (transcription), 198 (ET). Cf. also Müller, *Engellehre*, 310. "Balsamos" is also
found in a list of names which the Basilidian Gnostics pretended to take from Hebrew
sources, according to Jer. *Ep.* 75.3. The other names mentioned by Jerome are Armazel,
Barbelon, Abraxas, and Leusibora.

things which I reveal to you on most pure papyrus, incorruptible and insusceptible to worms."[78] The text goes on to say that this angel revealed many things and that Adam beheld angels and great powers. It also refers to other "writings" produced by Adam. The writings referred to may very well have been Jewish Adam books,[79] but the use of our Gnostic *Apocalypse of Adam* by Mani may perhaps be indicated in the following statement: "And he became mightier than all the powers and the angels of creation."[80] Be that as it may, it can hardly be doubted that the *Apocalypse of Adam* is closely related to the Adam cycle of Jewish literature which goes back, at the latest, to the first century C.E. Josephus is acquainted with such literature, and may be relying on an early testament of Adam when he tells of Adam's predictions of deluge and fire and the erection by the progeny of Seth of inscribed steles of stone and brick for the purpose of preserving their lore.[81]

Of course it cannot be doubted that the *Apocalypse of Adam* is a *Gnostic* text from beginning to end. It therefore has a far different slant in its interpretation of the Adam-Seth traditions from that of the other Jewish and Christian Adam books. This is already evident in its first section wherein Adam addresses Seth and gives him a biographical account of his and Eve's misadventures after their creation. A comparison with *Adam and Eve* is especially instructive. In *Adam and Eve* the two protoplasts have been banished from Paradise for their sin, and are duly repentant.[82] In the *Apocalypse of Adam*, on the other hand, Adam and Eve see themselves as naturally "higher than the god who had created us and the powers with him."[83] The Creator acts against Adam and Eve out of jealous wrath, in a manner quite reminiscent of the devil in *Adam and Eve*, banished from heaven because of his refusal to worship the newly-created Adam.[84] The author of this material is therefore not only dependent upon early Jewish Adam traditions, but is also critical of them, supplying a radically new perspective on biblical history.

This perspective is carried over into the revelation proper, which constitutes the bulk of the *Apocalypse of Adam* (II in the outline). In form this revelation is a "historical apocalypse" in which the salvation of

---

[78] 49.3–10. See Cameron-Dewey, *Mani Codex.* The text of pp. 1–72 of the codex was first published by Henrichs-Koenen, "Mani-Kodex."

[79] So e.g., Henrichs, "Mani Codex," 725; Stroumsa, *Another Seed,* 146.

[80] 50.1–4; cf. *Apoc. Adam* V,5:64,16–19. This would tell against the late third-century date for the *Apocalypse of Adam* proposed by Beltz, *Adamapokalypse.*

[81] *Ant.* 1.67–71; cf. the *Apocalypse of Adam,* II,E in our outline.

[82] Chs. 1–11.

[83] 64,16–18.

[84] Chs. 12–17.

the elect seed of Seth (the Gnostics) is the dominant concern. The three cataclysms from which the Gnostics are to be saved are the flood (II,B), a destruction by fire clearly identified as the destruction of Sodom and Gomorrah (II,C), and the final "day of death."[85] The elect are rescued from each catastrophe by the savior, who is Seth.

An Iranian background has been posited for the tripartite structure of this historical apocalypse.[86] But it is not necessary to posit a direct Iranian influence on this material since the Jewish sources provide an altogether adequate background.[87] The destructions by flood and fire are set forth in the Adamic traditions already referred to,[88] and there are (non-Gnostic) Jewish texts in which the destruction by fire is separated from the end-time, which constitutes the third and last catastrophic judgment. The Apocalypse of Weeks in 1 Enoch is an especially important example, inasmuch as that document might have influenced the Adam testament posited as the common source lying behind the Apocalypse of Adam and Adam and Eve.[89] The Apocalypse of Weeks has a threefold scheme of judgments: flood, fire, and final judgment.[90] Moreover the association of the fiery judgment with the destruction of Sodom and Gomorrah occurs not only in Gnostic texts,[91] but even in Philo.[92] To be sure, our Gnostic author has a slant on these traditions which would have been abhorrent to Philo or other non-Gnostic Jewish writers.

The essential point here, therefore, is that the Apocalypse of Adam is, from beginning to end, a Gnostic text in which the numerous Jewish traditions it inherits, including even the genre itself (apocalyptic testament), are thoroughly reinterpreted in the interests of a higher gnosis. With consummate irony our author sets forth the "real truth" concerning the heavenly origin of the spiritual "seed of Seth" (the Gnostics) and the utter folly of servitude to the Creator.[93] It is a Jewish Gnostic document in the sense that its genre and materials are derived from Judaism, and could only have been written by someone who was thoroughly acquainted with biblical and extra-biblical Jewish traditions. Yet in its

---

[85] II,D; see 76,16–17.

[86] Böhlig, "Adamapokalypse"; cf. Colpe, "Sethian Ages."

[87] See esp. Perkins, "Genre and Function," 387–89; and Stroumsa, Another Seed, 103–13.

[88] Adam and Eve 49.2–50.2; Jos. Ant. 1.68–70; Test. Adam (Syriac) 3.5.

[89] Nickelsburg, "Related Traditions," 535–37.

[90] 1 Enoch 93:4,8; 91:11–15. The judgment by fire (93.8) is interpreted as the burning of the Temple.

[91] Gos. Eg. III,2:60,9–18; Paraph. Shem VII,1:28,34–29,33.

[92] Vit. Mos. 2.53–58, 263; Abr. 1. See Stroumsa, Another Seed, 106.

[93] See Perkins, "Genre and Function," for a perceptive discussion of the Gnostic irony in the Apocalypse of Adam.

intentionality it is anti-Jewish in the extreme, a product of the Gnostic revolt against the Jewish God and his ordinances.

In our discussion of the *Apocryphon of John* we were able to distinguish its essential features from the thin Christian veneer which has been secondarily applied to it. The *Apocalypse of Adam* lacks such Christianizing features. The revelation is mediated not by Christ but by Adam. The "savior" (illuminator) is not Jesus Christ but *Seth*, who appears in various manifestations for the salvation of his seed.[94] To be sure, some scholars have thought they could find traces of Christian influence in the *Apocalypse of Adam*, particularly in the passage treating the final appearance of the Illuminator.[95] But this passage and its context can be interpreted without recourse to the New Testament or Christian tradition, for it adheres to a pre-Christian Jewish literary pattern based on OT traditions. The pattern in question deals with the persecution and subsequent exaltation of the righteous man, and has been convincingly delineated by G. Nickelsburg, with special reference to Wisdom 1-6 and other intertestamental Jewish literature.[96] This pattern is fully represented in the *Apocalypse of Adam*; it will also be noticed that it is disturbed by the interpolation on the competing views about the Illuminator:[97]

1. *Earthly persecution*	
Signs and wonders of the Illuminator	77,1-3
Conspiracy against him	77,4-15
Punishment of the Illuminator	77,16-18
2. *Exaltation, judgment*	
The peoples acknowledge their sin	83,4-84,3
Condemnation of the peoples	84,4-28
Exaltation of the elect	85,1-18

The author of the *Apocalypse of Adam* has taken over a well-established Jewish pattern, rooted especially in Isaiah 52-53 and

---

[94] "The imperishable illuminators who came from the holy seed: Yesseus, Mazareus, Yessedekeus" (85,28-31) may represent "the three avatars of Seth at each of his comings," according to Stroumsa (*Another Seed*, 102). The names are therefore mystical names of Seth. The last one, "Yessedekeus," could have been modelled on the name Ἰωσεδεκ in Jer 23:8 (LXX).

[95] Especially the sentence, "Then they will punish the flesh of the man upon whom the holy spirit has come" (77,16-18). See Yamauchi, *Gnosticism*, 107-15, esp. 110; Shellrude, "Adam," esp. 85-87.

[96] Nickelsburg, *Resurrection*, 48-111.

[97] II,D,3 in our outline; cf. discussion of the literary history of the *Apocalypse of Adam*, above. The pattern set forth here has also been noted with reference to the *Apocalypse of Adam* by Perkins, "Genre and Function," 390-91. Cf. also Nickelsburg, "Related Traditions," 537-38.

developed fully in Wisdom 1–6, in setting forth his prophecy concerning the final coming of the Illuminator. This pattern is especially apposite, for it corresponds to the "history" of the seed of Seth in the first two catastrophes of flood and fire: threatened with destruction they were rescued by heavenly intervention. In the final catastrophe a manifestation of Seth himself suffers with his seed, and with his seed achieves final victory and vindication. All of this is fully intelligible without reference to Christian history.

The references to baptism in the *Apocalypse of Adam* have also been interpreted in relation to Christianity. G. Shellrude, accepting the arguments of those who see in the *Apocalypse of Adam* a polemic against baptism,[98] sees in such passages as 83,4–8; 84,4–26; and 85,22–26 a polemic against orthodox Christianity and its baptismal practice. The Gnostics' opponents, according to Shellrude, claim the same redeemer as the Gnostic community, and baptism is associated with their acceptance of the redeemer, which can only be Christ.[99] But the spiritualization of "holy baptism" in the *Apocalypse of Adam* (85,25) does not imply a rejection of water baptism. And the main passage which has been taken as implying a rejection of baptism has more recently been seen to show just the opposite.[100] The Gnostics of the *Apocalypse of Adam* were, in fact, a baptismal sect (analogous to the Mandaeans),[101] and there is no reference to *Christian* baptism, either orthodox or heretical, anywhere in the text.

Is the *Apocalypse of Adam* therefore a "pre-Christian" Jewish Gnostic text? Here we must take up briefly the argument of G. Stroumsa, based upon the excursus on the competing views about the Illuminator, which he refers to as "the Hymn of the Child."[102] Thirteen "kingdoms" are listed in this passage, each with a different interpretation of the Illuminator, and each ending with the clause, "and thus he came to the water."[103]

---

[98] E.g., Morard, "Adam-interprétation" and "Adam-polémique"; cf. Hedrick, *Apocalypse,* esp. 192–215, on the redactor of the *Apocalypse of Adam.*

[99] Shellrude, "Adam," 88–90.

[100] 84,4–10. "Micheu and Michar and Mnesinous, who are over the holy baptism and the living water," are positive, not negative, figures. See MacRae, "Apocalypse of Adam," 191; H.-M. Schenke, "Sethianism," 598, 603; and Böhlig's remark in the seminar discussion printed in Layton, *Rediscovery,* 2. 557–58.

[101] Cf. Böhlig-Labib, *Apokalypsen,* 94–95. For an excellent summary of the evidence on ancient baptismal sects see now Rudolph, *Baptisten;* on the Mandaeans in this connection see 17–19.

[102] II,D,3 in our outline. See Stroumsa, *Another Seed,* 88–103.

[103] A number of interesting studies have been done on the religious background of the various "kingdoms." See e.g., Böhlig, "Adamapokalypse," 154–61, and Beltz, *Adamapokalypse,* 135–75. The "coming to the water" is probably a reference to the descent of the savior in each case, rather than to baptism. See Hedrick, *Apocalypse,* 145–47.

Stroumsa argues that the first twelve "kingdoms," to whom the savior comes in various forms, represent the twelve tribes of Israel, while the thirteenth kingdom represents the Christian church. The reference to the "word" (logos) which is said to have "received a mandate there"[104] is taken to reflect the Logos doctrine of early Christianity. The Gnostic community, on the other hand, is represented by the "generation without a king over it," those who alone have true knowledge concerning the identity of the savior (i.e., the heavenly Seth), and who alone constitute the "seed" who "receive his (the savior's) name upon the water."[105] The Apocalypse of Adam, therefore, represents a strain of Sethian Gnosticism resistant, and in reaction, to the Christianizing of Sethian gnōsis.[106]

It seems to me that Stroumsa's interpretation of the first twelve "kingdoms," as referring to Israel, is forced. Indeed the first twelve kingdoms may better be seen as elaborating on the "twelve kingdoms" of Ham and Japheth referred to earlier in the text.[107] The thirteenth would then presumably refer to the Shemites, and the "mandate" or "ordinance"[108] could be taken as referring to the Law.

If Stroumsa is correct, however, in his interpretation of the thirteenth kingdom, the Apocalypse of Adam, far from being a "pre-Christian" Gnostic text, is rather one in which the original themes of Sethian gnōsis, based on Jewish traditions, are retained against a tendency on the part of Gnostic opponents to see in Jesus Christ the true incarnation of the Gnostic savior. The Gospel of the Egyptians, with which the Apocalypse of Adam shares much material in common,[109] represents that other side of Sethian gnōsis, as does the Apocryphon of John.

It is therefore unimportant for our discussion whether or not the Apocalypse of Adam is chronologically a "pre-Christian" text inasmuch as it represents a very early type of Gnosticism in which the Jewish components are central, and in which no Christian influence occurs. Even if the Apocalypse of Adam were chronologically late, it would represent a form of Jewish Gnosticism which resisted the kind of Christianization we have noted in the case of the Apocryphon of John. Its possible relationships with Mandaean and Manichaean forms of the Gnostic religion deserve further investigation.[110]

---

[104] 82,13–15.
[105] 82,19–20; 83,4–6.
[106] Stroumsa, Another Seed, 94–103.
[107] 73,26–27.
[108] tōš, 82,15.
[109] See MacRae, "Apocalypse of Adam," 152.
[110] Cf. Beltz, Adamapokalypse, and Böhlig, "Adamapokalypse."

IV. Conclusions

The two documents chosen for special consideration here are intended to exemplify the problem of Jewish Gnostic literature. The *Apocryphon of John* shows how a Jewish Gnostic text, or collection of texts, could become Christianized in final form. The *Apocalypse of Adam*, on the other hand, shows how a Jewish Gnostic text could retain its essential features without taking on a Christian cast. To be sure, these are only two examples, albeit important ones; others could have been chosen to make the same point, e.g., the *Hypostasis of the Archons*[111] and the *Paraphrase of Shem*.[112] We have seen, in the documents we have chosen for examination here, how biblical and other Jewish texts and traditions have been radically reinterpreted in the service of a higher gnōsis which denigrates the Creator and his world and overthrows the centrality of the Law. The "building blocks" of this new gnōsis, as expressed in literature, are Jewish; yet the interpretation can be seen to be "anti-Jewish" in the extreme, if by "Judaism" we mean (at least) devotion to the Creator, his Law, and his people.[113] This new gnōsis quickly assumed Christian forms, as is illustrated by the *Apocryphon of John*, wherein Jesus Christ assumes the role of a revealer. But while there seems to be a necessary relationship between Gnosticism (at least in its earliest forms) and Judaism, there is no such necessary relationship between Gnosticism and Christianity. Nor is there a single trajectory running from Jewish to Christian forms of the Gnostic religion.

The early Gnostics utilized and created a great number of books, and had access to exegetical and other Jewish traditions which were in oral circulation. What we have available now, as the result of chance discoveries, is undoubtedly only the "tip of the iceberg." In the material at our disposal we can see how specifically *Jewish* literature (especially the Bible), *Jewish* exegetical and theological traditions, and *Jewish* literary genres have been utilized to express a drastic reorientation of values and perceived religious truth. A question inevitably arises: Who were the people who created these writings, and for whom did they write? Here, unfortunately, we are faced with a lack of external evidence, and the concomitant necessity of applying our imagination to the texts themselves in order to extrapolate some answers.[114] Intimate

[111] NHC II,4. See esp. Barc's edition, *L'Hypostase.*
[112] NHC VII,1. See esp. Wisse, "Redeemer Figure."
[113] We should recall, though, that "normative Judaism" did not begin to emerge until the end of the first century C.E., in connection with the post-Temple reorganization at Jamnia.
[114] Contrast the case of the Dead Sea Scrolls: We have not only the scrolls themselves but massive evidence for the community which utilized them, as a result of the

familiarity with specifically Jewish forms and traditions, an awareness of popular philosophy and pagan lore, a highly sophisticated and creative hermeneutical approach, a sensitivity to profound questions of human existence—such are the chief characteristics of the early Gnostic literature. We can readily posit as authors and avid readers of the Gnostic materials Jewish intellectuals who, estranged from the "mainstream" of their own culture and dissatisfied with traditional answers, adopted a revolutionary stance vis-à-vis their religious traditions, not by rejecting them altogether but by applying to them a new interpretation. These were *religious* intellectuals,[115] not secularized apostates such as those Jews with whom Philo was well acquainted in Alexandria.[116] In reinterpreting their Jewish religious traditions, however, they burst the bonds of Judaism and created a new religion.[117] We are thus presented with the anomaly of Jews who finally *intended* to be "no longer Jews."[118]

That, in a nutshell, is the problem of Jewish Gnostic literature.

excavations at Khirbet Qumran. The only "external" evidence we have for the Gnostics is the polemics of the heresiologists. *Caveat lector!*

[115] I would posit *groups* of Gnostics, perhaps at first still formally attached to the synagogue but developing their own religious life. Aspects of this religious life can be extrapolated from the documents, to some extent. Note e.g., the references to baptism in the *Apocalypse of Adam*. The *Apocryphon of John* contains material which could have been used in catechesis.

[116] See *Virt.* 182; *Conf.* 2–3. Philo's own nephew, the notorious Tiberius Alexander, is one of the most famous examples of a Jewish apostate in antiquity.

[117] Cf. our discussion at the beginning of this essay. In its Manichaean form Gnosticism became a world religion. See Rudolph, "Weltreligion."

[118] Irenaeus reports of the Basilidian Gnostics: "They say they are no longer Jews, but not yet Christians" (*Haer.* I.24.6).

2

THE RIDDLE OF THE THUNDER (NHC VI, 2): THE FUNCTION OF PARADOX IN A GNOSTIC TEXT FROM NAG HAMMADI

Bentley Layton

Bentley Layton is Professor of Ancient Christian History at Yale University. As a member of the Cairo team that prepared the official UNESCO edition of the Coptic Gnostic Library, Professor Layton has written scholarly editions of eight ancient gnostic works, as well as related commentaries and essays. He is also a leading expert on the language and manuscripts of Coptic Egypt, having served as president of the International Association for Coptic Studies. Bentley Layton is author of *The Gnostic Scriptures: A New Translation with Annotations and Introductions.*

Preface

One of the important components in the literary and theological background of earliest Christianity was the collection of wisdom sayings. Such collections must have been the direct ancestors of works like the Synoptic Sayings Source ("Q") and the *Gospel According to Thomas.* As the original Hellenistic Jewish genre (Sayings of the Wise) developed into various gnostic counterparts, one of its salient evolutionary features was the appearance of dark sayings, whose interpretation was not plain, was riddlesome, or was even said to be "secret" (*logoi apokryphoi*). At this point the line of development merged temporarily with the Greek riddle, until the genre was ultimately transmuted into outright obscure paradox. A few paradoxical sayings are already present in the *Gospel According to Thomas*; but not until the appearance of a little-known *Gospel of Eve* did one find relatively pure forms of the new genre, which we may call the Riddle Gospel. The present essay explores several works in the thrall of the *Gospel of Eve,* chief among them being *Thunder, Perfect Intellect* (NHC VI,2). At this ultimate stage in the line of development, the voice of Dame Wisdom has become the voice of a riddle, and traditional sapiential content has been totally neutralized by paradox, making way for the construction of a mythic *hyponoia* ("buried meaning") more typical of the symbolic world of gnosticism.

I. The Literary Character
of *Thunder, Perfect Intellect*

Thunder, Perfect Intellect (or simply, *Thunder*) is a powerful poem of some two hundred verses, originally composed in Greek. This poem has been called unique[1] in the surviving Mediterranean literature, primarily because of its combination of the rhetorical mode of omnipredication (best known from Isis aretalogy) with a logic of antithetical paradox that negates the possibility of taking predication seriously. A few lines from the opening of the poem can serve to remind us of the extraordinary impression made by this most bizarre of all works from the Nag Hammadi corpus:

It is from the power that I, even I, have been sent
And unto those who think on me that I have come;
And I was found in those who seek me.
Look upon me, o you (plu.) who think on me.
And you listeners, listen to me!
You who wait for me, take me unto yourselves,
And do not chase me from before your eyes.
. . . .
For, it is I who am the first: and the last.
It is I who am the revered: and the despised.
It is I who am the harlot: and the holy.
It is I who am the wife: and the virgin.
. . . .
It is I who am the mother of my father: and the
   sister of my husband.
And it is he who is my offspring.
It is I who am the servant of him who begot me:
It is I who am the governess of my (own) offspring.

[1] According to MacRae (*Thunder*, 1) "[The *Thunder*] presents an especially interesting challenge to the student of Gnostic literature. In its form and content it is unique in the Nag Hammadi collection and virtually unique as a distinct literary work in the context of literature from the Roman and Hellenistic periods. Though it shares features of both form and content with passages in several types of ancient religious literature, it has no counterpart as a separate work." MacRae's essay together with responses by B. Pearson and T. Conley printed in the same volume constitute the major pieces of scholarly discussion on this tractate.

. . . .
It is I who am incomprehensible silence:
And afterthought, whose memory is so great.

. . . .
For, it is I who am acquaintance: and lack of acquaintance.
It is I who am reticence: and frankness.
I am shameless: I am ashamed.[2]

This short sample makes clear all the poem's salient features. (1) *The text is a monologue*, concerned not with plot, but with the building up of persona. In ancient rhetorical practice, this is *ēthopoiia* ("delineation of character"). Time, place, and occasion are still relevant, but they must be deduced from the *ēthopoiia*.

(2) An important element of this *ēthopoiia* is *the speaker's use of the formula egō eimi, "It is I who am.. . . ."* This somewhat cumbersome English translation of the formula is meant to take account of a contrast, expressed in Greek and in Coptic, between pairs like *phōs eimi tou kosmou* versus *egō eimi to phōs tou kosmou*, "I am the light of the world" versus "it is I who am the light of the world."[3] The first option answers the question, "To what class of thing do you belong?"; while the second answers, "Who is the light of the world?" This second option, the *egō eimi* option, was the hallmark of Isis propaganda, used in advertising campaigns of the deity as she competed for adherents in a syncretistic milieu, where each divine being claimed to be all good things to all people. Thus Isis grandly claims, "Isis am I, mistress of every land. . . . It is I who overcome fate."[4]

(3) Another aspect of the speaker's *ēthos* ("character") is *what she predicates of herself*. On the one hand, there is the outrageous pairing of the predicates so as to express a paradox, often phrased in balanced antithesis. Since paradox is utterly foreign to the content of Isis monologues the strong disjunction between self-predicating (Isiac) rhetoric and paradoxical logic is the true exegetical crux of our text. On the other hand, the poem gives us specific details about the speaker's family relations, social status, moral and mythic attributes, and abilities.[5] These

---

[2] *Thund.* VI,2:13,2–14,30, trans. by Layton.

[3] John 9:5 versus 8:12.

[4] Isis aretalogy of Cyme, verses 3a and 56. I translate from the text in Bergman, *Isis*, 301–303.

[5] *Family relations*: wife, virgin, mother, daughter, barren, has many children, married, unmarried, midwife, lying-in-woman, bride, bridegroom, begotten by her own husband, mother of her own father, sister of her own husband, mother of her own husband, begotten by her own offspring. *Social status*: first, last, revered, despised, governess of her own offspring, servant of her own father, declared publicly, denied, spoken of with truth and with lies, recognized, unrecognized, wealthy, poor, has many images, has no images, male, female, restrained, pursued, collected, scattered, celebrated, uncelebrated, spared, smitten, citizen, alien, rich, poor, distant, nearby, unified, dissolved, persistent, weak, has

details may be clues that our gnostic author has left behind in setting up this riddle.

(4) Modern interpretation stresses the combination of *egō eimi* and paradox as the characteristic feature of this text;[6] yet, in fact, the same number of lines is given to a quite different rhetorical mode, the *philosophical sermon or gnostic diatribe*. Examples of gnostic diatribe are well known,[7] and one should not forget its resemblance to exhortations of Jewish Wisdom in texts like the eighth chapter of Proverbs.[8] In this mode, the monologuist addresses the audience, issuing commands and invitations, disparaging their actions and attitudes, and posing rhetorical questions of a damaging sort. Rhetorical antithesis is very typical, though paradox is not. Now, in our text about one-half of the verses belong more or less to this mode.[9] But many of them have also the paradoxical character of the *egō eimi* predications, suggesting that the audience as a whole shares in the paradoxical nature of the monologuist.[10]

---

descended, has ascended. *Moral and mythic attributes*: holy, harlot, afterthought, memory of afterthought, voice of manifold sound, discourse of manifold imagery, *gnōsis*, *agnōsia*, frankness, reticence, shameless, ashamed, peace, war, mighty, disgraced, merciful, cruel, continent, weak, bold, fearful, thriving, feeble, wise, foolish, speaks, silent, *sophia* of Greeks, gnōsis of non-Greeks, judgment, life, death, law, lawless, divine pantheon, godless. *Abilities*: source of power for her own offspring, dependent upon her own offspring in her old age, strong, afraid (i.e., weak), teacher, uneducated.

[6] MacRae, *Thunder*, 2.

[7] A classic example is *Corpus Hermeticum* VII, *Poi Pheresthe Ō Anthrōpoi*: "O men, whither are you being swept away? You are drunk! You have drained to the last drop the unmixed drink of the teaching of ignorance. You cannot carry it, but are even now vomiting it. Quit your drinking; turn sober; look upwards with the eyes of the heart, and if you cannot all do so, at least let those who can. For this evil of ignorance floods the whole earth; it corrupts the soul imprisoned in the body, not permitting it to anchor in the harbors of safety" (*Corpus Hermeticum* 7.1, trans. F. C. Grant in Grant, *Gnosticism: A Source Book*, 224–25, at 224). The Greek text is edited by A. D. Nock in Nock-Festugière, *Hermès*, 1. 78–84. A typical Sethian gnostic example of this literary mode occurs in the Nag Hammadi Library in Zost. VIII,1:130,14–132,5.

[8] E.g., Prov 8:4–7 LXX, "O people, I exhort you, and I send forth my voice unto the children of humankind. O you who are simple, consider subtlety. And you who are untaught, take in (wisdom of the) heart. Listen to me, for I am speaking of solemn things and uttering straight (thoughts) from my lips. For my throat is going to meditate on truth; and deceitful lips are abominable before me." MacRae (*Thunder*, 2) calls attention to such passages, although he is making a somewhat different point.

[9] I am not proposing here a hypothesis of isolatable sources behind the poem; I only mean to observe a constant shift among several literary modes or genres that characterizes the way our author writes. Indeed, some verses resist simple classification under one head alone: the uniquely first-person utterances are usually paradoxical; the uniquely second-person utterances (commands, rhetorical questions, accusations) are usually diatribic; but, for example, first-person utterances addressed to the second person are harder to classify (16:18 seq. "It is I who am what you have scattered: and you have collected me"). Note also the wise cautionary remarks by MacRae, *Thunder*, 4.

[10] Thus, e.g., "Why, o you who hate me, do you love me, And hate those that love me?

(5) Finally, there is a fragmentary *mythic framework*, comprising a mere twelve verses: at the beginning,[11] "It is from the power that I, even I, have been sent/ And unto those who think on me that I have come;/ And I was found in those who seek me"; in the middle,[12] "It is I who cry out:/ And it is upon the face of the earth that I am being cast out"; and at the end,[13] "For—many and sweet are the . . . passions . . . which people restrain,/ Until they become sober and flee up to their place of rest./ And they will find me there,/ And live, and not die again" (i.e., not become reincarnate in a prisonlike body).

Brief as it is, this summarizes a myth of the soul's descent into the body, its entrapment in a disastrous cycle of reincarnations, and the descent of a savior from another realm of power and rest, who suffers, recalls the soul to soberness and her proper home, and reascends, showing the way for those who will be saved.

To recapitulate: nearly half of the verses are *egō eimi* self-predications, mostly paradoxical; nearly another half are diatribic, and also of these very many are paradoxical; and only a few verses are elements of a mythic setting.

II. Paradox and Riddle

What can be said about the female persona built up by this curious intersection of rhetorical modes? First, she likes to talk! We may call her "she," but gender is ultimately irrelevant since she is only a traveling voice. She is the savior of mankind; she saves by preaching, demanding a reorientation of mind and heart. She invites comparison with the authority of Isis and thence Dame Wisdom. She is an element within those to whom she is sent: the instrument of broadcasting and the instrument of reception are one and the same.[14] She and they are in the same paradoxical situation,[15] so that self-knowledge and knowledge of the savior may at least partly be the same. Finally, she and the saved have the same home.

The exegetical crux, namely the meaning of the speaker's paradoxical self-predications, raises the acute question of whether or not one should take the text seriously (e.g., "It is I who am the mother of my father: and

Declare me publicly, o you that deny me: And deny me, o you who declare me publicly" (*Thund.* VI,2:14,15 seq.).

[11] *Thund.* VI,2:13,2–4.
[12] *Thund.* VI,2:19,28–30.
[13] *Thund.* VI,2:21,20–32.
[14] "I was found in those who seek me. . . . You listeners, listen to me!" (*Thund.* VI,2:13,4.7).
[15] Cf. the discussion above with n. 9.

the sister of my husband").[16] Or should one, with modern interpretation, attempt only an overall history of religions assessment and assert that "the use of paradox in the I style . . . implies the rejection of all value systems that are at home in the world"?[17]

The broad solution is discomfiting: first, because the critic has a duty to work, if possible, at the level of textual details; second, because there is no substantial connection between the paradoxical omnipredication of our text and, as commentators have claimed,[18] the philosophical method of *via negativa*. Few ancient Greek thinkers would have considered the *via negativa* and the assertion of antithetical paradox to be interchangeable in such a way.[19]

Consequently, one ought to ask, What was the normal locus of outrageous paradox in the ancient Mediterranean world? The very simplicity of the answer may explain why it has eluded earlier students of this text: it is the Greek riddle.[20]

While *egō eimi* language has nothing in common with the Greek riddle as a specific grammatical form,[21] paradoxical dichotomy is a very salient feature of the riddle genre, as Aristotle pointed out long ago.[22] After Aristotle, the Peripatetic school took a serious interest in the topic, and theorists of the early Christian period continued to analyze the riddle mode.[23] Since modern scholars are not always acquainted with

---

[16] Thund. VI,2:13,30–32.

[17] MacRae, *Thunder*, 3.

[18] MacRae, *Thunder*, 3, apparently accepted also by the discussants of the colloquy (*Thunder*, 25–26).

[19] I should note, however, that apophatic language was on rare (I think) occasion combined with assertions of divine polyonymy. Thus, an oracle text in an inscription found at Oenoanda and studied by L. Robert (CRAIBL 1971, pp. 597–619) tells us that [Α]ὐτοφυὴς, ἀδίδακτος, ἀμήτωρ, ἀστυφέλικτος, οὔνομα μή χωρῶν, πολυώνυμος, ἐν πυρὶ ναίων, τοῦτο θεός· κτλ (Robert, p. 602), which Robert translates "Né de lui-même, à la sagesse infuse, sans mère, inébranlable, *ne comportant pas de nom, aux noms multiples*, habitant du feu, voilà ce qu'est Dieu." It was Prof. H.-D. Saffrey who kindly drew my attention (in another context) to this interesting amplification of the *via negativa*. Needless to say, polyonymy in itself is old and fairly common in Greek religious philosophy; it is not the same as paradox.

[20] Basic studies include: Schultz, "Rätsel"; Schultz, *Rätsel aus dem hellenischen Kulturkreise*; Ohlert, *Rätsel*.

[21] So at least as we find the examples cited, collected, or rephrased in ancient sources. For the Hellenistic period one of our principal sources is the literary epigram in which popular riddles were recast for a literate audience.

[22] Po. 1458a26, αἰνίγματος ἰδέα αὕτη ἐστὶ τὸ λέγοντα ὑπάρχοντα ἀδύνατα συνάψαι· κατὰ μὲν οὖν τὴν τῶν ὀνομάτων σύνθεσιν οὐχ οἷόν τε τοῦτο ποιῆσαι. κατὰ δὲ τὴν μεταφορὰν ἐνδέχεται, which Ohlert (*Rätsel*, 18) translates "Der Begriff des Rätsels ist der, dass man, indem man von wirklichen Dingen spricht, unmögliches verbindet. Das kann man nicht durch die Verbindung der eigentlichen Ausdrücke, aber man kann es durch die Anwendung der Metapher."

[23] Ohlert, *Rätsel*, 17–22.

the form of Greek riddles—the surviving examples are often in verse—it may be useful to quote some typical riddles.

οὐδεὶς βλέπων βλέπει με, μὴ βλέπων δ᾽ ὁρᾷ·
ὁ μὴ λαλῶν λαλεῖ, ὁ μὴ τρέχων τρέχει·
ψευδὴς δ᾽ ὑπάρχω, πάντα τ᾽ ἀληθῆ λέγων.
No one seeing sees me, but one who does not see beholds me.
One who does not speak speaks; one who does not run runs.
And I am a liar, yet say all things true.
Solution—a dream.[24]

μητέρ᾽ ἐμὴν τίκτω καὶ τίκτομαι· εἰμὶ δὲ ταύτης
ἄλλοτε μὲν μείζων, ἄλλοτε μειοτέρη.
I give birth to my own mother, and I am born; and I am
Sometimes greater than she, sometimes lesser.
Solution—unfortunately, not preserved.[25]

παρθένος εἰμὶ γυνὴ καὶ παρθένου εἰμὶ γυναικὸς
καὶ κατ᾽ ἔτος τίκτω παρθένος οὖσα γυνή.
I am a virgin woman, and the daughter of a virgin;
And I give birth once a year, remaining a virgin.
Solution—a date palm.[26]

Riddling[27] was an ancient and important social game in Greek-speaking culture, and so the style features of a riddle would have been easily recognized by an ancient Greek reader.[28] Riddles had not only a recognizable set of conventional forms, but also a characteristic logic—Aristotle called it adynata synapsai, "conjoin as mutually exclusive things." Riddle style, then, was recognizable in the ancient world; and it is likewise a recognizable element among the literary conventions of our text.[29]

---

[24] AP 14.110 = Schultz, Rätsel, No. 4. Cf. also Ohlert, Rätsel, 178–79.

[25] AP 14.41 = Schultz, Rätsel, No. 6. Schultz, Rätsel aus dem hellenischen Kulturkreise, 1. 23 (differing from Ohlert, Rätsel, 96). I am told (by Victoria Lord) that this riddle is transmitted in modern Greek culture and that a traditional solution is "a child."

[26] AP 14.42 = Schultz, Rätsel, No. 90. According to a lemma in cod. Laurentianus, the solution is βάλανος φοινίκων (Schultz, Rätsel aus dem hellenischen Kulturkreise, 1. 62). Ohlert (Rätsel, 174) proposes "a grapevine" as the true solution.

[27] The principal terms for riddle were αἴνιγμα and γρῖφος. For ancient theorists' attempts to explain a difference between these two words, see Ohlert, Rätsel, 17–22 (other ancient Greek words for riddle are noted there on 22 n. 2).

[28] For details one can consult Athenaeus, Deipnosophistae X 448b–459b.

[29] This is not, of course, to say that our text is a riddle pure and simple. However, some passages sound quite like a series or list of short riddles. E.g., 16:3 seq., "For, it is I who am the wisdom [of the] Greeks: And the acquaintance of [the] non-Greeks. It is I who am judgment for Greeks: And for non-Greeks. I am he whose image is manifold in Egypt: And she who has no image among the non-Greeks. It is I who have been hated everywhere: And who have been loved everywhere. It is I who am called life: And whom you have called death. It is I who am called law: And whom you have called lawlessness. It is I whom you have chased: And it is I whom you have restrained. It is I who am what you have scattered: And what you have collected."

Thus the *Thunder* owes its peculiar character to the blending of three ordinarily unrelated literary modes: the Isis/Wisdom proclamation, asserting the power, sovereignty, and special knowledge of the speaker; the philosophical sermon, with its vision of life falling into two neat moral, intellectual, and anthropological options (Two Ways) and exhorting the listener to choose only the higher way; and the riddle, which demands, first, a solution and, second, a reexegesis of the entire text as riddle to see how the solution applies. Riddles often speak with a mythic[30] directness that demands the active application of the listener's intellect, in a way that sermons and aretalogies rarely do.

III. The Solution to the Riddle

A riddle is the occasion for rethinking the sense of what otherwise seems obviously impossible, a time for a shift in perspective, a search for a deeper meaning. Even when the solution has been revealed or recognized, the riddle itself must finally be reread—exegeted—to discover how the solution applies, how a seeming paradox is not really a paradox. This invitation to exegesis is part of the riddle game. Riddles share these features with gnostic ways of treating scripture and tradition. The hermeneutic of riddles compares with e.g., the rereading of Genesis proposed by texts such as the *Secret Book of John*, the *Reality of the Rulers*, or the *Revelation of Adam*.[31] In one important sense, the function of such texts is not so much to replace Genesis as to lead the reader into a new relationship with it. Riddles can make use also of monologue, as in the *Thunder*.[32] But riddles have one thing that most gnostic texts do not—namely, a definite solution. For this reason, to the extent that our text belongs to the riddle genre, it is not unreasonable to ask, "Who is the thunder?" External testimonia provide a narrative

---

[30] "The oldest riddles mostly have a mythical or cosmic origin, and hence they retain the oldest mythical view of nature in a purer manner than do many other branches of literature. Birth, growth, and decay in nature as well as in human life; the rising and setting of the stars; the struggle between light and darkness; the changing images formed by the clouds of heaven—all these were riddles which demanded a solution and which were reclothed in the garb of a riddle because the solution could not clearly and meaningfully be found. Most peoples also clothed oracles and proverbs in the obscure language of the riddle; these were viewed as utterances of superior, divine insight. Hence in earliest times, riddles, oracles, and proverbs had the character of a secret and sanctified treasure. Even in the riddles of later time, many traces of early mythic components lie hidden. But in the course of time, profound insight into their original meanings became blurred in the spirit of the people and gradually was lost" (Ohlert, *Rätsel*, 1).

[31] The *Apocryphon of John, Hypostasis of the Archons, Apocalypse of Adam*.

[32] The three Greek riddles quoted above are typical. Descriptive (third-person) riddles are also common.

context for the riddle material in the *Thunder*. Both these testimonia and the internal details of the text point to one and the same solution: Eve.[33] Six items are worth noting.

(1) First, in the untitled tractate commonly called *On the Origin of the World* (NHC II,5) virtually an excerpt from the *Thunder* (though probably not an actual quotation from our text) is sung by Sophia Zoe, alias Eve of Life, the celestial androgynous child of Pistis Sophia, at the moment when she creates the animate or psychic Adam (see Table 1). This creation, for the author of *On the Origin of the World*, is distinct from the creation of fleshly Adam and the extraction of a fleshly woman from his side.[34]

(2) Second, the *Reality of the Rulers* (*Hypostasis of the Archons*), a classic "Sethian" text in Schenke's terminology,[35] quotes the same material, although more briefly[36] and no longer as a monologue. The *Hypostasis of the Archons* narrates only a single creation of Adam, namely the fleshly one. Adam is originally a lifeless androgyne.[37] The female spiritual principle (*hē pneumatikē*) enters Adam's prone body and gives it life. When the rulers (archons) surgically excise the female half of the androgyne (that half is the fleshly Eve) the *pneumatikē* is excised along with her.[38] Adam, recovering from his post-operative trance, then addresses her with words of the same hymn that we find in *On the Origin of the World* (see Table 2). Because of its brevity, the paradoxical character of this second citation is much less obvious. But another element is now additionally present: a famous series of puns on Ḥawa (see Table 2), the Aramaic name of Eve.[39] The common source of these two texts probably contained both a riddle-like aretalogy and a

---

[33] Partly seen by Bethge, "Nebront," 99: "Nebront [i.e., *Thunder*] expliziert keinen Mythus, ist jedoch weitgehend nur dann in seinen Selbstaussagen verständlich, wenn hinter vielen der gegensätzlichen Aussagen ein Mythus vom Fall und der Errettung der Sophia steht." He goes on to refer to the split of Sophia in Valentinianism and the degrading fall of the divine female consort in Simonianism. For the mixture of contrary emotions in the Lower Sophia or Achamōth of Ptolemaean Valentinianism, see Iren. *Haer.* I.4.1–2.

[34] For the creation of animate (psychic) Adam, see *Orig. World* II,5:113,25, and for fleshly Adam see *Orig. World* II,5:114,29.

[35] H.-M. Schenke, "Sethianism," 588–616.

[36] Not, I think, from the *Untitled Tractate* but from a common source, whose reconstruction I shall discuss below.

[37] *Hyp. Arch.* II,4:88,4–6.

[38] According to the author of *Hypostasis of the Archons*, the rulers' or archons' motivation for this surgical procedure is their desire to extract and rape the female spiritual principle.

[39] First explained, I think, by Alexander Böhlig in Böhlig-Labib, *Schrift ohne Titel*, 73–75. For the philological details, cf. now my notes 57–69 in "Hypostasis" (*HTR* 69 [1976] 55–58).

TABLE 1

The Song of Eve in *Thund.* VI,2:13,19–14,8 and *Orig. World* II,5:114,4–15

Thunder (rearranged for comparison)	*On the Origin of the World*
	Eve, then, is the first virgin, who gave birth to her first offspring without a husband. It is she who served as her own midwife. For this reason she is held to have said:
I am the *melē* of my mother.	"It is I who am the *meros* of my mother.
It is I who am the mother: and the daughter.	And it is I who am the mother.
It is I who am the wife (? *shime*): and the virgin (*parthenos*).	I am the wife (*hime*) and the virgin (*parthenos*).
It is I who am the barren: And who have many children.	It is I who am pregnant.
It is I who am the one whose marriage is magnificent; and who have not married.	
It is I who am the midwife: And she who does not give birth;	It is I who am the midwife.
It is I who am consolation: of my own travail.	It is I who am consolation of travail.
It is I who am the bride: and the bridegroom.	
It is my husband who has begotten me.	
It is I who am the mother of my father: and the sister of my husband. . .	It is I who am his mother.
It is I who am the servant of him who prepared me. . .	And it is he who is my father and my master.
And my power (*dynamis*) comes from him.	And it is he who is my power (*čom*)
I am the staff of his power (*cŏm*) in his childhood;	
[And] it is he who is the rod of my old age, And whatever he wishes happens to me.	He says whatever he wishes reasonably, I become (it)."

series of riddlesome Aramaic puns on the name of Eve.[40] The aretalogical material is more fully quoted in *On the Origin of the World*, the puns in the *Hypostasis of the Archons*. Possibly the original setting is given by the *Hypostasis*, since *On the Origin of the World* distributes what ought to be one block of pun material—though not the aretalogy—over two episodes, that is, the two creations of Adam.[41] The true setting, then, might be a monologue of the saving spiritual principle (*hē pneu-*

[40] They are also present in *On the Origin of the World*.
[41] First episode, *Orig. World* II,5:114,8–15; second episode, *Orig. World* II,5:116,6–8 ("you have given me life" = Aramaic *ḥayyiṭani*).

TABLE 2

The Song of Eve in *Thund.* VI,2:13,15–22
and Song of Eve in *Hyp. Arch.* II,4:89,11–17

Thunder (selected vss. rearranged)	*Hypostasis of the Archons*
	And the spirit-endowed woman came to him and spoke with him, saying, "Arise, Adam." And when he saw her, he said: "It is you who have given me life; You will be called 'Mother of the Living.'
For— . . .	For—
It is I who am the mother. . .	It is she who is my mother.
It is I who am the midwife. . .	It is she who is the midwife,
It is I who am the wife (? *shime*) . . .	and the wife (? *shime*),
It is I who am the barren:	
And who have many children.	And she who has given birth."

NOTES: "you have given me life"—ḥayyiṭani
"mother of the living"—Gen 3:20
"my mother"—Gen 3:20, cf.
   Thunder
"midwife"—ḥayyᵉṭā'
"the woman"—cf. Gen 2:23 and
   Thunder
COMPARE slightly later:
"she became a tree"—the tree of
   ḥayyayyā' (life)
"the *pneumatikē* came [in] the
   snake, the instructor"
"snake"—ḥewᵉyā'
"instructor"—*ḥāwē' (hypothetical form)

matikē), spoken from within the body of the fleshly Eve after her separation from the masculine half of the Adam androgyne. It is a kind of encoded *euaggelion*, a good news riddle, which if solved will reveal the immanent but hidden presence of a savior principle within the world.[42]

[42] The hidden immanence of the divine within humankind appears to be an important theme also in the Sethian tractate *First Thought in Three Forms (Trimorphic Protennoia)*, which in other important ways, discussed below, has connection with our text: cf. *Trim. Prot.* XIII,1:35,2.10.13–20.24–25; 36,23; 37,1 (?); 40,31; 41,20; 42,12.25; 45,21; 46,17.22–24; 48,20. Taken in isolation, some of these passages might be understood alternatively as referring to a *Messiasgeheimnis* ("messianic secret").

It is easy to construct kinship riddles[43] based on Eve once we review
the cast of characters in the setting of the *Hypostasis of the Archons.*

Fleshly Adam:	the brother of Eve while they were an androgyne; her father or parent, because she was extracted from him; her husband, eventually; her son, because during her confusion with *hē pneumatikē*, she is (in the words of Gen 3:21) mother of the living, and Adam is alive.
Fleshly Eve:	the inverse of all the above.
The *pneumatikē*, the celestial Eve:	
	mother of Adam; mother of Eve (fleshly Eve); remains a virgin vis-à-vis the rulers when they rape the fleshly Eve.[44]

This paradoxical network of relationships will explain the kinship
riddles in the *Thunder*, once we allow that in gnostic Sethian myth two
figures are called by the name "Eve" (celestial Eve, fleshly Eve) and so
the attributes of both figures can be invoked in the answer to the riddle
("Eve").

(3) Third, there may be a reference to this common source in
Epiphanius' account of the *Gnōstikos* (or Sethian) sect who, he says, read
a *Book of Nōrea*,[45] a prophecy of Barkabbas, a *Gospel of Perfection*
(contents not summarized), and a *Gospel of Eve (Euaggelion Euas)*,
named after her on the grounds that she "discovered the food of *gnōsis*
(divine acquaintance) through revelation spoken to her by the snake."[46]
This is close to the setting of the *Hypostasis of the Archons*—since in the
latter, the female spiritual principle returns precisely in the snake to
teach the good news of liberation. Thus in the *Gospel of Eve*, or at least
in one part of it, the heavenly Eve or *pneumatikē*, speaking now from
within the snake, addressed the fleshly Eve. Epiphanius then goes on to
characterize the literary mode of the *Gospel*: its predications (*rhēmata*)
are self-contradictory (*ouk isa*)—one should recall Aristotle's definition
of riddle, *adynata synapsai* (conjoin as mutually exclusive things)—"as
though," says Epiphanius, "(uttered) in the unstable frame of mind of a
drunkard given to uncontrollable talk; some (predications) are made for

---

[43] This basic class of riddles is briefly investigated by Schultz, *Rätsel aus dem
hellenischen Kulturkreise*, 2. 22.

[44] *Hyp. Arch.* II,4:89,23–28. Even Epiphanius (*Pan.* 39.6.3) had to admit that in a
certain sense Adam's wife was his own sister, since she was formed of his own flesh and
blood. He adds that this was not illegal since at the time there were no other women to
marry.

[45] Explicitly cited by the author of *On the Origin of the World* (II,5:102,10.24) as one of
his sources of information.

[46] ὡς εὑρούσης τὸ βρῶμα τῆς γνώσεως ἐξ ἀποκαλύψεως τοῦ λαλήσαντος αὐτῇ ὄφεως
(Epiph. *Pan.* 26.2.6 = I 278,1–2 H.).

laughter, the others filled with weeping."[47] Epiphanius quotes from the opening frame story of the *Gospel*. The story is set on a high mountain—like Paradise, according to *On the Origin of the World*.[48] The speaker, presumably the fleshly Eve, hears a *phōnē brontēs*, a voice of thunder, and it—the voice of thunder[49]—speaks:

> I am thou, and thou art I,
> And wherever thou art, it is I who am there;
> And I am sown in all things.
> And whence thou wilt, thou gatherest me;
> But when thou gatherest me, then gatherest thou thyself.[50]

The first part of this quotation ("I am thou, etc.") disappointingly has no verbal parallel in our text. It can nonetheless be understood as a kinship riddle; indeed, it is the voice of one Eve addressing the other. But what the thunder says about her own paradoxical dispersion in the hearers is used in the Nag Hammadi *Thunder*: "I was found in those who seek me" (13,4); "It is I who am what you have scattered:/ And what you have collected" (16,18 seq.); "Do not cause greatnesses, (dispersed) in parts (or particulars), to turn away from smallnesses;/ For it is from greatnesses that smallnesses are recognized" (17,28 seq.). Here the words spoken by the thunder to fleshly Eve are generalized and extended to all the saved.

There is some chance that the *Gospel of Eve* used by Epiphanius' *Gnōstikoi* is the text that stands behind the two main testimonia (nos. 1 and 2 above) and the Nag Hammadi *Thunder*. If so, one is faced with a situation in which it is possible to detect ancient literary responses—all of them in mighty works—to what critics might call a presupposed "strong text." While one can point to some of its probable characteristics, a definite reconstruction of even a part of the text is out of the question.

Let me throw caution to the wind for a moment and speculate on these probable characteristics, realizing that some will probably be only incidental to our testimonia and not in the original. It is a riddle gospel, called *euaggelion*, in which the possibility of liberation is implied by monologues of the heavenly Eve or female spiritual principle. It uses the authoritative Isiac and/or Jewish Wisdom style, combined with the paradox of Greek riddle. It is set in Paradise atop a high mountain, where reference to thunder (*brontē*) is at home. It also contains riddle-

---

[47] καὶ ὥσπερ ἐν ἀστάτῳ γνώμῃ μεθύοντος καὶ παραλαλοῦντος οὐκ ἴσα εἴη τὰ ῥήματα, ἀλλὰ τὰ μὲν γέλωτι πεποιημένα ἕτερα δὲ κλαυθμοῦ ἔμπλεα (*Pan.* 26.2.6 = I 278,3–5 H.).

[48] Orig. World II,5:121,1, where the rulers expel Adam and drive him down (Coptic *epitn*) from Paradise to (Coptic *ejn-*) the adjoining land.

[49] And not, as Wilson translates, "he" (Hennecke-Schneemelcher, NT Apocrypha 1. 241).

[50] ἐγὼ σὺ καὶ σὺ ἐγώ, καὶ ὅπου ἐὰν ᾖς, ἐγὼ ἐκεῖ εἰμι, καὶ ἐν ἅπασίν εἰμι ἐσπαρμένος. καὶ ὅθεν ἐὰν θέλῃς, συλλέγεις με, ἐμὲ δὲ συλλέγων ἑαυτὸν συλλέγεις (*Pan.* 26.3.1 = I 278,8–13 H.).

some puns based ultimately on a Semitic language.[51] It is addressed in
the first place to one or both of the fleshly protoplasts, perhaps alter-
nately. The speaker also lapses into the style of the gnostic diatribe (it is
hard to imagine just how this transition was made, or how often—our
Thunder text was not necessarily arranged like the lost gospel). The time
is perhaps a series of moments between the vivification of Adam and the
birth of Nōrea and Seth, with whom a new incarnation of the spiritual
seed begins; perhaps it was at this point that the Gnostic *Book of Norea*
took up the story.

(4) The likelihood that such a text actually existed is strengthened by
the existence of a Hellenistic Jewish tradition of paradoxical Eve riddles
in Greek. An instance of this riddle type in the Planudean Appendix to
the *Palatine Anthology* combines the two main motifs of Greek riddle,
impossible kinship ties and self-contradictory predicates.

ἀνήρ με γεννᾷ, καὶ πατὴρ ὑπὲρ φύσιν·
ζωὴν καλεῖ με καὶ θάνατον προσφέρω.
A human being begot me, and my father is supernatural.
He calls me Life, and I bring him death.

The solution is given by Michael Psellus: Eve.[52]

(5) This riddle would be hard to date and call Jewish, were it not for a
similar turn of thought in Philo (*Quis Rerum* 11.52), who speaks of the
fleshly Eve—allegorized as sensory perception—whom Adam, the
earthbound intellect, saw just after her creation and "gave the name of
Life (Zōē) to his own death," i.e., to the eventual source of his sin and
death.[53] Schultz, the learned editor of the Greek riddle corpus, thinks
that this may be an allusion to an Eve riddle,[54] and I am inclined to
agree. The circulation of such an Eve riddle, and the theological
reflection surrounding it, could have been the seed from which the
Gospel of Eve developed.

(6) I am loath to comment upon the sixth item—the speech of a fallen

---

[51] As I have noted in "Hypostasis" (*HTR* 69 [1976] 53) the presence of such puns does
not in itself indicate that the work was originally composed in a Semitic language. The
circulation of etymological glossaries of Semitic biblical names, composed in Greek,
made the necessary philological information available to any interested Greek-speaking
readers. Ancient glossaries of such a type have been collected and edited by Wutz,
Onomastica. We can see their use reflected as early as the time of Philo.

[52] *APl* 7.44 = Schultz, *Rätsel aus dem hellenischen Kulturkreis*, no. 100.

[53] Cf. *Thund.* VI,2:16,11 seq. "It is I who am called life: And whom you have called
death."

[54] Referring, of course, to Gen 3:21 in the LXX, where Adam is said to call his wife not
"Eve" but "Zōē" (life). Schultz (*Rätsel aus dem hellenischen Kulturkreise*, 1. 65) does not
commit himself on the precise relationship of the Philonic passage to the riddle as
phrased in the Planudean Appendix.

Wisdom figure, Ewath-Ruha, in the Mandaean *Ginza*.[55] The *Ginza* is presumably much later than the hypothetical gospel, and may merely attest to the hardiness of the *Gospel of Eve's* influence, perhaps in mediated forms. Does the speaker's unusual Mandaean name (Ewath) encode the original solution (expressed not in Mandaean Aramaic but in Greek) to our riddle, namely *Eua* (Eve)?

IV. Conclusions

From this solution of the riddle of the *Thunder*, several conclusions can be drawn.[56]

(1) One is now closer to understanding the obvious resemblance of the *Thunder* to certain passages of the *Hypostasis of the Archons* and *On the Origin of the World*, and possibly even a part of Mandaean scripture. This resemblance can be explained by the hypothesis of a common textual antecedent, known and responded to by the authors of these works. But from another perspective, one is also talking about ancient authors' perception of a distinct and indelible persona belonging to the main feminine character of the gnostic Sethian spiritual drama, a persona developed at a stage before the composition of these four works and marked by such strength and rhetorical peculiarity that subsequent writers did not escape it when writing of this character's interventions in our world.

(2) The exploration of the persona's antecedent components—the self-predications of Isis-Wisdom, the paradoxes of the Eve riddle, the diatribic language of sapiential exhortation—allows one to postulate a concrete literary antecedent in which these strands were fused and against which we might measure other literary works. That this antecedent was the *Gospel of Eve* is by no means the only possible construction of the evidence, though it may be the simplest one. The specific literary hypothesis is unproven and unprovable. The real point

---

[55] Lidzbarski, *Ginza* (right), 205–207 (noted by MacRae, *Thunder*, 7).

[56] It is not within the scope of this essay to exegete the text in detail or to examine all the evidence for the speaker's identity. This evidence is summarized above in n. 5. For her paradoxical *family relations* see discussion above with n. 43; on this basis can be explained her paradoxical *abilities*. Both the speaker's puzzling genealogy and her *social* and *moral ambiguity* were first encapsulated in the vulgate tradition of Eve riddles (above, with n. 53) and no doubt given poignancy by the widespread belief that biblical Eve had on one occasion disported with the devil (*Tg. Ps.-J.* Gen 4:1; Klijn, *Seth*, 3–8); in gnosticism this ambiguity finds systemic expression in tandem pairs of female emanations called *pronoia:epinoia* (forethought:afterthought) or high and low wisdom *(sophia)*, who are (respectively) less and more involved in materiality. The speaker's *philosophical attributes* are discussed in the section that follows below. Pearson's remarks in MacRae, *Thunder*, 11, partially and unconsciously anticipate the correct solution.

of this essay is only to show the coherence and identity of the persona as such, and to assert that the presence of this persona in a certain body of ancient texts indicates that they are somehow genetically related.

(3) The ambiguous Eve (who is essentially the female spiritual principle or heavenly Eve) is another strand in the network of evidence that binds certain texts together in the so-called gnostic Sethian system. Establishing the identity of this persona might lead one to the conclusion that the *Thunder* is gnostic and Sethian to the same degree that the Ḥawa puns in the gnostic Sethian *Hypostasis of the Archons* are gnostic and Sethian.

(4) Probably this persona is also Jewish to the same degree that the *Hypostasis of the Archons* is Jewish. The literary mode of Eve texts is, however, not predominantly "targumic" but rather "Isiac" (biblical critics have for some time recognized Isis rhetoric as a characteristic of Hellenistic Jewish wisdom texts).

(5) From Epiphanius one knows to associate the persona as found in the *Gospel of Eve* with a sect called *Gnōstikos*. The relationship of this sect to the texts under discussion, and indeed to the whole gnostic Sethian cluster, needs careful consideration.

(6) Incidentally, one gains new awareness of a link between the Nag Hammadi corpus and a heresiological report in one of the antignostic fathers.

(7) Despite certain resemblances to Dame Wisdom of Hellenistic Judaism, the most obvious cross-referent of the persona was Isis—an essentially Egyptian or Egyptianizing feature within gnostic Sethianism. This feature constitutes a kind of evidence, though certainly inconclusive, that the persona was invented and known in Egypt. This Egyptian connection is suggested also by other kinds of evidence: Epiphanius knew the *Gnōstikos* sect from a personal visit to that country;[57] *On the Origin of the World* was obviously written in Egypt; all the texts under consideration in this essay, indeed all the texts in Schenke's gnostic Sethian cluster (except perhaps some excerpts in Irenaeus) were at least transmitted in Coptic-speaking Egypt.

(8) After hypothesizing that the *Thunder* belongs to the gnostic Sethian group, one is entitled to look for individual details or parallels in the *Thunder* that echo other texts of the Sethian group. There are a few obvious possibilities:

    a. *Thund.* VI,2:13,1 (title), "Thunder—Perfect Intellect."

       Trim. Prot. XIII,1:43,13–15, "The lots of destiny and those which traverse (or measure) the houses were greatly disturbed by a sharp thunderclap."

---

[57] *Pan.* 26.17.4 = I 297,15–21 H.

b. *Thund.* VI,2:18,9, "It is I, however, who am the [perfect] intellect."
   Trim. Prot. XIII,1:47,7–9, "And I taught [. . .] by the [. . .] by perfect
   intellect."
   Steles Seth VII,5:121,23–25, "O you (sc. Barbēlō) who are called
   perfect!"
   Ibid. 123,21, "You are intellect."
c. *Thund.* VI,2:13,4, "I was found in those who seek me."
   Trim. Prot. XIII,1 (cf. passages listed in n. 42; there are no
   verbatim parallels).
d. *Thund.* VI,2:14,4, "My power comes from him (my offspring).
   I am the staff of his power in his childhood."
   Ap. John II,1:22,32–23,2, "And it (the ruler) extracted a portion of
   his power from him and performed another act of modeling, in
   the form of a female . . . and into the modelled form of
   femaleness it brought the portion it had taken from the power
   of the human being."
e. *Thund.* VI,2:14,9–10, "It is I who am . . . afterthought, whose
   memory is so great."
   Ap. John II,1:30,24, "I, who am the memory of the forethought."
   (Cf. ibid. 28,1–2, "The afterthought of the luminous forethought.")
f. *Thund.* VI,2:14,12–14, "It is I who am the voice whose sounds are
   so numerous:/ And the discourse whose images (or kinds) are
   so numerous./ It is I who am the speaking: of my (own) name."
   Ibid. 20,30–31, "It is I who am the speaking that cannot be
   restrained./ It is I who am the voice's name, and the name's
   voice."
   Ibid. 19,9, "It is I who am . . . unrestraint."
   Ibid. 19,20–22, "It is I who am . . . the speaking that cannot be
   restrained."
   Ibid. 19,32, "It is I who am acquaintance with my name."
   Trim. Prot. XIII,1:37,20–24, "The sound that has derived from my
   thinking exists as . . . a voice.. . . It contains within it a verbal
   expression.. . ."
   Trim. Prot. XIII,1:38,11–16, "It is I who am . . . the unrestrainable
   and immeasurable sound."
g. *Thund.* VI,2:15,8, "You will find me in the kingdoms."
   Apoc. Adam V,5:77,27–82,19.
h. *Thund.* VI,2:16,6–8, "I am he whose . . . and she who.. . ."
   Trim. Prot. XIII,1:45,2–3, "I am androgynous."
   Ap. John II,1:27,33–28,2, "It is the mother-father who is greatly
   merciful . . . and the afterthought of the luminous forethought."
   Gos. Eg. IV,2:73,11–12 (=III,2:61,25–62,1) "The masculine female
   virgin, the Barbēlō."

  i. *Thund.* VI,2:20,1, "I am manifest [and . . .] travel [. . .]."
      Ap. John II,1:30,13–14, "I existed . . . traveling in every path of
      travel"; similarly 30,17; 30,23; 30,33.
On balance, this evidence is inconclusive. I regard the hypothesis as not
yet verified.

  (9) It is historically necessary to understand the literary background of
Thunder as including a traditional female figure known from religious
literature. Yet insofar as our text treats that figure as the solution to a
riddle, she no longer functions here as a persona but is reduced to a
mere word ("Eve"). It lies in the nature of riddle solutions that such a
word can be construed in various ways, that is, can have a multiplicity of
referents (see above with n. 43).

  (10) Finally, there are many predications in the *Thunder* that cannot
be explained by simple reference to the solution "Eve." It is undeniable
that the genuine riddle mode is mixed with traditional *topoi* from Jewish
sapiential tradition or Isiac propaganda, transmuted of course into
dichotomous paradox. This has a purpose. It strengthens the speaker's
claim to authority, but also undermines confidence in the content of the
actual Wisdom tradition. Much of gnosticism can be seen not as a revolt
against, but as a revision of, traditional religions, especially in their
textual manifestations. What the *Hypostasis of the Archons* does to
Genesis, what the *Treatise on Resurrection* does with second-century
Christian creeds,[58] and what the *Gospel According to Thomas* presumably would have us do with the sayings tradition[59] (if only it would
tell us how!), the *Thunder* does to traditional sapiential aretalogy. On the
one hand, it presupposes the normative authority of the sapiential
persona, while on the other hand, it hollows this traditional form of its
original meaning and refills it with what, for gnostics, always takes
precedence over scripture and tradition: namely, the gnostics' own myth
of the origin and fate of the soul, her salvation by a heavenly teacher,
and her ultimate return to her home.

  The mythic figure of Thunder says as much, in her own words (at least
in my translation):

  It is I who am the meaning of text,
  And the manifestation of distinction; . . .
  Behold, then,. . . all the texts that have been completed.[60]

It has generally been held that the *Thunder* contains no distinctive
Christian, Jewish, or gnostic allusions and does not seem clearly to
presuppose any gnostic myth. Perhaps this essay, for all its brevity, has
suggested another way out.

  [58] Layton, "Resurrection," 190–217, esp. at 209–17.
  [59] *Gos. Thom.* II,2:32,12–14.
  [60] *Thund.* VI,2:20,33–21,12.

3

SETHIAN GNOSTICISM: A LITERARY HISTORY

John D. Turner

John D. Turner is both Professor of Religious Studies and Professor of Classics and History at the University of Nebraska—Lincoln, having taught at that institution since 1976. Professor Turner has devoted much of his academic career to Nag Hammadi studies both in terms of writing and service.

He has served on the Society of Biblical Literature Nag Hammadi Seminar as well as on the Steering Committee of the Nag Hammadi Section of that society. From 1971–72 he was an associate of the Technical Subcommittee for the International Committee for the Nag Hammadi Codices of UNESCO and the ARE.

Written contributions to Nag Hammadi studies have included numerous articles on the relationship of Gnosticism to Platonic philosophy and the *editio princeps* of the *Book of Thomas the Contender.*

Preface

The following analysis of the literary dependencies and redactional history of the Sethian gnostic texts from Nag Hammadi and elsewhere allows one to assign them to various periods during the first four centuries of the Christian era. The texts thus dated seem to reflect a coherent tradition of mythologumena that includes: (a) a sacred history of Seth's seed, derived from a peculiar exegesis of Genesis 1–6; (b) a doctrine of the divine wisdom in its primordial, fallen, and restored aspects; (c) a baptismal rite, often called the Five Seals, involving a removal from the fleshly world and transportation into the realm of light through the invocation of certain divine personages; (d) certain Christological speculations relating Christ to prominent Sethian primordial figures such as Adam and Seth; and (e) a fund of Platonic metaphysical concepts relating to the structure of the divine world and a self-actuated visionary means of assimilating with it.

The result of the study suggests that Sethianism interacted with Christianity in five phases: (1) Sethianism as a non-Christian baptismal sect of the first centuries B.C.E. and C.E. which considered itself primordially enlightened by the divine wisdom revealed to Adam and Seth, yet expected a final visitation of Seth marked by his conferral of a saving baptism; (2) Sethianism as gradually Christianized in the later first century onward through an identification of the pre-existent Christ with Seth, or Adam, that emerged through contact with Christian baptismal groups; (3) Sethianism as increasingly estranged from a Christianity becoming more orthodox toward the end of the second century and beyond; (4) Sethianism as rejected by the Great Church but meanwhile increasingly attracted to the individualistic contemplative practices of third-century Platonism; and (5) Sethianism as estranged from the orthodox Platonists of the late third century and increasingly fragmented into various derivative and other sectarian gnostic groups, some surviving into the Middle Ages.

I. The Sethian Literature

Mainly following the lead of Hans-Martin Schenke of the *Berliner* (DDR) *Arbeitskreis für koptisch-gnostische Schriften*,[1] current scholarship considers the following literature to be representative of Sethian Gnosticism: The Barbeloite report of Irenaeus (*Haer.* I.29); the reports on the Sethians (and Archontics) by Epiphanius (*Pan.* 26 and 39–40), Pseudo-Tertullian (*Haer.* 2) and Filastrius (*Haer.* 3); the untitled text from the Bruce Codex (Bruce); and the following treatises from the Nag Hammadi Codices and BG8502: four versions of the *Apocryphon of John* (*Ap. John* BG8502, 2 and NHC III,1 [short version]; NHC II, 1 and IV, 1 [long version]); the *Hypostasis of the Archons*; the *Gospel of the Egyptians*; the *Apocalypse of Adam*; the *Three Steles of Seth*; *Zostrianos*; *Melchizedek*; the *Thought of Norea*; *Marsanes*; *Allogenes*, and *Trimorphic Protennoia*.

II. The Sethian Themes

So far as I can see, most of the Sethian documents cited above originated in the period 100–250 C.E. They seem to derive their content from five basic complexes of doctrines: (1) a fund of Hellenistic-Jewish specu-

---

[1] H.-M. Schenke, "System" and "Sethianism."

lation on the figure of Sophia, the divine wisdom; (2) midrashic interpretation of Genesis 1–6 together with other assorted motifs from Jewish scripture and exegesis; (3) a doctrine and practice of baptism; (4) the developing Christology of the early church; and (5) a religiously oriented Neopythagorean and Middle-Platonic philosophical tradition of ontological and theological speculation.

A. Sophia Speculation

As appropriated by Sethianism and the Gnostics in general, Sophia is a hypostatized form of Ḥokmah (i.e., the divine Wisdom of Proverbs 8, Job 28, Sirach 24) and is regarded as a female deity, perhaps also connected with the Spirit that moved over the water in Gen 1:2–3. In the gnostic texts, Sophia functions at many levels under various names in a highly complex way. She functions as a creator and savior figure on a higher level as the divine Thought, which increasingly distinguishes itself from the high deity through various modalities, and gives rise to the divine image in which man is made. But she also functions on a lower level as the mother of the ignorant demiurge and the enlightener and savior of the divine image captured by the demiurge in human form. N. A. Dahl, in this regard, stresses the role played by the thought of Philo in this complex of ideas, particularly the notion of Sophia as Mother of the Logos and as the Mother figure in a divine triad of God the Father, Sophia the Mother, and Logos the Son.[2]

B. Interpretation of Genesis 2–6

Given the existence of an upper (either undeclined or restored) and lower Sophia, conceived as Mother, and her upper and lower sons, the Logos and the Archon, the peculiar Sethian reinterpretation of Genesis 2–6 easily follows: the anthropogony; the inbreathing of the divine Spirit; the sending of Eve or her extraction from Adam; the eating from the tree of knowledge; expulsion from paradise; the birth of Cain, Abel, Norea, and Seth and his seed; the flood and intercourse between women and the angels, with the addition of the story of Sodom and Gomorrah; and a final judgment and salvation. These episodes are interpreted in terms of a series of moves and countermoves between the upper Mother and Son and the lower Son in a contest over the control of the divine Spirit in mankind. In a very early period, still within the context of a disaffected and heterodox Judaism (and working with Jewish materials and gnosticizing Hellenistic-Jewish principles of interpretation), the peculiar Sethian doctrines concerning the origin, incar-

---

[2] Dahl, "Archon," 2. 689–712; see in particular pp. 707–8, and n. 44 (p. 708).

nation, subsequent history, and salvation of these Gnostics were worked
out in terms of the upper and lower Adam, Seth, and seed of Seth. In
particular this involved the doctrines of heavenly dwellings (the four
Lights) for the exalted counterparts of the "historical" Sethians, and the
tripartitioning of history into four basic epochs of salvation. These
epochs could be delineated by events in the lower world, such as the
flood, the conflagration, and the final overthrow of the Archons (as in
the *Apocalypse of Adam* and the *Gospel of the Egyptians*). Or these
epochs could be marked by the three descents from the upper world of a
Savior (as Father, Mother and Son) involving (1) the inbreathing of the
divine Spirit into Adam, (2) the arrival of the luminous Epinoia (a Sophia
figure) in the form of Eve, and (3) the final appearance of Seth as the
Logos (or Christ; cf. the *Apocryphon of John*, and the *Trimorphic
Protennoia*). Other schemes or combinations of these episodes were also
worked out. If there is anything peculiarly Sethian in the tractates under
discussion, it would show itself here, since these speculations in fact
constitute the sacred history of the Sethian Gnostics.

C. *The Baptismal Rite*

In addition, it is clear that some form of baptismal ritual is peculiar to
the Sethians. In whatever baptismal tradition the Sethians stood, it is
clear that it was spiritualized as part of a general trend that shows itself
throughout the first century in both Christian and probably non-Christian baptizing circles. In particular, the Sethian baptismal water was
understood to be of a celestial nature, a Living Water identical with light
or enlightenment, and the rite itself must have been understood as a
ritual of cultic ascent involving enlightenment and therefore salvation.
This could also involve polemic against ordinary water baptism, as in
the *Apocalypse of Adam*.

D. *Christianization*

Gradually, but especially during the second century, Sethianism was
Christianized, particularly by the identification of the Logos (the last
member of the Father-Mother-Son triad) with Christ. This process could
move in a positive direction by adding explanatory Christological
glosses as in the *Gospel of the Egyptians*, or even casting Sethian
materials into the framework of a revelation dialogue between Christ
the revealer and a revered disciple as in the *Apocryphon of John*. Or it
could move in a more polemical direction, as in *Trimorphic Protennoia*.
So also the reverse movement could occur, in which Sethian materials
were built into originally Christian materials circulating among Sethians, as could be the case with *Melchizedek*.

E. *The Platonic Contribution*

Finally, during the late first and throughout the second and third centuries, Neopythagorean and Platonic metaphysics made a strong impact on Sethianism. They served to structure its world of transcendent beings by means of ontological distinctions, and to explain how the plenitude of the divine world might emerge from a sole high deity by emanation, radiation, unfolding, and mental self-reflection. Neopythagorean arithmology helped to flesh out the various triadic, tetradic, pentadic, and ogdoadic groupings of the transcendental beings. Besides metaphysics, there was also at home in Platonism a by-now-traditional technique of self-performable contemplative mystical ascent toward and beyond the realm of pure being, which had its roots in Plato's *Symposium* (cf. 210A–212A). Interest in this technique shows itself in such figures as Philo, Numenius, the author(s) of the *Chaldean Oracles*, and in Plotinus. This technique not only supplemented earlier apocalyptic notions of ecstatic visionary ascent (perhaps associated with the spiritualized Sethian baptismal ritual as in *Trimorphic Protennoia*, *Gospel of the Egyptians*, *Zostrianos*, and perhaps in *Marsanes*), but it also created new forms apparently independent of such a baptismal context as in *Allogenes* and *Three Steles of Seth*. Most importantly, though, the older pattern of enlightenment through gnōsis "knowledge," conferred by a descending redeemer figure, could be replaced by a self-performable act of enlightenment through contemplative or visionary ascent, whether for individuals (*Allogenes* and *Marsanes*) or for a community (*Three Steles of Seth*).

III. Chronology and Redaction

On the background of these basic complexes of ideas, the following reconstruction of the composition and redaction of the Sethian treatises is suggested, although it is impossible to know which version of a particular document may have been available at each stage to the composers of the various treatises. Thus one ought perhaps to speak more generally of the redaction and incorporation of doctrines and traditions rather than of the particular extant documents that today serve as their exponents or instances.

A. *Before 100 C.E.*

One might begin with the (already Christianized) Ophite system of Irenaeus (cf. *Haer.* I.30), where one finds the triad of beings Man, Son of Man, and Third Male, the first two of whom, as suggested above, may have been conceived as androgynous. There is also a lower mother figure, the Spirit, who emits Sophia-Prunicos, who by gravity descends to and agitates the waters below, taking on a material body. When she is empowered from above to escape this body and ascend to the height, she becomes the father of the Archon Yaldabaoth. The Archon produces seven sons named as in the *Apocryphon of John*, and boasts that he alone is God, to which his mother responds that "Man and the Son of Man" are above him. Then follows the making of the man and the woman both of whom are specially enlightened by Sophia, and the stories of the tree of *gnōsis*, the expulsion from paradise, the birth of Cain, Abel, Seth and Norea, the flood, and finally the incognito descent of Christ, the Third Male, through the seven heavens. He puts on Sophia and rescues the crucified Jesus. Many of these motifs are at home in the Sethian treatises, but especially in *Ap. John* BG8502,2:44,19ff.; NHC II,1:13,3ff. (similarly in other versions), which is not paralleled by the Barbeloite system of Iren. *Haer.* I.29. Much of this material common to the *Apocryphon of John* and the Ophites is connected with the interpretation of Genesis 2–6, and one also finds versions of this material in the *Apocalypse of Adam*, *Hypostasis of the Archons*, and summarized in the *Gospel of the Egyptians*. The Ophite system describes repeated salvific acts of Sophia: providing the divine model for the protoplast, enlightening of Eve, protecting her light-trace from conception through the Archon, aiding the conception through the Archon, revealing the significance of Adam and Eve's bodies, and aiding the conception of Seth and Norea and the birth of the wise Jesus. The final salvific act is the deliverance of Sophia and Jesus by Christ.

1. *Early Sethian Eschatology.* The Sethian versions of this activity structure it into four distinct epochs of saving history marked by the flood, the conflagration and the judgment of the powers as in the *Apocalypse of Adam* and *Gospel of the Egyptians*. Or the epochs are marked by three distinct manifestations of a being more exalted than Sophia who descends first in a male mode, then in a female mode as Epinoia, and finally as the Logos (as in the *Apocryphon of John*, *Trimorphic Protennoia* and *Gospel of the Egyptians*). What makes the Sethian versions' adoption of this history of deliverance distinctive is their stress on Seth and their self-identification with Seth's seed, "the unshakeable race," who since the flood and conflagration live simultaneously on earth and in the aeons of the four Lights until the judgment of the Archons by a dramatic eschatological manifestation of Seth as the Logos. Between the conflagration and the final judgment of the Archons, the Sethians keep in contact with their heavenly counterparts by means of: (a) revelations Seth left behind inscribed on steles of brick and clay,

or on wooden tablets, or in certain books, all preserved on a special mountain, as well as by means of (b) a ritual of celestial ascent conceived in baptismal imagery, which Seth conferred upon his seed for their enlightenment.

2. *Sethian Tripartitions.* In accord with their tripartition of the history of salvation and of the modes in which the redeemer appears throughout this history, the Sethians structured their transcendent world into Father-Mother-Son triads as a more distinctive way of conceiving the saving work of the transcendent (aspect of) Sophia than was the (more biblical) triad of Man (the high deity), Son of Man (the androgynous heavenly Adam), and a Son of the Son of Man (Seth; cf. the terminology of the non-Sethian *Eugnostos* and *Sophia of Jesus Christ*). The androgynous image of God could be conceived either as the heavenly Adam (Adamas, Geradamas) or, stressing its female aspect, as the Thought (Ennoia) of the high deity who could be conceived as the Mother of the Son of Man. Thus her voice reveals to the Archon the existence of her higher consort, Man or the Father, and of her offspring, the Son of Man. Of course, conceiving the second member of the triad as female, a transcendent Sophia-figure distinguished from the Sophia who worked below, meant a transformation of the second member into a Mother (still androgynous) figure distinguished from Adamas the Son of Man (who now takes third place). This duplication is reflected in the alternate but equivalent designations of the Mother as, for instance, male virgin, womb, Father of the All, first Man, and thrice-male. Note, for example, how the second part of the *Apocryphon of John* in NHC II prefers the designation Mother-Father (II,1:5,7; 19,17; 20,9; 27,33) instead of the designation "merciful Father" or "merciful Mother" as in BG8502,2 (but cf. 77,11 which has "Mother-Father"). While this might account for the identification of the Father and Mother portion of the triad, the identification of the Son is a more complex problem. Given the tripartite Sethian history of salvation, the Son would be involved in the third and finally decisive salvific manifestation of the divine into the world. He could be the third manifestation of the Illuminator (*Apocalypse of Adam*) or the Logos which puts on Jesus, which in *Gospel of the Egyptians* is identified with Seth or in *Trimorphic Protennoia* with Christ. Or he could be viewed as the Christ who has appeared to John the son of Zebedee after the resurrection (*Apocryphon of John*). Or he could be simply conceived as the third and finally effective saving manifestation of the divine as in the Pronoia-hymn at the end of the *Apocryphon of John* II,1 (not even distinguished as Son).

This divine triad could be conceived in two fundamental ways: as a vertically schematized ontological hierarchy that gives rise to and structures the transcendent world, or else as a horizontally schematized succession of three divine manifestations. In the latter case, the three manifestations might be conceived as three manifestations of a single being in three modes such as the Father-Voice, Mother-Speech, Son-Logos (*Trimorphic Protennoia*), or as three separate beings in some sense identical with but mythologically distinguished from a higher being, such as the Autogenes, the Epinoia of Light, and Christ, all sent by the (Mother-)Father in the *Apocryphon of John*. The vertical scheme is illustrated in the Invisible Spirit, Barbelo, and the Autogenes in *Allogenes*, *Zostrianos*, *Three Steles of Seth* and *Marsanes*. In the Christianized Sethian theogonies, the third level is called either Christ (Iren. *Haer.* I.29, *Apocryphon of John* and the first part of *Trimorphic Protennoia*) or the Thrice-Male Child of the Great Christ (*Gospel of the Egyptians*).

3. *Hymnic Accounts of the Savior's Descent.* A careful reading of the *Apocryphon of John* (longer version) reveals that *Trimorphic Protennoia* is, in part, an expansion of the concluding Pronoia hymn (*Ap. John* II,1:30,12–31,25). The hymn contains a brief aretalogical self-predication of the divine Pronoia speaking in the first person singular (31,12–16) followed by the narration of her three descents into Chaos or Hades taking on the form of the seed to save them (30,16–21; 30,21–31; 30,31–31,25). In the third stanza there is a sudden shift from a third person plural to a third person singular designation for her seed, introduced by a gloss in 31,4 identifying the prison of Hades as the prison of the body. This seems to introduce material originally foreign to the hymn (reflected once earlier in *Ap. John* II,1:23,30–31) employing the *topos* of awakening sleepers (cf. Eph 5:14) ensnared in the bonds of oblivion by reminding them of their predicament (31,4–10 and 31,14–22). It seems likely that the third stanza of the original hymn must have concluded:

> And I entered into the middle of their prison and I said: "I am the Pronoia of the pure light; I am the thinking of the virginal Spirit, he who raised you (plural) up to the honored place." And I raised them up and sealed them in the light of the water with Five Seals in order that death might not have power over them from this time on.

One finds a very close equivalent of this hymn in the second half of the Naasene Psalm (Hipp. *Ref.* 5.10.2), where Jesus says:

> Look Father: this prey (the fallen soul) to evils is wandering away to earth, far from thy Spirit, and she seeks to escape the bitter Chaos but knows not how to win through. For that reason send me, Father. Bearing Seals I shall descend; I will pass through all the Aeons; I shall reveal all the mysteries and I shall deliver the secrets of the holy way, calling them Gnosis.[3]

[3] See Marcovich, "Naasene Psalm," whose translation I adopt.

Clearly these two hymns have been influenced by the same complex of ideas: the descent of a revealer bearing seals into Chaos, and its bitterness, to rescue the soul below. While the Naasene Psalm also tells of the descent of the soul and displays the male Jesus as savior, the Pronoia hymn tells only of the threefold descent of the feminine Pronoia (or remembrance thereof), the last of which succeeds in raising up Pronoia's members, who are viewed as consubstantial with her.

4. *A Descent Hymn Elaborated: Trimorphic Protennoia.* The Pronoia hymn, or something much like it, then underwent expansion in its first stage as an aretalogy of Protennoia as Father-Voice, Mother-Speech, and Son-Word now found in *Trimorphic Protennoia.* Furthermore, another stage of composition was devoted to spelling out the "mysteries" communicated by the revealer as well as the nature of the (Five) "Seals" brought by him or her. A final stage saw to its Christianization.

Assuming that *Trimorphic Protennoia* finds its basis in the hymnic ending of the longer version of the *Apocryphon of John*, a closer analysis shows the following approximate compositional history for *Trimorphic Protennoia.* The underlying basis of the tractate can be seen in the consistent *egō eimi* "I am" self-predications of Protennoia which are structured into an introductory aretalogy (XIII,1:35,1–32) identifying Protennoia as the divine Thought (35,1–32) followed by three *egō eimi* aretalogies of about forty lines each in the same style. The second and third of these aretalogies form separate subtractates in *Trimorphic Protennoia* (Protennoia is the Voice of the Thought who descends first as light into darkness and gives shape to her fallen members [35,32–36,27; 40,29–41,1]; Protennoia is the Speech of the Thought's Voice who descends second to empower her fallen members by giving them spirit or breath [42,4–27; 45,2–12; 45,21–46,3]; and Protennoia is the Word of the Speech of the Thought's Voice who descends a third time in the likeness of the powers, proclaims the Five Seals, and restores her seed [members] into the Light [46,5–7; 47,5–23; 49,6–23; 50,9–20]). If this, or something like it, is what the author started with, it can be seen that he has expanded this tripartite aretalogy with six doctrinal insertions (36,27–40,29; 41,1–42,2; 42,27–45,2; 46,7–47,top; 47,24–49,top and 49,22–50,9). Three of these insertions are "mysteries" which Protennoia is said to have communicated to her sons. The first and longest insertion (36,27–40,29) narrates the story of the Autogenes Christ and his four Lights. The last of these Lights (Eleleth) emits Sophia (his Epinoia) to produce the demon Yaldabaoth who steals the Epinoia's power to create the lower aeons and man. It concludes with the restoration of Epinoia-Sophia who is regarded as completely innocent of fault. It is constructed in third person narrative.

The first of the "mysteries" (41,1–42,2) narrates the loosening of the
bonds of flesh by which the underworld powers enslave Protennoia's
fallen members. This mystery is announced in direct discourse to a
second person plural audience. The second mystery (42,27–45,2), called
the "mystery of the (end of) this age" (42,28), is addressed to a similar
group in the second person plural. It narrates an apocalyptic announcement of the end of the old age and the dawn of the new age with the
judgment of the authorities of chaos, the celestial powers, and their
Archigenetor. The third mystery (47,24–49,top), called "the mystery of
Gnosis" (48,33–34) is again addressed to a second person plural audience, now called the "brethren." It narrates the descent of Protennoia as
the Word who descends incognito through the various levels of the
powers and strips away the corporeal and psychic thought from her
brethren and raises them up to the Light by means of a baptismal-
celestial ascent ritual identified as the Five Seals.

It is clear that *Trimorphic Protennoia* has been secondarily Christianized. Three glosses identifying the Autogenes Son with Christ in the
first subtractate (37,[31]; 38,22; 39,6–7) probably derive from the traditional theogonical materials common to the *Apocryphon of John* and
Iren., *Haer.* I.29, upon which the author has drawn. But in the third
subtractate the situation is much different, and seems to suggest that
Trimorphic Protennoia has undergone three stages of composition.
First, there was the triad of aretalogical *egō eimi* self-predications of
Protennoia as Voice, Speech, and Word. Second, this was supplemented
by doctrinal insertions based upon traditional Sethian cosmological
materials similar to those of *Apocryphon of John* and Iren. *Haer.* I.29, as
well as upon (apparently non-Sethian) traditional materials treating the
harrowing of hell and the eschatological overthrow of the celestial
powers, and again upon Sethian traditions about the baptismal ascent
ritual of the Five Seals. After circulation as a Sethian tractate in this
form, the third stage of composition seems to have been the incorporation of Christian materials into the aretalogical portion of the third
subtractate.

Specifically, the narrative of the incognito descent of Protennoia as
Word, hidden in the form of the Sovereignties, Powers, and Angels,
culminating in the final revelation of herself in her members below,
seems to have undergone a Christological interpretation. In 47,14–15, it
is said that as Logos, Protennoia revealed herself to "them" (i.e.,
humans?) "in their tents" as the Word (cf. John 1:14). In 49,7–8 it is said
that the Archons thought Protennoia-Logos was "their Christ," while
actually she is the Father of everyone. In 49,11–15, Protennoia identifies
herself as the "beloved" (of the Archons), since she clothed herself as

Son of the Archigenetor until the end of his ignorant decree. In 49,18–20 Protennoia reveals herself as a Son of Man among the Sons of Man even though she is the Father of everyone. In 50,6–9, Protennoia will reveal herself to her "brethren" and gather them into her "eternal kingdom." In 50,12–16, Protennoia has put on Jesus and borne him aloft from the cross into his Father's dwelling places (cf. John 14:2–3). In this way traditional Christological titles such as Christ, Beloved, Son of God ("Son of the Archigenetor") and Son of Man are polemically interpreted in a consciously docetic fashion. By implication, the "orthodox" Christ is shown to be the Christ of the "Sethian" Archons; the "orthodox" Beloved is the beloved of the Archons; the "orthodox" Son of God is the "Sethian" son of the ignorant Archigenetor; and the "orthodox" Son of Man is only a human among the sons of men, while for the Sethians, the true Son of Man is Adamas, the Son of the supreme deity Man (the human form in which the deity revealed himself as in *Ap. John* II,1:14,14–24 and *Gos. Eg.* III,2:59,1–9), or perhaps he is Seth, the Son of Adamas as in *Ap. John* II,1:24,32–25,7. Therefore, the Protennoia-Logos is in reality the Father of everyone, the Father of the All who only *appears* as the Logos "in their tents" (*skēnē*; a gloss on "the likeness of their shape" in *Trim. Prot.* XIII,1:47,16 in what seems to be conscious opposition to John 1:14). That is, he *appeared* in the "likeness of their shape" but did not become flesh as the "orthodox" believe. In only disguising himself as the "orthodox" Christ, the Logos indeed had to rescue Jesus from the "cursed" (not redemptive!) cross and restore him to the "dwelling places of his Father." In what seems a conscious reference to John 14:2–3, Jesus did not prepare a place for his followers; instead, the Logos, invisible to the celestial powers who watch over the aeonic dwellings (i.e., the four Lights?), installs Jesus into his Father's dwelling place (*Trim. Prot.* XIII,1:50,12–16; perhaps in the Light Oroiael as in *Gos. Eg.* III,2:65,16–17).

Most of these polemical Sethian reinterpretations of "orthodox" Christology in *Trimorphic Protennoia* seem to depend on key texts from the Gospel of John in order to score their point in any acute fashion, although this has been a matter of scholarly dispute.[4] It seems that the

---

[4] Cf. the discussions of G. Schenke, "Protennoia"; Helderman, "Zelten"; H.-M. Schenke, "Sethianism," 607–12; and summarizing the debate, Robinson, "Sethians." My own position is that *Trimorphic Protennoia* underwent superficial Christianization in its second stage of redaction, but specific and polemical Christianization in its third stage of redaction. The superficial resemblances to the Johannine prologue scattered throughout *Trimorphic Protennoia* are to be explained by the emergence of both texts from gnosticizing oriental sapiental traditions at home in first-century Syria and Palestine, as suggested by Colpe, "Überlieferung," 122–24. The Christological glosses in the first sub-tractate are to be explained by the influence of the theogonical section of the *Apoc-*

key to the resolution of this dispute lies in the recognition that *Trimorphic Protennoia*, in its first two stages of composition, was a product of non-Christian Sethianism, drawing its Logos-theology from a fund of oriental speculation on the divine Word and Wisdom as did the prologue to the Gospel of John in a similar but independent way. But both the prologue and *Trimorphic Protennoia* later underwent Christianization in a later stage of redaction; the prologue in Johannine Christian circles, and *Trimorphic Protennoia* in Christianized Sethian circles. Indeed, *Trimorphic Protennoia* may have undergone Christianizing redaction in the environment of the debate over the interpretation of the Gospel of John during the early second century. This debate is reflected in the Johannine letters, and a bit later in western Valentinian circles is concerned with the interpretation of the Logos (e.g., The *Tripartite Tractate* of NHC I) and of the Gospel of John (e.g., Ptolemaeus in Iren. *Haer.* I.8.5 and the Fragments of Heracleon).

5. *The Early Sethian Baptismal Rite.* The spiritualized conception of baptism as a saving ritual of enlightenment reflected in the Sethian texts must also have been current in the first century, to judge from the complex of ideas in Col 2:8–15, where circumcision (regarded as a stripping off of the body of flesh) is connected with a baptism conceived as a dying and rising, and Christ's death is interpreted as a disarming of the principalities and powers. To judge from the Sethian baptismal mythologumena, the Sethians, wherever they derived their original rite, must have developed it in close rapprochement with Christianity. They must have sustained their initial encounter with Christianity as fellow practitioners of baptism, indeed a baptism interpreted in a very symbolic and spiritual direction. For example, the Sethian name for their Living Water, itself a conception found also in Johannine Christianity (John 4:7–15), is Yesseus Mazareus Yessedekeus, which seems very much like a version of the name of Jesus into which Christians were baptized, perhaps in a threefold way. Yet to adopt this name did not necessarily mean understanding oneself principally as a Christian, as the rather cryptic and concealed form of this name suggests. Indeed it was adopted by the redactor of the (apparently in all other respects) non-Christian *Apocalypse of Adam.*

In many respects, the baptismal rite seems to have provided the

----

ryphon of John. But the more striking parallels to the Gospel of John discussed here, as well as the explicit application of apparent Christological titles to Protennoia-Logos, seem to me to constitute deliberate "Christianization," although in a strictly polemical vein. Whether the redactor of the third compositional stage hypothesized by me is really Sethian or heterodox Christian is impossible to tell; in any case he is certainly not an "orthodox" or "apostolic" Christian, though perhaps he might be a "super Johannine" (heretic) of the sort suggested by Brown, "Sheep."

context or occasion for many of the principal Sethian themes to coalesce in various combinations. This is quite obvious in the case of the Sethian rite of cultic or individual ascent, and also in the theme of the descent of the redeemer bearing the Five Seals. Yet the web of interlocking themes could be even more complex, as in the case of *Apocalypse of Adam*, part of which seems to draw on an old mythical pattern to illustrate thirteen versions of the descent of the Illuminator. It exhibits a myth which could be developed in various ways to portray the origin of mankind, the origin of the Savior, and perhaps the origin of both water baptism and celestial baptism as well.

In a very illuminating article, J. M. Robinson[5] drew attention to a series of striking parallels between the structure and motifs of the thirteen kingdoms, i.e., thirteen opinions concerning the coming of the Illuminator "to the water," and a similar mythical structure to be found in the NT Apocalypse of John (Rev 12:1–17) and reflected in the baptism and "temptation" stories of Mark 1:9–13, and in some fragments from the *Gospel of the Hebrews*. As can be seen from Robinson's study, there underlies Mark 1, Revelation 12 and *Apoc. Adam* V,5:77,26–82,19 a basic mythical structure concerning a divine child and his divine mother who are threatened by an evil power, but who are rescued and find safety in the wilderness until the evil power is destroyed. This general pattern could be made to apply not only to Adam and his divine mother or to Seth and his mother Eve, but also to the birth of Jesus, to Mary and their flight to Egypt from Herod, and perhaps more remotely to certain aspects of the Isis-Osiris-Horus cycle.

For our immediate purposes, however, it is important to see that facets of such a myth were applied to baptism not only in Mark (where wilderness is also ultimately a place of safety) and in the fragments of *Gospel of the Hebrews* but also in *Apocalypse of Adam*. In Mark the Savior is baptized in the (ordinary) water to which he comes, after which the Spirit descends to the Savior together with a Voice that pronounces him Son of God. The parallel in Matthew agrees, but has reservations about the baptism in water by John. Luke omits explicit mention of Jesus' baptism by John, and has the Spirit descend on Jesus during his post-baptismal prayer. The Fourth Gospel suppresses Jesus' explicit baptism by John in mere water, demoting John to the Voice of one crying in the wilderness, whose only subsequent function is to witness to the descent of the Spirit upon Jesus. Instead, the Fourth Gospel (John 4:7–15) understands Jesus as the source of Living Water, which to drink means eternal life, and as the one who will baptize with the Holy Spirit,

---

[5] Robinson, "*Gattung* of Mark," 119–29.

which the author identifies with the Living Water (John 7:37–39). Like-wise, the second compositional stage of *Trimorphic Protennoia* regards the Logos, who descends with the Five Seals at the conclusion of the first-stage aretalogy, as the Logos-Son. He pours forth Living Water upon the Spirit below out of its source, which is the Father-Voice aspect of Protennoia, called the unpolluted spring of Living Water. So also *Gospel of the Egyptians* understands the descent of Seth as Logos to be the bestowal of a holy baptism, probably in Living Water. These baptismal descents of the Logos or Seth are initiated by Barbelo, the Father-Mother, an exalted Sophia figure, who communicates to those who love her by Voice or Word (the Johannine prologue, *Trimorphic Protennoia*). Jewish wisdom texts portray the exalted Sophia as the fountain or spring (cf. Sirach 24; Philo, *Fug.* 195) from which comes the Word like a river (Philo, *Somn.* 2.242; cf. *Fug.* 97), the Mother of the Word through whom the universe came to be (*Fug.* 109; cf. *Trimorphic Protennoia* and the Johannine prologue). To be baptized in her water is to receive true gnōsis. Thus her Voice (*bath qol*) is the revelation of the truth: e.g., "Man exists and the Son of Man" in the *Apocryphon of John* or the *Gospel of the Egyptians*; "This is my beloved Son" in Mark 1:11 (cf. 9:7), where the heavenly Voice comes down to water; similarly the Voices in *Trim. Prot.* XIII,1:40,8–9; 44,29–32 and *Apoc. Adam* V,5:84,4. Indeed it is likely that *Trimorphic Protennoia* derived its scheme of Voice, Speech, and Logos from such a complex of notions.

The conclusion to be drawn from these clusters of ideas is that the Sethian soteriology involving the saving descent of Barbelo, or of her Voice, or of Seth or of the Logos was most likely worked out in a baptismal environment characterized by speculation on the significance of words spoken and waters involved (cf. *Zost.* VIII,1:15) during the first century.[6] In this environment it rubbed shoulders with Christianity, but

---

[6] Gnostic Sethianism must have originated among the numerous baptismal sects that populated Syria and Palestine, especially along the Jordan valley, in the period 200 B.C.E.–300 C.E.: the Essenes/Dead Sea sect, the pre-Christian Nasareans of Epiphanius, John the Baptist and his followers, the Jewish-Christian Nazorenes, the Ebionites, Pauline and Johannine Christians, Naasenes, Valentinians/Marcosians, Elkasaites, Sabeans, Dosi-theans, Masbotheans, Gorothenians, Hemero-baptists, Mandeans, and the groups behind the *Odes of Solomon, Acts of Thomas, Pseudo-Clementines*, Justin's *Baruch*, etc. (cf. Thomas, *Mouvement baptiste*). These baptismal rites, often representing a spiritualizing protest against a failing or extinct sacrificial temple cultus (so Thomas), are mostly descendants of ancient Mesopotamian New Year enthronement rituals in which the king, stripped of his regalia, symbolically undergoes a struggle with the dark waters of chaos, cries for aid, is raised up and nourished by water or food, absolved and strengthened by a divine oracle, enthroned, enrobed, and acclaimed as king, acquiring radiance and authority (e.g., tablets III and IV of "I will praise the Lord of Wisdom," ANET 434–36). Similar imagery of struggle and exaltation can be found in Psalms 18, 30, 69, 80, 89, 110, 114 and 146 (cf. 1 Kgs 1:38–47; it may be that suffering in the water and baptism [or drink]

probably did not fully take the step of identifying their savior with Christ or Jesus, which it would soon do, but in a rather polemical fashion.

are two aspects of the function of water in these rites). In 2 Esdr 13:1–6 the rising of the Son of Man is accompanied by the issuance of his cosmic voice. In 2 Enoch 22, Enoch is raised up before God by Michael, stripped of his earthly garments, anointed and enrobed in glory so that he shines. In the Maccabean period, T. Levi 8:2–10 portrays the priest Levi as "a priest forever" (cf. Melchizedek); he is commanded to put on priestly garments (including the garment of truth), but then is invested as a royal figure (anointed, given a staff, washed, fed bread and wine, clad with a glorious robe, linen vestment, purple girdle and crowned). In T. Levi 18:6–7 at the advent of the eschatological priest, a star arises, emitting the light of knowledge; the Father's voice issues from the heavenly temple; the spirit of understanding rests on him in the water; the priest will open the gates of paradise, feed the saints from the tree of life and bind Beliar.

Baptismal and ascensional motifs occur frequently in patristic heresiological reports: the Sethians (Hipp. Ref. 5.19.21: washing in and drinking from living water, celestial enrobing); Justin's Baruch (Hipp. Ref. 5.27.2–3: drinking from and baptism in living water as opposed to earthly water); the Naasenes (Hipp., Ref. 5.7.19: washing in living water, anointing; 5.8.14–18: issuance of the divine voice over the flood, passing through water and fire, lifting up of gates; 5.9.18–20: drink of living water) and the Marcosians (Iren. Haer. I.21.3–5 baptism in the name of Achamoth, anointing in the name of Jao, anointing for heavenly ascent). Valentinian baptism is reflected in the baptismal appendices to A Valentinian Exposition and in the Gospel of Philip. Baptismal motifs occur in the Odes of Solomon, especially Ode 11:7–16 (drinking living water, stripping away of folly, enrobing with radiance and enlightenment) and Ode 24:1–5 (the voice of the Dove above the Messiah and the opening of the abysses; cf. Ode 17:1–16 and its parallels with Trim. Prot. XIII,1:41,4–42,2 which is interpreted as a baptism). The sequence of acts in the Five Seals of Trim. Prot. XIII,1:48,15–35 is very much like the sequence of acts in the Mandaean Masbūtā as summarized by Rudolph, Mandäer, 2.88–89: entrance into the "Jordan," triple self-immersion, triple immersion by the priest, triple sign with water, triple drink, crowning, invocation of divine names, ritual handshake, and ascent from the "Jordan"). In Trimorphic Protennoia, the one baptized is enrobed before baptism as seems to be the case among the Qumran sectaries, the Mandaeans, and later Christian rites (apparently only Elchasaites were baptized naked).

It is quite likely that the early Sethian baptismal milieu was the setting for the baptismal mythologumena in the Sethian treatises, and especially for the hymnic materials in Gos. Eg. III,2, pp.66–67, Apoc. Adam V,5, pp.78–82, Melch. XI,1, pp.5–6 and 16–18, and in the baptismal material of Trimorphic Protennoia. These materials seem to envision the descent of the savior into the world, corresponding to the descent of the king or of the one baptized into water or world of chaos, but also the spiritual visionary ascent of the one baptized out of the water, or world, into the light, corresponding to the enthronement and exaltation of the king, priest, or priest-king. Allogenes, Three Steles of Seth, and especially Zostrianos with its celestial baptism reflect in their visionary ascent scheme only the enthronement-exaltation-glorification aspect of the baptismal rite. There seems to be a close correspondence of the pattern of baptismal immersion and emergence with the humiliation and exaltation pattern of the ancient enthronement rituals. On such grounds certain of the NT Christological hymns employing a similar pattern may also be seen against a baptismal environment, especially the Johannine prologue, Phil 2:6–11, Col 2:9–15, 1 Tim 3:16, and 1 Pet 3:18–22. The portrayal of the deliverer or his forerunner as a light dawning (anatellein or anatolē) or entering the world is associated with the advent of the priest-king of T. Levi 18 and of John the Baptist (of priestly descent) in Luke 1:76–79 (and perhaps in the Johannine prologue if it once applied to the Baptist). Such texts may in part reflect the eschatological advent of the star and scepter of Num 24:17 (often interpreted as referring to a royal and a priestly messiah by the Dead

6. *The Earliest Sethian Compositions.*   Thus I would suggest that by
the end of the first century, Sethians possessed at least the following
sacred texts. First, several versions of a possibly hymnic narrative of the
threefold descent of the divine Mother like the one contained at the end
of the longer version of *Apocryphon of John* according to which the
third descent was finally effective and was understood to be the mythical origin of a Sethian baptismal rite called the Five Seals. This might
also have existed in the form now embedded as source B in C. W.
Hedrick's redactional theory of the *Apocalypse of Adam,*[7] in which three
men (!) appear to Adam in a dream to awaken him from the sleep of
death (V,5:65,24–66,12; 67,12–21). They speak of the third descent of the
Illuminator who performs acts that disturb the God of the powers. He
cannot recognize the power of this "man" and punishes his flesh only
after he has caused his elect to shine and he has withdrawn to the holy
houses (the four Lights?) in the great aeon from which he had come
(V,5:76,8–11; 76,14–82,17; 82,19–83,4). Indeed, the redactor leads us to
believe that prior to his withdrawal, he imparted to his elect a secret
gnōsis which is "the holy baptism of those who know the eternal

Sea sect; cf. 1 QM 11,6; 1 QSb 5,20–25; 4 QTestim 9–13; CD 7,9–21; also *T. Judah* 24 and
Rev 22:16).
    The judgment upon the sons of Seth reflected in Num 24:17, as interpreted in the
Damascus Document (CD 7,9–21) and the Samaritan tradition (*Asatir* II,3), that Seth
founded Damascus have been used to show that the Samaritans of Damascus claimed to
be the true generation of Seth (the people of the Northern Kingdom) whom the scepter,
the prince of the Qumran community, was coming to destroy (Beltz, "Samaritanertum").
Since no orthodox Samaritan traditions reflect this Qumran tradition, Beltz suggests it
was a Samaritan sectarian tradition, and that it was the Dositheans who thought of
themselves as sons of Seth, an identification perhaps reflected in the mention of
Dositheus in *Steles Seth* VII,5:118,10–19. While a connection between the Sethians and
Dositheans is only a suggestion, certain Dositheans apparently constituted a baptizing
sect of the first and second centuries C.E. (Vilmar, *Abulfathi annales,* 151–59; *Ps. Clem.
Rec.* 2.8 and *Hom.* 2.24; Origen, *Cels.* 1.57; 6.11; Euseb. *Eccl. Hist.* 4.22; cf. Montgomery,
Samaritans, 253–63). The Pseudo-Clementines link Dositheus with Simon Magus and
John the Baptist (*Rec.* 1:54–63; 2.8; *Hom.* 2.15–24; 3.22); these accounts are of doubtful
historical value, but they may reflect an original association of John or Simon or
Dositheus with Samaria. A possible connection between John (and Jesus!) and Samaria
occurs in the first four chapters of the Fourth Gospel, especially if his baptismal activity
at Ainon near Salim is to be located in Samaria as Scobie thinks (*John the Baptist,* 163–
77; 187–202; perhaps this Ainon=spring has to do with "ainon" in *Gos. Eg.* IV,2:44,25 and
"ainos" in *Trim. Prot.* XIII,1:39,1). These possible links between the Baptist, heterodox
Samaritanism, the Fourth Gospel and early Sethianism deserve further investigation. In
any case, both John the Baptist and Seth are portrayed as eschatological figures who
introduce a baptismal rite, as Jesus also is portrayed insofar as he is identified with Seth
in the Sethian literature. The introduction of this rite is connected with a cosmic
judgment, involves a passing through water and, in the synoptics, a pending baptism with
fire (or the Holy Spirit). These are complexes of ideas which in an early Sethian
baptismal environment might have been linked to the Sethian tripartite eschatology
marked by flood, fire and final judgment.
    [7] Hedrick, "Adam," and more fully, *Apocalypse.*

knowledge through those born of the word and the imperishable illuminators (the four Lights?) who came from the holy seed (of the celestial Sethians): Yesseus, Mazareus, Yessedekeus, [the Living] Water" (V,5:85,22–31). Furthermore, the tripartite narrative attributed above to the first redactional stage of *Trimorphic Protennoia* would belong here.

B. 100–125 C.E.

The first quarter of the second century must have seen the development of a theogonical account of the successive begettings of the triad Father-Mother-Son conceived as the Invisible Spirit, Barbelo, and their Son. Such an account underlies the Barbeloite system in Iren. *Haer.* I.29. By now, the basic triad has been embellished by the addition of an elementary set of hypostatized divine attributes, which themselves could form pairs so as to produce further beings, such as the four Lights which were probably objects of vision in the spiritualized Sethian baptismal rite of the Five Seals. The first quarter of the second century seems to have been a period of vigorous arithmological speculation on the first ten numbers, but especially the first four numbers, comprising the Pythagorean *tetraktys* "the sum of the first four numbers." This was carried on by such Pythagoreanizing Platonists as Theon of Smyrna and Nicomachus of Gerasa, who in turn depend in part on similar arithmological and mathematical theories produced by such early first-century Platonist figures as Dercyllides, Adrastos of Aphrodisias (a Peripatetic commentator on Plato's *Timaeus*) and Thrasyllos, a court philosopher under the Emperor Tiberius. The harmonic ratios produced by these first four numbers and the geometric entities of point, line, surface, and solid had been applied to the structure and the creation of the world soul long before by Plato and his successors in the old Academy, especially Speusippus and Xenocrates. Thus it is not necessary to assume that the Barbeloite system of Iren. *Haer.* I.29 is dependent upon Valentinus or his successors, Polemy and Heracleon, or vice versa, since this arithmological lore was by now readily available in the handbooks employed in the dense network of urban schools where anyone who wished to become literate might study them alongside the *Timaeus* itself. Although this Sethian "Barbeloite" theogonical material exists in a number of treatises each of which adds its own special touches (e.g., Iren. *Haer.* I.29, *Apocryphon of John*, *Gospel of the Egyptians*, *Allogenes*, *Zostrianos*, *Three Steles of Seth*, *Marsanes* and *Trimorphic Protennoia*), it seems that the material common to the *Apocryphon of John* and Iren. *Haer.* I.29 represents the earliest form.

In the early second century the principal emphasis of gnostic speculation on the beyond seems to be the explanation of how the current world came to be and how and whence the savior originated and descended with enlightening gnōsis. This speculation seemed to require a Father and Mother who produced and sent the Son. The peculiar exegesis of Genesis 1–6 with its emphasis on the primordial origins of the heavenly and earthly Sethians was the only obvious aetiology by which the Sethians could maintain any sense of separate identity as the elect ones. This mythology, presented in narrative as a temporal succession of successive human generations, required to be matched by a similar but less temporally conceived succession of the unfolding hypostases and offspring of the high deity.

1. *The Apocryphon of John.* To judge from Iren. *Haer* I.29 and the four versions of the *Apocryphon of John* (which represent already Christianized versions of the Sethian myth of Barbelo the Mother and the sender of both the primordial saviors, Autogenes and Epinoia [Sophia, Eve] and also the eschatological savior, the Autogenes [Christianized as Christ], the *Apocryphon of John* first exhibited the following profile. The Father, the invisible virginal Spirit, emitted his female aspect conceived as his Thought (Ennoia) which took shape as his First Thought (or Forethought) named Barbelo, who in Jewish tradition was probably a manifestation of the divine Name. Since (as her name suggests) God is in four, she requests the Invisible Spirit to realize four of her attributes as separate hypostases: Foreknowledge, Incorruptibility, Eternal Life and Self-begotten or Autogenes. The last of these is later identified with her Son Adamas, or Christ. Since Barbelo is the self-begotten divine Mind and wisdom of God, her Son should likewise possess similar powers and so his own attributes (Mind, Will, Logos and Truth) are manifested. At this point, there remains to be explained the origin of the four Lights, the celestial dwellings of Adamas, Seth, the celestial seed of Seth, and the future home of the historical Sethians. They are a traditional part of the Sethian's baptismal lore as shown in Gos. Eg. III,2:64,9–65,26 and in the baptismal prayer in *Melch.* IX,1:16, 16–18,7. The four Lights are explained by forming a tetrad of pairs composed of the hypostatized attributes of both Barbelo and her Son so that the "Autogenes" attribute of the Son and the Incorruptibility aspect of Barbelo produced the four Lights: Harmozel, Oroiael, Davithe, and Eleleth. At that point, to judge from the current versions of the *Apocryphon of John* and the *Gospel of the Egyptians,* Barbelo caused a further pairing of her attribute of Eternal Life and her Son's attribute of Will (Thelēma). They give rise to four further feminine attributes, Grace, Will (Thelēsis), Understanding, and Wisdom (the upper Sophia, perhaps called Phronesis; cf. *Hyp. Arch.* II,4:93,18–19 and 94,2–4). This sets the stage for the fall of Sophia, a lower aspect of the Mother. After giving

rise to the Archon, she projects the image of the Son, Adamas. Later still, she causes the conception of Seth and his seed, whom she also rescues, either by herself or, as in the *Apocalypse of Adam*, by angelic beings, perhaps the servants of the Lights. In order to provide even more primordial spiritual prototypes of these beings, a further pairing of attributes, the Mother's Foreknowledge and the Son's Mind, must have produced the archetypal patterns for Adam, Seth, and his seed. They are then placed in the first three of the four Lights, leaving the fourth as a dwelling for the restored lower Sophia.

The systems of Irenaeus and the *Apocryphon of John* each contain subtle departures from this hypothetical arrangement, either by way of simplification, confusion, or more likely, in the case of the *Apocryphon of John*, to enhance the position of Christ instead of Adamas as the Son in the wake of Christianization. As van den Broek has pointed out,[8] the birth of Autogenes from Ennoia and Logos found in Irenaeus is suppressed in the *Apocryphon of John* because Autogenes is identified with the Christ who has, in the extant versions of the Barbeloite system, become identified as the Son of the Father and Barbelo. He points out that while in the *Apocryphon of John* Christ the Son is identified with his Autogenes aspect, in Iren. *Haer.* I.29, this Autogenes and his son Adamas are lower beings produced by Ennoia and Logos. They receive, however, great honor in a way that would suit a much higher being. He shows convincingly that, since Irenaeus says all things were subjected to Autogenes, the Barbeloite system originally considered him little less than God, crowned with glory and honor and given dominion over all things, an application of Ps 8:4-6. Originally, therefore, Autogenes had a higher rank. This would be the rank that Christ the Son now holds in the Christianized system, although this presupposes a stage still prior to the Father-Mother-Son triad in which there was Man and the Son of Man, little less than God. Thus the development of the bisexual nature of the Son of Man into Mother and Son demoted the Son, the Autogenes Adam, one notch. The Barbeloite system preserved the rank of Autogenes by identifying him with Christ (*Ap. John* BG8502,2:30,6; but not in NHC II,1) but demoted Adamas. On the other hand, Irenaeus' version demoted both Autogenes and Adamas, leaving only Christ as the supreme Son.

The *Apocryphon of John* results from a combination of this theogony with the Sethian story of Yaldabaoth's creation of the protoplasts and the subsequent struggle between him and the Mother depicted in terms of Genesis 2-6. The entire work is then construed as the final revelation

[8] "Autogenes."

of the Mother who in the form of Christ reveals the whole thing to his disciple John. The source upon which the longer and shorter versions seem to depend may possibly have been produced during the first quarter of the second century. The long negative theology of the Invisible Spirit at the beginning seems quite in keeping with the interests of such thinkers of this period as Basilides, the Neopythagorean Moderatus and, farther afield, of Albinus. As E. R. Dodds showed in 1928,[9] this negative theology is only a natural development of Plato's doctrine of the Good "beyond being in power and dignity" in the *Republic*, 509B and of the speculations about the non-being of the One in the *Parmenides*, 137Cff.

Perhaps by the end of the first quarter of the second century, the shorter recension (BG8502,2 and NHC III,1), supplemented by the short excursus on the soul (BG8502,2:64,9–71,2) came into existence in the form of a dialogue between the resurrected Christ and his disciple John, son of Zebedee, together with the appropriate Christian glosses substituting Christ for the Autogenes Adam (cf. the similar phenomenon in the case of *Eugnostos* and the *Sophia of Jesus Christ*).

2. *Trimorphic Protennoia*. Perhaps at this time the second compositional stage of the *Trimorphic Protennoia* was also achieved by the addition of the four mysteries to the triple descent aretalogical narrative, as discussed above. The first of these mysteries indeed seems dependent on the already Christianized system common to the *Apocryphon of John* and Iren. *Haer*. I.29, and the fourth draws on the Sethian baptismal tradition of the Five Seals.

C. 125–150 C.E.

Toward the end of the first half of the second century, *Trimorphic Protennoia* may have reached its present (polemically) Christianized form. This period may also have seen the redaction of the longer version of the *Apocryphon of John* in Codices II and IV by the addition of a long section on the many angels that contributed parts to the body of the protoplastic Adam, claimed to be derived from a "book of Zoroaster" (II,1:15,29–19,11) and the inclusion of the Pronoia hymn at the end (II,1:30,11–31,25; discussed above).

1. *The Apocalypse of Adam* (Source B). The redactional combination of a triple descent narrative culminating in the Sethian rite of baptismal enlightenment with a major version of the Sethian history of salvation derived from an exegesis of Genesis 1–6 in the case of the *Apocryphon of John* may have occurred at about the same time that part

[9] "The *Parmenides* of Plato," esp. 132–33.

of a similar triple descent narrative (fleshed out with the opinions on the thirteen kingdoms) in source B of the *Apocalypse of Adam* was connected by its redactor with the Genesis-inspired Sethian salvation history of source A. At the same time he also incorporated Sethian baptismal tradition, but in a polemical way. Although the *Apocalypse of Adam* was not Christianized in an obvious way by the redactor, it is at least arguable that Source B contained concepts that originated in close contact with Christianity such as the punishing of the flesh of the man upon whom the spirit has come (V,5:77,16–18) and the (unsatisfactory) speculations on the origin of the Illuminator as the son of a prophet, or son of a virgin or son of Solomon attributed to the second, third, and fourth kingdoms (V,5:78,7–79,19). Just as is the case with the Christological motifs in the third subtractate of *Trimorphic Protennoia*, such concepts seem to be introduced in a polemical vein, suggesting that the triple-descent motif may have been developed in connection with an attempt to distinguish Sethianism from Christianity with its increasing stress on the once-for-all nature of Christ's redeeming activity. For Christianity, the period of Israel was one only of preparation for the advent of salvation in Christ, while for the Sethians, salvation had been in principle already achieved in primordial times, with the raising of Seth and his seed into the Aeon. Thus the first and second descents of the redeemer had actually already performed the fundamental work of salvation in primordial times and left witnesses to it on inscribed steles and in books. The third descent of the redeemer is therefore only to remind the earthly Sethians of what had been accomplished for them in the past, and to grant them a means of realizing this in the present through the baptismal ascent ritual.

That this third descent of the redeemer is identified with the preexistent Christ who brings salvation as *gnōsis* rather than salvation through his death on the cross should occasion no surprise. There were tendencies toward such views in Johannine Christian circles as well. One should bear in mind that also during this period (140–160 C.E.) Valentinus likewise developed the notion of a pneumatic Christ coming to waken the sleeping spirit in humankind, a notion which lies at the core of his system. Valentinus and his successors made Christ the focus of their system and thus were allied principally with Christianity. The Sethians, however, seemed to find their sense of uniqueness in opposition to the Church on the grounds just mentioned. Since various groups were not isolated from one another but freely made use of texts and ideas borrowed from other groups, the adoption of Christ into their system was only natural, but did not fundamentally change its basically non-Christian nature and inner cohesion.

2. *The Hypostasis of the Archons.*   Finally, it is also probable that in the mid-second century or slightly later, *Hypostasis of the Archons* reached its present Christianized form, perhaps derived from a hypothetical "Apocalypse of Norea," posited by H.-M. Schenke[10] as the source common to *Hypostasis of the Archons* (II,4) and *On the Origin of the World* (II,5). The prominence in this work of Norea as sister of Seth and offspring and earthly manifestation of Sophia through Eve may have inspired the short treatise *Norea*, which conceives Norea in two levels. She is the upper Sophia who cried out to the Father of the All (i.e., Adamas conceived as Ennoia) and was restored to her place in the ineffable Epinoia (perhaps the Light Eleleth to whom she cries in *Hypostasis of the Archons*) and thus in the divine Autogenes. Yet she is also the lower Sophia manifested as daughter of Eve and wife-sister of Seth who is also yet to be delivered from her deficiency, which will surely be accomplished by the intercession of the four Lights, or their ministers. It is interesting that here Adamas is himself the Father of the All, yet is also called Nous and Ennoia as well as Father of Nous, a set of identifications which recalls the bisexual nature of Adamas as both Father and Mother, or Man and Son of Man (which are perhaps the two names that make the "single name" Man).

In this presentation, I have urged an early dating (125–150 C.E.) for the *Apocalypse of Adam, Hypostasis of the Archons, Norea, Trimorphic Protennoia,* and the longer recension of the *Apocryphon of John;* earlier yet (100–125 C.E.) for the shorter recension, the first two compositional stages of *Trimorphic Protennoia* prior to its Christianization, and source B of the *Apocalypse of Adam;* and a still earlier date (prior to 100 C.E.) for the traditional materials they include: the Sophia myth, the exegesis of Genesis 1–6 and other OT traditions, and an already spiritualized Sethian baptismal rite. Christian influence was at work in all these periods and explicitly so in the last two, while Neopythagorean speculation becomes influential around 100–125 C.E. On the other hand, the polemical use of Christological motifs appears in the last period, 125–150 C.E., when explicit heresiological summaries and refutations of the gnostic systems begin to appear, e.g., Justin's lost *Syntagma*. All these documents stress the movement of salvation from above to below by means of descending redeemer revealers appearing at certain special points in primordial and recent history, bearing *gnōsis* and not infrequently conferring a baptismal rite (not in *Norea* or *Hypostasis of the Archons*).

---

[10] "Sethianism," 596–97.

D. *150–200 C.E.*

Aside from *Allogenes, Zostrianos, Marsanes,* and *Three Steles of Seth,* there are two of the Sethian works which I have not placed in this period: *Melchizedek* and *Gospel of the Egyptians.* The latter seems to me to have taken shape a bit later, somewhere in the second half of the second century, since it seems to presuppose the existence of the extant versions of the *Apocryphon of John, Trimorphic Protennoia,* and the baptismal nomenclature (especially Yesseus Mazareus Yessedekeus) known to the redactor of *Apocalypse of Adam. Melch.* IX,1:16,16–18,7 and 5,17–6,10 also seem to presuppose, especially in its baptismal doxology, the five doxologies in *Gos. Eg.* IV,2:59,13–29; III,2:49,22–50,17; 53,12–54,11; 55,16–56,3; 61,23–62,13. The key element is the mention of Doxomedon as first-born of the Aeons, a name apparently unattested elsewhere except in *Gospel of the Egyptians* and *Zostrianos.*

1. *The Gospel of the Egyptians.* As H.-M. Schenke has suggested, the emphasis of *Gospel of the Egyptians* seems to lie upon baptismal traditions and prayers which conclude it (cf. III,2:64,9–68,1), while the preceding sections seem to function as a mythological justification for them. Indeed the first part of the *Gospel of the Egyptians* seems to be built almost entirely on these five doxologies or presentations of praise which enumerate the origins of the principal transcendent beings of this treatise. These are the great Invisible Spirit, the male virgin Barbelo, the Thrice-Male Child, the male virgin Youel (a double of Barbelo), Esephech the Child of the Child (a double of the Triple Male Child), the great Doxomedon Aeon (containing the last three beings; cf. *Zost.* VIII,1:61,15–21 and *Gos. Eg.* III,2:43,15–16: the great aeon, where the Triple Male Child is), and various other pleromas and aeons. Apparently *Gospel of the Egyptians* understands the Invisible Spirit, Barbelo and the three beings (Thrice-Male Child, Youel and Esephech) contained in the Doxomedon aeon to constitute the Five Seals. This suggests a baptismal context for these doxologies, perhaps also suggesting Schenke's[11] notion of a divine pentad (cf. *Ap. John* II,1:6,2 and *Steles Seth* VII,5,120,20) of names (cf. *Trim. Prot.* XIII,1:49,28–32; "the Five Seals of these particular names") which are invoked in the course of the baptismal ascent (in five stages: robing, baptizing, enthroning, glorifying, rapture into the light, XIII,1:48,15–35). Thus the Son figure of the Father-Mother-Son triad of the *Apocryphon of John* has been subdivided into another Father-Mother-Son triad, leaving the Autogenes Logos dangling in this system, although still produced by the (Invisible) Spirit and

[11] H.-M. Schenke, "Sethianism," 603–4.

Barbelo ("Pronoia") and still establishing the four Lights by his Word. It would appear that the *Gospel of the Egyptians* has combined two traditions. They are the Invisible Spirit-Barbelo-Autogenes triad from the system of the *Apocryphon of John* and *Trimorphic Protennoia*, and another tradition of a pentad, derived from the Sethian baptismal tradition. Strikingly, *Gospel of the Egyptians* also seems to move towards the postulation of another triad (which is possibly developed, for example, by *Allogenes* into the Triple Power) between the Invisible Spirit and Barbelo, namely "the living Silence," an unspecified Father and a Thought (Ennoia, which in turn becomes the Father in the triad, Father/Ennoia, Mother/Barbelo, and Son/Thrice-Male Child). Finally, Adamas seems to occupy a still lower rank, as in the *Apocryphon of John* (where he is produced by Foreknowledge and Mind): Adamas follows and is separated from the Autogenes Logos, and is produced by "Man" (perhaps the Invisible Spirit) and a lower double of Barbelo, Mirothoe. In turn Adam conjoins with Prophania to produce the four Lights and Seth, who conjoins with Plesithea to produce his seed.

Gospel of the Egyptians seems also to know the myth of Sophia from the version found in *Trimorphic Protennoia* according to which a voice from the fourth Light Eleleth urges the production of a ruler for Chaos, initiating the descent of the hylic Sophia cloud, who produces the chief archon Sakla and his partner Nebruel, the makers of twelve aeons and angels and of man. After Sakla's boast and the traditional voice from on high about the Man and Son of Man, a double of Sophia (Metanoia) is introduced to make up for the deficiency in the Aeon of Eleleth due to Sophia's descent. She descends to the world which is called the image of the night, perhaps reflecting an etymology of Eleleth's name, perhaps Lilith or *lēylā* "night," and suggesting that Eleleth is ultimately responsible for the created order.

Gospel of the Egyptians also mentions the three parousias of flood, conflagration and judgment through which Seth passes, which seems to show awareness of the scheme of *Apocalypse of Adam* in its presently redacted form. Again this tradition is set in a baptismal context, since the third descent of Seth serves to establish a baptism through a Logos-begotten body prepared by the virgin (Barbelo?). And indeed this Logos-begotten body turns out to be Jesus, whom Seth puts on, as in *Trim. Prot.* XIII,1:50,12–15 (cf. the Ophite version of this theme in Iren. *Haer.* I.30.12–13).

Finally there is the lengthy list of the various baptismal figures (*Gos. Eg.* III,2:64,9–65,26) and the two concluding hymnic sections (*Gos. Eg.* III,2:66,8–22, and 66,22–68,1) which Böhlig-Wisse have adroitly reconstructed in the form of two separate hymns of five strophes each, perhaps again reflecting the tradition of the Five Seals. In this regard, the Five Seals tradition may even have given rise to the fivefold repetition of the doxologies (enumerated above) constituting the basis of the theogony in the first part of *Gospel of the Egyptians*. The concluding baptismal hymns are strongly Christian in flavor, especially the first one, mentioning Yesseus Mazareus Yessedekeus and, very frequently, Jesus. The list of baptismal figures preceding the prayers reveals a multitude of new figures (most of which show up in the baptismal sections of *Zostrianos*) alongside the more traditional ones, such as Micheus, Michar, Mnesinous, Gamaliel and Samblo (in *Apocalypse of Adam* and *Trimorphic Protennoia*), and Abrasax and Yesseus Mazareus Yessedekeus (in *Apocalypse of Adam*). Also included are Adamas, Seth and his seed, and Jesus residing in the four Lights Harmozel, Oroiael, Davithe, and Eleleth (as in *Apocryphon of John* and *Trimorphic Protennoia*).

Before passing on to the *Allogenes* group of treatises, one should also note the occurrence of Kalyptos in *Gos. Eg.* IV,2:57,16, a name which may be present in translated form also in *Trim. Prot.* XIII,1:38,10 as a cognomen for Barbelo. Likewise in *Gos. Eg.* IV, 2:55,25 there seems to occur the phrase "the First One who appeared," likely a translation of Protophanes (here apparently a cognomen for the Thrice-Male Child), a term occurring also in *Ap. John* II,1:8,32 as a cognomen for Geradamas, further suggesting an original connection between Adamas and the Triple Male Child. Perhaps also Prophania, who in *Gospel of the Egyptians* functions as Adamas' consort in the production of Seth and the four Lights, is a feminine variant of Protophanes, again suggesting the bisexual Adamas, the Son of Man, as the first to appear, doing so in Sethian terms as both female (Mother, Barbelo, the Ennoia of the First Man) and male (the Autogenes Son).

2. *Allogenes and Zostrianos*. *Zostrianos* is heavily indebted to the Sethian *dramatis personae* especially as they occur in *Gospel of the Egyptians*, and collects these into three rather distinct blocks (*Zost.* VIII,1:6; also pp. 29–32 and 47). But the bulk of *Zostrianos* is cast in a truly new scheme and conceptuality, which seems to have been developed independently by the author of *Allogenes* and adopted by *Zostrianos* in a somewhat confused way. This new scheme is the Sethian practice of visionary ascent to the highest levels of the divine world, which seems to be worked out for the first time by the author of *Allogenes* utilizing a large fund of philosophical conceptuality derived from contemporary Platonism, with no traces of Christian content. *Zostrianos* appears to be based on the scheme of visionary ascent and the philosophical conceptuality of *Allogenes*, but it makes a definite

attempt to interpret this ascent in terms of the older tradition of baptismal ascent and its own peculiar *dramatis personae*, especially as they occur in *Gospel of the Egyptians*.

The metaphysical structure of both *Allogenes* and *Zostrianos*, as well as *Three Steles of Seth*, appears to be centered on the triad Father-Mother-Son as is the case with the *Gospel of the Egyptians*, *Apocryphon of John*, and *Trimorphic Protennoia*. In *Zostrianos* this triad is conceived as a vertical hierarchy of beings. The Father at the metaphysical summit (perhaps himself beyond being) is the Invisible Spirit and is accompanied by his Triple Powered One. Below him, the Mother member of the triad is named Barbelo, who herself subsumes a triad of hypostases. The highest of these is Kalyptos, the Hidden One. The next lowest is Protophanes, the First-Appearing One, who has associated with him another being called the Triple Male (Child). The third of the triad is the Son called the divine Autogenes.

So also the various levels of the Aeon of Barbelo, the divine Mind (Nous), are described in terms of their content, again expressed in terms of the Platonic metaphysics of the divine intelligence ("noology"). As the contemplated Mind, Kalyptos contains the paradigmatic ideas or authentic existents; Protophanes, the contemplating Mind, contains a subdivision of the ideas ("those who exist together"), i.e., universal ideas, perhaps "mathematicals," distinguished from the authentic existents by having "many of the same" and being combinable with each other (unlike the authentic existents; cf. Plato, according to Aristot. *Metaph*. I. 6 and XIII. 6), and also distinguished from the ideas of particular things ("the perfect individuals"). The particular ideas ("the [perfect] individuals") are contained in Autogenes, a sort of demiurgic mind (the Logos) who shapes the realm of Nature (*physis*) below. Since the distinction between the "individuals" in Autogenes and "those who exist together" in Protophanes is rather slight for the author of *Allogenes*, the Triple Male Child fits nicely as a sort of mediator between them. This mediating function of the Triple Male also qualifies him for the title of Savior (*Allogenes* XI,3:58,13–15).

The doctrine of the Triple Powered One found in *Allogenes* also occurs in *Three Steles of Seth*, *Marsanes*, and *Zostrianos*. It is clearly the most intriguing feature of these treatises and perhaps the crucial feature by which they can be placed at a definite point in time (and in the Platonic metaphysical tradition). In *Allogenes*, *Three Steles of Seth*, and *Zostrianos*, the Triple Powered One of the Invisible Spirit consists of three modalities: Existence, Vitality or Life, and Mentality or Knowledge (or Blessedness). In its Existence modality, the Triple Powered One is continuous with (i.e., potentially contained within) and indistinguishable from the Invisible Spirit. In its Vitality modality, the Triple Powered One is the boundlessness of the Invisible Spirit proceeding forth in an act of emanation both continuous and discontinuous with the Invisible Spirit and its final product, Barbelo, the self-knowledge of the Invisible Spirit. In its Mentality modality, the Triple Powered One has become bounded as Barbelo, the self-knowledge of the Invisible Spirit. It has taken on form and definition as perceiving subject with the Invisible Spirit as its object of perception.

This is the same doctrine as is found in the anonymous Parmenides commentary (Fragment XIV) ascribed by Hadot to Porphyry,[12] where the Neoplatonic hypostasis Intellect unfolds from the absolute being (to einai) of the pre-existent One in three phases. In each phase the three modalities of the Intellect (namely Existence, Life, and Intelligence) predominate in turn. First as Existence (hyparxis), Intellect is purely potential, resident in and identical with its ideas, the absolute being of the One. In its third phase, Intellect has become identical with the derived being (to on) of Intellect proper (the second Neoplatonic hypostasis) as the hypostatic exemplification of its paradigmatic idea, the absolute being of the One. The transitional phase between the first and third phase of Intellect is called Life and constitutes the median modality of Intellect (boundless thinking). The same idea is also found in Plot. Enn. 6.7. 17,13–26:

> Life, not the life of the One, but a trace of it, looking toward the One was boundless, but once having looked was bounded (without bounding its source). Life looks to the One, and determined by it, takes on bound, limit, form . . . it must then have been determined as (the Life of) a Unity including multiplicity. Each element of multiplicity is determined multiplicity because of Life, but also is a Unity because of limit . . . so Intellect is bounded Life.

What is really original in Allogenes, besides the importation of Platonic metaphysics into Sethianism, is the scheme of visionary ascent experienced by Allogenes. Certainly Sethianism was familiar with accounts of the ecstatic visionary ascents of Enoch, Elijah, Abraham, Jacob, Paul and others contained in Jewish and Christian apocalyptic. Allogenes, however, is distinguished by a Platonically inspired visionary ascent of the individual intellect in which it assimilates itself to the hierarchy of metaphysical levels with which it was aboriginally consubstantial but from which it had become separated.[13] In Allogenes, one undergoes the ascent according to a prescribed sequence of mental states: earthbound vision; ecstatic extraction from body and soul involving a transcending of traditional gnōsis; a silent but unstable seeking of

---

[12] Hadot, Porphyre.
[13] See my "Threefold Path," 341–46 and Williams, "Stability."

oneself; firm standing; and sudden ultimate vision characterized as an ignorant knowledge devoid of any content that might distinguish between subject and contemplated object. Each stage is characterized by increasing self-unification, stability and mental abstraction, a movement away from motion and multiplicity to stability and solitariness.

The prototype of such an experience is found already in Plato's *Symposium* 210A–212A, where Socrates recounts his path to the vision of absolute beauty into which he had been initiated by Diotima. In such mysteries, ultimate vision or *epopteia* was the supreme goal, also expressed as assimilating oneself to God insofar as possible (Plato, *Theatetus*, 176B). This was a traditional quest of religious Platonism not only in Plato, but also later in such figures as Philo (who, however, shunned the notion of total assimilation to God), Numenius, Valentinus, perhaps Albinus, Clement of Alexandria, Origen, and many others besides. In the period under discussion, this tradition culminates in Plotinus.

In such a way, Allogenes achieves a vision of the Aeon of Barbelo and the beings comprising it (*Allogenes* XI,3:57,29–58,26), then transcends his earthly garment and even his own knowledge by means of a vacant ignorance and sees the Mentality, Vitality, and Existence aspects of the Triple Powered One of the Invisible Spirit (XI,3:58,27–60,37). At this point, Allogenes is suddenly filled by a primary revelation of the Unknowable One and his Triple Power (*Allogenes* XI,3:60,37–61,22). The rest of the treatise is mostly devoted to an interpretation of his visionary experience in terms of a negative theology (*Allogenes* XI,3:61, 32–62,13; supplemented by a more positive theology, XI,3:62,14–67,20). This negative theology contains a nearly word-for-word parallel with the one found in the beginning of the *Apocryphon of John*: *Allogenes* XI,3:62,28–63,23=*Ap. John* II,1:3,18–35=BG8502,2:23,3–26,13. *Allogenes* is thus likely to have borrowed from the *Apocryphon of John*.

E. 200–300 C.E.

When one realizes that *Allogenes* and *Zostrianos* are probably to be included in the "apocalypses of Zoroaster and Zostrianos and Nicotheus and Allogenes and Messos and those of other such figures" (Porph. *Vit. Plot.* 16) whose stance was attacked by Plotinus and whose doctrines were refuted at great length by Amelius and Porphyry himself in the period 244–269 C.E., one may date *Allogenes* around 200 C.E., with *Zostrianos* coming a bit later around 225 C.E. (Porphyry certainly recognized it as a spurious and recent work). *Allogenes* is also to be included among the various Sethian works under the name of Allogenes mentioned by Epiphanius around 375 C.E. (*Pan.* 39.5.1; 40.2.2). Furthermore, Plotinus, in his antignostic polemic (*Enn.* 3.8; 5.8; 5.5 and 2.9, tractates

30–33 in chronological order, which constitute the original complete antignostic tractate recognized by Harder, "Schrift Plotins"), probably has these tractates in view.

1. *Zostrianos.* While *Allogenes* (like *Three Steles of Seth*) takes no interest at all in the realm of Nature below Autogenes (mentioned only once at *Allogenes* XI,3:51,28–32 as containing failures rectified by Autogenes), *Zostrianos* and *Marsanes* do treat this realm. They seem to enumerate six levels of being below Autogenes, called the thirteen cosmic aeons (i.e., the world), the airy earth, the copies *(antitypoi* made by the Archon) of the Aeons, the Transmigration *(paroikēsis)*; the Repentance *(metanoia)* and the "self-begotten ones" (plural). Although it is unclear in *Zostrianos* as it now stands, the Untitled Text of the Bruce Codex (Schmidt-MacDermot, *Bruce Codex,* 263,11–264,6) allows us to conjecture that "the self-begotten ones" constitute the level at which *Zostrianos* is baptized in the name of Autogenes. It contains the Living Water (Yesseus Mazareus Yessedekeus), the baptizers Micheus, Michar (and Mnesinous), the purifier Barpharanges, a figure called Zogenethlos and, besides these, the four Lights Harmozel, Oroiael, Davithe, and Eleleth, together with Sophia. In *Zostrianos,* Adamas is found in Harmozel; Seth, Emmacha Seth and Esephech the Child of the Child, in Oroiael; and the seed of Seth, in Davithe. In addition, certain triads of beings are either residents in or cognomens of the four Lights (*Zost.* VIII,1:127,16–128,7). It is unclear whether the repentant souls (of the historical Sethians?) are contained in Eleleth, as would be expected, or in the level of Metanoia immediately below the self-begotten ones. It appears also that the figures of Meirothea (*Zost.* VIII,1:30,14–15) and Plesithea (*Zost.*VIII,1:51,12) and Prophania (*Zost.*VIII,1:6,31) also belong to the self-begotten ones. It seems that in comparison to *Allogenes,* *Zostrianos* really is guilty of multiplying hypostases, but these are no doubt derived from the Sethian baptismal tradition, not only from free invention. It seems fair, then, to see *Zostrianos* as a derivative from *Allogenes* and *Gospel of the Egyptians.*

2. *The Three Steles of Seth.* The *Three Steles of Seth* clearly represents the same system as *Allogenes;* yet it is constructed as a triptych of presentations of praise and blessing to Autogenes, Barbelo, and the pre-existent One in connection with a communal practice of a three-stage ascent and descent. After an initial revelation and various blessings rendered by Seth (*Steles Seth* VII,5:118:25–120,28) who praises the bisexual Geradamas as Mirothea (his mother) and Mirotheos (his father), the rest of the treatise uses the first person plural for ascribing praise to (1) the Triple Male, (2) to Barbelo who arose from the Triple Powered One (characterized by being, living and knowing, and is also called Kalyptos and Protophanes), and (3) to the pre-existent One who is

characterized by the existence-life-mind triad. The whole concludes with a rubric (*Steles Seth* VII,5:126,32–127,22) that explains the use of the steles in the practice of descent from the third to the second to the first; likewise, the way of ascent is the way of descent. The fact that the method of descent is mentioned first is strange (one notes that the Jewish Merkabah mystics called themselves Yordē Merkabah, "descenders to the Merkabah"). Another instance of the interdependence of these texts is a common prayer tradition: *Steles Seth* VII,5:125,23–126,17, *Allogenes* XI,3:54,11–37 and *Zost.* VIII,1:51,24–52,24; 86,13–88,bottom.

3. *Marsanes.* Last of all, *Marsanes* and the Untitled Text of the Bruce Codex should be mentioned as probably the latest of the Sethian treatises that we possess. Like *Zostrianos* and *Allogenes*, *Marsanes* records the visionary experience of a singular individual, probably to be regarded as one of the many manifestations of Seth. B. A. Pearson in his fine introduction to this tractate,[14] suggests that the name Marsanes, mentioned in the Untitled Text of the Bruce Codex (Schmidt-Mac-Dermot, *Bruce Codex*, 235,13–23) in connection with Nicotheos (and Marsianos by Epiphanius [*Pan.* 40.7.6] in his account of the Archontics), reflects a Syrian background for its author, and dates *Marsanes* in the early third century. But one might argue for dating it to the last quarter of the third century since it indeed posits an unknown Silent One above even the Invisible Spirit, in much the same way as Iamblichus during the same period posited an "Ineffable" beyond even the One of Plotinus.

As mentioned previously, the first ten pages of *Marsanes* present a visionary ascent to, and descent from, the highest level of the divine world. They depict the same basic structure as *Allogenes*, but with the omission of the Triple Male and the addition of at least the Repentance (perhaps in unrecoverable parts of the text one would find mention of the Transmigration and Antitypes) and the "cosmic" and "material" levels. From page 55 onward one notes the occurrence of a few baptismal terms, such as "wash," "seal," and perhaps "[Living] Water" (*Marsanes* X,1:65,22). Indeed the entire perceptible and intelligible universe is structured according to a hierarchy of thirteen seals. Aside from the narrative of the unfolding of Barbelo from the Triple Powered One (of the unknown Silent One, or of the Invisible Spirit?) and the plentiful occurrence of Platonic metaphysical terms such as "being," "non-being," "truly existing," "partial," "whole," "sameness," "difference" (esp. *Marsanes* X,1:4,24–5,5), one learns that Marsanes has not only come to know the intelligible world, but also that "the sense-perceptible world is [worthy] of being saved entirely" (X,1:5,22–26), an idea quite in line with *Allogenes* as well. These texts, *Allogenes*, *Zostrianos*, *Three*

---

[14] Pearson, *Codices IX and X*, 229–50.

Steles of Seth, and *Marsanes*, which I call the "*Allogenes* group," all exhibit a tendency not only toward an ontological monism, but also, save perhaps in the case of *Zostrianos* with its Sophia myth, a rather positive attitude toward the sense-perceptible world, the realm of Nature. Even *Zostrianos*, which affirms the existence of the demiurgic work of the Archon, its artificiality and its death-threatening bondage, concludes: "Release yourselves, and that which has bound you will be dissolved. Save yourselves, in order that it may be saved" (VIII,1:131,10–12).

4. *The Untitled Text of the Bruce Codex.* Finally, as previously mentioned, the Untitled Text of the Bruce Codex also belongs among the Sethian treatises, and seems to have affinity mostly with *Zostrianos* and *Gospel of the Egyptians*. It is almost entirely devoted to an elaborate cosmology involving the transcendent Sethian *dramatis personae* arranged into various levels and groups called "fatherhoods" and "deeps" consisting of myriads of powers. It narrates the descent of the light-spark and Christ through Setheus, bearing a salvation which seems to be effected by the baptismal rite already discussed. It is by all standards a most complex work defying any simple analysis. I can do no more than state that Schmidt[15] has dated it to the end of the second century, although I would be inclined to put it a bit later, around 350 C.E., but for no reason other than its extraordinary prolixity in comparison with the other Sethian treatises.

IV. Conclusion

It may be that the Sethians' gradual shift away from their original communal baptismal context, interpreted by means of a rich history of their primordial origins and salvation, towards the more ethereal and individualistic practice of visionary ascent contributed to the eventual decay and diffusion of those who identified with the Sethian traditions. Around 375 C.E., Epiphanius has difficulty recalling where he had encountered Sethians, and says that they are not to be found everywhere, but now only in Egypt and Palestine, although fifty years before they had spread as far as Greater Armenia (*Pan.* 39.1.1–2; 40.1). Perhaps the burgeoning pressure of officially sanctioned Christianity after Constantine drove them away from their former community centers. Their initial rapprochement with Christian ideas, alternating between positive in the case of *Apocryphon of John*, *Hypostasis of the Archons* and *Melchizedek*, and more negative and polemical in the case of *Trimorphic Protennoia*, *Gospel of the Egyptians*, and the *Apocalypse of Adam*, may have proved a liability. While Christological concepts could

---

[15] Schmidt, *Schriften*, 664.

clearly depict the eschatological advent of Seth in their own era, to adopt these meant also to reinterpret them in a Sethian way and thus challenge a more "orthodox" Christological interpretation. Although this preserved for a time their separate conscious identity as an elect body, in the long run it must have earned the hostility of the increasingly better organized, institutional, "orthodox" church. Certainly influential church fathers holding powerful positions in the church singled out the Sethians along with many others for attack. At first, this attack was perhaps rather pedantic, sarcastic, and theoretical, but in the case of a Tertullian or later an Epiphanius, it could become brutal and libelous. Though thrust away by the church, many Sethians no doubt held on to their own version of Christianized salvation history, but concentrated more and more on spiritualizing it along a vertical, transcendent axis. Such an emphasis on vertical transcendence at the expense of a sense of primordial history must have weakened their sense of traditional historical grounding and communal solidarity.

The final stage seems achieved in the *Allogenes* group, where the Sethians, if they thus identified themselves any longer, moved into rapprochement with pagan Platonism. Epiphanius tells us that the Archontic branch of Sethianism had rejected baptism and the sacraments associated with the church. This happened possibly around the inauguration of the Sassanide era, the time of the vision and mission of Mani, who also rejected baptism. Without some cultic or communal form of this rite, individual Sethians were left to their own devices. An increasing emphasis on self-performable techniques of spiritual ascent with its attendant possibilities for individualism possibly entailed a further weakening of communal awareness traditionally grounded in ritual and primordial history. While initially welcomed into Platonic circles, their insistence on enumerating and praising their traditional divine beings with hymns, glossalalia, and other forms of ecstatic incantation must have irritated more sober Platonists such as Plotinus, Porphyry and Amelius. Although the Platonists initially regarded the Sethians as friends, soon they too, like the heresiologists of the church, began writing pointed and lengthy attacks upon them for distorting the teaching of Plato which they adapted to depict their own spiritual world and the path toward assimilation with it. This rejection, coupled with the official sanction of Christianity under Constantine and the attendant pressure against the very paganism the Sethians had turned to, may have contributed to the fragmentation of the Sethian community into a multitude of sectarian groups (e.g., Audians, Borborites, Archontics; perhaps Phibionites, Stratiotici, and Secundians), some of which survived into the Middle Ages—a true scattering of the seed of Seth!

A photograph of the Nag Hammadi Codices taken by Jean Doresse in Cairo in 1949 prior to their early conservation in plexiglass by Martin Krause and Pahor Labib. *Institute for Antiquity and Christianity at Claremont, California (IAC) photo.*

Outside of the cover of Nag Hammadi Codex II. It is the most decorated of the leather covers. *IAC photo by Peggy Hedrick.*

In the courtyard of the Coptic Museum James M. Robinson and Charles W. Hedrick confer on a reading in Nag Hammadi Codex VI: The *Acts of Peter and the Twelve Apostles. IAC photo by Peggy Hedrick.*

Charles W. Hedrick at work in the Coptic Museum in Cairo on the reconstructed papyrus roll of Codex IV. *IAC photo by Peggy Hedrick.*

Behind the modern quarry (white area near the center of the picture) lie the "crocodile caves," where, at the beginning of this century, a discovery of papyri stuffed inside mummified crocodiles is reported. *IAC photo by Peggy Hedrick.*

Columns from the ancient Basilica of St. Pachomius lie scattered about the surface of the ground. In modern times the site served as a threshing floor for the village of Faw Qibli. Wheat is still winnowed as in biblical times. *IAC photo.*

In the background: the Jabal al-Tarif, the awesome cliff face at the base of which the Nag Hammadi Codices were discovered; in the foreground: three shadoofs, part of a primitive system of irrigation still in use in Upper Egypt. *IAC photo by Peggy Hedrick.*

The east wall of Tomb 8, cleared during the first and second seasons of excavation at the Jabal al-Tarif, was inscribed with the beginning lines of psalms, perhaps as a memory aid for monks who meditated in the cool tombs in the heat of the day. *IAC photo by Peggy Hedrick.*

PART II
GNOSTICISM, NEW TESTAMENT,
AND EARLY CHRISTIAN LITERATURE

4

GNOSTICISM AND
THE CHURCH OF JOHN'S GOSPEL

George W. MacRae †

Educated at Boston College, Johns Hopkins, and Cambridge University, George MacRae was Stillman Professor of Roman Catholic Studies at Harvard Divinity School from 1973 until his untimely death on 6 September 1985.

Professor MacRae served on the Editorial Board for the Hermeneia commentary series, was an editor for *New Testament Abstracts*, and had contributed articles to professional journals throughout his prestigious career. As an active member of professional societies like the international Studiorum Novi Testamenti Societas (member of the editorial board), the Council on the Study of Religion (vice-chairman, 1969–74), and the Society of Biblical Literature (Executive-Secretary), Professor MacRae offered invaluable counsel to sections of the academic community.

Preface

This presentation to the Working Seminar is a contribution to the discussion of "Primitive Christianity and Gnosticism." It focuses on issues in the scholarly discussion of possible Gnostic influences on the Gospel of John and Johannine Christianity, giving principal attention to points at which the Nag Hammadi Gnostic texts shed light on the issues. The Fourth Gospel has long been a pivotal text for investigating the interaction of Gnosticism and Christianity. This presentation does not aim at surveying the vast literature on the topic nor at arguing in detail the case, which it espouses, for Gnostic influence. Instead it lists a number of areas, some based on previous research, others programmatic suggestions for further study, in which the issue of Gnostic influence warrants discussion. The following points are raised:

(1) The relationship between the language and imagery of the Johannine Prologue and the Gnostic mythological structure of the Nag Hammadi tractate *Trimorphic Protennoia*.

(2) The genre of revelation discourse which is shared by John and many Gnostic writings.

(3) Patterns of Gnostic and Johannine Christology and soteriology.

(4) The theme of becoming children of the Father by virtue of revelation of the Father in the Son, a theme common to John and the *Gospel of Truth.*

(5) Johannine and Gnostic dualism, which of itself and in isolation is not seen as compelling evidence of Gnostic influence.

(6) The possible Gnostic interaction of the Johannine Christians who were rejected by the author of the First Epistle of John.

(7) As a suggestion for further study, the relationship of the Gnostic and the Johannine debt to the wisdom tradition.

I. Introduction

This presentation is intended to be a survey of selected issues in the discussion of the Fourth Gospel and Gnosticism. The title, however, may be somewhat misleading. It was chosen to be broadly representative of the relationship between the Johannine tradition and Gnosticism, not to focus on questions of Johannine ecclesiology as such. These latter questions depend, among other things, on different types of source and redaction criticism. The amount of modern scholarly literature that deals with John and Gnosticism is enormous and it is as diverse in its conclusions as one might imagine. It is by no means the intention of this brief survey to catalogue such literature. In fact, the viewpoint adopted here is that the study of Gnostic texts is indeed relevant to the under-standing of the Fourth Gospel, and that decision eliminates from the survey, though not of course from serious consideration, a good deal of the literature.

Since the work of Rudolf Bultmann in particular, the question of a relationship of the Fourth Gospel to Gnosticism has been a burning one and is well-reflected in commentaries, monographs, and the voluminous periodical literature. Consequently the chief focus of this presentation will be on what the discovery of the Nag Hammadi Gnostic texts has added to the discussion. No wholly new hypotheses will be propounded here, but what is suggested is presented in the hope that scholarly discussion may elicit points of consensus or clear rejection. As is well known, the Gospel of John has variously been characterized as Gnostic, gnosticizing, anti-Gnostic, or totally immune from the Gnostic debate. Are there any objective criteria for deciding among such options?

II. The Context of the Johannine Prologue

The most clearly focused and concrete contribution to the discussion of a possible Gnostic background to the Fourth Gospel is the suggestion that the Johannine Prologue is related to the mythological scheme of the Nag Hammadi *Trimorphic Protennoia* NHC XIII,1. We owe this suggestion to the work of the *Berliner Arbeitskreis für die koptisch-gnostische Schriften*[1] and in particular to the dissertation of Gesine Schenke.[2] Perhaps the discussion of this whole issue needs to go back to the observation of Bultmann that the figure of the Logos, especially in John 1:5, can be explained only by a mythological (i.e., Gnostic) context, not by a philosophical or even quasi-philosophical one.[3] The (apparently Sethian) Gnostic work *Trimorphic Protennoia* shows the concept of Logos as a revealer figure set in the context of a complex of divine emanations (apparently non-Christian despite the superficial and most likely secondary Christianization of the text): Voice, Sound, Word. The parallel is strengthened by a substantial list of common epithets including life, light, and others.[4] The heart of the argument invokes a principle that may be of wider significance in the comparison of ancient texts: "One has the impression that the relevant statements of *Protennoia* stand in their natural context, whereas their parallels in the Johannine prologue . . . seem to have been artificially made serviceable to a purpose really alien to them."[5] In any case, it is easier to envisage the spread of the relevant attributes in the Gnostic work as original, than to suppose that the author dismantled the narrowly focused Prologue of the Fourth Gospel to spread the attributes throughout a much broader mythological context. It is important to note here that no one seriously argues that the Fourth Gospel is indebted to the Nag Hammadi tractate as to a literary work. Clearly both are dependent on developments of the wisdom tradition and may simply have had a common ancestor. But whether that ancestor is already a Gnostic modification of the wisdom tradition is the question at stake.

---

[1] G. Schenke, "'Dreigestaltige Protennoia.'"

[2] "Protennoia." See also Colpe, "Überlieferung." The whole debate on this issue is treated by Robinson, "Sethians."

[3] *John*, 19–31.

[4] For lists of the alleged parallels see Robinson, "Sethians."

[5] G. Schenke, "'Dreigestaltige Protennoia,'" 733; translation by Robinson, "Sethians," 651.

III. The Revelation Discourse Genre

In a lucid and informative book Pheme Perkins has analyzed the form
and function of the Gnostic dialogue as a distinctive literary genre.[6] She
frequently deals with Gnostic interpretation of Johannine dialogic passages but does not investigate Gnostic influence on the Johannine
material. Such an investigation might indeed prove interesting, however. Here I would like to suggest a somewhat different genre of
discourse that is shared by both the Fourth Gospel and the Gnostic
sources. The model was sketched by Bultmann and in more detail by his
student Heinz Becker, whose dissertation was posthumously published
by Bultmann.[7] Becker attempted to account for the major discourses of
the Fourth Gospel by appeal to a (somewhat ideal) form of Gnostic
discourse (*Offenbarungsrede*) consisting of self-predication ("*Autodox-
ologie*") in the "I-style," invitation or call to decision, and promise of
reward or threat of punishment—all three elements loosely organized in
repetitive or "spiral" form and set against a background of cosmic
dualism. Though this style of discourse has its roots in the wisdom
tradition, it nevertheless seems to be a distinctively Gnostic genre. It is
represented in the Nag Hammadi collection in numerous works such as
Thunder NHC VI,2; the *Trimorphic Protennoia* XIII,1; the longer
ending of the *Apocryphon of John* NHC II,1:30,11–31,25, and others. It is
noteworthy that some of these examples show either no Christian
influence or at best a merely superficial Christianization.

   That this discourse genre appears in the Fourth Gospel in numerous
passages is quite clear (e.g., 6:35–51b; 8:12–47; 10:7–18). Frequently the
Gospel examples show the revelation discourses embedded in dialogues, but the similarity to what Becker described and to what we find
in many Nag Hammadi examples is clear. It should be noted that there
is no suggestion here that the Fourth Evangelist used a Gnostic revelation discourse as a *source* for the discourses of Jesus, but only that in
the composition of them he was influenced by the Gnostic genre.

IV. The Patterns of Christology and Soteriology

The most widely discussed claim of Gnostic influence in the Fourth
Gospel is in the area of Christology and soteriology, and in this survey
we can only allude to the discussion. Since the work of Bultmann many
have taken the Gnostic background of Johannine thought for granted;

---

[6] *Gnostic Dialogue.*
[7] *Reden.*

others have continued to emphasize the non-Gnostic elements of the Gospel. In any case, the Gospel portrays Christ as a pre-existent, in some sense divine, figure who descends from the world of the Father into the created world for the purpose of offering salvation to humanity by revealing the Father. Apart from the question of the origin of this type of thought, one must recognize the fact that it resembles nothing in the ancient world so much as the Gnostic revealer myth. The very concept of salvation as revelation to be appropriated by knowledge (John 17:3) is universally characteristic of Gnosticism and, in the New Testament, unique to the Fourth Gospel.[8] Here there are no metaphors of redemption, reconciliation, justification, sacrifice, and the like, but only the word of revelation.

It is possible to assume a radical position and assert that the Fourth Gospel is in this respect a thoroughgoing Gnostic reinterpretation of Jesus.[9] I am more inclined to side with Bultmann in the debate and see the notion of incarnation (John 1:14) and the reality of Jesus' death as brakes upon the tendency toward a consistent Gnostic view. However Gnostic its language and thought-structures, the Fourth Gospel is not docetic. Recent contributions to the discussion have tended to reinforce the Gnostic debt of the Evangelist without abandoning the idea that the Gospel falls short of outright Gnosticism and docetism.[10]

V. Children of the Father

The Nag Hammadi *Gospel of Truth* NHC I,3 affords an interesting parallel to an aspect of the Fourth Gospel that is not often alluded to. This Gnostic gospel clearly makes use of much of the New Testament by implicit quotations, exegesis of passages, and allusions. But a recent commentator has remarked that it is not clear that the work is familiar with the Gospel of John despite the fact that it contains some notable parallels to that Gospel (e.g., Christ as Logos, the Christology of the name).[11] The point of interest here is the way in which the *Gospel of Truth*, ostensibly a meditation on the role of Christ as Son and name of the Father, really focuses on the Gnostics themselves as children of the Father. Christ is the revealer of the Father, to be sure, but he is also a

---

[8] In addition to Bultmann's commentary see the excellent study of Forestell, *Word*.

[9] See among others Käsemann, *Testament*.

[10] See H.-M. Schenke, "Christologie." In the same volume Fischer ("Christus") argued for Gnostic influence on the basis of an exegesis of John 10 seen as best understood against the background of a typical Gnostic myth. This fascinating article confronts us with the classic question of whether a passage is written against a Gnostic background or is merely capable of a consistent Gnostic interpretation.

[11] Ménard, *L'Évangile de Vérité*, 8.

paradigm for the Gnostic. At the conclusion of the work the author says of the Gnostics:

> They rest in him who is at rest, not striving nor being involved in the search for truth. But they themselves are the truth; and the Father is within them and they are in the Father. . . . And his children are perfect and worthy of his name, for he is the Father: it is children of this kind that he loves.[12]

In the dynamic of the work the Gnostics become children of the Father by virtue of Christ's revealing the Father to them in himself.

The resemblance to the Fourth Gospel is close. The Prologue announces the theme in 1:12: "But to all who received him, who believed in his name, he gave power to become children of God." The body of the Gospel does not return to this theme of being children of God until the revelation of the Father by Jesus is complete (cf. 14:8–11; as part of the farewell discourses this passage is a proleptic comment on the passion narrative). In the resurrection appearance to Mary Magdalene the Johannine Jesus dramatically transforms the Easter message to say: "Go to my brethren and say to them, I am ascending to my Father and your Father, to my God and your God" (20:17). Those who believe in Jesus have become children of God.

The notion of a filial relationship to God is not, of course, unique to the Fourth Gospel in the New Testament. There is for example the importance of adoptive sonship in the theology of Paul. But the parallel between the Gospel of John and the *Gospel of Truth*, if indeed the latter is not dependent on the former, may be significant precisely in the role of revelation of the Father in bringing about the kinship.

VI. Dualism

Underlying most of the points raised so far is the much-discussed issue of Johannine dualism, which has been compared variously with Platonic thought, Qumran speculation, and, of course, Gnosticism. Taken in isolation, this issue is not in my view decisive for determining Gnostic influence on the Fourth Gospel, no matter how suggestive are the Johannine dualistic statements (e.g., 3:31; 8:23; etc.).[13] Though I think it probable that the dualistic pattern of Johannine thought is indebted to contemporary Gnostic ideas, it is clear that the Fourth Gospel has adapted a cosmic dualism to its own purposes, which are not ultimately

---

[12] NHC I, 3:42,21–28; 43,19–24.

[13] On this issue and other aspects of Gnostic influence on the Fourth Gospel, see the thesis of Langbrandtner, *Weltferner Gott*.

Gnostic. The rift between the world of light, the world above, the world of the Father on one hand, and on the other the world of darkness, the below, the fleshly, is not in the Fourth Gospel unbridgeable. The assertion that "God so loved the world that he gave his only Son" (3:16) is difficult to imagine in a thoroughly Gnostic context. If the Fourth Evangelist derived his dualistic perspective from contemporary Gnostic speculation, he clearly transposed it onto an ethical plane: "And this is the judgment, that the light has come into the world, and men loved darkness rather than light, because their deeds were evil" (3:19). Though the dualism of John by itself is not clear evidence of Gnostic influence, it may be very significant in the context of other arguments for such influence.

VII. The Johannine Church

There is at least one further stage that one should investigate in the study of the relationship of the Fourth Gospel to the Gnostic tradition, namely the role of the First (and Second) Epistle of John in the subsequent history of the Johannine community.[14] Without taking a clear position, I wish only to suggest some lines for further research. Everyone is agreed that the First Epistle rejects a docetic interpretation of the Gospel, but there remains disagreement about whether the interpretation of the Gospel among those Johannine Christians whom the Epistle opposes is already Gnostic or only tending in that direction. I am inclined to the former alternative—on the grounds that non-Gnostic docetism is difficult to identify in the early second century C.E. In my view, the Gospel itself clearly favors a Gnostic interpretation—and that was historically the case as we know from such Valentinian interpreters as Heracleon and Ptolemy. But whether the radical wing of the community itself was in fact Gnostic remains debatable.

VIII. Wisdom, Gnosticism, Johannism

It is clear from the foregoing survey that the root problem in identifying the background of the Fourth Gospel is the fact that the Jewish wisdom tradition can be used to account for much of what some interpreters regard as Gnostic. The real issue then becomes: is the Fourth Gospel an independent development from the wisdom tradition or is it part of a

---

[14] See Brown, *Community of the Beloved Disciple* and *Johannine Epistles*; Perkins, *The Johannine Epistles*.

larger movement of speculation in which Gnosticism also reinterprets wisdom? I suggest that this remains the central issue in Johannine studies, and the weight given to specifically Gnostic adaptations of wisdom, in comparison with the Fourth Gospel, will be determinative of the history of religions question.

5

GNOSTIC SAYINGS AND CONTROVERSY TRADITIONS IN JOHN 8:12-59

Helmut Koester

Professor Helmut Koester holds the significant distinction of being both the John H. Morison Professor of New Testament Studies and the Winn Professor of Ecclesiastical History at Harvard University. Born in Germany, Professor Koester studied under such noted scholars as Rudolf Bultmann, Heinrich Frick, and Wilhelm Mauer, and taught at the University of Heidelberg. In addition to academic service Professor Koester has also served as a minister to several congregations of the Lutheran Church.

A recognized authority on the history of early Christianity and its religious environment, Professor Koester has written many scholarly and professional journal articles, encyclopaedia entries, and books. His most recent major publication is a two-volume introduction to the New Testament.

His academic service has been marked by distinguished roles as the Chairman of the Committee on Advanced Degrees at Harvard, an Associate Trustee of the American Schools of Oriental Research, and a Trustee of the Albright Institute of Archaeological Research. He is a member of such notable professional societies as Studiorum Novi Testamenti Societas, the Society of Biblical Literature, and is a Fellow of the American Academy of Arts and Sciences. He is also Chairman of the New Testament Editorial committee of Hermeneia and Editor of the *Harvard Theological Review*.

Preface

The origin and composition of the Johannine discourses and dialogues are still among the major unsolved problems of New Testament scholarship. Rudolf Bultmann had argued for a major written source of revelation discourses that was used by the author of the Fourth Gospel.[1] This theory has been rejected almost unanimously by subse-

---

[1] Bultmann, *John*. The German original was first published in 1941.

quent scholarship. More recent commentators usually acquiesce in describing the elements of the characteristic style of these discourses and treat them as a whole as compositions of the author.[2] The effort to identify traditional sayings of Jesus incorporated in these discourses has so far brought very limited results because the Synoptic Gospels were used as the primary criterion in this search.[3] As I have argued elsewhere,[4] it seems to me that comparison with apocryphal gospels such as *Papyrus Egerton 2*, the *Gospel of Thomas*,[5] the *Dialogue of the Savior*, and the *Apocryphon of James* can give us some clues for understanding the process of composition of the Johannine discourses and for identifying the traditional sayings utilized in their composition.

In this study, I propose to use John 8:12–59 as a test case for two reasons. (1) Parallels to this chapter frequently occur in gospels of the Nag Hammadi corpus, especially in the *Gospel of Thomas*. (2) This Johannine section contains controversies of Jesus with his Jewish opponents. These controversies are of the same type as those of John 5:39–47 which are paralleled by a section of the "Unknown Gospel," i.e., they could possibly be identified as materials drawn from a written source.[6]

I. Composition of the Passage

Traditionally, the unit John 8:12–59 has been viewed as highly problematical and disjointed. Bultmann split this section into nine disparate smaller units which he assigned to various sections in his attempt to reconstruct the original order of John's Gospel.[7] Brown says: "An analysis of the structure of ch. viii (12ff.) is perhaps more difficult than that of any other chapter or discourse in the first part of the Gospel."[8] One may wonder, however, whether the interpreters have asked the right question. Well-organized discourses, like the discourse on the bread that has come down from heaven in John 6, have led to the assumption that the

[2] Cf. Brown, *John*, 1. cxxxii–cxxxvii (with literature).
[3] Dodd, *Historical Tradition*, 335–420.
[4] Cf. my *Introduction*, 2. 178–85; and my articles "Dialog und Sprachüberlieferung"; "Gnostic Writings."
[5] Brown ("The Gospel of Thomas") investigated in detail the parallels to the Gospel of John in the *Gospel of Thomas*, but he simply assigned these parallels to Johannine influence upon the second, i.e., gnostic, source of the latter Gospel. In his commentary, Brown repeatedly refers to those parallels in the *Gospel of Thomas*, but does not draw any consequences for the analysis of the Johannine discourses.
[6] Cf. my article "Apocryphal and Canonical Gospels."
[7] Cf. his *John*, passim. The various segments of 8:12–59 appear in the following order and context: 7:19–24; 8:13–20; 6:60–7:14; 7:25–29; 8:48–50; 8:54–55; 7:37–44; 7:31–36; 7:45–52; 8:41–47; 8:51–53; 8:56–59; 9:1–41; 8:12; 12:44–50; 8:21–29; 12:34–36; 10:1–12:32; 8:30–40.
[8] Brown, *John*, 1. 342. Cf. his comment on the first part of this section (p. 343): "Yet, within 12–20 the thought skips and jumps."

primary criteria of organization must be cohesion and logical progress of
the argument. The author may have achieved that in some of the
Johannine discourses, but the first stage in the process of composition
was the collection of originally independent smaller units which did not
necessarily have the same thematic orientation. Different sections of the
Gospel of John indeed represent very different stages of development
along the trajectory from the collection of oral materials to the composition of coherent literary units.[9] John 8:12–59 may belong to a comparatively early stage in this process. If this is the case, the more original
units will be more clearly recognizable in this chapter. Its disjointed
appearance, then, is simply an indication of a more original stage in the
development of this literature. It is, therefore, not surprising that materials used here for the composition are still more easily recognizable
than in other chapters of this Gospel.

The section begins with one of the characteristic *egō eimi* "I am" self-
predications of Jesus, followed by a promise:

I am the light of the world.
He who follows after me, will not walk in the darkness,
but will have the light of life. (John 8:12)

The structure of this self-predication (recognition formula)[10] and the
promise are exactly the same as in John 6:35:[11]

I am the bread of life.
He who comes to me, will not hunger,
and he who believes in me, will never thirst.

It has not been possible to demonstrate that sayings with the "I am"
formula in the Gospel of John are traditional.[12] Rather, one must assume
that the author of the Fourth Gospel employs the formula in order to
reshape, as self-predications of Jesus, materials which were available to
him in a different form. In John 6:35, such materials are at his disposal in
the form of a midrash on the manna from heaven. But for the metaphor
of the light utilized in the self-predication of 8:12, no such OT materials
are available. The fundamental contrast between light and darkness that

---

[9] I am referring to the model of composition in several stages, suggested by Brown. Cf.
his *John*, 1. xxxiv–xxxix; id. *Community of the Beloved Disciple*, 17–24.

[10] Cf. Bultmann, *John*, on John 6:35.

[11] Cf. also 10:9; 11:25; 16:5. There are several modifications of this formula: 6:51; 10:7,
11, 14; 14:6; 15:1. All of these are products of the author of the Fourth Gospel.

[12] Becker (*Reden*) has demonstrated that the form of the "promise" is clearly
traditional. But he is less convincing in his attempt to show the traditional character of
the *Johannine* "I am" formula—notwithstanding the fact that self-predications are, of
course, widespread in the religions of the time. See on the whole question Brown, *John*,
1. 535–38.

appears here has parallels in the literature from Qumran,[13] but it is
missing in the sayings of Jesus in the Synoptic Gospels.[14] It can be found,
however, in sayings of Jesus preserved in writings from Nag Hammadi.
Compare the following:

Dial. Sav. III,5:127,1–6

If one does not [. . . the] darkness, he will [not] be able
to see [the light]. Therefore [I] tell you [. . . of the]
light is the darkness. [And if one does not] stand in [the
darkness, he will not be able] to see the light.

Gospel of Thomas logion 24:

There is light within a man of light,
and he lights up the whole world.
If he does not shine, he is darkness.

That such sayings were known to the author of the Fourth Gospel is
evident from John 11:9–10:

If someone walks in the day, he does not stumble,
because he sees the light of this world. But if someone walks in the night, he stumbles, because the light
is not in him.[15]

In John 8:12, the fundamental contrast ("not walk in the darkness"—
"have the light of life") corresponds to the contrast expressed in these
sayings. One can, therefore, assume that the entire "I am" saying,
together with the promise, is a Johannine reformulation of a traditional
saying about light and darkness.

The subsequent discussion about Jesus' martyria "testimony" continues earlier debates of Jesus with his opponents in the Gospel of John,
in particular the debate of John 5:35–47.[16] It seems to me that all
discussions about the martyria ultimately rely upon traditions originating in the debates of the early Johannine community with its Palestinian Jewish opponents. References to Scripture, Moses, the Law, and
to John the Baptist dominate these traditions.[17] The close relationship to

---

[13] Brown, John, 1.340.

[14] "You are the light of the world" (Matt 5:14) uses the word "light" only as an image,
but lacks the contrast of light and darkness as metaphors for the realms of good and evil.

[15] Variants of this saying are present in John 12:35f.; 9:4. It is typical for the style of
such sayings that they play with the ambiguity of the metaphor and shift from its use as
an "image" to its understanding as a principal metaphysical designation. Cf. also 1 Thess
5:4–6.

[16] Bultmann (John, on 8:13–20) considers the section beginning with 8:13 as the
conclusion of the complex comprising John 5:1–47 and 7:15–24.

[17] On the "midrashic" structure of these traditions, cf. Martyn, Fourth Gospel.
Although the term martyria is typically Johannine, it is hardly a creation of the author of
the Gospel. It also occurs in this context in Papyrus Egerton 2; see below.

these traditions is also evident in the formulation of John 8:14a ("And even if I testify to myself, my testimony is true")—a deliberate contradiction to John 5:31 ("If I testified to myself, my testimony would not be true"). For one portion of the debate about *martyria* in 5:31–47, there is external confirmation for the hypothesis that the author of John was using older, and indeed written materials. *Papyrus Egerton 2*, the fragment of an "Unknown Gospel" published in 1935,[18] reproduces a debate between Jesus and the lawyers and rulers of the people about the testimony of the Scriptures and Moses that was most probably the source for John 5:39 and 45.[19]

John 8:14b ("because I know whence I came and where I am going, but you do not know whence I come and where I am going") cannot be ascribed to the same source. Rather, it is an adaptation of a traditional saying of Jesus. Its character is patently gnostic, and while it is used elsewhere in John with respect to Jesus,[20] it can also be used of the believers who share his origin and destiny.

Compare the following:

Gospel of Thomas logion 49:

Blessed are the solitary and elect
for you will find the kingdom.
For you are from it,
and to it you will return.

Gospel of Thomas logion 50:

If they say to you,
"Where did you come from?"
say to them,
"We came from the light . . . ."

John 8:15–16 resumes the discussion of the realized eschatology of 5:22–24. These verses belong to the author's own reinterpretation of the expectation of a future judgment by God (or by Jesus) which was widely held in early Christian circles.[21] The purpose of this "flashback" to 5:22–24 is perhaps only to introduce a statement about the unity of Jesus and the Father. The preparation for this statement is further supplemented

[18] Bell-Skeat, *Unknown Gospel*; for further literature, cf. my article "Apocryphal and Canonical Gospels," 119.

[19] For further discussion of the relationship of *Papyrus Egerton 2* to the Gospel of John see "Apocryphal and Canonical Gospels," 119–21.

[20] Cf. John 16:28: "I have gone out from the Father and have come into the world; again I leave the world and I am going to the Father."

[21] On John's critical reinterpretation of traditional Christian eschatology, cf. Bultmann, *John*, on John 3:19 and 5:21.

by another fragment from the tradition of earlier debates with Judaism from which John had already drawn 8:13–14a. The reference to the law is explicit in 8:17 ("and it is written in your law") and there is no doubt about the conscious reference to the legal rule of two witnesses (Deut 17:6; 19:15). That John 8:18 (where Jesus is pointing to himself and to the Father as the two witnesses) contradicts this rule which requires two witnesses *in addition to* the person concerned, should not lead to the surprise question why Jesus "does not mention John the Baptist who was sent to testify to the light," nor can it be explained by reference to exceptions in rabbinic jurisprudence.[22] Rather, this sentence is formulated by the author in order to provoke the question "where is your father?" (8:19a), which in turn gives the opportunity to quote once more a traditional saying that concludes this section.

John 8:19b ("You do not know me nor the Father; if you knew me, you would also know my Father") reflects the saying that is most fully preserved in Matt 11:27 and Luke 10:22:

> No one knows the Son except the Father,
> and no one knows the Father except the Son
> and anyone to whom the Son chooses to reveal him.

This saying is cited in several other passages of the Gospel of John, all of them certainly independent of the Synoptic Gospels (cf. especially John 14:7–10)[23] and it also appears in *Dial. Sav.* III,5:134,14–15:

> And if he does not know the Son,
> how will he know the [Father]?

Compare
Gospel of Thomas logion 69:

> Blessed are they who have been persecuted within themselves.
> It is they who have truly come to know the Father.

John 8:20 seems to be entirely redactional.[24] Although 8:21 introduces a new theme, the explicit remark that "no one arrested him, because his hour had not yet come" interrupts the context more than necessary. I would suggest that at this point the author returned to his source from which he had drawn the debates of Jesus with his Jewish opponents. *Papyrus Egerton 2* confirms this: in this fragmentary papyrus the first preserved section, containing the parallels to John 5:39 and 45 (see

---

[22] Brown, *John*, on John 8:18.

[23] Cf. my article "Gnostic Writings."

[24] Bultmann (*John*) finds in this verse the conclusion of the entire section that began in 5:1 (see above, n. 16).

above), was followed—after a lacuna of uncertain length—by a fragment that begins as follows:

> [to gather] stones together to stone him. And the
> rulers laid their hands on him that they might arrest him
> and [deliver] him to the multitude. But they [were not
> able] to arrest him because the hour of his betrayal [was]
> not yet [come]. But he himself, the Lord, escaped out of
> [their hands] and turned away from them.

This was obviously the conclusion of the debate with the lawyers and
rulers preserved in the first fragment of the papyrus. In John 8:20, the
author of the Fourth Gospel used only a part of this conclusion. Other
sentences from this report of an attempted arrest of Jesus appear in John
7:30, 44; 10:31, 39.[25]

II. Tradition History

Rather than proceeding with a detailed analysis of the subsequent
sections of John 8, I shall give a brief survey of John 8:21–59, indicating
those instances in which one can assume either the utilization of traditional sayings or the dependence upon other source materials.

John 8:21–22: A traditional saying:

> I am going away and you will seek me . . .
> Where I go, you cannot come.[26]

Cf. *Gospel of Thomas* logion 38:

> There will be days when you will look for me and not find me.

Ap. Jas. I,2:2,22–27:

> "Have you departed and removed yourself from us?"
> But Jesus said: "No, but I shall go to the place whence I
> came. If you wish to come with me, come."[27]

John 8:21b, 23–24: "You will die in your sins," and the discussion about
"being from below/the world" and "being from above/not from the
world" is the interpretation of the author of the Gospel.

---

[25] It is far more likely that John utilized this report repeatedly (in order to create the
impression of an increasing hostility of the Jews) than to assume that the passage in
Papyrus Egerton 2 was pieced together from passages in three different chapters of the
Gospel of John.

[26] The same saying is used in John 7:34, 36 ("You will seek me and not find me, and
where I am you will not be able to come") and John 13:33 ("You will seek me, and as I
said to the Jews, where I am going you will not be able to come").

[27] Cf. *Ap. Jas.* I,2:14,20–21: "I shall ascend to the place whence I came."

John 8:25–26a: A traditional saying:

They said to him:
"Who are you?"
Jesus said to them:
"First of all, what I say to you. [28]
I have many things to say and to judge about you." [29]

Cf. *Gospel of Thomas* logion 43:

His disciples said to him:
"Who are you that you should say these things to us?"
[Jesus said to them:]
"You do not realize who I am from what I say to you,
but you are like the Jews. . . ."

John 8:26b–29 is the interpretation of the author of the Fourth Gospel, using the typical Johannine motif of the *egō eimi* in relation to the "raising up of the Son of Man," i.e., the crucifixion of Jesus (cf. John 3:14; 18:5,6,8; but also 8:58). It is clear from this interpretation that the author understands very well the identity of Jesus' person with his speaking: "You will recognize that it is I (*egō eimi*) and that I do not do anything from myself, but that I *speak* as my father has taught me" (8:28).

John 8:30: A composition of the Evangelist.
John 8:31–32: A traditional saying:

If you remain in my word,
you will truly be my disciples,
and you will know the truth,
and the truth will make you free.

Gospel of Thomas logion 19:

If you become my disciples,
and listen to my words,
these stones will minister to you.
There are five trees in paradise . . .
Whoever becomes acquainted with them,
will not experience death.

John 8:33–36: This section could be assigned to the same source from which John drew other materials of debates of Jesus with his Jewish

---

[28] On the notorious difficulties of translating this sentence, cf. Brown, *John*, note on 8:25. The point seems to be the same as the one of the parallel in *Gospel of Thomas* logion 43, i.e., that whatever Jesus says represents his identity.

[29] How difficult this passage is, if one does not recognize the dependence upon a traditional saying, is clearly expressed in Bultmann's statement that a decision is not possible (*John*, on 8:25–27).

opponents. C. H. Dodd[30] has argued that John 8:35 ("The slave does not remain in the house forever; the son remains forever") is a traditional saying. He also points to the fact that "The truth will set you free" and "He who commits sin is a slave" are "Stoic maxims."[31] This suggests that the final phrase of the saying of John 8:31f. may have been added by the author of John in view of his interpretation offered here. Indeed, this final phrase has no parallel in the possibly more original form of the saying as quoted in *Gospel of Thomas* logion 19.

John 8:37–50: The analysis of this section is difficult, and I am not able to present a convincing solution. It seems to me, however, that further efforts in isolating more traditional sayings in the gospel literature of the Nag Hammadi writings would result in further clarification. The problem in this section is twofold. (1) Traditional sayings are modified by the author of John. (2) They are very closely interwoven with fragments of the Fourth Gospel's source, relating debates of Jesus with his Jewish opponents. What follows are just a few suggestions, all questionable.

John 8:37: Reference to John's source reporting attempts to arrest Jesus.

John 8:38: "What I have seen from my father that I speak." Possibly a variation of a saying quoted in 8:26–27.

John 8:39–41: Comments on the source containing debates of Jesus with his opponents.

John 8:42: "I have come from God . . .": Traditional saying.

John 8:43: Johannine expansion of the discourse.

John 8:44: Quote of a tradition about the devil as murderer.[32]

John 8:45–46: Johannine expansion of the discourse.

John 8:47: "He who is from God hears God's words": Variation of a traditional saying.

John 8:48–50: "You are a Samaritan and you have a demon": From a source containing Jesus' debates with opponents; cf. Mark 3:20–22.

The last section is more readily recognized with respect to its components.

John 8:51: A traditional saying:

Truly, truly I say to you:
Whoever keeps my word,
will not see death into eternity.[33]

---

[30] *Historical Tradition*, 379–82.

[31] Dodd, *Historical Tradition*, 380; cf. 330.

[32] Bultmann (*John*, on 8:44) has made it very likely that such a tradition is used here as well as 1 John 3:8, 15.

[33] Cf. John 6:63: "The words which I have spoken to you are spirit and life."

Cf. *Gospel of Thomas* logion 1:

Whoever finds the interpretation of these sayings
will not experience death.

Dial. Sav. III,5:147, 18–20:

[   ] understands this
[   ] will live for [ever].

John 8:52–59, the interpretation, clearly uses the same source of Jesus'
debates with Jewish opponents which I posited for several preceding
sections. This is confirmed by 8:59, "They took up stones to throw them
at him. But Jesus hid himself and went out of the temple"; cf. the passage
from *Papyrus Egerton 2* quoted above.

In conclusion, let me reiterate that the disjointed appearance of this
chapter of the Gospel of John seems to result from the use of two types
of traditional materials which have not been fully developed into a
logical discourse: (1) traditional sayings of Jesus; most of them have
parallels in gospels that are usually called "gnostic," although there are a
number of parallels in the Synoptic Gospels. The history of these
sayings, however, still needs to be integrated into the history of the
sayings of the Synoptic tradition; (2) a (written) source of debates of Jesus
with his Jewish opponents of which a sample has been preserved in
Papyrus Egerton 2. The character of these debates and of their relationship to the Synoptic controversy stories still needs further clarification.

III. Nag Hammadi Parallels to John

Future analysis of the discourses of the Gospel of John will profit from
the search for further traditional sayings preserved in Nag Hammadi
writings. I will simply list some of the Johannine passages to which
striking parallels exist in the *Gospel of Thomas*, the *Dialogue of the
Savior*, and the *Apocryphon of James*. The list does not claim to be
complete,[34] and traditional sayings of John documented from other
sources have not been included.[35]

---

[34] I am not listing all possible parallels between John and the *Gospel of Thomas* which
Brown assembled in his article (see above, note 5), but only those instances in which the
same traditional saying seems to be used.

[35] E.g., the saying of John 3:3, 5 which is also quoted in Justin, *Apol.* 1.61.4. On other
Synoptic materials, cf. Dodd, *Historical Tradition*, 335–65.

John 3:35:

The Father loves the Son and has given everything into his hand. [36]

Cf. *Gospel of Thomas* logion 61:

I am he who exists from the Undivided.
I was given some of the things of my Father.

John 4:14:

He who drinks from the water that I give him,
will never thirst into eternity.
But the water that I will give him
will become in him a spring of bubbling water
    for eternal life. [37]

Cf. *Gospel of Thomas* logion 13:

You have drunk, you have become intoxicated from the
bubbling spring that I have measured out.

John 6:63: See above, on John 8:51.
John 7:33–34 (see above on John 8:21–22):

I am going to the one who sent me.
You will seek me and not find me,
and where I am you cannot come.

John 7:37–38: See above, on John 4:14.
John 9:4: See above, on John 8:12.
John 10:29: See above, on John 3:35.
John 11:9–10: See above, on John 8:12.
John 12:35–36: See above, on John 8:12.
John 13:33: See above, on John 8:21–22.
John 14:2–3 (2–12): A close parallel to this discourse, probably a more original variant, is preserved in *Dial. Sav.* III,5:132,2–19;[38] cf. also *Ap. Jas.* I,2:2,24–26.
John 14:9:

Such a long time I have been with you,
and you have not known me, Philip?

Cf. *Ap. Jas.* I,2:13,39–14,2:

I have revealed myself to you (sg.), James,
and you (plu.) have not known me.

[36] Cf. also John 10:28–29; 13:3.
[37] Cf. also John 7:38–39.
[38] For a more detailed analysis cf. my article "Gnostic Writings," 250–51.

John 16:23–24:

Truly, truly, I say to you,
Whatever you ask the Father,
he shall give to you in my name . . .
Ask and you will receive,
so that your joy will be full. [39]

Cf. *Gospel of Thomas* logion 92 (cf. 94):

Seek and you will find.

Dial. Sav. III,5:129,14–16:

And he who [knows, let him] seek and find and [rejoice].

Ap. Jas. I,2:10,32–34 and 10,39–11,1:

Invoke the Father,
implore God often,
and he will give to you. . . .
Rejoice and be glad as sons of God.

John 16:23a, 30 (in the form of a question of the disciples):

23: And on that day you will not ask me anything.
30: Now we know that you know everything,
and have no need that someone ask you.

Cf. *Gospel of Thomas* logion 92:

Yet what you asked me about in former times
and which I did not tell you then,
now I do desire to tell,
but you do not inquire after it.[40]

John 16:25 (cf. 16:29):

Those things I have spoken to you in parables.
The hour is coming, when I shall no longer speak
to you in parables,
but I shall speak to you about the father openly.

Cf. *Ap. Jas.* I,2:7,1–6:

At first I spoke to you in parables,
and you did not understand;
now I speak to you openly,
and you do not perceive.[41]

John 16:28: See above, on John 8:14.

---

[39] Koester, "Gnostic Writings," 238–40.
[40] Cf. also *Dial. Sav.* III,5:128,1–5; *Acts of John*, 98.
[41] This version of the saying resembles Mark 4:10–12 more closely than John 16:25.

John 17: There are numerous parallels to passages in gnostic gospels and discourses[42] as well as to sayings already quoted above. In its genre and style, however, John 17 resembles literary gnostic discourses much more closely than other parts of this Gospel. Therefore, this chapter would require an investigation involving different methodological criteria.

John 20:29:

> Blessed are those who have not seen
> and yet believe.

Cf. *Ap. Jas.* I,2:12,38–13,1:

> Blessed will they be who have known me;
> woe to those who have heard and have not believed.
> Blessed will they be who have not seen yet [have believed].[43]

IV. Conclusion

In conclusion, let me point out a few challenging problems concerning my hypothesis.

(1) In most of the gnostic texts traditional sayings are already embedded in dialogue and discourse. It is difficult to isolate them, and the exegete's eyes are not sufficiently trained for this task.

(2) The type of sayings tradition which confronts us here is fundamentally different from the one that we are accustomed to in the Synoptic Gospels, because interpretations are not *added to* traditional sayings; rather, they are expressed in the transformation of the sayings themselves. E.g., *Dial. Sav.* III,5:125,19 "The light of the body is the mind" has replaced the traditional term "eye" by the interpretive term "mind." Thus, original metaphors can disappear in favor of their new epexegetical equivalents.

(3) There seems to be little respect for the original "form" of a saying; i.e., basic formulations ("There is light within a man of light, and he lights up the whole world") can be transformed into I-sayings ("I am the light of the world").

(4) Compared to the Synoptic tradition, there is an ever increased tendency to attract materials which are not true "sayings," but rather

---

[42] E.g., John 17:9–10; cf. *Gospel of Thomas* logion 100; John 17:23; cf. *Ap. Jas.* I,2:4,40–5,5.

[43] Cf. also *Ap. Jas.* I,2:7,17–25.

creedal statements, catechisms, wisdom lists, and formulations of biblical exegesis.

(5) We know too little about "gnostic hermeneutics." What are the rules and criteria of interpretation, and how have they been applied in the process of transmission and exegesis of traditional materials?

Success in solving at least some of these problems will certainly lead to the realization that there was a much broader base to the first-century sayings tradition than the Synoptic Gospels would suggest.

6

THE FUNCTION AND BACKGROUND
OF THE BELOVED DISCIPLE
IN THE GOSPEL OF JOHN

Hans-Martin Schenke

Hans-Martin Schenke, Professor of New Testament Literature and Theology at Humboldt University, Berlin, GDR (East Germany), holds doctorates both in theology (1956) and philosophy (1960); his lectureship in theology was also completed at Humboldt (1960).

Professor Schenke has distinguished himself in such prestigious societies as Studiorum Novi Testamenti Societas, the Association Internationale d'Études des Patristiques, and the Société d'Archéologie Copte.

His special interests concern the value of the recent Nag Hammadi manuscripts for the history of religion in late antiquity. Professor Schenke is a prolific writer in these areas and has made many invaluable contributions to Nag Hammadi studies.

Preface*

This paper raises and addresses the following question: is it possible to solve the special problem of the function and background of the Johannine Beloved Disciple with the help of the gnostic parallels found in the Nag Hammadi documents and related texts? This question of identity appears as a specific query within the larger question—which,

* The present contribution was not specifically prepared for the Working Seminar on Gnosticism and Early Christianity. Originally it was a lecture given at Princeton Theological Seminary and at the State University of California in Long Beach on a lecture tour across this country from October 11 to November 20, 1982. But now I place it at the disposal of this seminar. For, in my opinion, it fits nicely with the topic of the seminar. Nevertheless, in this new context and as a contribution to the discussion on the relationship between Primitive Christianity and Gnosticism the paper receives another bias. I should like to thank my colleagues James M. Robinson, Robert Hodgson, Jr. and Harold W. Attridge for their advice and assistance in improving the English style of the present paper.

according to the program of the seminar will be addressed by the Working Seminar in a variety of approaches—namely, the question of the overall importance of the Nag Hammadi texts for understanding the Gospel of John and Johannine Christianity. Consequently, I feel compelled to outline or to restate my own position regarding the larger general question.

During my work two Nag Hammadi texts have surfaced as especially relevant for the exegesis of the Gospel of John, namely, the *Book of Thomas* (=*Thomas, the Contender*), which has previously been recognized as significant to such discussion, and the *Trimorphic Protennoia*. Regarding the relevance of the *Book of Thomas* (NHC II,7) there are two further points. On the one hand, the material of the *Book of Thomas* displays striking parallels to some obscure passages of John 3. *Book of Thomas* II,7:138,21–36 contains parallels to John 3:12 and 3:21 (plus 1 John 1:6). *Book of Thomas* II,7:140,5–18 throws light on John 3:11. On the other hand, the dialogue framework of the *Book of Thomas* as a whole proves attractive for Johannine scholarship since the *Book of Thomas* and John are obviously linked by the phenomenon that the Savior's dialogue partner(s) frequently misunderstand him.[1]

For my general view regarding the importance of the *Trimorphic Protennoia* (NHC XIII,1) for the understanding of the prologue of the Gospel of John—a view identical with that of our group, the *Berliner Arbeitskreis für koptisch-gnostische Schriften*—I may simply refer to James M. Robinson's contribution to the Yale Conference ("Sethians") and the respective discussion.[2]

Beyond this it may be worth noting that Christoph Demke's interpretation[3] has subsequently caused me to change my earlier literary-critical analysis of the prologue of John together with the corresponding reconstruction of its source.[4] That earlier analysis was characterized by the understanding that the source extended only to 1:12b and by the hypothesis of a double redaction (evangelist and ecclesiastical redactor). But now I think that it is necessary to attribute also John 1:14, 16, and 18 to the source. There are five reasons for this:

1. The parallel to *Trimorphic Protennoia* with its threefold revelation,

---

[1] For the details cf. H.-M. Schenke, "Book of Thomas," sections 1, 2, 4.

[2] Layton, *Rediscovery*, 2. 643–62 and 662–70.

[3] Cf. Demke, "Logos-Hymnus." Compare especially p. 64: "By this we can conclude the research of the shape of the source. Our result is: As sources for the prologue the evangelist uses (1) a song of the 'celestials,' which used to be performed in the service of the congregation (vss 1, 3–5, 10–12b); (2) the confession of the 'terrestrials' of the congregation, responding to this song (vss 14, 16)" (author's translation).

[4] Cf. H.-M. Schenke, "Christologie," 226–27.

where the Christianization also occurs only *within* the third part (the keyword "tent" σκηνή, e.g., appears in the third part).

2. My own argument in the Melchizedek paper[5] that John 1:14a ("And the Word became flesh") could very easily have been conceived in a gnostic way. At the very least this possibility cannot be excluded.

3. My vivid impression that among the numerous explanations of the insertion of John the Baptist (1:6–8), the explanation of Rudolf Bultmann —with its implication (namely, that the "prologue" was originally a hymn on John the Baptist)—is the best one after all. Especially in view of the role of the Baptist as it now appears from Nag Hammadi texts, Bultmann's interpretation seems quite conceivable. (In this case 1:15 also comes from the evangelist.)

4. My view of the Sethians, from which the possibility emerges of seeing Sethians, Mandaeans, and the disciples of John the Baptist in a certain parallel development, appears to support Bultmann's analysis.

5. In principle the new and different style of 1:14, 16, 18—including the "we," which, as an element presumably coming from the evangelist, repeatedly took me into increasing difficulties—could be sufficiently explained along the lines of Demke's view. But I would prefer to conceive of a poetic structure in which just the style changes between stanzas two and three. Such a shift of style—and of the person imagined as the speaker—is well known from the Nag Hammadi texts (and, e.g., also from the *Odes of Solomon*).

Finally, I cannot avoid asking a very subtle but irresistibly suggestive question, although I feel unable to judge whether it warrants pursuit: is the relationship between *Trimorphic Protennoia* and the prologue of John only a specific example of a much more general relationship between Sethianism and the whole Gospel of John? This suggests that Sethianism could be understood as the gnostic background of (the discourses of) the Fourth Gospel. For the time being it seems as if this might explain several obscure aspects of the Fourth Gospel from one common root. These aspects are, above all, the following four:

1. *The polemic against John the Baptist and his disciples.* The rivals of the Johannine community would have been Samaritan baptists who considered their founder, John the Baptist, to have been an incarnation of the celestial Seth as the Logos.

2. *The specific Johannine conception of the Son of Man.* This "Son of Man" would be in principle the celestial Seth as the son of the celestial Adamas or his incarnation.

---

[5] Cf. H.-M. Schenke, "Melchisedek," 124–25.

3. *The Paraclete figure.* The "other" Paraclete would be the next form in which the celestial Seth will assist his race.

4. *The prominent role of the Samaritan motif in the Fourth Gospel* (provided that Sethianism is actually rooted in Samaritanism).

I. Introduction

The figure of the Beloved Disciple is admittedly one of the great puzzles in the mysterious Fourth Gospel. The expression "Beloved Disciple" usually refers to that nameless and shadowy disciple of Jesus whom John alone denotes according to the pattern "the disciple whom Jesus loved"[6] (John 13:23; 19:26; 20:2; 21:7, 20). The problems raised by this figure in the Fourth Gospel are both numerous and complex. Who or what is the Beloved Disciple? Is he a real figure or an ideal one? If real, is he an eyewitness to all that is reported in the Gospel or only the guarantor of certain episodes and facts? In this latter case, is he identical with one of the known followers of Jesus, such as John, the son of Zebedee; John Mark; the Ephesian John; Lazarus; Matthias; Paul? If ideal, is he a symbol for Gentile Christianity or for the charismatic function of the church? Is it the purpose of this figure, in either case, to project back into the life of Jesus the Christian group which forms the social basis of the Fourth Gospel? Has the figure two levels of meaning such that the ideal witness simultaneously serves as a literary monument to a key figure in the history of the Johannine circle? How is 21:24, the final statement that the Beloved Disciple, having died in the meantime, is the author of the Gospel related to the preceding passages about the Beloved Disciple? How is this statement to be understood at all? How many passages actually referring to the Beloved Disciple are there? Does the figure appear even where the stereotyped designation does not? How can the strange distribution of the Beloved Disciple passages be

---

[6] 13:23 ἦν ἀνακείμενος εἷς ἐκ τῶν μαθητῶν αὐτοῦ ἐν τῷ κόλπῳ τοῦ ᾽Ιησοῦ, ὃν ἠγάπα ὁ ᾽Ιησοῦς: "One of his disciples, whom Jesus loved, was lying close to the breast of Jesus" (RSV).

19:26 ᾽Ιησοῦς οὖν ἰδὼν τὴν μητέρα καὶ τὸν μαθητὴν παρεστῶτα ὃν ἠγάπα: "When Jesus saw his mother, and the disciple whom he loved standing near. . ." (RSV).

20:2 καὶ ἔρχεται πρὸς Σίμωνα Πέτρον καὶ πρὸς τὸν ἄλλον μαθητὴν ὃν ἐφίλει ὁ ᾽Ιησοῦς: ". . .and went to Simon Peter and the other disciple, the one whom Jesus loved" (RSV).

21:7 λέγει οὖν ὁ μαθητὴς ἐκεῖνος ὃν ἠγάπα ὁ ᾽Ιησοῦς: "That disciple whom Jesus loved said. . ." (RSV).

21:20 ᾽Επιστραφεὶς ὁ Πέτρος βλέπει τὸν μαθητὴν ὃν ἠγάπα ὁ ᾽Ιησοῦς ἀκολουθοῦντα: "Peter turned and saw following them the disciple whom Jesus loved" (RSV).

explained; that is, why does he not appear (at least distinctively) before 13:23? Do the formulae in 13:23; 19:26; 20:2; 21:7, 20 referring to the figure of the Beloved Disciple belong to the same literary stratum in the Gospel of John, or are they distributed among two different layers? What claim is made by the designation "Beloved Disciple"? How should one understand this claim? There is, after all, a considerable difference between a sentence like "Jesus loved the disciple so-and-so"[7] and a sentence like "It is the disciple so-and-so whom Jesus loved." The difference would seem to be between an instance of general love and one of exclusive love, the latter ultimately assigning the other disciples to the category of "non-beloved." But even if the designation "Beloved Disciple" does not denote a radical exclusivity, it does at least connote a comparative one ("the disciple whom Jesus loved more than all the others").

The questions are numerous, and so too the answers—numerous, and embarrassing. But a history-of-research would be out of place here, for the reader may easily go and read it in the relevant literature.[8]

All these problems are interlaced one with another, although the intersections are not equidistant at every point. The question about the *function* of the Beloved Disciple in the Fourth Gospel, however, is a point in the network of questions where especially many lines converge, and one may conveniently start here. There are also some new things to be said here. First of all, what is new is a general change of view within German Johannine research with respect to the question of function, a change which can be noticed and should be taken up, though one must try to keep it from getting out of hand. The second part of the present paper will later, under the ambiguous rubric "background," raise the following question: is it possible that new light can be thrown upon the set of problems concerning the Beloved Disciple from outside the Gospel of John and Johannine research?

II. On the Function
of the Beloved Disciple

Even in addressing only one of the major issues regarding the Beloved Disciple, it would be impossible within the scope of a paper to take up all the individual problems connected with it. That would, indeed, mean to start from zero once again. So one must avoid devoting the same

[7] Cf. 11:5 ἠγάπα δὲ ὁ ᾽Ιησοῦς. . .τὸν Λάζαρον: "Now Jesus loved. . .Lazarus."
[8] Cf. Kragerud, *Lieblingsjünger*; Roloff, "Lieblingsjünger"; Schnackenburg, "Jünger"; id., *Johannesevangelium*, 3.449–64; Lorenzen, *Lieblingsjünger*; Thyen,"Johannesevangelium"; id., "Entwicklungen."

amount of attention to others' points of view as one does to one's own or to those of one's particular scholarly tradition.[9] Thus it becomes increasingly necessary to reveal one's own premises. The bases from which the following remarks begin are the—certainly widespread—views (1) that neither the Gospel of John as a whole nor certain parts of it can be thought of as guaranteed by a historically trustworthy person or regarded as written by an eyewitness; and (2) that the whole of chapter 21 is redactional. Starting from these premises, the question about the function of the Beloved Disciple hinges on the stratum or strata to which one assigns the Beloved Disciple passages. The Beloved Disciple clearly appears, it is true, in the supplementary chapter of the redaction (21:1–14 and 15–24) but also in three earlier sections (20:1–10; 19:25–27; 13:21–30). In the tradition of New Testament scholarship in which this writer is rooted it is usual to reckon the Beloved Disciple passages in chapters 13, 19, and 20 to the stratum of the evangelist, who speaks here rather vaguely of the Beloved Disciple. It is thought that either the evangelist introduces here an ideal or symbolic figure into the history of Jesus; or, that he appeals in these places to a real person as guarantor of the pertinent events. But the editor, while trying to imitate the evangelist on the whole, has in chapter 21 blatantly and recklessly identified the Beloved Disciple as the author of the Gospel. This tradition of scholarship appears most markedly in the commentary on John by Rudolf Bultmann and it is, accordingly, almost a matter of course both in the Bultmannian school and in the wider sphere of its influence.

This hypothesis, however, does not fit, and ends ultimately in a dilemma, as the pertinent literature clearly shows. There seems to be only one way out of the dilemma, a way which is practical without much ado and follows from the assumption that the Beloved Disciple is already redactional in chs. 13, 19, and 20. The Beloved Disciple would have penetrated into the Gospel from behind, that is to say, from ch. 21. This theory would have to say, then, that all the Beloved Disciple passages belong to the same stratum, namely to the latest, or that of the redactor. The Beloved Disciple, thus, is a redactional fiction who functions to give the Fourth Gospel the appearance of being authenticated and written by an eyewitness. But this is, in principle, only the resumption of an earlier theory under now modified conditions.[10]

---

[9] Recently an article appeared, the title of which is almost identical with the title of this paper, but its author is rooted in a different scholarly tradition and so in fact approaches other problems. Cf. Hawkin, "Beloved Disciple." Prof. Paul-Hubert Poirier, director of BCNH and a participant in the Working Seminar, kindly provided me with a copy of this article.

[10] Cf. Kragerud, Lieblingsjünger, 11–12 and add to his survey: Goguel, Introduction, 2. 361–64; Harnack, Studien, 126 n. 2.

Interestingly, however, this earlier view, appropriately modified, frequently reappears as a "new" solution to the Beloved Disciple problem in that part of German Johannine scholarship which is wrestling with the Bultmann heritage. Two sentences from Hartwig Thyen evidence the feeling that such a general change of view has made some headway. He writes in the first instance: "We shall see that—contrary to Bultmann's explanation—in current research the awareness of the uniformity of all the Beloved Disciple passages in the Gospel, including chapter 21, is more and more keenly felt."[11] In the second instance he writes: "After all, a growing and by no means uncritical consensus holds that the literary figure of the Beloved Disciple as located on the level of the text must correspond with a concrete person on the level of the real history of Johannine Christianity."[12] Advocates of this new view are, in addition to Thyen himself, his student Wolfgang Langbrandtner, and above all Ernst Haenchen.[13]

In the Thyen school, however, this return to an older basic assumption about the purely redactional character of the Beloved Disciple assumes a specific form which the present writer is unable to accept. In Thyen's view of the Beloved Disciple one meets two basic tendencies in German Johannine scholarship of the era after Bultmann; or, at least, one suspects that Thyen's view is being developed against the background of these tendencies. On the one hand, the extent of the material ascribed to the redactor is increasing to such an extent that the evangelist is about to disappear. On this hypothesis the work of the evangelist in a sense takes on the function of Bultmann's conjectural source consisting of revelation discourses (Offenbarungsreden). For the work of the evangelist becomes itself a gnosticizing source, whereas the role of the Bultmannian evangelist is conferred upon the redactor, who thus becomes the main level of interpretation. On the other hand (and at the same time), the Fourth Gospel and Johannine literature as a whole are no longer seen as the intentional creation of one author (or, if necessary, of more than one author); instead, the Gospel as a whole and all the material contained in it are seen primarily as the product of a special Johannine tradition, of a Johannine history of preaching, or of a Johannine "trajectory."[14] What triggered these two tendencies is one and the same factor, namely, the

---

[11] Thyen, "Johannesevangelium," 222 (author's translation).
[12] Thyen, "Johannesevangelium," 223 (author's translation).
[13] Cf. Thyen, "Johannes 13"; id., "Johannesevangelium"; id., "Entwicklungen"; Langbrandtner, Weltferner Gott; Haenchen, Johannesevangelium, 601–5.
[14] Cf. Becker, "Aufbau"; id., "Abschiedsreden"; Robinson-Koester, Entwicklungslinien, 233–35; Müller, "Parakletenvorstellung."

rejection, even in the Bultmann school, of a source of revelation discourses.

In this context, then, the redactional fiction of the Beloved Disciple, in the view of Thyen, receives a second dimension (cf. the second quotation above). The Beloved Disciple is taken to be a fiction only on the literary level of the Gospel. On the level of the real history of Johannine Christianity, however, a real person (who enjoyed general veneration) corresponds to him. A literary monument has been set up to the memory of this person in the Gospel by devising the Beloved Disciple figure. The historical role and appreciation of this person, as Thyen sees it, emerged from his settling a serious crisis within Johannine Christianity over Christological issues, which crisis ended in schism.

Against Thyen's extension and evaluation of the jointly shared basic assumption, the present writer wishes to retain as much as possible of Bultmann's model of literary criticism. Accordingly, one ought not to assign more of the Beloved Disciple passages to the redactor than is absolutely necessary. Moreover, provided it is correct to read the Beloved Disciple passages, so to speak, backwards, it follows that the technique used by the redactor in editing the Beloved Disciple into ch. 21 is possibly the same as in other places where the Beloved Disciple appears with Peter. In other words, the most likely assumption is that, as in ch. 21, the figure of Peter in 13:21–30 and 20:1–10 belonged already to the text that the redactor edited. Thus, in the supposed text of the evangelist in chapter 13, it would have been Peter himself who asked Jesus to disclose the traitor and to whom the traitor was revealed. Accordingly one would have to imagine the original form of the section as follows:

> When Jesus had thus spoken, he was troubled in spirit, and testified, "Truly, truly, I say to you, one of you will betray me." The disciples looked at one another, uncertain of whom he spoke. One of his disciples was lying close to the breast of Jesus, Simon Peter. Therefore they beckoned to him, that he should ask who it is of whom he spoke. So lying thus close to the breast of Jesus he said to him, "Lord, who is it?" Jesus answered, "It is he to whom I shall give the morsel, when I have dipped it." So when he had dipped the morsel, he gave it to Judas Iscariot, the son of Simon. Then after the morsel Satan entered into him. Jesus said to him, "What you are going to do, do quickly." Now no one at the table knew why he said this to him. Some thought that, because Judas had the money box, Jesus was telling him, "Buy what we need for the feast"; or, that he should give something to the poor. So, after receiving the morsel he immediately went out; and it was night.

Along the same lines, in ch. 20 (in the *Vorlage* prior to its redaction) Peter would have run together with Mary Magdalene to the empty tomb. It is easier to describe the work of the redactor in ch. 20 than in ch. 13. One simply needs to transpose the ready-made results of literary-critical analysis from the relation source/evangelist to the relation evangelist/ redactor.[15] One would reconstruct the original form of the section 20:1–10 as follows:

> Now on the first day of the week Mary Magdalene came to the tomb early while it was still dark, and saw that the stone had been taken away from the tomb. So she ran, and went to Simon Peter and said to him, "They have taken the Lord out of the tomb, and we do not know where they have laid him." Peter then came out (with her) and they went toward the tomb. Stooping to look in, Peter saw the linen clothes lying and the napkin, which had been on his head, not lying with the linen clothes, but rolled up in a place by itself. And he saw, and wondered in himself; for as yet he did not know the scripture, that he must rise from the dead. Then the disciple went back to his home.[16]

The third Beloved Disciple passage (apart from the supplementary ch. 21) is 19:25–27. Located shortly before a (widely accepted) editorial gloss (19:34, 35), it is the only Beloved Disciple scene in the Fourth Gospel with a theme other than the superiority of the Beloved Disciple to Peter. One may without difficulty attribute the whole double verse 19:26/27, which is in any case clearly discernible as an insertion into an earlier context, to the redactor (instead of the evangelist). In this case 19:26–27 and 19:34b, 35 belong to the same stratum and the "eyewitness" of 19:35 denotes directly and "originally" the Beloved Disciple mentioned before. The intention of 19:26–27 is to have the Beloved Disciple, in the dying-hour of Jesus, appointed his successor on earth.[17] But, as Anton Dauer has convincingly pointed out, the essential point here is that this appointment as successor is accomplished by making the Beloved Disciple, in a sort of adoption, the brother of Jesus.[18] We will have to return to this point in the third part.

Contrary to Thyen, therefore, the Beloved Disciple passages are only a simple fiction of the redactor. Reference is made to the alleged Beloved Disciple in the same way as the Pastorals refer to Paul. The function of the Beloved Disciple is to ground the Fourth Gospel (and the tradition of the Christian group in which it originates and has its influence) in the eyewitness testimony of one who was especially intimate with Jesus. This kind of deception may find its explanation and, what is more, its justification, only within a particular historical situation of conflict. The circumstances, however, do not point to a conflict within the group, but rather to a confrontation with another Christian (Petrine) tradition.

---

[15] Cf. esp. Schnackenburg, "Jünger," 102–5; Hartmann, "Vorlage."
[16] Cf. the reconstruction of the Greek text in Hartmann, "Vorlage," 220.
[17] Cf. Thyen, "Johannesevangelium," 225.
[18] Cf. Dauer, "Wort des Gekreuzigten"; id., Passionsgeschichte, 192–200, 316–33.

III. On the Background
of the Beloved Disciple

Turning to the question of the background of the Beloved Disciple
fiction, possible sources of light from outside the Gospel will be considered. The Beloved Disciple nomenclature appears outside John in the
special material of the so-called Secret Gospel of Mark, a gospel used on
certain occasions in the church of Alexandria. This material is quoted in
a recently discovered letter of Clement of Alexandria to a certain
Theodore.[19] In a quotation from the narrative of the resurrection of a
young man, one reads: "Then the young man, having looked upon him,
loved him" (III,4).[20] And in a second quotation from this special material
the young man is referred to as: "(the young man) whom Jesus loved"
(III,15).[21] If the letter of Clement be genuine it is probable that the
resurrection story of the anonymous youth in the Secret Gospel of Mark
represents an earlier stage, in terms of the history of tradition, of the
narrative we know as the resurrection of Lazarus in the Fourth Gospel.
So the question could be raised whether the new evidence does not
prove that those scholars were right who have always taken Lazarus to
be the Beloved Disciple.[22] On the other hand, this resurrected youth who
submits himself to the mystery of initiation six days after his resurrection
assumes the symbolic role of an ideal figure. And it is this role that
seems to connect the resurrected youth once again with the Johannine
Beloved Disciple.

The two parallels between the Beloved Disciple of the Gospel of John
and the resurrected youth of the Secret Gospel of Mark are, however,
not really quite parallel. First, one should note that there is a difference
between Jesus doing the loving in the Gospel of John and the resurrected youth doing the loving in the Secret Gospel of Mark. Actually,
this motif of loving Jesus fits perfectly the context in the Secret Gospel of
Mark and, therefore, seems to be original here. The resurrected youth
has every reason to be grateful to Jesus for raising him, and hence to say
"he loved Jesus" fits the flow of the narrative. To be sure, there is a later
reference in the Secret Gospel of Mark to Jesus loving the resurrected
youth. But this shift from the youth loving Jesus to Jesus loving the youth
makes sense in this second reference. For here Jesus is refusing to
receive some women who are related to the resurrected youth, and

[19] Smith, Secret Gospel of Mark; id., Secret Gospel: Discovery.
[20] ὁ δὲ νεανίσκος ἐμβλέψας αὐτῷ ἠγάπησεν αὐτόν.
[21] (ὁ νεανίσκος) ὃν ἠγάπα αὐτὸν ὁ Ἰησοῦς.
[22] E.g., J. Kreyenbühl, R. Eisler, W. K. Fleming, F. V. Filson, J. N. Sanders, K. A.
Eckhardt.

hence it needs to be made clear that Jesus is not also rejecting the youth by affirming that Jesus did in fact love him. There is a second difference between the Beloved Disciple in the Gospel of John and the resurrected youth in the Secret Gospel of Mark: the love for the Beloved Disciple has an exclusive overtone; or, at least a comparison is made which favors the Beloved Disciple over against the others. For by calling the beloved person a disciple, the suggestion is that Jesus did not love the other disciples as much as he did the Beloved Disciple. But when the resurrected youth in the Secret Gospel of Mark is loved by Jesus, this suggests only that Jesus cared for the deceased and raised him from the dead. There is implied no diminution of all the other young men or of the disciples of Jesus. A third difference between the two stories is that the fiction or role differs in the two cases. The context of the resurrected youth in the Secret Gospel of Mark is cultic—a sacrament is involved, probably the baptism and higher initiation of the youth. The resurrected youth is thus a symbolic portrayal of the validity of a secret initiation, since it projects the initiation back into the life of Christ. But the Beloved Disciple in the Gospel of John is something quite different. While both figures are fictional (indeed the resurrected youth in the Secret Gospel of Mark is a mere phantom), the Beloved Disciple in the Gospel of John is portrayed as a person of flesh and blood, and, consequently much more historicized.

A more promising starting point for elucidating the background of the Johannine Beloved Disciple is the assumption that the redactor in modeling the fictitious Beloved Disciple had in view a special legendary disciple-figure of Jesus who, advanced in years, had died a natural death and about whom various legends had arisen.[23] The question, then, would be whether it is possible to identify this figure. To begin with, the typology of the "Beloved Disciple" takes one a step further, since the designation "the disciple whom Jesus loved" means no less than "the disciple whom Jesus loved more than all the other disciples." Now, there is a passage in the *Gospel of Philip* that may present a fuller context for such a view:[24]

> [As for Ma]ry Mag[da]lene, the S[avior lov]ed he[r] more than [all] the disciples [and used] to kiss her [oft]en on her [mouth]. The rest of [the disciples wen]t to [them in order to] make [dema]nds. They said to him: "Why do you love her more than all of us?" The Savior answered and said to them: "Why do I not love you like her?"

The type of disciple-figure to whom this applies is one who is loved by Jesus more than all the other disciples. Such figures representing *this*

[23] Cf. Bultmann, *Johannes*, 554.
[24] Section 55b; NHC II,3:63,33–64,5.

type of the "Beloved Disciple" appear often in the apocryphal tradition, the most prominent ones being Mary Magdalene (as in the quotation above), James, the brother of the Lord, and Judas Thomas. Mary Magdalene appears as the "Beloved Disciple" also in another passage of the Gospel of Philip:[25]

> There were (only) three (women) always keeping company with the Lord: Mary his mother and h<is> sister and Magdalene, the one who was called his consort. His sister and his mother and his consort were each a Mary.

In this connection it is worth noting that this view of Mary Magdalene has provided the framework as well as the title for the Gospel of Mary (BG8502,1). From this text two passages are cited:

> Peter said to Mary: "Sister, we know that the Savior loved you more than the rest of women. Tell us the words of the Savior which you remember—which you know (but) we do not, nor have we heard them." Mary answered and said: "What is hidden from you I will proclaim to you" (10,1–9).

> Peter answered and spoke concerning these same things. He questioned them about the Savior: "Did he really speak with a woman without our knowledge (and) not openly? Are we to turn about and all listen to her? Did he prefer her to us?" Then Mary wept and said to Peter: "My brother Peter, what do you think? Do you think that I thought this up myself in my heart, or that I am lying about the Savior?" Levi answered and said to Peter: "Peter, you have always been hot-tempered. Now I see you contending against the woman like an adversary. But if the Savior made her worthy, who are you indeed to reject her? Surely the Savior knows her very well. That is why he loved her more than us" (17,15–18,15).

James, the brother of the Lord, also serves as a type of the "Beloved Disciple," as the three Nag Hammadi tractates that bear the name "James" reveal: the Apocryphon of James (NHC I,2), the (First) Apocalypse of James (NHC V,3), and the (Second) Apocalypse of James (NHC V,4). There is also saying 12 of the Gospel of Thomas (NHC II,2), which makes the "Beloved Disciple" James appear to be the sole foundation of the church:

> The disciples said to Jesus: "We know that you will depart from us. Who is to be our leader?" Jesus said to them: "Wherever you came from, you are to go to James the righteous, for whose sake heaven and earth came into being" (34,25–30).

Judas Thomas, too, embodies the "Beloved Disciple" idea, and one may first of all refer to the entire Syrian Judas Thomas tradition, especially in the light of Helmut Koester's research.[26] Two passages deserve special attention here. One is the section of the Gospel of Thomas dealing with the creed-like statement of Thomas:[27]

---

[25] Section 32; NHC II,3:59,6–11.
[26] Robinson-Koester, Entwicklungslinien, 118–34.
[27] Logion 13a; NHC II,2:34,30–35,7.

Jesus said to his disciples: "Compare me to someone and tell me whom I am like."
Simon Peter said to him: "You are like a righteous messenger." Matthew said to him:
"You are like a wise philosopher." Thomas said to him: "Master, my mouth is wholly
incapable of saying whom you are like." Jesus said: "I am not your master because
you have drunk (yourself) and become intoxicated from the bubbling spring which I
have measured out."

Even more suggestive for the "Beloved Disciple" character of Judas
Thomas is the beginning of the *Book of Thomas* (NHC II,7). The
framework for the first part of its parenetic materials is a revelation
discourse delivered by Jesus to Thomas (138,4–21). In it Thomas is
addressed or mentioned three times as the (physical) brother of Jesus.
There are also the following words which bear on the character of Judas
Thomas: "You are my twin and my true friend" (138,7–8). Against Peter
Nagel[28] one can show that the second predicate of the sentence really
means "my true friend" and not "my fellow contender." One is thus
justified in supposing a Greek original with this meaning "you are . . . my
true friend" behind the Coptic.[29] Transposed into a form parallel with
that of the Gospel of John, this would read "you are the one I truly love,"
or, in the third person singular, "he is the one whom Jesus truly loved."[30]

On the whole two considerations seem important. On the one hand, it
lies in the nature of these "Beloved Disciple" figures that they claim
superiority to Peter. This is evident in some of the quoted examples. In
the *Apocryphon of James* this goes to the extent that Peter, as the foil of
James within this pair of disciples, has to play the fool.[31] On the other
hand, the "Beloved-Discipleship" seems to connote certain family ties
between the respective disciple and Jesus. One is inclined to ask
whether the natural predisposition to love among family members might
not have facilitated the conceiving and applying of the "Beloved
Disciple" idea.

In this connection the observation about John 19:26–27, where Jesus
entrusts his mother to the Beloved Disciple, reveals its full relevance.
While all the other Beloved Disciple scenes of the Fourth Gospel are
designed to reveal the superiority of the Beloved Disciple to Peter, this
scene serves "only" to make the Beloved Disciple the brother of Jesus.
Here the question suggests itself whether Judas Thomas, the most
mysterious of all the brothers of Jesus, might not have been the historical
model (in terms of history of tradition) for the Beloved Disciple figure of
the Fourth Gospel. In other words, has the redactor of the Fourth Gospel

---

[28] Nagel, "Thomas."

[29] σὺ εἶ . . .ὁ φίλος μου ὁ ἀληθινός.

[30] σὺ εἶ ὃν φιλῶ ἀληθῶς, or: αὐτός ἐστιν ὃν ἐφίλει ἀληθῶς ὁ ᾽Ιησοῦς.

[31] Cf. H.-M. Schenke, "Jakobusbrief," 117–18.

made use here of one of the versions of the Thomas legend? This seems to be particularly plausible if Johannine Christianity be localized in Syria, which is otherwise known as the home of the Thomas tradition. What is needed in order to make this theory really plausible is evidence to the effect that Jesus promised Thomas that he would tarry till he comes, i.e., that he would not die before the return of Christ. Perhaps it is possible to understand logion 1 in the *Gospel of Thomas* and the strange tradition about the mysterious "three words" in logion 13b[32] as such evidence, or at least the remains of this supposed promise.

Turning to the *Gospel of Thomas*, one may note that after the confession of Thomas in logion 13, acknowledged by Jesus as being the truth, the text continues:

> And he took him and withdrew and told him three "words." When Thomas returned to his companions, they asked him: "What did Jesus say to you?" Thomas said to them: "If I tell you one of the 'words' which he told me, you will pick up stones and throw them at me; a fire will come out of the stones and burn you up" (35,7–14).

Only this second part of the logion has a parallel in the *Acts of Thomas* 47, where Thomas addresses Jesus in a prayer thus: "Who did set me apart from all my companions and speak to me three words, wherewith I am inflamed, and tell them to others I cannot!"[33] It does not require much to imagine that one of these three "words" could have been something like: "You will remain until I come"[34] or "you will not experience death until I come."[35] At any rate a promise of this sort would lead understandably to the anticipated jealousy of the other disciples.

Logion 1 of the *Gospel of Thomas* reads: "And he (Jesus [?]) had said: 'Whoever finds the explanation of these sayings will not experience death'" (32,12–14). This could easily be taken to be a transformation (like John 21:23b) of "Jesus had said to Thomas: 'Since you have found the explanation of my sayings, you will not experience death.'"

If this suggestion be correct, the redactor of the Fourth Gospel would in fact have doubled the figure of Thomas. For Thomas appears in the Gospel of John also under his own name, especially in the part of the Gospel written by the Evangelist,[36] and then reappears in the part of the Gospel added by the editor as the anonymous Beloved Disciple. But this duplication would not necessarily disprove such an hypothesis. There are several possible reasons for the doubling, e.g., the redactor could

---

[32] Cf. *Acts of Thomas*, 47.

[33] ὁ ἀφορίσας με κατ'ἰδίαν ἐκ τῶν ἑταίρων μου πάντων, καὶ εἰπών μοι τρεῖς λόγους ἐν οἷς ἐγὼ ἐκπυροῦμαι, καὶ ἄλλοις εἰπεῖν αὐτὰ οὐ δύναμαι.

[34] σὺ μένεις ἕως ἔρχομαι.

[35] σὺ οὐ μὴ γεύσῃ θανάτου ἕως ἔρχομαι.

[36] Cf. John 11:16; 14:5, 22(?); 20:24, 26, 27, 28; 21:2.

have done it without realizing it; or, he could have done it deliberately and, for that very reason, have chosen the mysterious paraphrase. After all, Thomas appears in two roles even in the *Gospel of Thomas*: as he *who reports*, i.e., as the (alleged) author (in the incipit), and as a person *who is reported on* (logion 13). Finally it seems easy to reverse the whole question and to look upon the conspicuous role that Thomas plays in the text of the unrevised Fourth Gospel as created under the influence of the same Syrian Judas Thomas tradition, which, then, would have affected the Fourth Gospel at two stages in its development.

7

ON BRIDGING THE GULF
FROM Q TO THE GOSPEL OF THOMAS
(OR VICE VERSA)

James M. Robinson

James M. Robinson is currently the Director of the Institute for Antiquity and Christianity at the Claremont University Center, Professor of Religion at the Claremont Graduate School, and Affiliate Professor of Theology and New Testament at the School of Theology at Claremont, California.

Among his various academic and professional duties, Professor Robinson is a member of the New Testament Board of the Hermeneia commentary series. He is a member of such prestigious professional societies as the Society of Biblical Literature and the International Association for Coptic Studies.

Professor Robinson is internationally known for his work in Gnostic and New Testament studies. He has written numerous journal and dictionary articles and perhaps is best-known for being the general editor of the highly regarded *Nag Hammadi Library in English*. Significant books by Professor Robinson include *A New Quest of the Historical Jesus*, *The Problem of History in Mark*, and *Trajectories through Early Christianity*, which he co-authored with Helmut Koester.

Preface

The problem of the relation of gnosticism to early Christianity is all too complex, and progress toward a solution of the various intertwined problems has been too slow and convoluted. The discovery of the Nag Hammadi Codices and the making of them accessible has not provided a simple solution. In a sense the flood of new source material has so engrossed scholarly energy that our generation seems to be lost in the detail of translation and interpretation with the broader questions in part lost from view.

The present paper addresses the problem area first by assessing the relevance of the Messina definition of gnosticism for this problem.

127

Rather than that definition facilitating the solution of the problems, it is argued below that it solidified them by creating additional language difficulties. A second section introduces a somewhat new ingredient into the usual discussions of gnosticism, by working not back from second-century gnosticism, where one is sure to be talking about gnosticism, but rather forward from Jesus' immediate Galilean followers (for whom the same surely cannot be said) in search of a hypothetical sociological roadbed for a trajectory from Jesus to gnosticism. Third, two documents of similar genre near the two poles of such a roadbed, Q and the *Gospel of Thomas*, are brought into focus, and it is argued that they cannot be kept apart, as those seeking to keep the New Testament and gnosticism apart would maintain. For in the kind of dating that applies to them they overlap, and thus produce a continuum, putting, so to speak, rails on the roadbed. Then in a final section the discussion of the problem of the genre of such sayings collections, a discussion I had initiated some twenty years ago, is brought more nearly up to date.

This paper thus does not solve the problems posed by the topic of our colloquium, but it does seek to blaze a trail for an important discussion that could track the course of the trajectory from Jesus to gnosticism.

I. The Messina Definition of Gnosticism

The Messina Colloquium on "The Origins of Gnosticism" set up a committee composed of Geo Widengren, Hans Jonas, Jean Daniélou, Carsten Colpe, and Ugo Bianchi, aided also by Marcel Simon and Henri Irenée Marrou, to prepare during the meeting a draft of a "proposal for a terminological and conceptual agreement with regard to the theme of the Colloquium." Their draft was then debated, emended, and adopted at a final three-hour session of the Colloquium. Since both the draft and the debate were in French, I was asked to be the English translator of the document, which meant I was to read the final English translation at the conclusion of the discussion. Thus, though the English is mine, I was involved neither in the preparation of the draft nor in the discussion itself, during which time I was more than busy emending my draft translation back and forth as the debate wound its way through the draft document. For at each turn of the debate I had to be certain that I had noted the formulation finally agreed upon and had correctly translated it into English. The published English translation is as I read it at the end of the lengthy discussion.[1]

---

[1] Bianchi, "Proposal," xxvi–xxix. It had already been published in the brief announcement by Bianchi, "Colloque." Carsten Colpe, who had been entrusted with preparing the

The document began with the stated purpose, "to avoid an undiffer-
entiated use of the terms gnosis and gnosticism." This proposal is already
in its inception a problem, in that especially German language sensitivities (and the German part of English-language sensitivities) have a
built-in pejorative feeling for -isms, perhaps to an extent Romance
languages do not. Ugo Bianchi, whose own introductory essay at the
Colloquium had in view the final document, dismissed such a pejorative
note found in German literature, as exemplified in a comment by Hans-
Martin Schenke:

> Incidentally, in research one not infrequently uses instead of or alongside of "gnosis"
> also the concept "gnosticism." Here one occasionally means by gnosticism Christian
> gnosis in distinction to pre-Christian pagan gnosis. The concept gnosticism is in any case
> pejorative and basically is on a level with the terminology of the heresiologists.[2]

Yet Bianchi himself, while distancing himself from this pejorative usage,
does not favor using the term gnosticism of "the true gnosis established
by the orthodox in polemic with the gnostics." He merely extends its
usage to mark the distinction both from that orthodox gnōsis and from
other more neutral kinds of gnōsis. Thus "gnosticism" becomes a purely
descriptive, phenomenological term—that nonetheless is not to be identified with mainline Christianity!

In past usage the German noun Gnosis and the English term gnosticism have been largely synonymous, one translating the other, although Germans have sometimes had a broader definition of the phenomenon itself than have the English. Thus confusion is invited by the
potentiality of applying the new distinction between the terms to older
literature where they were roughly synonymous, and indeed in applying
it to ongoing usage which has not been basically changed by the action
at Messina. For the German discussion has by and large rejected the
Messina distinction:

> On the other hand the ripping apart of gnosis and gnosticism is unfortunate and
> dangerous, since both terms are already so closely connected with the well-known
> phenomenon of late antiquity. "Gnosis" itself was employed by the Christian heresi-
> ologists to designate it. With the term "gnostics" (gnostikoi) the connection has been
> made to the central idea and in part to the self-designation. . . .[3]

German translation, asked, understandably enough, that his presentation of the German
translation be deferred until after the Colloquium. Hence it is absent from that preprint
but was included in the Messina volume itself, pp. xxix–xxxii, and was reprinted:
"Messina-Kongress," 129–32.

[2] Bianchi, "Problème," 4, n. 2, citing H.-M. Schenke, "Gnosis," 375.

[3] Rudolph, "Gnosis, ein Forschungsbericht" (1971) 18–19. He reports H.-M. Schenke, in
his review of Bianchi, Origini, as saying one "cannot do much" with this expanded sense
of gnosis (ThLZ 93 [1968] 905) and Karl Schubert as questioning whether the distinction
between the two terms "helps us further" (Origini, 527). He reports A. Böhlig as

As the last sentence suggests, a by-product of the problem is that the noun and adjective "gnostic" have become ambiguous. In actual practise they are used to refer to gnosticism. What would the adjective be to go with the noun gnōsis? What noun would one use to refer to a person whose religion was gnōsis but not gnosticism?

A few illustrations of the chaos in translation that would arise in implementing the clear terminological distinction between gnōsis and gnosticism will suffice to indicate how impractical the Messina proposal actually is. When for example Rudolf Bultmann wrote: "Der Kampf gegen die Gnosis . . . ," Kendrick Grobel rightly translated: "The struggle against gnosticism. . . .[4] When in 1924 Hans Leisegang entitled his gnostic anthology Die Gnosis and in 1961 Robert M. Grant entitled his comparable book Gnosticism, they were writing source books on the same phenomenon, gnosticism.[5] When Leisegang's work was superseded a generation later by a three-volume work produced by a team of Germans under the leadership of Werner Foerster with the title Die Gnosis, it was the same subject matter, gnosticism, that was covered (with of course the addition of material that had become available in the intervening period).[6] When an English translation edited by R. McL. Wilson,[7] used the English title Gnosis, this usage was inappropriate, if it was taken to mean not what Bultmann, Leisegang and Foerster meant, but some distinct, much broader thing legislated by the Messina Colloquium. For the collection contains only what the editors took to be gnosticism, rather than including the broader phenomenon gnōsis. Thus, the English title is a mistranslation, if one is to think in Messina terms. The same is true of Robert Haardt's volume on gnosticism entitled in German Gnosis, with the English translated by J. F. Hendry also entitled Gnosis.[8] All these works are collections of what the German authors consider gnostic texts in the sense of gnosticism, just as much as Grant's collection Gnosticism is meant in the sense of gnosticism.

The Messina definition of gnosticism proposes "beginning methodologically with a certain group of systems of the Second Century A.D.

welcoming the distinction as something that can "in fact help," but then conceding that "what gnosis as a religious world view might mean is not yet grasped concretely" (Origini, 703).

[4] Bultmann, Theologie des NT (1st ed.), 168 = 3rd ed. 1958, 172; ET=Theology, 1.168.

[5] Leisegang, Gnosis; Grant, Gnosticism: A Sourcebook.

[6] Die Gnosis, vol. 1: Zeugnisse der Kirchenväter, ed. W. Foerster with E. Haenchen and M. Krause; vol. 2: Koptische und Mandäische Quellen, ed. C. Andresen and W. Foerster with M. Krause and K. Rudolph; vol. 3: Der Manichäismus, by A. Böhlig with Jes Peter Asmussen.

[7] Foerster, Gnosis.

[8] Haardt, Gnosis; ET=Gnosis: Character.

which everyone agrees are to be designated with this term."[9] The definition of that phenomenon is quite specific:

> The gnosticism of the Second Century sects involves a coherent series of characteristics
> that can be summarized in the idea of a divine spark in man, deriving from the divine
> realm, fallen into this world of fate, birth and death, and needing to be awakened by
> the divine counterpart of the self in order to be finally reintegrated. Compared with
> other conceptions of a "devolution" of the divine, this idea is based ontologically on the
> conception of a downward movement of the divine whose periphery (often called
> Sophia or Ennoia) had to submit to the fate of entering into a crisis and producing—
> even if only indirectly—this world, upon which it cannot turn its back, since it is
> necessary for it to recover the pneuma—a dualistic conception on a monistic back-
> ground, expressed in a double movement of devolution and reintegration.[10]

It is, of course, to be welcomed when any phenomenon in the history
of religions is defined with relative precision on the basis, as here, of
typological and historical study. But the problems begin to emerge when
one moves toward language for the penumbral areas surrounding this
crisp phenomenon. For, "in distinction from this [second-century phe-
nomenon], gnosis is regarded as 'knowledge of the divine mysteries
reserved for an elite.'" This very broad definition of gnōsis, however,
makes it rather useless, in that many religions would qualify as such
gnōsis. To describe something as gnōsis in this sense would say no more
than that is is like apocalypticism, Qumran, John the Baptist, Paul, and
Mark. One might compare the terms pietism and piety—to describe a
religion as pietism provides a relevant characterization, but to describe
it as piety is so general as to be hardly worth saying. But according to the
Messina document one cannot go beyond this vague gnōsis unless a
religious phenomenon "is conditioned by the ontological, theological
and anthropological foundations indicated above." Since the definition
to which this refers is very specific and doctrinal, there is no middle
ground between the extremes, no bridge, to use the metaphor of the title:

> Not every gnosis is gnosticism, but only that which involves in this perspective the idea
> of the divine consubstantiality of the spark that is in need of being awakened and
> reintegrated. This gnosis of gnosticism involves the divine identity of the knower (the
> gnostic), the known (the divine substance of one's transcendent self), and the means by
> which one knows (gnosis as an implicit divine faculty [that] is to be awakened and
> actualized. This gnosis is a revelation-tradition of a different type from the Biblical and
> Islamic revelation-tradition).[11]

Thus, the Messina document has already ruled that the biblical tradition
does not include the gnōsis of gnosticism, at which point the basic
problem of our Working Seminar on Gnosticism and Early Christianity

[9] Bianchi, Origini, xxvi.
[10] Bianchi, Origini, xxvi–xxvii.
[11] Bianchi, Origini, xxvii.

would be conveniently solved for us, if we were simply to appropriate the Messina document.

If one nonetheless has the temerity to inquire about gnosticism before the second century, one is given an option between *pre-gnosticism* and *proto-gnosticism*:

> If it is a matter of *pre-gnosticism* one can investigate the pre-existence of different themes and motifs constituting such a "pre-" but not yet involving gnosticism. But if it is a matter of *proto-gnosticism*, one can think to find the essence of gnosticism already in the centuries preceding the Second Century A.D., as well as outside the Christian gnosticism of the Second Century.[12]

Yet *pre-gnosticism*, like *gnōsis*, is so broad as to include almost anything and hence to say almost nothing, whereas *proto-gnosticism* may be found, by those who so choose, anywhere from Iran to Orphism, except *not*, by definition, in normative Judaism and Christianity:

> Some scholars have also inquired as to the position of Christianity in relation to pre-gnosticism or proto-gnosticism. In this regard it seems to the authors of this report that, if gnosticism as defined in I above involves the "devolution" of the divine, it is impossible to classify it as belonging to the same historical and religious type as Judaism or the Christianity of the New Testament and the *Grosskirche*.[13]

Thus, in practise, the purely descriptive definition of second-century gnosticism and its substantive precursor, proto-gnosticism, are by definition ruled out of first-century Christianity. Hence, rather than the study of gnosticism and early Christianity over the next generation being in an open situation due to the discovery of the Nag Hammadi Codices, the Messina definition has in effect ruled that the most recent assured result to which scholarship should be bound as it seeks to adjust previous scholarship to the new situation created by the Nag Hammadi Codices is the traditional view dominant up to the turn of the last century: Christian gnosticism is after all only a second-century phenomenon, a view immortalized in the English language world a generation later by F. C. Burkitt's *Church and Gnosis: A Study of Christian Thought and Speculation in the Second Century*[14] (although to be sure he was not yet a party to the terminological maneuvering and hence did not realize that he should have said "gnosticism"). Thus, to the extent that matters of historical fact can be settled by committee action and definition, our problem is again solved before we actually get into it. Here one can only agree with Hans-Martin Schenke:

---

[12] Bianchi, *Origini*, xxvii.
[13] Bianchi, *Origini*, xxviii.
[14] Burkitt, *Church and Gnosis*.

I am of the opinion that clarity of concepts can under certain conditions also obscure the issue at stake (and does so here). . . . With regard to the proposed concept "gnosticism," in my view this is after all a step backward, insofar as here not only does the old view of gnosticism [German: *Gnosis*] = Christian heresy appear conserved (even if only terminologically), but also and especially what belongs materially and historically together with the systems of the second century, and which has been recognized as such (certain heresies of the NT, Simon Magus, Menander, Hermetica, Mandeans), is artificially separated off (again), so that then the origin of this "gnosticism" actually presents only a sham problem.[15]

But, since the final solution arranged for us at Messina has not yet actually been imposed, the problem may still be investigated briefly in terms of pre-postmodern historical method. It is to this purpose that the present paper is dedicated.

The solution to the traditional problem of gnosticism and early Christianity has not been solved by the publication of the Nag Hammadi Codices. For the early heralding of such a gnostic text as the *Apocalypse of Adam* as "pre-Christian" proved somewhat premature, in that Alexander Böhlig has clarified his usage of that term in the *editio princeps* to mean no more than that the text was not yet under Christian influence, irrespective of the century of its composition.[16] To be sure, a much later dating of that text has subsequently been retracted by Hans-Martin Schenke.

I should like to take this opportunity formally to reject my earlier objection to Böhlig's evaluation of the *Apocalypse of Adam* as a product of pre-Christian gnosis. I must also retract my counter-hypothesis that the *Apocalypse of Adam* should be regarded as a late product of gnosis; this former view of mine, which now seems unjustified in the broader perspective, is still occasionally attributed to me in the literature, to my regret.[17]

And the possibility of sources imbedded in it suggests a still earlier origin for its mythology;[18] yet, neither it nor the other Nag Hammadi texts have settled the question in favor of pre-Christian gnosticism to the satisfaction of those whose argument rests its case on the positivistic observation "no texts, no history."

Furthermore, one only need recall the complexity of the definition of gnosticism in the Messina document to see how hopeless it would be to try to demonstrate that the full system was, item for item, in Pauline congregations of the 50s or the like. To be sure, if one were, in analogy to the Messina procedure, to define orthodox Christianity in second-cen-

---

[15] H.-M. Schenke, "Review."

[16] Böhlig-Labib, *Apokalypsen*, 95: "The writing comes from pre-Christian Gnosticism." The subsequent clarification was in a personal communication.

[17] H.-M. Schenke, "Sethianism," 2.607. He is there retracting the view he had expressed in his review of Böhlig's *editio princeps*, OLZ 61 (1966) 31–32.

[18] Hedrick, *Apocalypse*. See in this regard the critique by Birger Pearson in the present volume.

tury terms, for example in terms of the Apostles' Creed, there would be
as little orthodox Christianity as gnosticism in primitive Christianity and
the New Testament, thereby reopening the discussion in an original
way. Hence, the strategy implicit in limiting gnosticism to the second
century and thereafter, namely the resultant allocation of first-century
Christianity to orthodoxy, cannot be carried through, lest on the same
logic the absence of second-century orthodoxy in the first century lead to
the allocation of first-century Christianity to—heresy! Yet when such a
leading authority on Nag Hammadi and the New Testament as Hans-
Martin Schenke fails to find gnosticism in Pauline congregations during
Paul's lifetime, one should take note of this fact,[19] even if he has re-
opened the question in the light of Dennis R. MacDonald's argument
that Paul is opposing a gnostic concept of baptism in Gal 3:26–28.[20]

Although for the question of the origins of gnosticism it would be very
important to know whether gnosticism were present in the Christianity
of the 50s, for example, in Pauline congregations, this may not only be a
moot question, but also a less relevant way to pose the question, if the
inquiry is directed less to the problem of gnosticism than to the problem
of the development of early Christianity, which is in fact the point of
departure for the research of most of us here. If one may assume that
there must be some lead time to any movement in the history of ideas,
then one may legitimately inquire as to what there was in primitive
Christianity that would have provided a congenial point of departure, a
seedbed, an impetus, which, once gnosticism began to emerge in the
environment, would have invited that trend to express itself in some
strands of Christianity rather than in others. Thus, rather than straining
to argue on the basis of inadequate evidence whether full-blown gnosticism was or was not presupposed at any given point, one would turn to
the documentation that does exist and inquire whether materials that
are not clearly gnostic are nonetheless what could develop into Christian gnosticism, given the necessary incentives in that direction. To be
sure, such an approach would not explain how "gnosticism began to
emerge in the environment" or the origin of the "incentives in that
direction," and to this extent a solution to the origins of gnosticism would
not be attained. But such an approach would conform to the recent
recognition that gnosticism is a "parasite" religion grafting into "host"
religions such as early Judaism and Christianity:[21] Where is one to locate
the "hospitality" of primitive Christianity that was greater than, for

[19] Schenke-Fischer, *Einleitung.*
[20] MacDonald, "Male and Female."
[21] Rudolph, "Gnosis, ein Forschungsbericht" (1971) 23, with reference to Bianchi as the
originator of the concept.

example, that of the imperial cult, which did not develop a gnostic wing? Such an approach might make it possible, to an extent not yet achieved, to trace the trajectories in early Christianity leading into gnosticism and thus might provide a major contribution to our understanding of the beginnings of Christianity and of Christian gnosticism. The present paper is intended to help launch such an undertaking.

II. The Sociological Substructure

The sociological substructure presupposed in gnosticism, namely an ascetic life style, seems particularly related to the bearers of the sayings of Jesus: wandering, begging charismatics. Gerd Theissen has characterized their life style as lack of home, family, possessions, and protection, in distinction from the village life of the sympathizing Jews or Jewish Christians who made that life style possible.[22] Luise Schottroff has emended this presentation to argue that there was not much difference between the economic plight of the wandering charismatic and that of the sedentary peasant, whose misery produced hobos as a by-product.[23] Wolfgang Stegemann has drawn attention to the distinction in class structure between Jesus' followers in Palestine before 70 C.E., who were dirt poor (his idiom is "beggar-poor," Greek ptōchoi), poor to where it hurt, with all the physical and social consequences of real privation, and the Christians outside Palestine, with whom we are more familiar through the books of the New Testament, beginning in the 50s C.E. with Paul. Here the Christians are from the lower and middle classes of handworkers (penētes), but hardly desperately poor.[24] Paul's churches were able to take up collections for Jerusalem-based Christians, which may suggest not only "Peter's pence," a kind of loyalty oath, but also an economic distinction. Now it is primarily from Q that we know about these Palestinian "poor."[25] They are "blessed" (Q 6:20, to make use of the Lucan numeration), and it is to them that "the good news is preached" (Q 7:22).

Another dimension of this same reality has to do with itinerant beggar charismatics who would of necessity wander from hamlet to nearby hamlet, each no more than a day's journey from the other. For they were

---

[22] Theissen, *Followers* = *Sociology;* cf. especially 10–14; German original: *Soziologie.* This was first worked out in Theissen, "Wanderradikalismus," 249–52, reprinted in *Studien,* 83–86; ET = "Itinerant Radicalism."

[23] Schottroff-Stegemann, *Jesus,* 64, 66–67. She considers Theissen's presentation in part improved in "Nachfolge und soziale Entwurzelung" (reprinted in Theissen, *Studien,* pp. 106–41).

[24] Stegemann, *Das Evangelium und die Armen,* 17–25.

[25] Stegemann, *Das Evangelium und die Armen,* 17, 23.

unable to involve themselves in grandiose Pauline-like travel plans, based on a portable job, or make use of "public transportation." By way of contrast, Diaspora Christianity was comprised of widely separated metropolitan centers, provincial capitals, travel to which involved not only overland trips of considerable distances, but especially necessitated the use of commercial traffic by ship from port to port. The shift from fishing boat to passenger ship prefigured that from farm to slum. No sooner would wandering charismatics from the hamlets sail to such a port and find themselves in the slums of the port area than a new life style would come upon them, with all the unintentional but very real shifting of the Christian message that this entailed.

It is to such a wrenching in the sociological reality of primitive Christianity that Gerd Theissen appeals to explain the shift from Q to the *Gospel of Thomas;*

> The sayings tradition could extend itself beyond its original situation in places where it changed its character. Where it was not possible to practice its ethical radicalism, it was possible to transform it into gnostic radicalism. The radicalism in action became in this way a radicalism in knowledge which did not necessarily require concrete results in behavior. We find a sayings tradition modified in just such a direction in the *Gospel of Thomas. . . .*[26]

By means of this theory Theissen supplies a much-needed sociological supplement to my presentation worked out too exclusively in terms of the history of ideas:

> Not only is the *Gospel of Thomas* a modified sayings tradition, but it is also a tempered gnosticism. The concrete demands are softened and transformed into a speculative mode. This change is not simply inevitable in the sayings tradition form (as J. M. Robinson proposes in "LOGOI SOPHŌN"), but probably presupposes a change in the carriers of the tradition, another social milieu in which the words of Jesus were no longer practical in their concreteness.[27]

It is, of course, the case that the genre of the sayings collection will not automatically end in gnosticism. Wisdom literature continued as wisdom literature; Pirke Aboth is not a gnostic text. That the sayings collection lacks the flesh and bones of a narrative framework, and hence a biographical cast such as the canonical Gospels present, does mean, however, that it might well be congenial to gnostic docetism, since only the message of the gnostic Redeemer, even in the form of a letter (the Hymn of the Pearl), is all that is actually needed. But it should have been obvious without having to be said that the gnosticizing proclivity of the sayings collection does in fact need some catalyst to go into effect.

---

[26] Theissen, "Wanderradikalismus," 269 = *Studien* 103 = "Itinerant Radicalism," 90.

[27] Theissen, "Wanderradikalismus," 269 = *Studien,* 103 = "Itinerant Radicalism," 93, n. 24, citing Robinson, "LOGOI SOPHŌN," *Zeit und Geschichte,* 77–96. Enlarged ET in *Future of Our Religious Past,* 84–130, and in Robinson-Koester, *Trajectories,* 71–113.

Yet the main trajectory of the sayings collection in primitive Christianity, which one might traditionally mock up as Q, QMt, Matthew, *Didache*, the *Gospel of Thomas*, need not have involved such a geographical-sociological jolt as Theissen suggests, as one moves beyond the Galilean Jesus movement into the Diaspora (although this would indeed be the case if one were to move from Chorazin and Bethsaida to Ephesus, Corinth, Alexandria and Rome). Rather, there was one direction in which the expansion of Christianity could have been by osmosis, from hamlet to nearby hamlet: toward Syria.

Theissen has made the point that one of the shifts involved in moving from the hamlet to the city had to do with language—the native languages persisted for centuries in the countryside long after the metropolitan centers had become functionally Greek, or at least with a Greek hegemony in a multi-lingual cosmopolitanism.[28] Thus, the shift from Aramaic to Greek is less a matter of from Palestine to the Diaspora than from the hamlet to the metropolitan center, where in the case of the Diaspora the movement would tend to get stuck. For once arrived at a provincial capital, the itinerant Galilean charismatic could not move back into the rural life style of hamlets outside the metropolitan area, where the native languages of the hamlets would now also be foreign— except in the area of Aramaic hegemony.

This consideration points clearly in one direction on a map, where the only land bridge for expansion out of Galilee hamlet by hamlet is through the Fertile Crescent, into Syria. Here the Aramaic mission could expand by small increments without any real awareness of provincial frontiers, indeed without any real need for a metropolitan point of departure. To whatever extent Jerusalem might at first have functioned as a sort of headquarters for the itinerant mendicant mission, it could readily have been replaced by Antioch. The shift of the itinerant leader Peter from Jerusalem to Antioch might serve as a symbol for this option. To be sure, in view of its prominence throughout the Synoptic gospels (Q 7:1), Capernaum might seem to have played that role. Perhaps that is why things came to a crisis there leading to the woe pronounced on that town when it stamped out the Jesus movement (Q 10:15). For, in spite of the presentation in Acts, one need not think of a single centralized headquarters even for a particular brand of early Christianity such as the sayings tradition seems to represent. From Chorazin and Bethsaida (Q 10:13) or from Capernaum to Tyre and Sidon or to the Decapolis (Mark 3:8; 5:20; 7:24.31) is a progression that would have been relatively imperceptible. There need have been no sudden wrenching of the

---

[28] Theissen, "Wanderradikalismus," 267 = *Studien* 101 = "Itinerant Radicalism," 90.

sayings tradition, once it could presuppose the literacy and Greek reflected in the redaction of Q, as it moved between Q and the *Gospel of Thomas*, even if this meant between (the regions of) Antioch and Edessa. This evolution, rather than cultural revolution, is in fact suggested by Theissen's characterization of Thomas as "tempered gnosticism."

It may be that the contrast between "conduct radicalism" in Q and "epistemological radicalism" in the *Gospel of Thomas* has also been overdrawn, as Kendrick Grobel has tended to argue in the case of the *Gospel of Thomas*:

> In several places Jewish subject-matter is detectable. I cannot convince myself that Thomas' "make the Sabbath Sabbath" (27) is to be spiritualized into vapour as it is by most commentators. After all, Jewish Christians—and some Gentile Christians, too?—continued literal Sabbath-observance long after they were Christian. There is also evidence in Thomas for a social concern which it would not surprise us to find among either Jews or Christians but which, so far as I am aware, is unknown among gnostics. Usury (a Jewish topic!) is explicitly forbidden in 95: "If you have coins, do not lend at usury but give them to him from whom you shall not get them (back)," which by omitting any reference to "hope" or "expect" apparently goes beyond even Luke vi. 34, 35 in enjoining generosity. Concern for one's fellow man is crystal clear in 25 (". . . protect—or : keep—him as the pupil of thine eye"), and so, as I understand it, is 69b: "Blessed are they that go hungry in order that they may fill the stomach of him who desires (to be filled)." The Coptic has some ambiguities here, but I think this translation is justifiable.[29]

Thus the sociological substratum of the trajectory from Q to Thomas may help to explain the way in which the gnosticizing proclivity in the genre of sayings collections was activated. But, on just these terms, the shift in context may not have been as sudden or drastic as Theissen would seem to suggest, corresponding to the fact that the actual difference between the two texts in terms of conduct versus speculation may not have been as great as he has indicated. The trend already perceptible in Q to mark off an unbelieving Judaism as a hopeless last "sinful and adulterous generation" is already a head start in the direction in which the *Gospel of Thomas* may have moved toward a gnostic perception of reality, without there being a real rupture in the curve of the trajectory.

M. Eugene Boring has defined the early Christian prophet as the primary bearer, moulder, and creator of the sayings tradition.[30] This provides an important supplement to our understanding of its sociological substructure. But he, like Schottroff, yet in a somewhat different way, seeks to break down the distinction between the charismatic prophet and the local congregation:

---

[29] Grobel, "Thomas," 373. This passage is quoted by Davies, *Thomas and Wisdom*, 7.
[30] Boring, *Sayings of the Risen Jesus*.

Gerd Theissen in particular has argued that the sayings of Jesus were transmitted in part by prophetic bands at the edge of society and church. Theissen's view that traditions were transmitted by charismatics is well-documented and is to be accepted. His view that sayings of Jesus which include a call for radical abandonment of home and family could only have been handed on by a homeless group on the fringe of society and church need not be accepted.[31]

The itinerant approach is attributed to a misreading and over-gener-alizing on the part of Adolf von Harnack of the then newly discovered *Didache*. Boring argues that the association of prophets with itinerant apostles in *Didache* 11 does not necessarily imply that the prophets were also itinerant, even though false itinerant apostles are called "false prophets." For Boring takes this to be "a general pejorative term that may be applied to a variety of types of fraudulent church leaders."[32] Even the arrival of a prophet from outside in *Did.* 13:1 need not imply itinerancy, since the prophet may be coming from a settled life else-where to settle in the new location.

This somewhat strained interpretation, and similar remarks about admittedly itinerant prophets in other sources, seem to be intended to avoid an inference from itinerancy that is not necessary. Boring uses such pejorative extreme terms as "a 'wandering' stranger who does not belong within the churches he addresses"; "an outsider to the local churches"; "a traveling prophet who intrudes his oracles into a commu-nity to which he does not essentially belong"; "a 'wandering' itinerant who troubles the life of the 'settled' churches"; "wandering bearers of an individualistic charisma"; an "individualistic anthropology"; "wander-ing, individualistic prophets"; "an extra-church transient loner on the fringes of stable congregational life."[33] The mission of the Twelve/ Seventy would seem not to presuppose congregations in the hamlets to which the itinerant went, but rather unevangelized Jewish communities with a town synagogue and varying degrees of hospitality and sympa-thizers. To be sure, ultimately congregations would have emerged in at least some of these hamlets, and there may have been a congregation from which the itinerant took his or her departure and to which they from time to time returned, as Boring insists:

This speech implies a somewhat settled, structured community, from which wandering missioners are sent out and to which they return. The very existence of the Q-tradition that precipitated a Q-document also implies a settled community. We should probably think of a scene resembling Acts 13:1–3 as a representative event in the life of this community and the setting for such a missionary charge as this speech.[34]

[31] Boring, *Sayings of the Risen Jesus*, 77.
[32] Boring, *Sayings of the Risen Jesus*, 59.
[33] Boring, *Sayings of the Risen Jesus*, 59–62.
[34] Boring, *Sayings of the Risen Jesus*, 149.

Yet it seems to go a bit too far when Boring suggests that it may not have
been those who were sent out who were the bearers of the Q sayings:

> Some of these messengers may themselves have been prophets, but not necessarily all
> of them. The mission is seen from a prophetic point of view, but this is because the
> speaker is a prophet. In view of the frequent assertion that early Christian prophets
> were "wandering," it should be noted here that it is those who are addressed who
> "wander," not necessarily the prophet-speaker of this mission charge himself.[35]

Yet the itinerant messengers are instructed to say "The kingdom of God
has come near to you" (Q 10:9), which fits Boring's definition of the
prophet as re-presenting Jesus' sayings (Mark 1:15).[36] This is more
explicit in Mark 6:11: "And if any place will not receive you and they
refuse to hear you ..." (Matt 10:14 "... listen to your words ..."). At this
Marcan position Luke 9:2 presents in indirect discourse ("And he sent
them out to preach the kingdom of God and to heal") the Q saying that
he quotes in direct discourse at the Q position (Luke 10:9), but that
Matthew quotes in direct discourse in this Marcan context (Matt 10:7).
And, of course, the prototype on whose tongue the Q community put its
message was himself itinerant, with "nowhere to lay his head" (Q 9:58).

Boring is most comfortable with what he takes to be the Matthean
situation:

> But the Matthean community also knows a relatively small number of "wandering"
> prophets, prophets who were not independent free lancers but delegated missioners of
> the Matthean church. In addition, there was a larger group of congregational leaders in
> the church, who were not "wandering" but resident in the congregation, who recog-
> nized that discipleship to Jesus was to be practiced in prophetic terms. They performed
> prophetic functions in the community, including speaking in the name of the risen Lord.
> These are not sharply distinguished from the disciples in general but they did form a
> recognizably distinct group. This is the picture of prophecy in the Matthean church that
> I accept. It would seem, therefore, that peculiarly Matthean statements about Christian
> prophets, and traditions representing the Matthean church, might be used in character-
> izing prophecy in Palestine-Syria in the last third of the first century.[37]

Though this may be the goal and the outcome of the charismatic
prophetic movement, it may well be somewhat anachronistic to read Q
in terms of it. The situation may be conceptualized in analogy to a more
familiar discussion: infant baptism could hardly have predominated in
the first generation, due to the lack of Christian parents to produce
Christian children, even though infant baptism may have been known at
the time in instances of the conversion of a whole household. But a
generation or so later the practice that might have begun as an exception

---

[35] Boring, *Sayings of the Risen Jesus*, 149.
[36] So already Theissen, "Wanderradikalismus," 253=*Studien*, 87="Itinerant Radicalism," 86.
[37] Boring, *Sayings of the Risen Jesus*, 45.

became more nearly the rule, as the sociological reality of Christianity shifted into that of a religion with a tradition and a culture of its own. Just so itinerant prophets may initially have wandered from pillar to post, with at best a home base to which to return as part of a "circuit," but with nowhere to rest their heads or to be sure of a square meal while out "in the field." But a generation or so later some of the households that had taken them in had become house churches, until the network of such local congregations would gradually come to represent the rule rather than the exception. Thus the itinerant charismatic would increasingly become an exception, to be monitored and ultimately to be given an honored, limited, and thereby domesticated role in the development that led to Christian monasticism—and gnosticism. One may compare the later experience of emergent monasticism; there the rigors of asceticism were acceptable as long as limited to the monks but heretical if universalized as conditions for admission to salvation on the part of all Christians (the heresy of the Egyptian ascetic Hieracas; see already Matt 19:12).

In Boring's detailed characterization of the charismatic prophet as bearer of the tradition of Jesus' sayings various aspects, though surely not necessarily gnostic, do, like the "wandering radicalism" of Theissen, provide a congenial trunk into which gnosticism could be grafted, a proclivity that could under certain circumstances be developed in a gnosticizing way. One is instinctively reminded of the Pauline opponents of 1 Corinthians when one reads of these prophets:

> Being subject to the judgment of the community does not relativize the authoritative form of the prophet's speech, which is delivered with a sense of absolute authority. Consequently, the form and tone of such sayings would be very like the sayings of Jesus himself (Matt. 7:29) and distinguishable from the sayings of ordinary Christian teachers and scribes.[38]

Or, to return to the encratite life style:

> Paul understands that apostles and the brothers of the Lord have the right to marry, and as an apostle he has that right. However, he and the prophet Barnabas are not married (I Cor. 9:5), which may reflect their prophetic ministry, though Paul himself does not make this connection explicitly. The successors of Paul, claiming the authority of prophetic revelation, *opposed* abstinence from marriage (I Tim. 4:1–5), but this may be because Paul's earlier prophetic-eschatological idealization of the unmarried state (I Cor. 7:25–40) was no longer understood eschatologically, but as a part of the general gnostic rejection of the world.... There is some significant evidence, then, that early Christian prophets typically were committed to poverty and sexual abstinence, and we may expect to find that sayings originating from, or shaped by, such prophets may sometimes manifest this commitment.[39]

[38] Boring, *Sayings of the Risen Jesus*, 90.
[39] Boring, *Sayings of the Risen Jesus*, 94.

Thus one may conclude that both in terms of the sociological analyses of wandering charismatics by Theissen, Schottroff, and Stegemann and in terms of Boring's clarification of early Christian charismatic prophets a religious type tends to emerge that would be intelligible as the sociological substratum of the trajectory from the sayings tradition reflected in Q and the *Gospel of Thomas* on into gnosticism and monasticism.

III. The Dating of Q and the Gospel of Thomas

Bernard P. Grenfell and Arthur S. Hunt reported in 1897 concerning Papyrus Oxyrhynchus 1 (*Gospel of Thomas* Sayings 26–33, 77a):

> Since the papyrus itself was written not much later than the beginning of the third century, this collection of sayings must go back at least to the end of the second century. But the internal evidence points to an earlier date. The primitive cast and setting of the sayings, the absence of any consistent tendency in favour of any particular sect [!], the wide divergences in the familiar sayings from the text of the Gospels, the striking character of those which are new, combine to separate the fragment from the "apocryphal" literature of the middle and latter half of the second century, and to refer it back to the period when the Canonical Gospels had not yet reached their pre-eminent position. Taking 140 A.D., then, as the *terminus ad quem*, and postponing for the present the question of the *terminus a quo*, we proceed to consider the possibility, which the provenance of the papyrus naturally suggests, that our fragment may come from the "Gospel according to the Egyptians." This Gospel, of which only a few extracts survive, was probably written about the beginning of the second century, and seems for a time to have attained in Egypt and even elsewhere a high degree of authority. . . .
>
> A more satisfactory view, though not free from difficulties, is that this fragment is what it professes to be, a collection of some of our Lord's sayings. These, judging from their archaic tone and framework, were put together not later than the end of the first or the beginning of the second century; and it is quite possible that they embody a tradition independent of those which have taken shape in our Canonical Gospels. . . .
>
> Of the peculiar tenets of developed gnosticism we have here not a vestige. Even if the prevailing judgment of these sayings should be that they were preserved in gnostic circles, and themselves show some trace of the tendencies out of which gnosticism developed, it does not follow that they are therefore inventions. And, whether free or not from gnostic influence, the genuine ring of what is new in this fragment, and the primitive cast of the whole, are all in favour of its independence of our Gospels in their present shape.[40]

They concluded "that they were earlier than 140 A.D., and might go back to the first century."[41]

With the discovery a few years later of P. Oxy. 654 (*Gospel of Thomas* Prologue and Sayings 1–7) there was no basic change in their view:

> Accordingly, we should propose A.D. 140 for the *terminus ad quem* in reference to 654 with greater confidence than we felt about 1 in 1897.[42]

---

[40] Grenfell-Hunt, *LOGIA*, 16,18,20.
[41] Grenfell-Hunt, *Papyri I*, 2.
[42] Grenfell-Hunt, *Papyri IV*, 15.

To be sure, they did not realize that P. Oxy. 655 was also part of the *Gospel of Thomas* (Sayings 24, 36–39), and did give it on its own terms a somewhat later date, suspecting that it might presuppose the canonical Gospels:

> The Gospel from which 655 comes is likely to have been composed in Egypt before A.D. 150, and to have stood in intimate relation to the Gospel according to the Egyptians and the uncanonical source used by the author of *II Clem*. Whether it was earlier or later than these is not clear.[43]

If Grenfell and Hunt had known only less primitive segments of the *Gospel of Thomas*, they might well have dated it later than they did. Perhaps for this reason the standard edition of the Coptic *Gospel of Thomas* introduced the modern discussion in language that opted for the "*terminus ad quem*" rather than the turn-of-the-century date actually favored within the spectrum earlier proposed:

> We are dealing here with a translation or an adaptation in Sahidic Coptic of a work the primitive text of which must have been produced in Greek about 140 A.D., and which was based on even more ancient sources.[44]

A much different assessment of the chronological situation was proposed in 1971 by Helmut Koester, and in a way that would seem to put Q and *Gospel of Thomas* side by side. In Koester's view the *Gospel of Thomas* is a second edition of a "sayings gospel," a gospel similar to the one of which Q is also the second edition.

> The basis of the *Gospel of Thomas* is a sayings collection which is more primitive than the canonical gospels, even though its basic principle is not related to the creed of the passion and resurrection. Its principle is nonetheless theological. Faith is understood as belief in Jesus' words, a belief which makes what Jesus proclaimed present and real for the believer. The catalyst which has caused the crystallization of these sayings into a "gospel" is the view that the kingdom is uniquely present in Jesus' eschatological preaching and that eternal wisdom about man's true self is disclosed in his words. The gnostic proclivity of this concept needs no further elaboration.
>
> The relation of this "sayings gospel," from which the *Gospel of Thomas* is derived, to the synoptic sayings source Q, is an open question. Without doubt, most of its materials are Q sayings (including some sayings which appear occasionally in Mark). But it must have been a version of Q in which the apocalyptic expectation of the Son of Man was missing, and in which Jesus' radicalized eschatology of the kingdom and his revelation of divine wisdom in his own words were dominant motifs.
>
> Such a version of Q is, however, not secondary, but very primitive. At least Paul's debate with his opponents in 1 Corinthians seems to suggest that the wisdom theology which Paul attacked relied on this understanding of Jesus' message. These opponents propagated a realized eschatology. They claimed that divine wisdom was revealed through Jesus. And at least one saying which Paul quotes in the context of his refutation is indeed found in the *Gospel of Thomas* 17 (1 Cor. 2:9).
>
> This would prove that such sayings collections with explicit theological tendencies

---

[43] Grenfell-Hunt, *Papyri IV*, 28.
[44] Guillaumont, *Thomas*, vi.

were in use quite early, and not only in Aramaic-speaking circles in Syria; that the source "Q," used by Matthew and Luke, was a secondary version of such a "gospel," into which the apocalyptic expectation of the Son of Man had been introduced to check the gnosticizing tendencies of this sayings gospel; and that the *Gospel of Thomas*, stemming from a more primitive stage of such a "gospel," attests its further growth into a gnostic theology.[45]

Koester's presentation would seem to postulate a four-stage procedure: (1) a pre-apocalyptic (written? Greek?) precursor of Q without the Son of Man but oriented to radicalized realized eschatological and sapiential traditions; (2) usage of (1) by the *Gospel of Thomas* with similar traits; (3) a bifurcation of the trajectory, with our Q using a Son-of-Man apocalypticism to oppose the gnosticizing proclivity to which (4) the *Gospel of Thomas* in effect yielded.

Meanwhile Koester has developed his position in considerably more detail. This is somewhat less apparent in his most recent publication, where his presentation is in the context of a vast survey where specifics cannot be itemized:

Q certainly had preliminary stages, such as occasional collections of sayings for catechetical, polemical, and homiletical purposes. But in its final composition and redaction, Q became an ecclesiastical manual which sought to bind the churches for which it was written to a particular eschatological expectation, and to conduct which was in keeping with this expectation. Its central feature was the waiting for the coming of Jesus as the Son of Man (Luke 17:22–37). This expectation, which seems to be missing in the oldest stages of the Synoptic sayings of Jesus, is derived from Jewish apocalyptic concepts (Dan 7:13–14). In Q it has become the key christological concept for the understanding of Jesus as the redeemer of the future. In contrast, the older expectation of the coming of the rule of God recedes into the background. . . .

Another tradition of interpretation of the sayings of Jesus, which also originates from the realm of Syria/Palestine, renounced the eschatological expectation which looks to the future. Characteristic for this tradition are sayings in which Jesus appears as a teacher of wisdom, or in which he speaks with the authority of the heavenly figure of Wisdom. With such words Jesus grants salvation to those who are able and prepared to hear and understand them. Similar sayings of Jesus are also preserved within the Q tradition (Matt 11:25–30; Luke 11:49–51), but they are unimportant in comparison with the dominating expectation of Jesus as the Son of Man. Through the discoveries of Nag Hammadi it has become possible to identify more clearly the interpretation of Jesus' sayings in terms of revealed wisdom, a tradition which apparently goes back to the earliest period of Christianity. The *Gospel of Thomas* . . . was probably written during I CE in Palestine or Syria. The absence of any influence from the canonical gospels and the location of the Thomas tradition in Syria are strong arguments for this date and provenance (cf. the later *Acts of Thomas*, which are certainly Syrian).

In contrast to other writings from the Nag Hammadi Library, the *Gospel of Thomas* shows no trace of the kerygma of the cross and the resurrection of Jesus. It is more sparing than Q in its use of christological titles; even the title of Son of Man is missing. . . . The contrast between Thomas and Jesus' brother James, which appears in Sayings 12 and 13 of the *Gospel of Thomas*, allows the conjecture that the author of this gospel belongs to Christian circles which sought to strengthen and defend the right of the tradition of Thomas against the authority of James, without denying the latter's

---

[45] Robinson-Koester, *Trajectories*, 186–87.

claim to leadership in ecclesiastical matters. This seems to reflect a politico-ecclesiastical situation in Palestine in I CE better than a controversy from a later period.[46]

In the Introduction to his forthcoming edition of the Gospel of Thomas Koester goes into considerably more detail concerning his understanding of the composition and dating of this text. And here he provides more specific reasons for his views. Relevant excerpts are with his permission here presented for discussion:

> [The Gospel of Thomas] was written in Syria between A.D. 70 and 100. . . . If the canonical gospels of the New Testament were used in the Gospel of Thomas, it could be classified as a writing of the second century which combined and harmonized sayings drawn from Matthew, Mark, and Luke. Examples of such sayings collections appear in 2 Clement and Justin Martyr (ca. A.D. 150). But in the Gospel of Thomas no such dependence can be demonstrated . . . , nor is any other early Christian writing used. Rather, the Gospel of Thomas is similar to the sources of the canonical gospels, in particular the synoptic sayings source (Q). Therefore a date of composition in the first century A.D. is likely. . . .
>
> A comparison with the Synoptic parallels . . . demonstrates that the forms of the sayings in the Gospel of Thomas are either more original than they or developed from forms which are more original. The biographical framework of Matthew, Mark, and Luke and their editorial changes are not reflected in the Gospel of Thomas. Parallels in the Synoptic gospels appear most frequently in those sections which reproduce older collections (Matthew 5–7 and Luke 6; Mark 4 and Matthew 13; Mark 4:22–25; Luke 12:35–56). . . .
>
> Sayings which Matthew and Luke have derived from their common source, the Synoptic Sayings Source (Q), occur frequently in the Gospel of Thomas (cf. especially Matthew 5–7 and Luke 6). However, the sayings about the future coming of the Son of Man which Q seems to have added to the older tradition of the sayings of Jesus are missing (in saying 86, "son of man" means "human being"; cf. saying 106). On the other hand, sayings about the kingdom ("of the father") are very frequent in the Gospel of Thomas (sayings 3, 20, 22, 27, 46, 49, 54, 57, 82, 96–99, 109, 113–114). If the sayings of Jesus about the kingdom indeed belong to an older stage of the sayings tradition than the Son of Man sayings, the sayings of the Gospel of Thomas derive from a stage of the developing sayings tradition which is more original than Q. This implies also that some of those sayings in the Gospel of Thomas which have no parallels in the Synoptic gospels could derive from the earliest stage of the tradition of sayings of Jesus. . . .
>
> Analogous to the Gospel of Thomas, however, is the earlier sayings tradition which preceded the final redaction of Q, in which the title Son of Man was introduced.
>
> With respect to the development of ecclesiastical authority, the Gospel of Thomas reflects the authority position of James, the brother of Jesus (saying 12; cf. Gal. 1:19; 2:9, 12; Acts 15:13; 21:18). His authority, however, is superseded by that of Thomas, who is entrusted with the secret tradition (saying 13). At the same time, Thomas's authority is contrasted with that of Peter, which was well established in Syria (Gal 1:18; 2:7–9; Matt 16:15–19), and that of Matthew, whose name may have been associated with the sayings tradition at an early date. . . . The authority of figures such as James and Peter (as also of Paul) would have been recognized during their lifetime in areas where they actually worked. In order to confirm these apostles' authority after their death, pseudonymous writings were produced under their names as early as the last three decades of the first century, especially when apostles were quoted on different sides of controversial issues (cf. 2 Thess 2:1–2). The Gospel of Thomas is intended to confirm Thomas's authority in contrast to claims made on behalf of ecclesiastical traditions under the authority of

---

[46] Koester, Einführung, 584, 586–87; ET=Introduction, 2.147–48, 150, 152–53.

James, Peter and Matthew—not because an apostolic name was needed to confirm the authority of Jesus, the author of the sayings, but in order to safeguard the special form of the tradition of churches which looked back to Thomas as their founder or as the guarantor of their faith.

The ascription of an early Christian wisdom book, composed of sayings of Jesus, to Matthew constitutes important evidence for the transmission of secret wisdom under apostolic authority. 1 Cor 1:11–17 attacks claims to possess special wisdom under the authority of Peter, Paul, Apollos and Jesus. This establishes an early date for the claiming of apostolic authority for secret wisdom. An "apocryphal" saying quoted by Paul in 1 Cor 2:9 is also preserved in the Gospel of Thomas (saying 17). We do not know how early the name of the apostle Thomas was associated with such traditions. But the ascription of wisdom books to the authority of an apostle is certainly an early form of pseudepigraphical literary production in the history of Christianity.[47]

In his Shaffer Lectures at Yale in 1980, still unpublished and hence also excerpted with his permission here for discussion, Koester described the relation of Q to the Gospel of Thomas or its major source as follows:

In that source [behind the Gospel of Thomas] as well as in the Gospel of Thomas one finds the same type of sayings materials: prophetic sayings, wisdom sayings and proverbs, metaphors and parables, I-sayings, and community regulations. It is striking, however, that the sayings about the coming Son of Man which are characteristic of the Synoptic Sayings Source do not appear in the Gospel of Thomas. Furthermore, apocalyptic sayings are comparatively rare, while wisdom sayings and revelation sayings— not absent from the Synoptic Sayings Source—predominate. The Gospel of Thomas is thus an old Christian sayings collection, or else based upon an older collection, which is more closely related to the genre of the wisdom book than the second common source of Matthew and Luke.[48]

Then this nuanced comparison of Q and the Gospel of Thomas is worked out in considerably more detail:

Sayings of Jesus must have been widely used in the first decades of the early Christian communities, and they were certainly collected and perhaps even written down at an early time. One of the several interests which prompted such collections was the need for instruction of the members of the churches. Sayings of Jesus were thus composed into catechisms, often combined with sayings and proverbs which had been drawn from the Jewish catechism of the "Two Ways," the way of life and the way of death. Paul already knew such catechetical materials, perhaps also collections of rules for the community composed of sayings. . . .

A second type of early collections of sayings concerns the wisdom sayings. The beginnings of such collections cannot be described with any certainty. But traces can be discovered very early. Wisdom sayings were known in the church in Corinth as early as its foundation by the apostle Paul. It is interesting that one of these wisdom sayings is

---

[47] Koester, "Thomas," in Nag Hammadi Codex II, para. 1, 3, 10, 7, 12, typescript pp. 1, 3, 9–10, 6–7, 15.

[48] Koester, "Tradition and History," II.3, typescript, p. 55. Since the Shaffer Lectures were in large part a translation and adaptation of a German article written by then, but only published in 1984, reference to it will provide further details: Helmut Koester, "Überlieferung und Geschichte."

quoted by Paul as "scripture" in 1 Cor 2:9. . . . Whatever the origin of this saying—it probably comes from a Jewish wisdom book—the *Gospel of Thomas* demonstrates that it found entrance into the tradition of wisdom sayings of Jesus (*Gospel of Thomas* 17). Moreover, there are some striking terminological similarities between the vocabulary of 1 Cor 1–4 and wisdom sayings preserved elsewhere as sayings of Jesus, especially with Matt 11:25–30 and Luke 10:21–24. . . . Such sayings may have been current among the Corinthians who spoke of Jesus as the revealer of heavenly wisdom. Indeed, in these sayings of the Synoptic Gospels, Jesus speaks in the first person singular with the voice of heavenly wisdom. The close relationship to traditional Jewish wisdom sayings is evident in Luke 11:49–51 where such a saying is quoted. . . . Matthew 23:34–35 simply omits the quotation formula and thus changes this quotation from a wisdom book into a saying of Jesus. In another instance, the origin of a saying in the wisdom tradition is evident from the conclusion "Yet wisdom is justified by all her children" (Luke 7:35; cf. Matt 11:19). Another wisdom tradition appears in Matt 23:37–39 (Luke 13:34–35) in which heavenly wisdom recalls all she has done in the past to save Jerusalem. The widespread occurrence of such sayings leads to the conclusion that the earliest wisdom books circulating in early Christian communities seem to have been collections of Jewish wisdom sayings. Once these sayings or the whole book were ascribed to Jesus, Jesus became the teacher of wisdom; this seems to have been the case in the Corinthian church. The further development of this tradition, however, shows that Jesus was more and more identified with the figure of heavenly wisdom.

1 Corinthians 1–4 indicates that the wisdom teaching of Jesus was understood as a secret teaching for the perfect; it is exactly this point that is attacked by Paul. A similar perspective has also been connected with the transmission of the parables of Jesus. A written collection of parables was included in Mark's Gospel (Mark 4). Twice in this collection it is emphasized that the mystery of the kingdom of God is given solely to the disciples, not to those "outside." Only to the disciples does Jesus explain the parables (Mark 4:10–12, 33–34). That this concept was not an isolated phenomenon and that it predates the Gospel of Mark, is now confirmed by the *Gospel of Thomas*, where the reproduction of a group of parables is introduced by the saying: "It is to those who are worthy of my mysteries that I tell my mysteries" (*Gospel of Thomas* 62). The parables of the kingdom are no longer understood as prophetic proclamation of the coming of a new age, but in analogy to the wisdom theology as special revelation to the elect which had been hidden until now and remains hidden for those outside. The concept of wisdom hidden and revealed also occurred in the wisdom sayings of Matthew 11 mentioned above; Paul explicitly refers to it in 1 Cor 2:6–7; and it is expressed in numerous other wisdom sayings (e.g., Mark 4:21–22; Luke 12:2–3).

In addition to the composition of catechisms and community regulations and to the written collections of wisdom materials in analogy to the Jewish wisdom books, there is evidence for a third development which resulted in the written composition of sayings of Jesus. This latter development is closely associated with the eschatological expectation of early Christian communities, perhaps even specifically with the Christian community in Jerusalem. But it must also be presupposed for the Pauline mission. . . . This apocalypse in Mark 13 is one of the cases where one can be fairly certain that Mark used a written source, probably a brief writing composed for purposes of instruction or propaganda. Part of the apocalyptic orientation expressed here is the expectation of the coming of the Son of Man on the clouds of heaven (Mark 13:26). The same expression dominates the apocalyptic sayings which the Synoptic Sayings Source has combined with older wisdom materials (cf. especially Luke 17:22–37). This particular Jewish expectation, ultimately deriving from the book of Daniel, may have been the catalyst for the collection of apocalyptic sayings of Jesus, including those materials which are determined by the quite different, and probably older, expectation of the coming of the kingdom of God.

Smaller written collections of wisdom sayings and of apocalyptic traditions, both transmitted under the authority of Jesus, must be presupposed for the first Christian sayings gospel for which we have some more tangible evidence: the so-called Synoptic Sayings Source. The dual character of this sayings gospel is evident, both in its attestation in the Gospel of Matthew and in the Gospel of Luke. Wisdom material occurs repeatedly in the parallel passages of these two gospels, and a major collection of wisdom sayings in the form of a wisdom book seems to have been the basis of this sayings gospel and originally determined its genre. But the final redaction of this book is dominated by those sayings which proclaim the coming of the Son of Man (e.g., Luke 17:22–37). . . . Admonitions in view of the unexpected coming of the parousia occupy the center stage (Luke 12:35–46). Even materials which belong to the genre of church order express this eschatological orientation. The Christian missionary is requested to reject all material possessions and not to settle anywhere (Luke 10:1–16; Matt 9:35–10:16). If Matt 10:23 ("You will not have gone through all the towns of Israel, before the Son of Man comes") can be assigned to the Synoptic Sayings Source (there is no parallel in Luke), the hypothesis of the localization of this writing in the Christian mission in Palestine as well as the urgency of the eschatological expectation would find a strong support. At the same time, the Synoptic Sayings Source clearly differentiates between the Christian expectation and the national and political messianism of contemporary Palestinian Judaism: the emphasis upon the commandment of loving one's enemies rejects indisputably all apocalyptic movements which want to force the coming of God's rule by hostile actions against the enemies of God (Luke 6:27–30). For the relation of the Synoptic Sayings Source to Judaism, two points are characteristic: The question of the Law does not seem to play any role; but the originally inner-Jewish polemic against the leaders of the people as the murderers of the prophets has been incorporated into the sayings of Jesus (Luke 11:49–51; cf. Matt 23:37–39). Also this indicates that the circles which produced this book must be located in Palestine, and that these Christians had indeed experienced persecution by Jewish authorities; cf. also the macarism of those who are persecuted because of the Son of Man (Luke 6:22–23). In this apocalyptic orientation which tries to establish a critical distance to the social and religious environment of Palestinian Judaism, the wisdom element of the tradition incorporated in this writing plays only a minor role in comparison with the dominant eschatological orientation.

In the *Gospel of Thomas*, however, a closely related sayings gospel, the wisdom element predominates. . . . Many of the sayings of the Synoptic Sayings Source also appear in the *Gospel of Thomas*. But the apocalyptic sayings about the coming of the Son of Man are missing completely, while wisdom sayings are more numerous than eschatological and prophetic sayings. Thus this gospel is more true to its genre, the wisdom book. For the genre of the wisdom book it is typical that many sayings are formulated as general truths (*Gospel of Thomas* 31–35, 47, 67, 94), that admonitions to recognize oneself occur repeatedly (2, 29, 49, 50, 67, 111), and that also the figure of heavenly wisdom appears and speaks about herself. However, instead of wisdom, it is now Jesus who speaks about himself in the style of I-sayings. The most striking of these I-sayings presents Jesus in analogy to wisdom who came into the world but did not find either an abode for herself, nor people who wanted to listen to her voice (*Gospel of Thomas* 28). . . . Parables of Jesus, most of them originally prophetic announcements of the coming of the kingdom, as well as prophetic sayings are interpreted as expressions of the presence of the kingdom of the heavens (or: kingdom of the Father). It is present in the person of Jesus for the disciples (*Gospel of Thomas* 3, 51, 52, 91). But the future expectation is never emphasized. . . . A typical example is the reformulation of the Parable of the Fishnet, which is used in Matt 13:47–48 as an illustration of the coming judgment; in the *Gospel of Thomas* (8) it is a parable about the finding of the treasure of wisdom. . . . That the parables are understood as secret instruction (*Gospel of Thomas* 62) corresponds to the understanding of the parables in Mark 4, and the general concept of the wisdom words of Jesus as secret words (*Gospel of Thomas* prologue) has its analogue in the understanding of wisdom teaching among the Corinthians against whom Paul argues in 1 Corinthians 1–4. Thus, so far the *Gospel of Thomas* presents an understanding of the wisdom sayings of Jesus which is in agreement with the principles of the wisdom book that was the catalyst for the earliest written collections of these sayings.[49]

The position of Koester has found its most direct echo in a collection of non-canonical gospels edited by his pupil Ron Cameron, who acknowledges that Koester "helped me establish a set of methodological questions with which to explore their treasures," and that it was "at his recommendation I was able to undertake this project."[50] Indeed in a Foreword Koester himself explains:

> Some would argue that these gospels add little to our picture of the historical Jesus. Our picture, however, is dependent upon our understanding of the transmission of traditions about and from Jesus and of the process of the formation of written gospel texts. The non-canonical gospels are important witnesses to these developments. In many instances, they are directly dependent upon the earliest stages of the collections of sayings of Jesus and stories about him; and they show little, if any, influence from the gospels of the New Testament. Students of early Christian literature will be greatly enriched if they utilize these materials as they learn to understand how the earliest oral traditions of Jesus were used and transformed in Christian communities: how they were collected, put into writing, edited, and repeatedly revised.[51]

In his Introduction Cameron spells out criteria for dating, which one may assume are derived from Koester's orientation:

> One of the most vexing problems in the study of gospel literature is determining with any sort of precision the date of composition of a particular document. This is no less a problem in seeking to date the gospels of the New Testament than it is in dating the non-canonical gospels. There are, however, techniques available that permit one to suggest, with a reasonable degree of confidence, a plausible date of composition:
> 1. Form criticism provides a means of ascertaining the relative dating of discrete pieces of the tradition. Texts whose literary forms are relatively spare can generally be dated to a period earlier than those which exhibit a more elaborate, developed stage of the tradition.[52]

The relative position of a given saying from the *Gospel of Thomas* within the morphology of the form of that saying may have implications for the relative chronology of the saying when it received this particular form. One might think of the parables that in the *Gospel of Thomas* occur in a non-allegorical form that is presumably "relatively spare" compared to the allegorical form of these parables in the canonical Gospels. Thus they represent what is often called a "pre-Synoptic" layer. But the *Gospel of Thomas* also presents sayings in "a more elaborate, developed stage of the tradition," when compared with their canonical equivalents, such as Saying 22. It is precisely the presence in the same document of sayings that are "relatively spare" as well as of sayings that

---

[49] Koester, "Tradition and History," III.2, typescript, pp. 83–93.
[50] Cameron, *The Other Gospels*, 11.
[51] Cameron, *The Other Gospels*, 9.
[52] Cameron, *The Other Gospels*, 17.

are "a more elaborate, developed stage of the tradition" that should
warn us against assuming that the chronological implications of an
individual saying can be generalized to apply to the document as a
whole. One may not assume that every saying received the form it has in
a given document at the time the document itself was composed. Of
course the more sayings from the *Gospel of Thomas* that can be placed
at a relatively early date, the more appealing an early date for the basic
composition of the *Gospel of Thomas* becomes, in which case segments
pointing to a late date come to seem more like secondary accretions in
the process of the transmission of the already-composed document. But
this is at best a cumulative and relative argument.

> 2. Compositional parallels in the gospel tradition furnish additional evidence. When
> the history of a saying or story in one text can be paralleled in another whose develop-
> ment can be determined and to which a date can be assigned, then a contemporaneous
> date of composition can generally be given to both texts.[53]

Even if the parallel has to do with the composition of the whole rather
than the form of the individual unit, contemporaneity is not necessarily
evident. Matthew and Luke share compositional traits without being
necessarily contemporaneous, at least not for Koester, who says of
Matthew that it was composed "in the last [the German edition only
inserts: two] decades of I CE," but of Luke that it "cannot have been any
later than ca. 125.[54] Nor do the compositional parallels between Mark
and John make them strictly contemporaneous, for they are usually
dated a generation apart. Hence compositional parallels between Q and
the *Gospel of Thomas* need not make them strictly contemporaneous.
But compositional parallels would in a sense shift the burden of proof
upon the side of the argument that seeks to separate the parallel texts
widely in time. For arguments for the perseverance of the compositional
trait through a period of time as well as extenuating circumstances
suggesting the parallel texts are not contemporaneous, would need to be
provided.

> 3. The role given to persons of authority, whose position in a particular community
> serves to authenticate its transmission of the tradition, supplies further confirmation of a
> likely date of composition. At a certain point in the history of early Christianity,
> communities began to appeal to revered figures of the past in order to legitimate the
> traditions of their own groups. The period in which the community that fostered the
> Gospel of John began to revere the memory of the Beloved Disciple and Peter by
> looking to them as the guarantors of its traditions, for example, was most likely
> contemporary with the time when the community of the *Gospel of Thomas* began to
> esteem Thomas and James by appealing to them as authorities in the transmission of its
> traditions.[55]

[53] Cameron, *The Other Gospels*, 17.
[54] Koester, *Einführung*, 608 and 749 = *Introduction*, 2.173, 310.
[55] Cameron, *The Other Gospels*, 17–18.

Parallel stages in the morphology of the social structuring of communities behind gospels, in such matters as authority figures accrediting
gospels, an argument to which Koester himself had appealed, do not
date the documents themselves unless the relevant evidence can be
shown to have been introduced at the redactional stage. Sayings 12 and
13 in the *Gospel of Thomas* could have been sensed in their relevance
for authenticating the tradition as early as the time when the Beloved
Disciple and Peter were introduced in a comparable role in the trajectory of the Gospel of John. But whereas John 21 is on other grounds
known to be redactional, so that the interaction of the Beloved Disciple
and Peter in that chapter can be located chronologically at the time of
the Johannine redactor (which is of course later than the date which one
ascribes to the basic composition of the Fourth Gospel), Sayings 12 and
13 of the *Gospel of Thomas* are not known to coincide chronologically
with the time of the author. The references to Thomas in the title and
opening line of the text may well have Saying 13 in view, but such an
appeal to apostolic authority for the *Gospel of Thomas* by the author
could have taken place later than the formulation of the competitive
Sayings 12 and 13. Perhaps one could argue that the choosing of these
two sayings and the placing of them side by side would indicate on the
part of the author a sensitivity comparable to that of John 21, although
the author's decision not to place them at an emphasized position such
as the beginning or end of the text may illustrate the inconclusiveness of
such reflection.

4. Literary dependence of one document upon another, datable one establishes the
earliest possible date at which the dependent document was composed. Thus, the date
of the composition of the Gospel of Matthew and the Gospel of Luke is later than that of
the Gospel of Mark, since Mark was used by Matthew and Luke as a source of their
respective writings.[56]

The view that the *Gospel of Thomas* is independent of the canonical
Gospels, apart from secondary accretions after the basic composition, for
example when translated into Coptic, has gained ground over the past
generation, with the result that the automatic dating of the *Gospel of
Thomas* after the canonical Gospels and hence necessarily into the
second century must be considered increasingly an anachronism in the
history of research. But there are individual instances that must be
considered on their merits, and, if dependence on the canonical Gospels
seems more probable to certain instances, one must weigh whether this
indicates that a reversal of this scholarly trend is in order or whether
one has to do with isolated secondary interpolations.

[56] Cameron, *The Other Gospels*, 18.

5. When a text refers to historical events, the text must have been composed sometime during or after those events took place. The Gospel of Mark's reference to the destruction of the Temple in Jerusalem in 70 c.e., for example, means that this document in its final form could not have been composed before that time.[57]

The *Gospel of Thomas* hardly refers to historical events, so that this criterion for dating is hardly applicable, although the argument of Jacques-É. Ménard (see below) that Saying 53 presupposes a second-century debate would perhaps fall within this category. Koester's argument (see above) that the *Gospel of Thomas* does not cite early Christian literature might fall also in this category in the sense of an *argumentum e silentio*.

6. The existence of external witnesses to a text gives fairly reliable confirmation of at least the latest possible date of composition of the text.[58]

Manuscript evidence providing a latest possible date is not relevant for the position of Koester, who is concerned with an earliest possible date. But when one considers the dating of those who advocate as late a date as possible (see below), then one may wonder how late they might have been if one only had the fourth-century Coptic copy of the *Gospel of Thomas* and not the early third century Oxyrhynchus Papyrus 1. And when would one date the Gospel of Mark?

When Cameron comes to introducing specifically the *Gospel of Thomas*, it is the methodological principles he has enumerated that presumably lie behind the formulation:

Most of the sayings in the *Gospel of Thomas* have parallels in the "synoptic" gospels of Matthew, Mark, and Luke in the New Testament. Analysis of each of these sayings reveals that the sayings in the *Gospel of Thomas* are either preserved in forms more primitive than those in the parallel sayings in the New Testament or are developments of more primitive forms of such sayings. The particular editorial changes which the synoptic gospels make, including the addition of a narrative structure and the inclusion of traditional sayings and stories within a biographical framework, are totally absent from the *Gospel of Thomas*. All of this suggests that the *Gospel of Thomas* is based on a tradition of sayings which is closely related to that of the canonical gospels but which has experienced a separate process of transmission. The composition of the *Gospel of Thomas*, therefore, is parallel to that of the canonical gospels. Its sources are collections of sayings and parables contemporary with the sources of the canonical gospels. In this respect, the *Gospel of Thomas* can be profitably compared with the Synoptic Sayings Source, common to Matthew and Luke, generally referred to as Q. . . . Since the composition of the *Gospel of Thomas* parallels that of the gospels of the New Testament, the most likely date of its composition would be in the second half of the first century, almost certainly in Syria.[59]

This assessment thus tends to coincide with that of Koester himself, as

---

[57] Cameron, *The Other Gospels*, 18.
[58] Cameron, *The Other Gospels*, 18.
[59] Cameron, *The Other Gospels*, 24–25.

is to be expected, in that "he read various drafts of this manuscript with critical insight and consummate skill; the final draft has benefited immeasurably from his comments."[60]

If Helmut Koester's presentation is unmistakably in the German tradition, he has found an advocate with regard to dating whose instincts are in effect in the British tradition, Stevan L. Davies, whose information about Koester's position is up-to-date only as of 1971:

> In this book I shall first argue that in no meaningful sense is Thomas "gnostic." Then I shall show that although Thomas is by no means a systematic document, it does have a comprehensible set of ideas, which are, for the most part, drawn from the Jewish Wisdom and apocalyptic traditions. Finally, I shall place Thomas in its context in the very early church. It is a collection of sayings used to instruct newly-baptized Christians. It appears to reflect an early form of Johannine preaching and probably came into being at about the same time as the Q document.... Thomas should be dated ca. A.D. 50–70.[61]

The question as to whether the *Gospel of Thomas* is gnostic or not is in Davies's view decisive as to whether the *Gospel of Thomas* is to be taken seriously:

> Unfortunately, almost immediately after the publication of the Gospel of Thomas, books and articles were written which dismissed Thomas as "gnostic." Because of these books and articles, there has been very little discussion of Thomas during the past fifteen years. If Thomas is "gnostic" then perhaps Christians need pay little attention to it. But if it is not "gnostic" in any meaningful sense, then Christian scholarship has falsely denigrated and subsequently ignored a text of great importance.[62]

Thus Rudolph's view that the term gnosticism is no longer pejorative[63] seems a bit premature, although one may recall that Grenfell and Hunt had already in 1897 pointed out that if the *Gospel of Thomas* should turn out to be gnostic "it does not follow that they [the sayings] are inventions." Of course Koester himself is an instance of a contemporary (and Christian) scholar who considers the *Gospel of Thomas* as gnostic but does not for that reason dismiss it, but considers it of utmost importance.

Davies comes to identify the pejorative view of "gnostic" that he originally limited to "Christians" and "Christian scholarship" as that of scholarship as such, namely, as an overarching euphemism for "heresy":

> As it is most commonly used today, "gnostic" in the language of scholarship does not so much describe a sect or set of ideas as pronounce upon the orthodoxy or acceptability of certain texts over against others.... As the term "heresy" became one which scholarship decided not to use, the term "gnostic" has come to serve as a substitute.[64]

[60] Cameron, *The Other Gospels*, 11.
[61] Davies, *Thomas and Wisdom*, 4.
[62] Davies, *Thomas and Wisdom*, 3.
[63] Rudolph, "Gnosis, ein Forschungsbericht," 36 (1971) 19, citing U. Bianchi (see n. 1 and 2 above).
[64] Davies, *Thomas and Wisdom*, 32–33.

This view is apparently characteristic of Davies's own usage, but hardly that of many critical scholars, who would seek a more objective descriptive usage free of such value-laden overtones.

Davies's polemic against defining *Gospel of Thomas* as gnostic is due not only to these pejorative overtones, but also to the implications they have for him with regard to a late dating:

> The reason usually, if not always, given for dating Thomas in the second century is once more the supposition that Thomas is a gnostic document.... Arguments for an early or mid-[second-]century date are based entirely (to the best of my knowledge) on the idea that since Thomas is gnostic it must necessarily be a second-century text. If Thomas cannot be said to be gnostic in any meaningful sense, its date may be considerably earlier than A.D. 140. It may well have been written in the mid-first century.[65]

Koester had also associated the unexamined assumption of a mid-second-century date with the association of the *Gospel of Thomas* with gnosticism. Koester's response is to affirm that gnosticism may well be present in the first century, as may other traits traditionally treated as secondary because apocryphal. But Davies seems to share the traditional second-century association of the concept of gnosticism. Indeed he considers some instances, where an affinity to gnosticism may be present, such as Sayings 111b and 114, as a later gloss or an addition by a later redactor.[66]

Davies rightly points out that it was premature to assume that because the *Gospel of Thomas* is in the Nag Hammadi Library it is necessarily gnostic, in that subsequent study has shown that the library contains non-gnostic material in a few cases, and specifically in the case of wisdom literature (the *Teaching of Silvanus* and the *Sentences of Sextus*).[67] He also points out that the earlier view of the dependence of the *Gospel of Thomas* on the canonical Gospels has been largely abandoned, with the result that the *Gospel of Thomas* need not on this ground be dated later than the canonical Gospels.[68] He, like Koester, appeals to the pre-Synoptic material in the *Gospel of Thomas* as "one of the strongest indications that the Gospel of Thomas is of first century date."[69] Further, he argues that collections of Jesus' sayings are characteristic of an early period, rather than being a second-century phenomenon, by which time such collections occur only imbedded in other documents.[70] For the imbedding of Q in Matthew and Luke was not a

---

[65] Davies, *Thomas and Wisdom*, 18, 33.
[66] Davies, *Thomas and Wisdom*, 22, 30, 149–55.
[67] Davies, *Thomas and Wisdom*, 4, 22–24.
[68] Davies, *Thomas and Wisdom*, 5.
[69] Davies, *Thomas and Wisdom*, 5.
[70] Davies, *Thomas and Wisdom*, 13.

pair of isolated events, but part of an all-encompassing trajectory that Davies characterizes as follows:

> Mark also did this as his parable collection in chapter four indicates. Independent collections of Jesus' sayings were a form of written tradition quickly succeeded by narrative gospels, dialogues of the resurrected Christ, parenetic letters, apologies, etc., some of which served as frames for sets of sayings.[71]

Thus Davies finds my earlier reasoning, which was in terms of an uncritical assumption of the conventional date, "a curious conclusion."[72] Of course, the question is whether all of early Christianity went the route of submerging the sayings collection in a narrative framework, or whether the admittedly early genre of sayings collection was continued in one strand of Christianity in the second century. The latter alternative would not require a second-century date for the Gospel of Thomas, but would render intelligible a continuity of genre between Q and the Gospel of Thomas, even if there were a time spread, rather than requiring that the two texts reflect quite independent genres, as was assumed by the view of Kümmel I was then opposing. To consider the two texts to be contemporary would of course serve the same purpose even more effectively, if it could be substantiated.

Davies also presses the point that having traditions superior to the Synoptics

> would probably not have been possible much later than the year A.D. 90. Are there any sayings of Jesus in second-century writings which are considered superior to their parallels in the synoptics?[73]

He further argues that parables, wisdom sayings, and proverbs "are certainly not characteristic of second-century Christian texts,"[74] though one might think of the role of parables in the Apocryphon of James. Thus Davies concludes, partly in dependence on Koester:

> Thomas appears to be a document from very early times, roughly the time of Q. It has an early format; it has much early material. In some ways (in terms of Wisdom speculations) Thomas may be "later" than Q; in some ways (in terms of apocalyptic Son of Man speculations) Q may be "later" than Thomas. . . . Thomas may be as old as, or even older than, Q.[75]

Davies exploits Koester's observation that the Gospel of Thomas lacks the apocalyptic Son of Man and the Pauline kerygma to query: "Might Thomas have come into being before these trends became wide-

---

[71] Davies, Thomas and Wisdom, 15.
[72] Davies, Thomas and Wisdom, 14, referring to Robinson-Koester, Trajectories, 102. See more recently Robinson, "Collections," 389–94.
[73] Davies, Thomas and Wisdom, 16.
[74] Davies, Thomas and Wisdom, 16.
[75] Davies, Thomas and Wisdom, 17.

spread?"[76] He argues that "First Corinthians 1–4 is testimony to the antiquity of many of the central ideas in the Gospel of Thomas."[77] Of course by this time the Pauline kerygma was widespread, though the Q and Thomas communities may have been exceptions.

Davies even speculates that the Synoptics may be dependent on the *Gospel of Thomas*:

> There may be instances of radical revision of Thomas' sayings in the synoptics, instances where mystagogic sayings have been transformed into parenetic sayings (Logion 22 and Mark 9:42–10:15?, Logion 24 and Matthew 6:22–23 and Luke 11:34-36?, Logia 6 and 14 and Matthew 6:2–18?, Logion 13 and Mark 8:27–30?).[78]

To be sure, this is a possibility difficult to take seriously, in that one would tend to prefer to conjecture, if not the reverse procedure, at least a sharing of common traditions. Hence Davies adds:

> As these sayings in their canonical form are so utterly familiar and those in Thomas so seemingly strange it is unlikely that any contemporary critical methodology will provide means to determine *radical* reworking.[79]

Thus Davies concludes with a basic reorganization:

> The Christology, or Jesusology, of Thomas is complex but it does not stem from decades of Christian theological speculation. It derives from a naive application of manifold Wisdom speculations to Jesus. The lack of Manichean or Marcionite dualism, the absence of any mythology of Sophia's fall or of Christ's ascent or descent through hostile realms populated by inimical Archons indicate that Thomas' sophiological Christology existed prior to or in ignorance of what many call gnosticism. . . .
>
> Its background is that of Jewish Wisdom speculation. It is wholly independent of the New Testament gospels; most probably it was in existence before they were written. It should be dated A.D. 50–70. . . .
>
> Thomas does not presuppose the Johannine or synoptic gospels or the theology of Paul; even less does it presuppose the mythologies of second-century theologians such as Valentinus or Heracleon. In reference to the sayings of Jesus, the synoptic gospels depend upon and incorporate sayings which first circulated in Thomas' and Q's *logoi sophon* form. In reference to baptism, Paul's eschatological reservations may presuppose Thomas' orientation to present fulfillment in baptism. In reference to a dualism of light/dark, world/"world," and to *ego eimi* discourses of Jesus, John may be a later development of what we find here and there in Thomas.
>
> The Gospel of Thomas is a mid-first-century text. It is an early document of sophiological Christianity oriented toward baptismal initiation, and it can be considered gnostic in no meaningful sense. When the time comes that Thomas is understood to have come into being ca. A.D. 50–70, our knowledge of the history of the early church will immeasurably increase.[80]

Thus Koester and Davies present arguments for quite early datings of

---

[76] Davies, *Thomas and Wisdom*, 29.
[77] Davies, *Thomas and Wisdom*, 145.
[78] Davies, *Thomas and Wisdom*, 145.
[79] Davies, *Thomas and Wisdom*, 145.
[80] Davies, *Thomas and Wisdom*, 146.

the *Gospel of Thomas* on the alternate assumptions that it is an instance of early gnosticism or that it is in effect pre-gnostic.

The way in which Koester has for all practical purposes placed the *Gospel of Thomas* back into the time of the canonical Gospels, Q, or even earlier, has not gone uncontested. Howard Clark Kee has taken Koester to task for rearranging the source material to fit his preferences:

> Or again, one may be uncomfortable with the apocalyptic expectation that pervades the Q material as we have it in the gospels, and one may correctly observe that the Q material as incorporated into the *Gospel of Thomas* has been deeschatologized. But that provides no basis for the historical conclusion that Q was originally non-eschatological, and that the element was later introduced into the tradition by those combatting gnosticism by apocalyptic counterclaims. The discovery of the immensely important Nag Hammadi gnostic library vastly increased knowledge of second and third century gnosticism, but it sheds no clear light on the question as to whether there was a pre-Christian gnosticism. Instead, it seems to confirm the theory that gnosticism was a growth on second century Christianity. The *Gospel of Thomas* is a prime example of the adaptation of earlier Christian tradition to portray Jesus as a gnostic revelatory figure, just as the Q material is thoroughly eschatological, rather than manifesting a sprinkling with later apocalyptic condiments. It is against backgrounds which exist in tangible form, rather than in terms of conceptual anachronisms, that the christological images are to be perceived and analyzed. . . .
>
> The task of christological research . . . demands holistic study of New Testament texts, rather than surgical analysis of hypothetical components or sources. It can perhaps avoid the foolish stance that, while it is fine for "all flesh to see God's salvation," they ought to see it our way.[81]

Of course the basis of Koester's view is not an uncomfortable feeling about Q being pervaded with apocalypticism, as if he were the victim of his dogmatic prejudices, but rather the view first worked out by Philip Vielhauer[82] that has gained considerable ground of late to the effect that Jesus had an eschatology oriented only to the kingdom of God, with the concept of the Son of Man being first introduced by the church. This view has had an impact on Q studies, to the effect that its apocalypticism, in the sense of its Son-of-Man Christology, not in the sense of its kingdom-of-God eschatology, has for some become a late ingredient in the tradition.[83] The absence of a Son-of-Man Christology perhaps

---

[81] Kee, "Christology," 236, 242.

[82] Vielhauer, "Gottesreich und Menschensohn" (reprinted in Vielhauer, *Aufsätze*); and "Jesus und der Menschensohn" (reprinted in *Aufsätze*).

[83] Schulz, Q, lists among "the more recent Q traditions" "apocalyptic sayings and even an apocalypse," although "the expectation of the apocalyptic arrival of the Son of Man Jesus determined the life and proclamation of the very earliest congregation in a decisive way." Lührmann, "Liebet eure Feinde," 425, follows Koester, and speaks of a "reapocalypticizing of the proclamation of Jesus" in Q. Strecker, "Bergpredigt," 67, note 95: "The question remains contested, whether and to what extent one can demonstrate for Q, along side of a strict expectation of judgment (Polag, *Christologie der Logienquelle*, 155), also an acute imminent expectation of the parousia (thus Hoffmann, *Theologie der Logienquelle*, 34–39). But it is certain that later Q layers are oriented apocalyptically to a high degree."

from the Sermon on the Mount/Plain in Q[84] is, for example, an indication that this "Sermon," which on other grounds may be a very old
sayings collection imbedded in Q, may have been oriented only to the
kingdom of God, and thus tends to document Koester's hypothesis. This
possibility is too serious a matter to be dismissed with invidious language about source criticism, which is after all a generally accepted and
highly successful method in our discipline. Koester is not so foolish as to
think everyone should see it his way, but he is seeking to carry through
methodically the important form-critical task of expanding in terms of
small collections the history of the Synoptic tradition, a purpose for
which he should only be commended, irrespective of the degree of
success one attributes to his efforts thus far.

An analogous criticism was levelled by Joseph A. Fitzmyer against
Koester's pupil Elaine Pagels and against gnostic gospels in general, as

> the schlock that is supposed to pass for "literature". . . . It has been mystifying, indeed,
> why serious scholars continue to talk about the pertinence of this material to the study
> of the New Testament.[85]

Hence it may be no coincidence that Fitzmyer has supported for the
Gospel of Thomas the latest possible date:

> The Greek copies are dated roughly to the first half of the third century A.D., but the
> Gospel itself may well have been composed toward the end of the second century.[86]

Indeed a further argument used by Koester for dating the Gospel of
Thomas earlier than the traditional dating is that the latter reflects just
such prejudice:

> The terms "apocryphal" and "canonical" reflect a traditional usage which implies deep-
> seated prejudices and has had far-reaching consequences.[87]

Fitzmyer's dating coincides with that of Jacques-É. Ménard who, in
fact, argues

> that the milieu to which the Gospel of Thomas belongs is that of the New Testament
> apocrypha. . . . From this rapprochement with the Naassenes it seems to us that one can
> conclude that the Gospel of Thomas belongs in its ensemble—the exceptions will come
> to confirm the rule—to the milieu of the New Testament apocrypha, and one must say
> of it as of the other writings of this genre that it depends on the canonical Gospels. In its
> case in particular one must add that these canonical Gospels reached it by the
> intermediary of the Syriac versions.[88]

---

[84] Jeremias, "Schicht," 159–72; Fitzmyer, Luke, 635.
[85] Fitzmyer, "Gnostic Gospels," 123, cited by Koester, "Apocryphal and Canonical
Gospels," 106.
[86] Fitzmyer, Luke, 85.
[87] Koester, "Apocryphal and Canonical Gospels," 105.
[88] Ménard, L'Évangile selon Thomas, 3.

The view that the *Gospel of Thomas* is dependent on Syriac versions
of the canonical Gospels has also been suggested by Antoine Guillaumont in his recent judicious sorting of the semitisms of the *Gospel of
Thomas* into various distinguishable categories.

> There are a number of cases, however, where the Aramaic substratum, far from
> remaining a pure conjecture, takes on for us tangible form. Many semitisms of the
> *Gospel of Thomas* seem indeed to have their source in the Syriac versions of the New
> Testament, with which the text of this apocryphon presents evident affinities. . . .
> The *Gospel of Thomas* presents, in addition, in the logia that have Synoptic parallels,
> a certain number of variants in relation to the Greek text of the New Testament that are
> quite well explicable if one considers them as translations of ambiguous terms em-
> ployed in the Syriac versions, or in one or the other of them. . . .
> The *Gospel of Thomas* presents, nonetheless, in relation to the text of the Synoptics,
> variants that are not found in the Syriac versions of the New Testament nor are they
> explicable, in terms of the ambiguity of a term, on the basis of them. They seem to have
> their explanation in an Aramaic substratum other than the known Syriac versions and
> are, for this reason, of great interest. . . .
> Indeed the existence of a Syriac state of the collection, earlier than the Coptic state
> that has been preserved, is proven by a certain number of facts: first of all, the close
> affinities that we have seen between the Coptic text of the logia and the old Syriac
> versions of the New Testament; further, a large number of Aramaisms listed above
> could equally well be Syriacisms; finally, there are some linguistic particularities that
> are incontestably Syriacisms. . . .
> Hence the study of the semitisms preserved in the Coptic text of the *Gospel of
> Thomas* leads to important conclusions. It shows, on the one hand, the close ties that
> exist between this work and the milieu of the Syriac tongue and leads one to think that
> there must have been prior [to the Coptic translation] a redaction in this tongue. On the
> other hand, some of them permit, it would seem, to go beyond that and to perceive,
> particularly for the logia that have Synoptic parallels, an Aramaic substratum that they
> would have in common with the latter.[89]

Here it is not clear why one need assume a dependence on a Syriac
translation of the New Testament to explain the instances where the
Syriac canonical Gospels and the *Gospel of Thomas* share a variant from
the Greek New Testament or where the Syriac canonical Gospels
present an ambiguous term with one of its meanings found in the Greek
New Testament and one in the *Gospel of Thomas*. For the Syriac
translations of the canonical Gospels no doubt made use of oral traditions of the sayings of Jesus in Syriac or Aramaic, which in given
instances could have influenced the author of the *Gospel of Thomas*, but
not the canonical Gospels; or, ambiguous semitic terms could have been
translated by the canonical Gospels one way, by the *Gospel of Thomas*
the other. That variants between the canonical Gospels and the *Gospel
of Thomas* can at times be explained as translational variants of ambiguous Syriac or Aramaic terms that do not occur in the extant Syriac
translations of the canonical Gospels indicates that the phenomenon at

---

[89] Guillaumont, "Semitismes," 197–99, 201, 203–204.

times occurs where it cannot be argued that the *Gospel of Thomas* was dependent on the canonical Gospels in Syriac translation.

Ménard infers from the dependence of the *Acts of Thomas* (beginning or middle of the third century) on the *Gospel of Thomas* that the latter "could hence date from the end of the second century,"[90] thereby elevating the *terminus ad quem* into the *terminus a quo*. He supports his late dating with the following argument:

> The uselessness of physical circumcision in Saying 53 of the *Gospel of Thomas* picks up the debate between Tineius Rufus and Rabbi Akiba, in which the former emphasized that if circumcision were necessary children would be born circumcised. Now Tineius was governor of Judea in 132 and Akiba died in 135, and the rescription of Hadrian making circumcision like castration a crime subject to capital punishment was one of the causes of the revolt of 132.[91]

Even if it were clear, however, that the *Gospel of Thomas* were dependent on this incident, one must consider here as elsewhere the option of late interpolations. The latest trait in a sayings collection is far from being an assured indication of the date when the basic collection was made.

B. Dehandschutter has presented in its most extreme and explicit form an antithesis to the position of Koester:

> One wonders whether the solution of Koester (and of those who have followed him) does not lose too much from view that the problem of Q is in the first place a problem of the literary criticism of the Synoptics, whereas the *Gospel of Thomas* is in the first place an apocryphal "gospel" dating from the end of the second century.[92]

Dehandschutter seeks to carry out this contrast in terms of genre, but in the process does no more than reveal again the dogmatic point of departure of this late dating (see below).

It should be clear from what has been said thus far that a distinctive problem of dating the *Gospel of Thomas* has to do with the fluidity of the text of a non-canonical sayings collection in translation. This problem is recognized by Koester:

> It is quite likely that the Coptic text of the *Gospel of Thomas* does not directly reflect the original text of this gospel; differences between the Coptic version and the Greek fragments from Oxyrhynchus show that the text was not stable; similar observations can be made for the transmission of other gospels during the 2d century.[93]

Not only does the *Gospel of Thomas* share a fluidity of text with other non- or not-yet-canonical literature, but also a fluidity of text particularly characteristic of sayings collections, where there is no train of

[90] Ménard, *L'Évangile selon Thomas,* 156.
[91] Ménard, "Datation," 12.
[92] Dehandschutter, "L'Évangile de Thomas," 510.
[93] Koester, "Apocryphal and Canonical Gospels," 116.

thought or causal nexus to stabilize the text from saying to saying. A saying can be added or subtracted, a sequence can be altered, quite imperceptibly.

There is in fact some indication that some dependence of the *Gospel of Thomas* on the canonical Gospels may have been introduced at the level of the translation into Coptic. A comparison of the Greek fragments P. Oxy. 1, 654, 655 with the Coptic *Gospel of Thomas* by Wolfgang Schrage shows "that the translator has assimilated the *logion* [*Gospel of Thomas* 33] to the Synoptics."[94] He describes the relation of the two versions to each other as follows:

> The translator [Schrage concedes he could also speak of the redactor or copyist] did not proceed slavishly in his work of clothing the *logia* in a different linguistic dress, but permitted himself the freedom of additions and deletions of various kinds in translating the New Testament quotations, which he fully recognized as such. In general he translated exactly and retained differences from the Synoptic form of the *logia*. . . . In individual cases he distanced himself further from the New Testament or left out quotations. . . . But there is no indication that the Coptic *Gospel of Thomas* represents an advanced stage of gnostification. The translator even partially assimilated the *logia* to the canonical sayings of the Lord. . . . This assimilation, however, is also not motivated by greater faithfulness to the New Testament biblical text, nor is it to be understood as a compromise with "orthodoxy." Rather it indicates that the translator, where he could, made use of an already known Coptic Gospel version. . . . Whether this familiarity of the translator with a Coptic Gospel version goes back to a form already fixed in writing is difficult to say. In view of the brevity of the quotations it is more probable that the translator himself had this Coptic translation in his ear or his memory rather than in his hands. It is striking that in individual cases the Coptic *Gospel of Thomas* stands nearer to the original New Testament text than does the Sahidic. . . .[95]

To be sure, this does not seem to indicate that the Sahidic *Gospel of Thomas* was directly dependent on the Sahidic New Testament, as Kurt Rudolph, following Peter Nagel, has pointed out:

> A series of important grammatical differences speak against a dependence of *Gospel of Thomas* on the Sahidic New Testament.[96]

Yet the way in which the Sahidic translation of the *Gospel of Thomas* seems to have been free to interact with the New Testament should warn against assuming automatically that such canonical parallels argue in favor of the original Greek *Gospel of Thomas* having been dependent on the canonical Gospels, as Schrage does in his monographic comparison of the Sahidic *Gospel of Thomas* with the Sahidic New Testament.[97]

---

[94] Schrage, "Evangelienzitate," 266.

[95] Schrage, "Evangelienzitate," 267–68.

[96] Rudolph, "Gnosis, ein Forschungsbericht," 34 (1969) 361. He refers there to Peter Nagel, "Codex II," 447, n. 24; 453–54, 462.

[97] Schrage, *Verhältnis*.

The fluidity of the text has other implications with regard to the assessment of the text and hence by implication to its dating, as a summary of secondary literature by John Dominic Crossan illustrates:

> Detailed comparisons between the Greek and Coptic texts make it evident, however, that the latter is not just a straight translation of the former but is, minimally, a deliberate redaction of it, "an adapted translation" (Fitzmyer,1974:416), or, maximally, both are "very different recensions of the Gospel of Thomas" (Marcovich:64). On this point the combination of Gospel of Thomas 30+77b in Oxy P 1 is very significant since that conjunction is a special indication "that the Coptic version is not a direct translation of the Greek, for we have here a tripartite saying, whereas the Coptic has preserved the two parts separately" (Fitzmyer,1974:398). It is of course a separate question whether it was the Coptic translation that redactionally separated an originally unified Greek saying (Hofius:187; Kuhn:1960:317–18), or, whether it was the Greek recension in Oxy P 1 that did so [i.e. united two sayings] while the different and more original Greek recension translated into Coptic did not (Marcovich:69). That former interpretation seems preferable, and in that case the Coptic would be a much more gnosticizing version of the Greek (Jeremias,1964:106–111).[98]

Harold W. Attridge has, however, warned against inferring from the scant evidence the necessity of postulating different recensions:

> Yet it also remains possible that the recension which the Coptic represents was based on one of the P. Oxy. texts; none of the differences between the Greek and Coptic versions necessarily precludes this possibility.[99]

If in fact the text of the Gospel of Thomas (or Q) was never stable, but continued its own life throughout the whole period from the earliest sources imbedded in it down to the copying of the Gospel of Thomas in Codex II (or of Q in Matthew and Luke), one must reconceptualize the procedures for dating: rather than the whole text of the Gospel of Thomas (or Q) being read synchronically, so that all the sayings contribute to establishing the one date of authorship and all the sayings are interpreted in terms of that one dating, one must learn to read diachronically, placing the individual sayings and indeed specific traits in them along the trajectory of the life of the text. This is, of course, not a completely new methodological insight, but it has not been implemented systematically, and indeed the modalities for, and the implications of, its implementation have not yet been worked out.

Perhaps the most important thing to be said about the relative dating of Q and the Gospel of Thomas is that they overlap, in that at least the "pre-Synoptic" versions of such canonical sayings as the parables in Gospel of Thomas are as old or older than at least the composition of Q (in that, e.g., they probably include authentic sayings of Jesus), although

---

[98] Crossan, In Fragments, 32–33.

[99] See "Appendix: The Greek Fragments," prepared by H. W. Attridge in Layton, Nag Hammadi Codex II.

of course the Q trajectory itself also goes back in part to authentic sayings. Koester's appeal to a source imbedded in the Gospel of Thomas consisting of such "pre-Synoptic" parables, if its status as a written source could be established, would, as a pendant to the source imbedded in Mark 4, illustrate the point.

Conversely, it is an asymmetrical comparison to compare Q with the Gospel of Thomas as we have it in Nag Hammadi Codex II. For in talking about Q, scholarship has in view a source two stages behind the manuscript evidence, (the canonical Gospels of Matthew and Luke). First, one separates out Q^{Mt} and Q^{Lk}; second, one separates out Q as the common precursor to which the symbol Q traditionally refers. Thus one would be comparing this reconstructed source at more than one remove from the manuscript evidence with the Gospel of Thomas in its last, late-fourth-century stage represented by the one relatively complete manu-script to have survived. In the comparison of two different stages in the morphology of texts as fluid as sayings collections, it is not at all sur-prising that a temporal spread can be demonstrated. But no more is proven by such an observation than the truism regarding a single sayings collection, that one stage is older than the other, e.g., that Q as the common ancestor of Matthew and Luke is earlier than e.g., Q^{Mt} or Matthew itself, or, in terms of the Gospel of Thomas, that the text of the late fourth-century Coptic Gospel of Thomas is later than that of the fragmentary third-century Greek texts from Oxyrhynchus.

Of course it is a valid scholarly objective to assign a date to a major compositional activity in the trajectory of a sayings collection such as the moment when it was put in writing; or, the moment when smaller written and oral collections were brought together into something like its present size; or the moment when editing went beyond the inter-pretation implicit in the selection and ordering of the sayings and introduced redactional comments created by the author in order to make explicit the given interpretation. But to argue, as scholarship has tradi-tionally done, that some such event or events in the case of the Gospel of Thomas is later than in the case of Q, may not, even if it were true, be the relevant chronological observation. Of course it might be an impor-tant fact in a chronicle of early Christian literature. But it might not be of great significance for most other purposes, such as tracing the history of the transmission of the sayings attributed to Jesus. Any "history of the Synoptic tradition" of the future must include among its primary source material much of the Gospel of Thomas along with Q and Mark 4, as well as oral traditions established by form criticism in its description of what lies behind the Synoptic Gospels. Unfortunately one does not have in the case of the sources imbedded in the Gospel of Thomas two

documents in which any of them are imbedded, as one does in the case
of Q. As a result, a reconstruction of sources lying behind the *Gospel of
Thomas* would be more like the problem of reconstructing the Signs
Source used by John, and hence calls for more detailed argumentation
than has thus far been provided. But, just as some kind of Signs Source
should in my view be included in any future "history of the Johannine
tradition," just so must some kind of assessment of the older layers in the
Gospel of Thomas be included in any such study of what lies behind the
canonical Gospels. The late date of [the translation of, interpolations
into, the final redaction of, the scribe of ?] the *Gospel of Thomas* cannot
be validly used as an argument for leaving this text out of the study of
the Synoptic tradition, any more than it would be legitimate to eliminate
the Synoptic Gospels themselves, dating from the last third of the first
century, from discussions of a person who lived in the first third of that
century, about whom they contain traditions going back to his lifetime.

IV. The Genre of Q and the Gospel of Thomas

Apart from the discussion in my essay "LOGOI SOPHŌN" scant attention has been devoted in the study of Q and the *Gospel of Thomas*
during the past generation to the question of the literary genre to which
they might be attributed. Other than the general recognition that Q is not
just a paraenetic supplement to the gospel, as had earlier been assumed,
but is in effect a gospel of a different kind than the canonical Gospels,
little has been done. One may mention, however, that in 1970 Ernst
Bammel associated Q with testamentary literature.[100] But this view
depends on the testamentary motif with which Q is thought to have
terminated, Luke 22:29, 30b. Verse 29, however, which Bammel considers decisive, is not in Matthew, and hence is on methodological
grounds difficult to treat as decisive for establishing the genre of Q. One
may merely recall the blunt comment of Hans Conzelmann: "But: the
last section did not stand in Q."[101] Even if this verse should be attributed
to Q, such a testamentary motif may be more relevant as a partial
explanation for the absence of a "theology of the cross" and hence of a
resultant passion narrative than as a positive explanation of the structure of the body of the work as a testament's collection of sayings.

In 1979 Robert Hodgson, Jr., our co-host at the Springfield Seminar,
had sensed that my "history of the *Gattung* 'Sayings of the Sages' from
Jewish wisdom literature to gnosticism revealed a development not un-

---

[100] Bammel, "Q," 39–50, esp. 49–50.
[101] Conzelmann, "Literaturbericht," 243. Jeremias (*Sprache*, 290–91) considers the
verses redaction because of their Lucanisms.

related to the history of the OT testimony tradition,"[102] to which his own study is largely directed. But this dimension of his work has not yet been fully developed at the time the present paper was completed, so that an evaluation of its implications seemed premature. Thus one may turn to the often tacit assumptions regarding genre that the essay "LOGOI SOPHŌN" was opposing and the discussion of that proposal thus far.

One of the major views about the Gospel of Thomas held that it consisted of material abstracted from the canonical Gospels so as to conform to the gnostic perspective that only the knowledge imparted by the gnostic redeemer was relevant. The result was that the narrative framework of the sayings of Jesus and other materials in the canonical Gospels were deleted. But this derivation of the form of the Gospel of Thomas presents various problems. Other gnostic texts from Nag Hammadi indicate that gnostics would not need to eliminate the narrative framework as thoroughly as one would have to assume to have been the case in the Gospel of Thomas. For they were able to impose a gnosticizing tendency on narratives such as the passion and resurrection, as well as the baptism. Furthermore it is not reasonable to assume that sayings in a meaningful context with one another in the canonical Gospels would be scattered randomly throughout the Gospel of Thomas. If one has had to give up the assumption that since the Gospel of John is a "spiritual" Gospel it could use the Synoptic Gospels in a way that mere mortals cannot make sense of, one needs also to give up the assumption that gnostics were so unreasonable that they too acted in ways that one need not seek to comprehend rationally. Finally, the distinctive editorial traits of the canonical Gospels are not present in the Gospel of Thomas to indicate that its sayings went through that editorial process. The Gospel of Thomas comes from a period in time (irrespective of whether one dates it at 140 C.E. or earlier) when sayings of Jesus were still being transmitted orally. Hence dependence on the canonical Gospels is not yet the normal assumption when sayings of Jesus are cited.

The disassociation of the genre of the Gospel of Thomas from that of the sayings collection in preference for explaining the form of the Gospel of Thomas as the outcome of the removal of the narrative and other undesirable ingredients from the canonical Gospels (without really reflecting on the resultant postulation of something like a reductionist genre) seemed in some cases to reflect at least in part a perhaps unconscious desire to disassociate the heretical Gospel of Thomas from apostolic Christianity, represented in this instance by Q. This came

---

[102] Hodgson, "Testimony Hypothesis," 361–78, esp. 375, n. 74. Cf. now Hodgson, "Dialogue with J. M. Robinson."

forcefully to my attention in the following statement of 1963 by Werner Georg Kümmel.

> But whether or not a very old tradition parallel to the Synoptics is at the basis of the *Gospel of Thomas*, the writing as such is doubtless no late form of the same literary genre as Q, but a later stage of a different kind in the development of the transmission of sayings of Jesus. . . . This results not only from the complete absence of any narration and substantive ordering, but especially from the absence of any Christology at all, and thus of any connection with the development of gospels that first becomes visible in Mark. The *Gospel of Thomas* presupposes the reinterpretation of the person of Jesus into the role of the Gnostic revealer and thus shows itself to be a literary form of a later time.[103]

B. Dehandschutter recognizes that Kümmel "has contributed greatly to disseminate this point of view," and that *Trajectories through Early Christianity* by Koester and myself was "decisive" in presenting the alternate thesis that seeks to trace "the 'prehistory' of the *Gospel of Thomas* as a collection of sayings."[104] Dehandschutter's essay is in effect an attempt to vindicate Kümmel's position especially over against that of Koester. It is for this reason that he sets up the antithesis between, on the one hand, "the 'Sayings Collection' as a particular genre, designed to conserve these sayings in their original form," "constituted of sayings well separated," and on the other, a "'mixed' genre," characterized by "incoherence." In the case of the latter he emphasizes "the secondary character of these compositions," a genre that "distances itself from the first Christian tradition," by "creating" sayings and "not for themselves, but to support a doctrine." Dehandschutter thus underscores especially the tendentious and creative nature of the latter process, a deficiency he assumes was not characteristic of the Synoptic tradition.[105] Thus, Dehandschutter has constructed a pure genre of discrete authentic sayings of Jesus without doctrinal tendency, a genre that never existed in fact, either as Q or otherwise, as a foil over against which the *Gospel of Thomas* becomes more like the typically second-generation gnostic genre of dialogues of the Resurrected with his disciples—a genre completely unrelated to Q. The antithesis between a genre to "*conserve*" authentic sayings and a genre to "*form*" inauthentic sayings is rather a

---

[103] Kümmel, *Einleitung*, 41; ET of the 14th edition of 1965, *Introduction*, revised edition based on the 17th edition of 1973, trans. Howard Clark Kee, 1975, 75–76. Quotation is from the 1963 edition.

[104] Dehandschutter, "L'Évangile de Thomas," 508.

[105] Dehandschutter, "L'Évangile de Thomas," 510–15. This view had been worked out in 1975 by Dehandschutter in a Leuven thesis, "Thomasevangelie," which was echoed by his Leuven professor Frans Neirynck, "Q," 716.: "This is, however, a gnostic composition which borrows from the canonical gospel, and its literary genre is more probably of a later origin. The Q source may represent a primitive Christian genre *sui generis*. Since it is not a mere 'collection of sayings' (Logienquelle), Schürmann prefers to call it a 'discourse source' (Redequelle)."

product of the modern conservative repudiation of critical scholarship, as is the antithesis between a genre with no theological tendency and a genre sold out to a theological tendency. No such antitheses exist in the primary sources. The irony of this effort is that one is thus presented with a sharp contrast between two pure genres, to which neither Q nor the *Gospel of Thomas* belongs. Neither is a chain of isolated logia, both are instances of a "'mixed' genre" with fused logia and the beginning of discourse traits; and both reflect theological tendencies. Thus both fall between these imaginary extremes, and in this sense . . . fall together.

It was largely in response to this view of Kümmel that the article "LOGOI SOPHŌN: On the *Gattung* of Q"[106] was composed. That the *Gospel of Thomas*, like Q, depends primarily on the living oral tradition, even though smaller collections, perhaps even written collections, may have been incorporated in either or both, has become the growing edge of subsequent scholarship, especially in the work of Koester.

Hans-Martin Schenke has recognized this aspect of Koester's work on the *Gospel of Thomas* as the most important reconceptualization that the discovery of this text has produced:

> For this too is to be said of the twenty years of research on the *Gospel of Thomas*: There has been a wealth of insights and new bits of information, but in my view only one ingenious and convincing conception for the whole—and this comes precisely from Helmut Koester, and says in essence that the *Gospel of Thomas* is to be seen within the framework of the living process of the transmission of the *sayings* of Jesus, which presupposes as bearer a special, indeed a onesided variant of early Christianity, namely sapientially determined Christianity.[107]

Thus, Schenke sees Koester transcending the then current debate as to whether the *Gospel of Thomas* was dependent on the canonical Gospels or on apocryphal gospels, by seeing it in the same position as Q in the morphology of Jesus traditions, directly feeding upon and growing out of the oral tradition of Jesus' sayings and smaller collections.

Koester's view in 1971 in *Trajectories* was that the basic source behind Q had been a sapiential collection such as the genre title "logoi sophōn" suggested, without the Son-of-Man apocalypticism characteristic of Q as we know it, but much like the postulated point of departure for the *Gospel of Thomas*. In the Shaffer Lectures of 1980 this view is resumed:

> The *Gospel of Thomas* is thus an old Christian sayings collection, or else based upon an older collection, which is more closely related to the genre of the wisdom book than the second common source of Matthew and Luke. . . . But the apocalyptic sayings about the

---

[106] Robinson, "LOGOI SOPHŌN," 77–96; *Future of Our Religious Past*, 84–130; *Trajectories*, 71–113.
[107] H.-M. Schenke, "Review of Ménard," 262.

coming of the Son of Man are missing completely [from the *Gospel of Thomas*], while wisdom sayings are more numerous than eschatological and prophetic sayings. Thus this gospel is more true to its genre, the wisdom book.[108]

This then raises the question as to the deviation of Q from the genre of the wisdom book. Koester wrote in his *Introduction*:

Q certainly had preliminary stages, such as occasional collections of sayings for catechetical, polemical, and homiletical purposes. But in its final composition and redaction, Q became an ecclesiastical manual. . . . [109]

But the basic ingredient in Q according to the Shaffer Lectures is a Jewish, non-Christian wisdom book (see above). In connection with the *Gospel of Thomas* Koester had spoken in the Shaffer Lectures similarly of "the wisdom book that was the catalyst for the earliest written collections of these sayings." Thus Q and the *Gospel of Thomas* would seem to have received their first written impetus, initially determinative of their genre, from sapiential books. But the secondary intrusion of an apocalyptic Son-of-Man Christology is for Koester responsible for the final redaction of Q (see above). Koester would hence seem to conjecture at least two written stages in the composition of Q, one at least in part under sapiential influence, one under apocalyptic.

Boring has put in question the Christianizing of a Jewish wisdom book by pointing out that the Bultmannian interpretation of the quotation formula in Luke 11:49 as referring to a wisdom book has given way in recent Q studies to other interpretations.[110] Boring also questions the post-Bultmannian assumption that the Son of Man title was not part of Jesus' own vocabulary, even when the term refers to the final judge as someone other than Jesus, a view rather important in relegating the Son-of-Man sayings to a secondary stage in the Q tradition:

Jesus did speak of the Son of Man who was to come in the future, a transcendent, eschatological figure with whom he did not identify himself, yet with whom he did associate himself very closely. It is only within this category of sayings that we may look for authentic sayings of Jesus [about the Son of Man]. I am myself unable to account for the distinction between the Jesus who speaks in these sayings and the Son of Man who is to come in the future (Mark 8:38 par.; Luke 12:8–9 par.; 17:22, 24, 26, 30 par.; 18:8; Matt. 19:28; 25:31) on any other basis than that it (the distinction, not necessarily these sayings) goes back to Jesus himself. As Tödt so succinctly states: "What is stated here is constructed as a soteriological correlation, not at all as a Christological continuity." The fact that Jesus did speak of the Son of Man as someone other than himself, who, in the eschatological drama, would vindicate discipleship to Jesus, does not mean that all sayings that evince this distinction are from Jesus. The genuineness of any particular saying must be settled from case to case, not *a priori* because it belongs in a particular formally-defined group. . . .

---

[108] Koester, "Tradition and History," II.3, typescript, p. 55; III.2, typescript pp. 90–91.
[109] Koester, *Introduction*, 2.147.
[110] Boring, *Sayings of the Risen Jesus*, 157–58.

In attributing even the sayings that make this distinction to the early church, thus making the distinction between Jesus and the Son of Man both *originate* in, and, when it becomes problematic, *be dissolved* by, the early church, Vielhauer and those who hold his view labor under an insuperable difficulty. To the objection that the church would not have distinguished Jesus and the Son of Man, Vielhauer replies "so long as 'Son of Man' had an apocalyptic meaning, it could not be applied to an earthly being. Thus the church had to distinguish between the earthly Jesus and the Son of Man" ("Jesus und der Menschensohn," pp. 143, 170ff). But this very argument militates against Vielhauer's other key point, that it was Christian prophets who first spoke Son-of-Man sayings in Jesus' name. The prophets did not, however, retroject sayings into the *Sitz im Leben Jesu*; it was not the earthly Jesus to whom they were attributing their sayings. The Jesus-ego with which they spoke was that of the exalted Lord, not the earthly Jesus, so they would not have distinguished Jesus from the Son of Man on the grounds given by Vielhauer. Thus the sayings that distinguish Jesus and the Son of Man must be either genuine, modeled on genuine words of Jesus, or secondary but non-prophetic. But if they are non-prophetic, they must belong to that later stratum of secondary Son-of-Man sayings that are dependent for their Son-of-Man terminology on the earlier, prophetic sayings. In Vielhauer's view this cannot be, for he properly regards these sayings as the oldest precisely because of the distinction they make between Jesus and the Son of Man. These are then used as the pattern for the later, secondary Son-of-Man sayings, thereby accounting for the fact that "Son of Man" occurs only in the third person in them. Unless the sayings in which the distinction between Jesus and the Son of Man is made are prophetic, the whole structure of Vielhauer's reconstruction collapses—yet they cannot be regarded as prophetic on his grounds.

In the light of our hypothesis, an apparent explanation for this constellation of phenomena immediately suggests itself: not only did Christian prophets contribute sayings to the developing synoptic tradition of Jesus' words by promulgating individual sayings in the name of the exalted Son of Man, but they stand at the transition-point between the sayings of the historical Jesus *about* the Son of Man and the sayings of the post-Easter Jesus who speaks through his prophets *as* the Son of Man. If this hypothesis is true, there is a sense in which explicit (titular) christology, and therefore Christian theology, began in the immediately post-Easter revelations of Christian prophets; these experiences may have been very closely related to the Easter experiences of the first disciples, or even identical with them.[111]

Such a return to Bultmann's attribution of such Son-of-Man sayings to the historical Jesus is reminiscent of another unexpected advocate of attributing more sayings in the Q tradition to the historical Jesus—Gerd Theissen:

If one understands by "church" congregations settled in one place together with their institutions, then there is no sociological continuity between Jesus and primitive Christianity. But it is different with wandering charismatics. Here the social situation of Jesus and a branch of primitive Christianity is comparable: Jesus was the first wandering charismatic. The transmitters of such sayings took over his life style, the *tropous kuriou* (*Did.* 11.8). What was shaped by their life style is hence for that reason far from being "inauthentic." Their wandering radicalism goes back to Jesus himself. It is authentic. Probably more sayings are "suspect" of being authentic than many modern sceptics would like.[112]

---

[111] Boring, *Sayings of the Risen Jesus*, 241, 292 (n. 13), 242–43.
[112] Theissen, "Wanderradikalismus," 257=*Studien*, 91="Itinerant Radicalism," 87.

Thus the problem of the genre of Q becomes intertwined with the layering of Q, which in turn becomes a question of the first steps in primitive Christian theology, which then becomes a question of where Jesus left off and primitive Christianity took over. To be sure, the well-worn authenticity question loses some of its theological freight once one recognizes that in terms of wandering radicalism and charismatic prophets, that is to say, in terms of the Christianity represented by Q and *Gospel of Thomas*, not only is less shift to be expected as one moves from Jesus to this "church." Also that Jesus is less an isolated or unique phenomenon, as subsequent Christology made him, and is more imbedded in the Jesus movement of Palestinian Judaism during the half-century that straddled the middle of the first century, of which New Testament Christianity, i.e., Diaspora and ultimately Gentile Christianity—Christianity as a historical movement—is a broken derivative. The familiar question of the legitimacy with which the proclaimer became the proclaimed may resolve itself into the question of faithfulness to the canon *behind* the canon—and to what is behind Q and the *Gospel of Thomas*.

As a result of these disagreements with the position worked out by Koester, Boring has argued that Q is less a sapiential book than a prophetic book:

> Likewise, the Q-materials are not well described by the term "Words of the Wise" (LOGOI SOPHŌN). While it is true that Q has many points of contact with the wisdom tradition in both form and content, Q is in no sense a "Christian Book of Proverbs" [Vincent Taylor]. Over against those who claim to live by traditional wisdom, the Q-community knows itself to live by revelation (Luke 10:21–22). The manner of address of wisdom materials is that of a "timeless truth," which speaks to the hearer because of its inherent validity, although it may be incidentally attached to a figure of the past: Solomon, Ahikar, Sirach. We have seen that Q does contain expressions of what was once gnomic wisdom, just as it contains teachings appropriate to a rabbi but, as proclaimed and heard in the Q-community, these tend to be transformed into the prophetic address of the exalted Jesus who is imminently expected as the Son of Man and judge of the world. . . . More than one mode of address is thus still present in Q, representing the literary remains of struggles to perceive Jesus as rabbi or teacher of wisdom, as well as exalted Lord, but the fundamental orientation of the Q-sayings as they came to Matthew and Luke is neither the timeless mode of wisdom nor the traditional mode of rabbinica but the present/future mode of prophecy.
>
> In addition to the analysis of particular sayings, there are some general features of the Q-complex of materials that relate it to Christian prophecy. Streeter has pointed out that the form of the "book" itself is prophetic, beginning with the baptism and temptation stories analogous to a prophetic "call" and continuing with a collection of oracles and a minimum of narrative, somewhat like Jeremiah. While the point may not be pressed, Q is probably closer to Jeremiah than to Proverbs, related more to traditional prophetic forms than to wisdom.[113]

[113] Boring, *Sayings of the Risen Jesus*, 180–81.

It may well be the case that the sapiential material in Q had lost the banality we usually associate with that concept, as indeed William A. Beardslee has pointed out, for example, that the wisdom sayings ascribed to Jesus have taken on an acuteness not typical of this genre.[114] To this extent one might say that Q is moving toward the "secret sayings" version of this genre, to which Mark 4 ("riddles") and the *Gospel of Thomas* belong, and which Irenaeus (*Haer.* I.1.5; I.28.7) associated with gnostic usage. Boring documents the revelation motif precisely by material usually held to be late in the development of Q. And it has been recognized that Q, in beginning with the baptism and temptation, indicates, precisely because of Mark, some modulation out of the sapiential tradition toward a more "historical" or "biographical" cast such as one finds also in Jeremiah. But Boring himself has pointed out "that prophecy in the early church manifests some wisdom features,"[115] so that "wisdom and prophecy are not alternatives."[116] And, although Koester has attributed the Son-of-Man apocalypticism to a secondary stage in the Q tradition, he has attributed to the earlier sapiential phase a radicalized eschatology, so that here, too, no either-or alternative seems to be involved. The efforts to bring to light the sapiential strand in primitive Christianity are not intended as a replacement of other strands that have been firmly established in the scholarly tradition, but rather to include in our total overview a strand that has been neglected.

Boring's most important contribution to the discussion of genre may be his tracking of a gradual bifurcation in the transmission of traditions about Jesus that led to sayings collections on the one hand and historical narrations or biographies on the other, alternatives represented at the outset by Q and Mark. With regard to Q:

> The historical Jesus was indispensable for the theological understanding of the Q-community. He had been the decisive prophetic messenger of transcendent Wisdom and had been exalted to become the Son of Man. His words, and a few of his deeds, had formed the original nucleus of the Q-materials. But the prophetic understanding of the Q-community tended more and more to focus on the post-Easter exalted Jesus. What Jesus of Nazareth had said became dissolved in what the post-Easter Jesus said through his prophets. If these two categories of material were ever distinguished, they had ceased to be by the time of the redaction of the Q-materials. While the dissolution of the word of the historical Jesus into the word of the heavenly Jesus had not yet occurred in Q, the center of gravity had shifted, so that Q was moving in the direction of a collection of "sayings of the living Jesus" such as the *Gospel of Thomas*.[117]

---

[114] Beardslee, "Wisdom Tradition," 231–40; "Proverb," 61–73; "Insight," in Beardslee, *Literary Criticism* 39–41.

[115] Boring, *Sayings of the Risen Jesus,* 141.

[116] Boring, *Sayings of the Risen Jesus,* 281, n. 141.

[117] Boring, *Sayings of the Risen Jesus,* 182. See also Robinson, "Narrative."

Or, as Boring puts it with regard to Q 12:4–7:

> Even if the sayings, or some elements from them, derive from Jesus himself, these
> words would be heard in the Q-community as the address of the exalted Jesus to the
> current situation of the threatened Q-community. . . . Rather than sayings of the risen
> Jesus being placed in the mouth of the historical Jesus by the Q-community, it appears
> that the tendency was the other way: traditional, even pre-Easter sayings of Jesus are
> claimed for the risen Lord.[118]

Over against this tendency in Q Boring squarely places Mark:

> The study of the sayings of the risen Jesus in Q and Mark respectively has revealed an
> important difference that is fundamental to understanding the relation of Christian
> prophecy to the canonical gospels. Whereas Q contains a considerable number of
> prophetic sayings, is tending to be understood as a whole as sayings of the risen Jesus
> and by its nature is open to continued expansion by the addition of new revelatory
> sayings, Mark contains only a few prophetic sayings, which are entirely contained
> within the historicizing pre-Easter framework, closing the door to further prophetic
> expansion. . . .
>
> It might be assumed that Mark has few prophetic sayings as a result of including only
> a few of any kind of sayings. The hypothesis being proposed here is that precisely the
> opposite relation obtains: the paucity of sayings in Mark is to be explained on the basis
> of Mark's view of the prophetic sayings. . . .
>
> Mark has so few sayings of Jesus because he is suspicious of Christian prophecy as it
> is present in his community and expressed in the sayings-tradition. He creates a new
> prophetic form intended as an alternative.
>
> We have seen that Q contained substantial prophetic materials and was coming to be
> regarded as altogether "sayings of the risen Jesus." It was not a rabbinic Q against which
> Mark was reacting but a prophetic Q. . . .
>
> The most probable reason for Mark's hesitating use of the Q-material is to be found
> in his suspicion of the genre that it represents the post-Easter revelations of the risen
> Lord. . . . But the message of the risen Lord is now bound to, and contained with, the
> tradition of Jesus of Nazareth as this is contained within a narrative presented entirely
> in a pre-Easter framework.
>
> What he opposes is the view that the risen Lord comes to speech in the collections of
> sayings such as Q that were so open to being considered the post-Easter address of the
> exalted Lord, an address no longer grounded in history. Such collections were not only
> composed of material much of which did in fact come into being after Easter, they were
> open to this interpretation in toto and to continued growth and expansion by the risen
> Lord.
>
> To counteract this tendency, Mark took a step at once paradoxical and radical: he
> presented the message of the living Lord in a narrative form in which the post-Easter
> Jesus, in the narrative story-line, says nothing. His message is confined entirely to the
> pre-Easter framework of the gospel form that Mark devised for this purpose. There is
> an intentional dialectic here. It is no accident that Mark ends at 16:8 with the announce-
> ment that Jesus is risen, but without his having appeared. To tell an appearance story is
> to have the risen Lord speak in an undialectical way and to open the door to a flood of
> post-Easter revelations of which Mark is very critical. . . . Mark is absolutely unwilling
> to tell the story in such a way that the risen Lord continues to speak in the story-line
> after Easter.[119]

---

[118] Boring, Sayings of the Risen Jesus, 167–68.
[119] Boring, Sayings of the Risen Jesus, 195–202.

If Mark stands thus clearly one step to the "right" of Q, the fact that it is only one step to the right is illustrated by comparing Mark with the next step, Luke, where the orthodox outcome is already evident:

> The relation of the power of God to the unfolding mission of the church in Acts is conceived by Luke in a different way than as the continuing ministry of Jesus, as we have seen above. The point may be seen by comparing Luke to Mark in this regard. In Mark, the "then" of Jesus' ministry is dialectically represented as the "now" of Mark's and his reader's own time. For Luke, Jesus' word and ministry are past history; but all revelations of the Spirit, all new communications from heaven, must be judged by the recollection of the life, teaching, death and resurrection of Jesus. God leads his community forward, but not along a line contrary to his definitive revelation in Jesus. . . . This is clearly illustrated, for example, in the ways in which Mark and Luke respectively handle the missionary charge of Jesus to his disciples. Mark 6:8–11 changes the original radicality of the instructions to make them more realistically applicable to Mark's own day, because he intends them to be heard as the present address of the risen Lord. The missioners are thus permitted to take a staff and to wear sandals. In Luke, on the other hand, the original radicality of the Q-form of the saying is preserved in the instructions of the disciples during Jesus' ministry (9:3; 10:4) but is "corrected" by Jesus at the end of his ministry (22:35–6). The teaching of Jesus is *directly* applicable only during the "midst of time," the historical time when Jesus was on the earth. The teaching of Jesus is still authoritative but no longer addressed the reader directly as the word of the living Lord.
>
> We are thus faced with the conclusion that Luke, who pictures the church as guided by the Spirit and frequently addressed by Christian prophets, does not understand these prophets to have produced new words of Jesus. . . . The form of Christian prophecy in Acts is not that of "sayings of the risen Jesus" (11:28; 21:11). We have seen that this is not a result of accurate historical tradition but of Lukan *Tendenz*.[120]

This could well throw new light on the background of Luke's innovation in adding to his Gospel an Acts of the Apostles, a step of far-reaching consequences to which Franz Overbeck first drew sharp attention. Prior to Luke, it was still possible for Mark to contemporize the narration about Jesus to such an extent that the implications for the church of the evangelist's time were transparent. But not only did this put severe limitations about what guidance could be provided the present in such a refracted medium, it also would have continued the strain on the traditional sayings of Jesus, which was the problem charismatic prophets posed to Mark, as Mark's own updating of Jesus' sayings indicates. Luke solved both these problems by replacing the resurrected Christ with the Holy Spirit as the church's contemporary authority. Thus the traditions about Jesus could be left back in the past as a venerable authority no longer directly binding on the present, but all the more securely fixed as an unchanging if indirect authority (on the way to canonicity). The presentation of the life of the church could then be brought out from behind the veil of the life of Christ into the light of day as the life of the Holy Spirit. The ambivalence of the proclamation of charismatic proph-

---

[120] Boring, *Sayings of the Risen Jesus*, 228–29.

ets in the name of the resurrected Christ is replaced by the less ambiguous leadership of the Holy Spirit.

Boring drew my attention to the fact that his thesis of the bifurcating
trajectory between the sayings collection of the living and speaking Lord
and the narrative biography of the Jesus of the past, which he arrived at
by means of his analysis of early Christian prophecy, converges in a
striking way with the implications I drew from an analysis of the
diverging visualizations of the resurrected Christ in my presidential
paper at the Society of Biblical Literature which he heard in December
1981:

> This ambivalence of the sayings tradition and hence of early sayings collections was not
> fully satisfactory to either side in the emerging polarization. If the orthodox manage to
> use and lose Q and to block the canonization of the *Gospel of Thomas*, opting for the
> biographical pre-Easter cast provided by the canonical Gospels, the gnostics, while
> accepting the *Gospel of Thomas*, really prefer another genre of gospel, the dialogue of
> the resurrected Christ with his disciples. It is this trajectory from the sayings collection
> to the gnostic dialogues, as well as its pendant in the orthodox trajectory from Q to the
> canonical Gospels, that is now to be sketched. . . .
>
> Thus both Mark and John seem aware of the pair of contrasting terms ["in parables"/
> "openly"], and both agree in placing the shift from one level to the other before rather
> than after Easter. . . .
>
> Wrede failed to recognize that Mark has, apparently intentionally, shifted that
> turning point back into the middle of his Gospel.
>
> This may indeed be the key to the perennial problem of the gospel genre. The fact
> that Mark and John transfer the shift to the higher level of meaning back prior to the
> crucifixion may be their most explicit rationale for playing down didactic revelations at
> Easter and filling almost their whole books with the period prior to Easter, the period
> when Jesus was teaching in his physical body on earth. Luke would in his way carry this
> to its logical outcome in defining the qualifications of an apostle so as to include not just,
> à la Paul, the resurrection, but the whole period since John the Baptist (thus reaching
> the position made standard in the English language tradition through the idiom "public
> ministry" Acts 1:21–22).[121]

Boring and I both take satisfaction in this convergence, not only in that
we are pleased to agree with each other, but also because we both
consider such a converging of views worked out independently of each
other and primarily in terms of independent source materials (in his
case the sayings of Jesus, in my case the appearances of Jesus) to be an
unexpected supplemental confirmation of the basic validity of this
position. It is also interesting to notice that much the same relationship
of Q and Mark has been worked out in terms of the shift from orality to
textuality by Werner H. Kelber,[122] who has already sensed the affinity of
his results to those of Boring. Thus it may be that in this area new
insights are converging that can be fruitful in the continuing study of the
genre of primitive Christian literature and the implications of the study

[121] Robinson, "Jesus from Easter to Valentinus," 22, 36.
[122] Kelber, *Oral and Written Gospel*.

of the question of genre for the understanding of the history and theology of primitive Christianity.

The most recent and comprehensive analysis of the genre of Q is the 1984 Toronto dissertation of John S. Kloppenborg. After a survey of genres of sayings collections in antiquity and a tracing of the stages through which Q went, he reaches the conclusion:

> Though Q, like any of the other instructions, gnomologia, and chriae-collections surveyed, has its peculiarities, idiosyncracies and unparalleled aspects, it is at the same time intelligible against the background of antique sayings genres. The shifts which have occurred in the course of Q's literary evolution from instruction to proto-biography do not present serious anomalies when viewed in terms of the generic typicalities and inner dynamisms of instructions, gnomologia and chriae collections. Both the instruction and the gnomologium had the potential for a gnosticizing hermeneutic as the Pythagorean *acousmata* and the *Teach. Silv.* show.... While the association of the speaker of the wise words with a divine agent (Sophia or God) is present both in the initial formative stage, and in the second recension, the editing of Q strengthened the historicizing side of the dialectic, first by introducing chriae, and then by the use of a biographical/narrative preface. These movements, it should be emphasized, do not represent a violation of the genre, or an attenuation of the "natural" development of Q as a wisdom collection.[123]

Such a detailed analysis can only serve to lead further and in a more nuanced and documented way the interest of twenty years earlier that came to expression in my essay *"LOGOI SOPHŌN."*

---

[123] Kloppenborg, "Synoptic Sayings Source," pp. 423–24=*Formation of Q.*

8

THE USE OF EARLY CHRISTIAN LITERATURE AS EVIDENCE FOR INNER DIVERSITY AND CONFLICT

Frederik Wisse

At the present time, Frederik Wisse is Associate Professor of New Testament at McGill University in Montreal. Born in the Netherlands, Dr. Wisse received his theological education in the United States and eventually was awarded a Ph.D. in Religion from Claremont Graduate School. He has done post-graduate work at Tübingen and Münster, Germany.

Dr. Wisse's research interests and publications are in the areas of Textual Criticism, Nag Hammadi Studies, Coptology, and the History of Early Christianity. He is co-editor of the Nag Hammadi Studies monograph series.

Preface

The historian of early Christianity faces serious methodological difficulties in the attempt to reconstruct the inner diversity and conflicts within the church before 200 C.E. The few surviving historical accounts of the Christian movement during this period offer only partial and often questionable information, as well as a theologically biased picture of the earlier conflict situations which they include. Thus the historian must resort to other early Christian writings in order to reconstruct the actual situation. It is difficult enough to evaluate the historical information which can be gleaned from these diverse writings even if the larger historical framework were clear. In the current state of research, however, even the framework itself must be inferred from writings which are ill-suited for this purpose.

Major steps towards the reconstruction of a satisfactory historical framework were taken during the last 150 years, particularly by F. C. Baur and W. Bauer. Nonetheless, serious difficulties remain in placing many of the early texts in this framework; this is true for some canonical

177

otridriS

and early patristic writings as well as for gnostic and apocryphal texts. The present essay argues that the nature of the conflict between orthodoxy and heresy during the third and fourth centuries C.E. mistakenly was assumed to apply also to the earlier period. This led to the false assumption that early Christian texts reflected the doctrinal diversity of competing factions or communities. This assumption is particularly inappropriate for gnostic texts, but it also does not apply to most other early Christian writings. In the heterodox situation which characterizes primitive Christianity, authors were not confined by community standards of orthodoxy. Thus conflicts usually arose over issues of practice and ecclesiastical authority. This recognition has profound implications for the historical analysis of early Christian and gnostic texts.

I. F. C. Baur's Categories of Early Christian Literature

Beginning with F. C. Baur, the central importance of locating and defining individual writings in terms of diverse or competing branches of the early church has been recognized in the critical study of early Christian literature. Baur took his starting point from such occasional, polemical writings as Paul's Corinthian correspondence and letter to the Galatians, which, he thought, gave proof of a conflict between competing Christian ideologies represented by Paul, on the one hand, and Judaizing Christians on the other.[1] With this basic division in primitive Christianity established on firm exegetical grounds, it became necessary to explain why the book of Acts presents a much more harmonious picture of the same period. Baur answered this by means of *Tendenzkritik*, "tendency criticism." He argued that the author of Acts could not admit to a state of disunity and conflict in apostolic times and thus made the conflict appear relatively minor, local, and temporary.

Baur realized that there was a third category of early Christian literature which needed to be explained in terms of the two factions in the church. In addition to polemical writings like Galatians and histories like Acts, there are a significant number of early Christian writings which are not overtly polemical and thus cannot be assigned readily to either the Pauline or Petrine parties. These books he assigned to an irenic or mediating faction. He claimed that from the Jewish Christian side the letter of James shows this mediating spirit, while Hebrews and 1

[1] For the following summary of Baur's position see the excerpts from Baur's writings and the bibliography in Kümmel, 127–40.

Peter tried to mediate from the Pauline side. He located the Gospel of John a step beyond the fusion of the two factions into the early Catholic church.

We are indebted to F. C. Baur for a clear understanding of the task and problematics of the history of early Christianity. The standard had been set: to explain an early Christian text historically is to locate it in terms of the different movements and controversies which characterized the early church. His own reconstruction of this period remains one of the high points of historical analysis.

For obvious reasons, the polemical writings and passages have a primary claim to our attention for they present direct evidence of diversity and conflict. They set the stage; all other literary evidence must be defined with reference to them. Nonetheless, polemical writings pose a special set of difficulties for the historian. Polemics are often highly personal and limited in scope. The position defended or attacked need not involve more than one person; one cannot, without further ado, assume that it characterized a larger group or faction. Baur was well aware that Paul's polemics against the Judaizers were, to a large extent, a self-defense. His letters appear to be as much the cause of a division between Jewish and Gentile Christianity as the result thereof. Had they been written by a lesser figure, and had they remained without positive response among Gentile Christian readers, they would have become an idiosyncratic phenomenon on the fringes of primitive Christianity.

We cannot assume that the relationship between the few surviving pieces of early Christian polemical literature and the main instances of conflict and factions in the church was a simple and direct one. In most cases we lack the corroborating evidence to determine whether the conflict reflected in our literature was widespread or local, major or incidental, lasting or of short duration. The role that the writing in question played in the conflict is often obscure and open to various interpretations. The reconstruction of the larger picture of diversity and conflict from such writings is a highly speculative, if not an impossible, undertaking.

Particularly for those canonical and other early Christian writings which soon found wide acceptance and use, it is important to distinguish between the historical situation which they *reflect* and the historical situation they *created*. For the former we need clear internal or supportive external evidence to conclude that the position defended or attacked is shared by a larger group or community. Religious books are generally not written to state what *is* but what the author thinks *should be*. The historian who ignores this runs the danger of creating parties or

religious communities which never existed or which did not yet exist
when the book was written. Even if the polemicist refers to all those
who support his position, one should evaluate such claims critically. The
tendency is to portray one's own position as that of the majority and as
being in keeping with the apostolic tradition, while that of the opponent
is by definition aberrant and isolated.

This touches on the second problem the historian must face in
evaluating polemical literature. One cannot expect that the position of
the other side has been represented fairly and completely in the heat of
the controversy. What is claimed about the opponents may well have
been quoted out of context, misconstrued, wrongly inferred or slan-
derous. This well-known drawback of polemics is particularly unfor-
tunate if, as is often the case, our knowledge of certain movements in
early Christianity is limited to refutation by opponents. As a consequence our knowledge of the refuted individuals or groups may be so
limited and distorted that the historian has difficulties identifying correctly surviving or newly found literature stemming from the refuted
party. One is tempted to assign such writings to a previously unknown
group. As a result, the ancient misrepresentation will have been com-
pounded through the creation by a modern interpreter of a ficticious
party in early Christianity.

The second category of ancient Christian literature for which the
historian must account is comprised of the ancient historical accounts.
As Baur correctly recognized, these accounts are hostile witnesses to
diversity and conflict within primitive Christianity, and their vision has
been distorted by what the author thinks should have been. It is very
modern to look at diversity as something positive, to make the necessity
of change into a virtue and to stress the salutary effects of conflict. In
contrast, ancient Christian historians from the author of Acts to Eusebius
tended to explain diversity in terms of truth and falsehood: change was
seen as falsification and conflict as instigated by demonic forces. Insofar
as they were aware of diversity in the primitive church they would try to
ignore it, make it look innocuous, or exploit it for their own partisan
purposes. This makes such histories of dubious value for modern
historians. Our knowledge of the first three centuries of the church,
however, is so limited and haphazard that we cannot do without these
histories. Nevertheless, this predicament is not as bad as it sounds, for if
the special theological bias of these histories is taken into account, they
prove to be invaluable witnesses for diversity and conflict in spite of
themselves.

The third, and by far the largest, group of early Christian texts which the historian must place in the historical framework of early Christian literature are those which are not overtly involved in inner Christian polemics. This large and diverse group reflects a great variety of beliefs and practices. For this category F. C. Baur's evaluation has not proven satisfactory. He wrongly assumed that all early Christian literature was somehow related to the main conflict he perceived. Though we cannot preclude the possibility that some early Christian books intended to mediate between competing factions, such a function is far from obvious for the New Testament books he mentions. As with polemical writings, mediating literature can only be identified as such—and could only have been effective as such—if it identified itself as such. If a writing lacks the expected features and references germane to its polemical or mediating purpose, then the historian must try to explain it in some other way. The real purpose of such literature may be catechetical, homiletical, exegetical, apologetic, speculative or propagandizing rather than an attempt to mediate between opposing views.

To account historically for this group of writings is far more difficult than is generally realized. Some of them may fit comfortably into one of the factions identified on the basis of polemical and historical texts, but many do not. This is particularly true for the earliest among them. It is far from clear what the relationship of such writings was to the different theological, ethical, ritual and organizational positions current in Christian churches at the time of their writing. As in the case of polemical literature, one may not assume that the views advocated in these writings reflect the beliefs and practices of a distinct group. There are, of course, documents commissioned by a larger group which represent community views. These, however, are relatively rare and the reader is normally informed of the special background of the document. If these clues are absent from the texts the burden rests upon the historian to give sufficient reasons as to why the text in question ought to be taken as representative of a larger group or faction. In practice this means that one must show compelling reasons why the author reflects in the writing the beliefs and practices of a wider community. As we shall see, the reflection of the faith and practice of a wider community presupposes a *Sitz im Leben* "life situation" of an established "orthodoxy." If no such controlled "orthodox" environment can be assumed for a text—and this is more the rule than the exception in early Christianity—then it becomes very questionable to attribute the special features of the text to a certain, otherwise unknown, branch of early Christianity.[2]

---

[2] I have argued this in greater detail in "Prolegomena," 138–45.

II. W. Bauer's Use of Early Christian Literature

Even though F. C. Baur's reconstruction of the history of early Christianity has made the traditional view untenable, it still took more than a
century before W. Bauer gave it the *coup de grâce* in his *Rechtgläubigkeit und Ketzerei im ältesten Christentum.*[3] He proved that there is no
historical basis for the traditional claim that orthodoxy preceded heresy
logically and chronologically. The pure beginnings of the church were
not a historical fact, but a theological concept imposed on the facts by
the author of Acts, Hegesippus, and Eusebius. What the church fathers
called heresy was not necessarily a deviation from the earliest form of
Christianity. In stating this W. Bauer clarified what F. C. Baur and others
had already said, or implied.

The new contribution W. Bauer made was his use of early Christian
literature to prove that second-century orthodoxy was not the majority
view but was a view largely limited to the churches in Rome, Corinth,
Antioch, and Western Asia Minor. He argued ingeniously that elsewhere various forms of "heresy" held sway and that they were even able
to threaten the outposts of orthodoxy outside of Rome. It is not my
purpose here to question Bauer's conclusions about the various geographical areas in which the church was located. Rather, we must see
how he uses early Christian literature as evidence for inner diversity
and conflict.

Little needs to be said about Bauer's uses of polemical literature. It
was not his intention to reinterpret the literary evidence for ancient
Christian heresies nor to give a comprehensive picture of the diversity in
belief and practice during the second century. By limiting himself
largely to second-century heresies for which there is multiple attestation, such as Montanism, Marcionism, and Gnosticism, he was able to
escape the difficulties and pitfalls which early Christian polemical
literature presents to the historian.

In contrast, a reexamination of ancient Christian historical accounts is
central to Bauer's thesis. Much of his book, and especially ch. 8, is
preoccupied with questioning the chief "hostile" witness for the second
and third centuries, Eusebius' *Ecclesiastical History*, and the earlier
historical sources which it incorporates. Both Eusebius and Bauer
appeal to second-century Christian literature in order to support their
understanding of the relationship between orthodoxy and heresy, but
they come to opposite conclusions. Eusebius refers to a significant

[3] Bauer, *Rechtgläubigkeit.* References are to the English translation of the second
German edition of 1964: Bauer, *Orthodoxy.*

number of orthodox authors and titles from the period prior to 200 C.E.[4] It is clear from the titles that some of these books were anti-heretical but for others this is not so certain. Eusebius claims repeatedly that these orthodox writings and many others like them "are still preserved to this day by a great many brethren."[5] In other words, Eusebius gives the impression that from early days on there was a large and widely dispersed body of orthodox literature which defended the truth and refuted heresy. By comparison, the heretics of the same period stood isolated and condemned.

Bauer quite rightly questions the evidence Eusebius presents.[6] It appears Eusebius has grossly inflated the list of orthodox authors and books by repeatedly referring to "very many others" of whom he cannot recount the names.[7] His claim that these works "have reached us" and can still be examined cannot be taken seriously. Though he was associated in Caesarea with what was likely one of the most extensive Christian libraries of that time, he shows no knowledge of the contents of most of the writings to which he refers. Bauer has good reasons to suspect that they did not survive. Eusebius assumed that many more orthodox books survived. But if he had evidence for this why did he not present it?

The question remains why most of the orthodox writings of the second century did not survive until the first half of the fourth century when Eusebius wrote his *Ecclesiastical History*. Harnack suggests that these "writings were no longer suited to the later dogmatic taste."[8] Bauer proposes another reason. He believes that the orthodox writers rather than the heretics stood isolated, and that their writings were suppressed by the "heretical" majority well before the "dogmatic taste" changed.[9] Thus Eusebius' evidence is turned against him and is used to support the opposite of what he wanted to prove.

It is noteworthy that Bauer does not seriously question Eusebius' claim that the second-century writings he lists were indeed orthodox, even though Eusebius most likely knew the content of only a few of them. He shares with Eusebius the belief that second-century Christian literature was either doctrinally orthodox or heretical; there is no third option. Bauer does not challenge Eusebius' assumption that second-century authors who wrote against the heretics must have been doctrinally orthodox in their other writings. Both assume that all Christian literature

---

[4] *Eccl. Hist.* 4.8 and 21–28.
[5] *Eccl. Hist.* 4.25.
[6] Bauer, *Orthodoxy*, 149–59.
[7] *Eccl. Hist.* 5.27.
[8] *Altchristlichen Literatur*, 1/1.248.
[9] Bauer, *Orthodoxy*, 166.

of that period was in some way part of an ideological struggle between competing "orthodoxies."

A second piece of evidence which Bauer takes from the *Ecclesiastical History* and turns against its author is the curious scarcity of anti-orthodox polemics in the heretical literature.[10] Though it would appear that second-century heretical authors were far more prolific than their orthodox counterparts, they appear uninterested in refuting the orthodox position. The Nag Hammadi texts tend to confirm this impression.[11] In terms of Eusebius' understanding of the situation in early Christianity, this lack of anti-orthodox polemic would be due to the numerical and theological superiority of the orthodox, who isolated the heretics and put them on the defensive.

For Bauer the evidence points in the opposite direction. He argues that the absence of anti-orthodox polemics was due to the fact that the heretics were dominant and secure in large geographical areas during the second century.[12] There was no need for them to refute orthodox teaching. In contrast, the orthodox churches were hard-pressed, and were forced to attack the heretics wherever and whenever they could. According to Bauer, behind the anti-heretical struggle stood the church of Rome with its aggressive, imperialistic policies.[13]

III. The *ad hominem* Nature of Early Christian Polemics

There is another factor which needs to be taken into account in order to evaluate properly the evidence which early Christian literature gives of inner diversity and conflict. The focus of Christian polemics in this period is basically *ad hominem*, i.e., directed against persons, rather than *ad doctrinam*, i.e., directed against teaching. Bauer was not unaware of this,[14] but he is mainly interested in proving the numerical superiority of the heretics in most areas. This predominant focus seems strange if the conflict was mainly due to a clash between different doctrinal positions. What is easily forgotten is that at this early period there was no comprehensive and widely accepted rule of faith which could function as a standard for truth and falsehood. Hence polemics were hardly possible at the level of doctrine. As a consequence, heresy at this time was not so much a teaching that was at variance with established doctrine, as it was the teaching—any teaching!—of someone

---

[10] Bauer, *Orthodoxy*, 169f.
[11] The few cases of anti-orthodox polemic are discussed by Koschorke, *Polemik*.
[12] Bauer, *Orthodoxy*, 170.
[13] Bauer, *Orthodoxy*, ch. 6.
[14] Bauer, *Orthodoxy*, ch. 7.

who was either unauthorized by the leadership or who for some reason or other was considered unworthy and unacceptable. The converse also applies: whatever was taught by someone who was approved by the leadership, or by the author in question, was by definition orthodox.[15]

This means that "orthodoxy" must have begun as orthocracy, i.e., the truth claim of a teaching depended on the accepted authority of the person who taught it. Even at the time of the Pastoral Epistles "sound doctrine" does not appear to have had a clear and stable content, but "sound doctrine" was basically the teaching of sound people, such as the apostles of old and the official church leadership of that time. This also explains the many pseudepigraphical writings from this period. It was not just an ancient "sales gimmick" or a way of honoring an admired member of the apostolic circle; rather, it was a necessity. Since there was not yet a standard by which to judge the truth claim of a writing on the basis of its content, soundness came to depend on the reputation of the author. Thus also, conflict and refutation had to focus on the author, though not just of necessity, but more likely because the conflict itself at this early period centered on persons and their functions.

The *ad hominem* polemics which characterized conflict in early Christianity exhibit the following features:[16]

(1) The opponent was associated with villains from the Old Testament (e.g., Cain, the Sodomites, Balaam, Korah, Jezebel), or with reported opponents of the apostles (e.g., Judaizers, Simon Magus). Just as the opponent was guilty by association, so the protagonist claimed trustworthiness by associating himself with the apostolic circle and other acknowledged heroes of the past.

(2) The opponent was pictured as a fulfillment of the prophecies about the eschatological false prophets or antichrists.[17] This meant that he was a tool of Satan.

(3) Immoral practices were often attributed to the opponent. Any sign of virtue must be a pretense for deceiving unsuspecting believers. Though this claim would have been in most cases untrue, it cannot simply be called slander, since it was not considered possible for a false believer to speak the truth and live a genuinely moral life.[18]

(4) The opponent must have gotten his ideas from pagan sources, and as such was not really "of us." Falsehood could not issue from truth or from a true believer.[19]

[15] See my discussion in "Prolegomena," 139-40.
[16] See also my discussion in "Epistle of Jude," 133-43.
[17] E.g., 1 John 2:18f.
[18] See Wisse, "Die Sextus-Sprüche," 55-86.
[19] This is the basic premise on which Hippolytus based his *Refutatio omnium haeresium*.

(5) In case heretical teachings are mentioned, these tended to be the already refuted heresies of the past (e.g., Jewish law) or the denial of generally accepted truths (e.g., 1 John 2:22).

(6) Opponents are said to reject proper authority (Jude 8). For Thebutis, Valentinus, and Marcion it was claimed that they turned to falsehood because their aspirations for high church office were frustrated.[20] There can be little doubt that the recognition of authority played a central role in the conflicts of this period.

In this kind of polemic there is no need to refute the opponent's teaching. It is, therefore, also impossible to reconstruct his teaching on the basis of the polemic. The few beliefs attributed to the opponents were not really descriptive but merely part of the *ad hominem* attack.[21] This is even true for Irenaeus and later heresiologists who refute their opponents by exposing heretical "teaching." The idea is that to see heretical teaching is to reject it. By listing details from heretical books which most Christians would consider foreign or grotesque, the author and readers of such books have been discredited. The place of these details in the thinking of the author often remains obscure.

Even when actual refutation was attempted, the arguments the heresiologist could muster were far from conclusive. The appeal to revelation and the gift of prophecy was not limited to one side in the conflict. One could try to discredit the prophet but it was not possible to rule out prophecy. Also appeals to Scripture could not easily be falsified, since there were no established standards for interpretation, and allegorization opened up unlimited possibilities for the interpreter. The best argument would seem to be the one based on reason. It is already present in Paul's arguments against the Judaizers in Galatians and the enthusiasts in Corinth, but it is only fully developed in Irenaeus' writings.[22] The truth is characterized by coherence, inner logic, and unity, while falsehood is incoherent, confusing, and contradictory. Irenaeus' description of heretical teaching in *Adversus haereses* I is designed to show this.

It is only in terms of an appeal to "reason" that we can speak of orthodoxy in the true sense of the word. The rational coherence of ideas provided an internal standard of truth. Only what coheres with traditional dogma is acceptable; what does not cohere with it is heresy. What stood over against this emerging understanding of orthodoxy was not a rival or internally coherent ideology but rather heterodoxy, i.e., an open and eclectic situation allowing for wide ranging theological speculation,

[20] *Eccl. Hist.* 4.22.5; Tertullian, *Adversus Valentianos*, 4.

[21] I have argued this for Jude, "Epistle of Jude," 133–43.

[22] Esp. in *Adversus haereses*, II–V.

and tolerating diversity. This heterodoxy was firmly rooted in the charismatic beginnings of gentile Christianity. It presented a major and long-lasting threat to the emerging orthocracy. The established leadership could not tolerate theological speculation outside of its control, and heterodox "teachers" could not tolerate this ecclesiastical control. The appeal to reason presented a way to reject heterodox speculation on the basis that it did not cohere logically with generally accepted tenets of the faith, rather than that it came from an unapproved author. There was now an objective basis to evaluate "new" teaching; if it proved to cohere it was not really new but already implied in apostolic teaching and if it did not cohere it had to be heresy. The appeal to reason went hand in hand with the claim of catholicity. Some of Irenaeus' views may well have been as peculiar and novel as those of Valentinus, but insofar as he could claim that they were derived from traditional and widely accepted dogma they could be called the teaching of true believers everywhere.

IV. Implications for the Reconstruction of Early Christian History

We must now state what the implications of this reconstruction are for the relationship between early Christian literature and the diversity and conflict in the church. W. Bauer was right in arguing that "heresy" appears to precede "orthodoxy" in most areas. He continued to use, however, the traditional terms "orthodoxy" and "heresy" and thus confused the picture. He can be misunderstood to say that the traditional view of primitive Christianity was correct; only the terms must be reversed. Heresy rather than orthodoxy came first and orthodoxy is really a late foreign element which was able to win only because it had as its spokesman the powerful and aggressive church in Rome; yet, the evidence would indicate that not heresy but heterodoxy preceded orthodoxy, and that it continued to be the majority view through most of the second century except where orthocracy had been able to establish itself. Orthodoxy evolved from orthocracy as a result of the conflict with heterodoxy.

The existence of a large number of writings from this period which were not overtly polemical is no longer a problem. Bauer is not far off the mark by implying that they were written in areas where "heresy" was not challenged by "orthodoxy." The situation becomes clearer if we pose a heterodox milieu for them which was conducive to theological innovation and speculation, and in which a diversity of views was tolerated. Some of this heterodox literature found wide acceptance and became part of the New Testament canon and orthodox collections, but most of it was later considered suspect or heretical. This heterodox literature was not written within clear limits of tolerance, nor was there a need for the authors to reflect the beliefs and practices of Christian communities.

It is not really possible to separate heterodox literature into orthodox and heretical texts. Such categories apply if at all, only in retrospect. Thus it is no surprise that not much of this literature survived until the time of Eusebius. Even writings of authors who were later considered orthodox because of their heresiological reputation were unlikely to fit the fourth-century standards for orthodoxy.

If indeed most Christian literature before 200 C.E. was written in a heterodox milieu, this has major consequences for the historian. It means that the beliefs and practices advocated in these writings, insofar as they vary from those reflected in other Christian texts, cannot be attributed to a distinct community or sect. Rather, these writings were more likely idiosyncratic in terms of their environment. The "teaching" they contain was not meant to replace other teaching but to supplement. They did not defend the beliefs of a community but rather tried to develop and explore Christian truth in different directions. In this heterodox milieu there were few limits to such private speculation. There was room for the prophet and the visionary. One heterodox writing would inspire the creation of another.

Christian-gnostic literature offers us the most extreme examples of heterodox literature. The orthodox heresiologists did not understand this. They assumed that the gnostic books contained the teachings of different sects. Since no two writings agreed in their teaching, they pictured the gnostics as hopelessly divided among themselves. With generally only literary evidence available to them, they were not able to see their mistake.[23]

Because gnostic texts were produced as heterodox literature in a syncretistic situation conducive to speculative thought, they were part of a literary rather than a sectarian phenomenon. Similar in origin and function to Orphic, Neo-Pythagorean, and Middle Platonic literature, they presuppose no organized sect in the background, as is becoming increasingly clear.[24] These writings reflect only the visions and speculations of individuals and the literature they used and imitated. One expects to find such individuals among itinerant preachers, sages, magicians, ascetics, visionaries, philosophers, and holy men.

---

[23] See Wisse, "Prolegomena," 140–41.
[24] Cf. Burkert, "Craft versus Sect," 183–89.

V. Conclusion

In conclusion I want to return to the beginning. F. C. Baur discovered in Paul's writings evidence for two opposing factions in the primitive church. It would appear that this conflict arose against the background of heteropraxis, i.e., a situation in which diverse practices were tolerated. Both Gal 2:3 and Acts 15:19 agree that the leaders of the Jerusalem church allowed gentile Christians to be free from the obligations of circumcision and the law which remained valid for Jewish Christians. By implication, Paul must also have agreed to this double standard. By the time of the Antioch incident, however, orthopraxis had gained the upper hand in the Jerusalem church. Paul saw the behavior of Peter, Barnabas, and the other Jews in the church of Antioch as a breach of the earlier agreement. In the letter to the Galatians Paul in turn was no longer willing to tolerate heteropraxis, for he argues now that also the Jewish Christians are free from the law.

How the Jewish Christians were able to integrate the law and faith is unclear. Most likely they did not try to integrate them theologically. The fact that Paul does not refute a coherent Jewish-Christian theology would indicate that there was no Jewish-Christian orthodoxy at this time. The Jewish Christians from their side used *ad hominem* polemic against Paul by challenging his authority as an apostle and by claiming that he incited believers to sin (Rom 3:8). Thus the conflict appears to be between orthopraxis and Paul's idiosyncratic teaching on faith and works.

Paul did not impose a strict orthopraxis on his churches but argued for tolerance and freedom except in the case of immorality. There was no established leadership and the stress on spiritual gifts created a profoundly heterodox situation. Divergent views in the congregation were not treated as heresy, but Paul tried to curb factions by arguing that edification of the community should be the common goal. The situation has changed drastically in the Pastoral Epistles. The need for orthocracy is obvious to the author. The readers are warned against false teachers, most likely itinerant preachers who try to impress women (2 Tim 3:6) and are, among other things, adept in speculative myths. He even associates them with the "heretics" of old, the circumcision party (Titus 1:10), the teachers of the law (1 Tim 1:7), which the great apostle had already refuted. The situation is now dominated by the conflict with gnostic heterodoxy.

Thus for the earliest Christian period (i.e., before the middle of the second century C.E. in Rome and well beyond that elsewhere) it would be a mistake to try to define its remaining literature in terms of competing theological positions or the conflict between orthodoxy and heresy. In the heterodox situation which prevailed at this time there was considerable tolerance to doctrinal diversity, partly of necessity, because on most issues the theological structure needed for refutation was lacking. The relative isolation of Christian communities and the lack of knowledge about sister churches no doubt contributed to this heterodox milieu and apparent tolerance for diversity. This explains the absence of clear polemic in some of the writings from this period. W. Bauer's thesis that it was due to the fact that heresy was dominant and unopposed in most areas would appear to be an anachronistic explanation. Conflict and polemics in this early period had their basis mainly in diversity of practice, both ethical and liturgical, and claims of authority. Attributing false doctrine to one's opponents at this point is usually an *ad hominem* polemical device.

Orthodoxy arose out of the increasing conflict between heterodoxy and orthocracy. The ecclesiastical leadership in such cities as Rome, no longer willing to tolerate heterodox teachers in its midst, attached the teaching function to its own office. The heterodox side was represented mainly by Montanists and various gnostics. In this conflict, the appeals to the rational coherence of ecclesiastical teaching and its assumed catholic and apostolic nature began to play an increasing role. Only at this point can we speak of orthodoxy and heresy. Orthodox writings are those which have been written consciously within the limits of doctrinal tolerance set by the ecclesiastical hierarchy. Earlier heterodox literature becomes orthodox retrospectively if it falls within these limits of tolerance, or heretical if it does not. The disappearance of most early Christian writings by the time of Eusebius, even the non-polemical writings of reputed heresiologists, would be explained if most of these books did not meet the later standards of orthodoxy. If this reconstruction of early Christianity is correct it will set clear limits and guidelines to the use of early Christian literature as evidence for inner diversity and conflict.

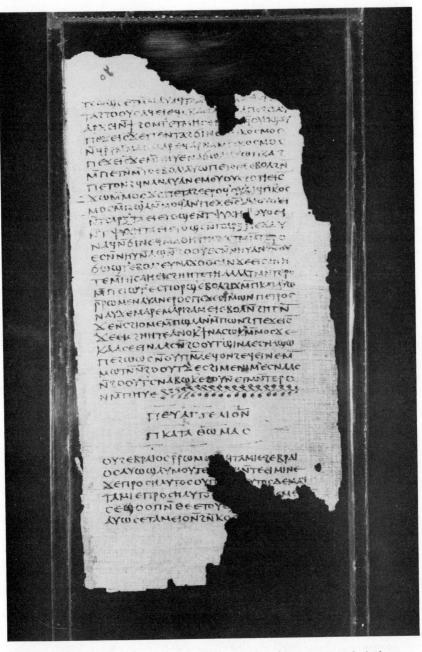

Coptic page 51 of Nag Hammadi Codex II showing the title of the *Gospel of Thomas*, an ancient collection of the sayings of Jesus. *IAC photo.*

Mahmoud, a professional digger from the village of Kuft in upper Egypt, was the principal "digger" in the excavation of Tomb 8. Note the adz he used in his work. *IAC photo by Peggy Hedrick.*

The face of the Jabal al-Tarif near the site of the discovery of the Nag Hammadi Codices. Camels are still used in Upper Egypt as a principal means of transportation. *IAC photo by Peggy Hedrick.*

A group of villagers from Hamra Dom, a village near the site of the discovery. The man in the dark garment serves as a chief guard for the Egyptian Antiquities organization. *IAC photo by Charles W. Hedrick.*

Jeff Purcell drawing a balk (unexcavated area between excavated squares) during the excavation of the Basilica of St. Pachomius at Faw Qibli. Pachomius is credited with establishing the first communal monastery in the fourth century C.E. *IAC photo by Charles W. Hedrick.*

Conference participants. Seated left to right: Harold W. Attridge, Stephen Gero, Douglas M. Parrott, Elaine H. Pagels, James M. Robinson, Helmut Koester. Standing left to right: Robert Hodgson, Jr., Paul-Hubert Poirier, Hans-Martin Schenke, John Sieber, John D. Turner, Birger A. Pearson, Bentley Layton, George W. MacRae, Frederik Wisse, Charles W. Hedrick. *Southwest Missouri State University photo by Patricia Goslee.*

PART III
GNOSTICISM AND THE EARLY CHURCH

9

GNOSTIC AND ORTHODOX DISCIPLES IN THE SECOND AND THIRD CENTURIES

Douglas M. Parrott

As an Associate Professor of Religious Studies at the University of California-Riverside, where he teaches courses in the Bible, Douglas Parrott's area of expertise covers both Gnosticism and New Testament Christianity.

Dr. Parrott is the editor of *Nag Hammadi Codices V,2–5 and VI, with Papyrus Berolinensis 8502, 1 and 4*, in the Coptic Gnostic Library Series. He also contributed to various of the tractates included in that volume. In addition, he is the editor of the forthcoming critical edition of the gnostic tractates *Eugnostos* and the *Sophia of Jesus Christ*, to be published in the same series. He is currently at work on a commentary on the two tractates.

Dr. Parrott participates in the Society of Biblical Literature, the American Academy of Religion, the Catholic Biblical Association, and the Institute for Antiquity and Christianity (Claremont).

Preface

The question to be dealt with here is whether there were two groups of disciples recognized in the second and third centuries, the one gnostic, the other orthodox. The first part of the discussion (sections I and II) examines the *Sophia of Jesus Christ* and deals with the problem of why the five disciples named in that tractate are the only ones named, since they are only a portion of the twelve men and seven women present. The four men identified are the second group of four in the lists of disciples in the Synoptic Gospels. It will be argued that they are named because they are not associated with the particularistic grounding of revelation with which the first four disciples are connected; that, it will be suggested, would have made them more acceptable to non-Christian Gnostics, to whom the *Sophia of Jesus Christ* was directed.

The second part (sections III and IV) explores whether the influence of the concept of two groups of disciples, the one orthodox and the other

193

gnostic, can be seen in other literature of the period as well as in the oral traditions.

I. An Examination of the Sophia of Jesus Christ

The *Sophia of Jesus Christ* is found in BG8502, where it is the third tractate (77,8–127,12), and also in NHC III, where it is the fourth tractate (90,14–119,18). The *Sophia of Jesus Christ* is a Christianized gnostic text. The case for this was first argued by Jean Doresse[1] and was supported with further argumentation by Martin Krause[2] and the present writer.[3] Although there were early doubters (W. C. Till[4] and H.-M. Schenke[5]), at present there is a consensus on its character. The case is based on the similarity of large parts of the text with the non-Christian gnostic text *Eugnostos* (NHC III,3 and V,1).[6]

The text presents oral teaching of Christ, sometimes identified as "savior," to the twelve disciples and seven women who continued to follow him after his resurrection. The teaching occurs in the time period between the resurrection (NHC III,4:90,14–16) and the ascension (III,4: 119,10), and takes place on a mountain identified only as "Divination and Joy" in Galilee (III,4:91,1–2). The writer is represented as an eye-witness ("But his resemblance *I* must not describe. No mortal flesh could endure it, but only pure and perfect flesh like that which he taught us about on the mountain called 'of olives' in Galilee" [III,4:91,14–20]). It may be that we are to think of him (or her) as one of the named disciples. An alternative would be to think of the disciples taking turns writing, at least during the dialogue portion of the text, as in *Pistis Sophia* I–III (71,18–72,20). In either case, the reader is clearly expected to think of the *Sophia of Jesus Christ* as coming directly from the immediate followers of Christ.

As to date, a fragment of the Greek version of the *Sophia of Jesus Christ* (P. Oxy. 1081) has been dated as late third or early fourth century,

---

[1] "Livres gnostiques," 150–54.

[2] "Eugnostosbriefes."

[3] "Relation between Gnosticism and Christianity," 405–6.

[4] Till-Schenke, *Papyrus Berolinensis 8502*, 54.

[5] "Studien II," 264–67. Schenke has since changed his views and now accepts the priority of *Eugnostos*.

[6] R. McL. Wilson has found in *Eugnostos* a number of parallels to words and phrases in the New Testament (*Gnosis*, 115–16). From these he suggests the possibility of Christian influence. None of them, however, are confined to the New Testament, and they are most likely explained as having come from a common stock of vocabulary and ideas.

thus providing a *terminus ad quem.*[7] H.-Ch. Puech suggests the tractate might have been composed in the second half of the second century C.E., or at the latest, in the third century, but he gives no reason.[8] Jean Doresse places the *Sophia of Jesus Christ* close to the first books of *Pistis Sophia.*[9] Till suggests a relative dating between the *Apocryphon of John* (NHC II,1; III,1; IV,1; BG8502,2) and *Pistis Sophia.* He argues that in the *Sophia of Jesus Christ* the understandable philosophical viewpoint found in the *Apocryphon of John* and its consistent development is diminished, while it represents an early stage in the development of a *Weltbild* (philosophical system) that ends in *Pistis Sophia.*[10]

As to the position of Doresse, a comparison of the *Sophia of Jesus Christ* and *Pistis Sophia* shows that the former is much more restrained than the latter. The points of contact, as far as the systems go, are only of the most general nature. One would certainly want to say that the *Sophia of Jesus Christ* was considerably earlier. As to Till's dating of the *Sophia of Jesus Christ* after the *Apocryphon of John,* a comparison of these texts reveals that the systematic material is more developed and the mythic material is much more developed in the *Apocryphon of John.* That suggests that the *Sophia of Jesus Christ* is earlier, although one must be cautious about any effort at relative dating, since it cannot be assumed that Gnosticism presents us with a single straight-line development. About all that can be said from these conclusions is that the arguments for a late dating of the *Sophia of Jesus Christ* are not persuasive.

Another approach is suggested by the idea proposed by P. Perkins that the *Sophia of Jesus Christ* was written not to convince non-gnostic Christians to accept gnostic Christianity but to convince non-Christian Gnostics to accept Christian Gnosticism.[11] Supporting that conclusion is the allusive nature of the references to gnostic teachings that are not specifically Christian in the *Sophia of Jesus Christ,* while the doctrine of Christ is quite fully developed. That suggests that the intended audience knew non-Christian gnostic teachings, but did not know the teaching about Christ.[12] If Perkins is correct, then the *Sophia of Jesus Christ* could be dated near the time when Christianity appeared in Egypt as a new

---

[7] Puech in Hennecke-Schneemelcher, *NT Apocrypha,* 1.245.

[8] Hennecke-Schneemelcher, *NT Apocrypha,* 1.248.

[9] "Livres gnostiques," 159.

[10] *Papyrus Berolinensis 8502,* 56.

[11] "Soteriology," 177; *Gnostic Dialogue,* 98.

[12] For further elaboration cf. the introduction to my forthcoming critical edition of *Eugnostos and the Sophia of Jesus Christ* to be published by E. J. Brill in the Coptic Gnostic Library series.

religious vitality.[13] An early date is also suggested by the fact that it seems free of anti-orthodox polemics and moreover seems not to have been influenced by any of the great Christian Gnostic systems, although, conversely, one finds elements that could have come from the *Sophia of Jesus Christ* in those systems—elements that seem to be elaborated or modified. In addition, the text it is based upon, namely *Eugnostos*, may be dated to the first century. A date early in the second century for the *Sophia of Jesus Christ*, then, does not seem unreasonable.

The basic pattern of thought in the *Sophia of Jesus Christ* is the same as that in *Eugnostos*. It begins with a theogony: Unbegotten Father; Self-begotten; Begetter (Immortal Man); First-begotten (Son of Man); and All-begetter (Savior; also identified as Son of Son of Man). All except Unbegotten Father and Self-begotten are androgynous, and the female part is called Sophia in each case. Each one creates various elements with which to furnish their respective aeons (other aeons, angels, firmaments, etc.). Finally the aeon of Immortal Man that appeared in chaos is described. It provides the patterns for everything that comes to be subsequently. It should be noted that the use of the name Adam (III,3:81,12; V,1:9, [23]) points to familiarity with Jewish tradition.

Insertions into this pattern at various points in the *Sophia of Jesus Christ* seem designed to do three things: (1) establish that Christ is now the great Savior (III,4:94,13–14), i.e., revealer, by virtue of his having come from Infinite Light (III,4:93,8–12); (2) describe in detail the salvific role of Christ in relation to the fallen pleromatic drop (III,4:106,24–108,14; BG8502,3:103,10–106,14; and again in III,4:114,13–118,25; BG8502, 3:118,1–126,5); (3) place Christ in the theogony, where he is identified with First-begotten, Son of Man (III,4:104,20–22).

II. The Problem

In the *Sophia of Jesus Christ* the revelation is given to the twelve disciples and seven women. They all participate in the dialogue, but only five disciples are named: Philip, Thomas, Mary (Mariam), Matthew, and Bartholomew (listed in order of their appearance). Of all the revelation dialogue tractates, gnostic or orthodox, *Sophia of Jesus Christ*

---

[13] That Egypt is the probable provenance of the *Sophia of Jesus Christ* is based upon research I have done on *Eugnostos*, which will be published in the forthcoming edition of the *Sophia of Jesus Christ* and *Eugnostos* in the Coptic Gnostic Library series. The crucial bit of information in *Eugnostos* is the reference to the 360-day year, which was commonly accepted in our period only in Egypt. The close relationship between *Eugnostos* and the *Sophia of Jesus Christ* would then suggest an Egyptian origin for the latter as well. Other, less likely, possibilities exist for the 360-day year; see, Przybylski, "Calendrical Data."

is the only one with this particular configuration of names. Two questions arise from this: Why are these disciples named and not the others? And why are the twelve and the seven mentioned at all? The second question will be dealt with later in the paper. It is to the first question that we now turn.

The presence of Mary (presumably Magdalene) in other gnostic dialogues (*Dialogue of the Savior, Gospel of Mary, Pistis Sophia*) and her absence from tractates that are orthodox, and probably orthodox, suggests that she functioned in gnostic circles simultaneously as the representative of the female followers of Jesus and as a symbol of the importance of women among the Gnostics.[14] Occasionally, to be sure, other women are mentioned (*Pistis Sophia; Gospel of Thomas*, logion 61), but Mary predominates. In the *Sophia of Jesus Christ* the representative character is quite clear, since she is the only one of the seven named.

But why are Philip, Thomas, Matthew, and Bartholomew named, and none of the other men? There appear to be four possibilities:

(1) The choice could have been simply randomly made by the writer from an available list. But why just four? After all there are thirteen questions, and if one assumes those questions had been framed before the choosing of the names, it is strange that he did not simply use the whole list of disciples and add Mary. There is no special virtue in the naming of four male disciples in gnostic circles, judging from other gnostic literature—the *Sophia of Jesus Christ* is the only one with four. Random choice is not an adequate explanation.

(2) *Pistis Sophia* I–III contains a tradition that Philip, Thomas, and Matthew are the "official scribes," and as such, in a special sense the three witness to "everything of the Kingdom of God" (71,18–72,20). That might provide an explanation, if one were to assume the existence of that tradition at the time of the composition of the *Sophia of Jesus Christ*—but only for the presence of those three disciples. Bartholomew would remain unaccounted for.

(3) One might think that the use of these names is related to their common usage in other gnostic literature. Certainly Philip, Thomas, and Matthew are found frequently, but Bartholomew appears only in *Pistis Sophia* IV and 1 *Jeu*, and in neither of these is his name found with all the others (which might have suggested a grouping), even if one were somehow to overcome the problem of the probable dating (*Sophia of Jesus Christ* early; *Pistis Sophia* IV and 1 *Jeu* late).

---

[14] See Elaine Pagel's excellent discussion of the place of women in Gnosticism, in her *Gnostic Gospels*, 59–69.

(4) The one place where these names are grouped together is the list of disciples in Mark; the same list is followed by Matthew and Luke. They come immediately after Peter, James, John, and Andrew. In the absence of other possibilities, it seems likely that the synoptic list is the source used by the author of the *Sophia of Jesus Christ*. But that does not explain *why* these names are used.

In the synoptics, this group disappears. Their names never appear after they are named in the list. Philip and Thomas, of course, appear in John, but Matthew and Bartholomew do not. None plays any special role in Acts. There is nothing, then, in the Gospels or Acts that gives a hint about why this group was chosen. If nothing in the source itself suggests a reason for the choice, we must look elsewhere. The choice may have been related to the context of the composition, particularly those whom the author wanted to influence, namely, the intended audience.

As indicated above, the intended audience probably was made up of non-Christian Gnostics. Their religious position was without doubt understood by the writer of the *Sophia of Jesus Christ* to be reflected in *Eugnostos*. One can assume that from the fact that he used *Eugnostos* as his basic source for *Sophia of Jesus Christ*. It is also implied by the way *Eugnostos* in Codex III has been edited to lead into the *Sophia of Jesus Christ*, which is the next tractate ("All I have just said to you, I said in the way you might accept, until the one who need not be taught appears among you, and he will speak all these things to you joyously and in pure knowledge" [III,3:90,4–11]). Someone, whether the author of the *Sophia of Jesus Christ* or another, thought that one who accepted *Eugnostos* might well be interested in hearing the same things repeated by "the one who need not be taught." It is reasonable to conclude, then, that *Eugnostos* represents the position of the non-Christian Gnostics to whom the writer of *Sophia of Jesus Christ* wanted to appeal.

In the largest sense, *Eugnostos* is an effort to ground religious affirmations in universal cosmic structures rather than in particular and particularistic religious traditions.[15] The effort to move from the particular to the universal in religion has a long history in antiquity and can be traced in the development of the use of the allegorical method, which began with Theagenes of Rhegium in the second half of the sixth century B.C.E. He used it to defend Homer against those who opposed his theology. Later the Stoics used it in the interests of philosophy. It

---

[15] I am indebted in what follows to the discussion of A. von Harnack on the difference between the second-century orthodox apologists and the Gnostics. Even though his view of the origin of Gnosticism is outdated, he very clearly understood the struggle between particularism and universalism during the period. See *Dogma*, 2.169–77.

allowed them to develop the conception that the gods were personified natural forces.[16]

The urge to universalize was a special problem for Judaism, because Judaism was particularistic as well as particular; that is, it was not only a separate and distinct religious tradition, but it asserted the absolute superiority of its tradition over all others. Ben Sira attempted to bridge the gap between Judaism and universal concepts by identifying Torah with wisdom (Sirach 24). Aristobulus used the allegorical method to demonstrate the reasonableness of Torah. The writer of the Wisdom of Solomon moved beyond Ben Sira and separated Wisdom (now fully personified) from Torah. Wisdom is what makes it possible to understand Torah in universalistic terms (Wis 9:9–17). As David Winston has put it, "She (Wisdom) was the perfect bridge between the exclusive nationalist tradition of Israel and the universalist philosophical tradition which appealed so strongly to the Jewish youth of Roman Alexandria."[17] Philo attempted to reconcile on a grand scale the particularism of Judaism with the universalism of the Hellenistic philosophical tradition through the use of the allegorical method.[18] There were, however, those who were not satisfied with these efforts, but who felt that the gap was unbridgeable. They concluded that the particular and particularistic tradition simply had to be relinquished. Philo possibly had such people in mind when he wrote:

> It is best to trust in God and not in obscure reasonings and insecure conjectures: "Abraham put his trust in God and was held righteous" and Moses holds the leadership since he is attested as being "faithful in all of God's house." But if we mistakenly trust our private reasonings we shall construct and build the city of the mind that destroys the truth: for Sihon means "destroying." For this reason one who has had a dream finds on awakening that all the movement and exertions of the foolish men are dreams devoid of reality. Indeed, mind itself was found to be a dream. For to trust God is a true teaching, but to trust empty reasonings is a lie. An irrational impulse issues forth and roams about both from the reasonings and from the mind that destroys the truth; wherefore also he says, "There went forth a fire from Heshbon, a flame from the city of Sihon." For it is truly irrational to put trust in plausible reasonings or in a mind that destroys the truth (L.A. 3.228–229).[19]

Philo is in this instance contending that mental speculations can go wild unless rooted in the tradition; such rootage would allow the speculations to be in some measure controlled.

---

[16] For a brief but valuable discussion of Greek allegory with helpful notes, cf. Winston, *Philo*, 4–7. See also Tate, "Allegory." For the origin of the interest in universalism among the Greeks, cf. Jaeger, *Paideia*, ch. 9 ("Philosophical Speculation: The Discovery of World Order").

[17] *Wisdom of Solomon*, 37.

[18] Winston, *Philo*, 4.

[19] Winston, *Philo*, 150–51. The translation is by Winston.

Eugnostos is a speculative system that at first glance resembles what Philo is speaking against. But there is a difference. The problem of control is addressed but in a way Philo had not anticipated. *Eugnostos* writes: "Now, if anyone wants to believe the words set down (here), let him go from what is hidden to the end of what is visible, and this Thought will instruct him how faith in those things that are not visible was found in what is visible" (III,3:74,12-19; see also V,1:3,29-4,7). In other words, one is able to check the correctness of statements about invisible things by examining visible things with the aid of Thought (Ennoia). This is because visible things are thought of as reflections of the invisible. Codex V, puts it this way: "For the higher faith is that those things that are not visible are those that are visible" (V,1:4,5-7). Thus the answer to the problem of control in mental speculation is not an ancient tradition but visible experience, enhanced or clarified by a divine revelatory element (Thought).

Eugnostos then is a speculative system cut free of any particular or particularistic tradition. The *Sophia of Jesus Christ* is calculated to appeal to those who accepted that kind of system. It is an attempt to "win them for Christ," to speak in modern evangelistic terms. Christ is placed in the system, by being identified with one of the major cosmic powers. Further, his role as savior is extensively described and is seen in the context of a universal arrangement directly related to the cosmological structure. At no point is he related to the particularistic traditions of the Old Testament.

If Christ is the ultimate revealer, then the revelation about him, to be fully authoritative, must not come from some third party, but from his own mouth. This requires the setting as we have it in the *Sophia of Jesus Christ*—after the resurrection (when his divinity is fully revealed) and before the ascension, with disciples present so the revelation can be transmitted. But who are to be identified among those transmitters?

One might think of the first disciples in the synoptic list, Peter, James, John, and Andrew, as obvious choices. The first three are the disciples most mentioned in the synoptic accounts. To cite but the most prominent examples: Peter confesses that Jesus is the Christ (Mark 8:29); Peter, James, and John alone accompany Jesus when he restores Jairus' daughter (Mark 5:37), when he goes up the Mount of Transfiguration (Mark 9:2), and when he enters the garden of Gethsemane (Mark 14:33). Moreover, Peter, James, John, and Andrew are the recipients of the "secret revelation" contained in Mark 13 (see 13:3).

But on the other hand, Peter and John, and probably Andrew and James, through close connection with them, were identified with the grounding of Christ in the Jewish tradition. Peter and John were pillars of the church in Jerusalem (Gal 2:9 and 1:18), the bastion of Jewish Christianity. Peter's speeches in Acts are exercises in the grounding of Christ in the scriptural traditions of Judaism (note the frequent references to the prophets and such phrases as "the God of Abraham and of Isaac and of Jacob" [3:13]—see particularly 2:14–35 and 3:12–26; 4:11; 10:43), and the Petrine letters continue that understanding of Christ (see e.g., 1 Pet 1:10–12; 2 Pet 3:1–2). Also the Gospel of John, in spite of the prologue, that equates Christ with universal Logos-Wisdom, primarily understands him in the categories of Jewish tradition (e.g., the pascal Lamb [1:29], Messiah [1:41], Son of God—King of Israel [1:49], and Prophet [4:19]). In all likelihood these disciples had already been used by early Christian evangelists as authorities for the understanding of Christ according to Jewish tradition. Perhaps writings ascribed to them or thought to have been influenced by them (e.g., Mark) were circulating— writings that were Judaistic, in the sense we have been speaking of. Perhaps those whom the writer of the *Sophia of Jesus Christ* wanted to influence had already been exposed to the Judaistic approach and disliked it. Whatever the reason, however, it is clear that he did not choose Peter, James, John, and Andrew as bearers of the universalistic interpretation of Christ.

The next four disciples on the synoptic list are, however, not connected with the Judaistic interpretation of the post-resurrection period. In John's Gospel during Jesus' life, Philip places Jesus in the context of Jewish tradition when he speaks to Nathanael: "We have found him of whom Moses in the law and also the prophets wrote, Jesus of Nazareth, the son of Joseph" (1:45). But this is prior to the post-resurrection/pre-ascension time during which the full truth was to be revealed (see Iren. *Haer.* I.30.14).

Matthew, of course, is associated with the very Jewish-tradition-oriented gospel bearing his name. But that association is obviously late. The earliest suggestion of it comes from Papias, who claimed that Matthew "compiled the sayings (of Jesus) for (those of) the Hebrew language" ('Εβραΐδι διαλέκτῳ τὰ λόγια συνετάξατο, Euseb. *Eccl. Hist.* 3.39.16). This seems to be followed by Irenaeus (cf. *Haer.* III.1.1). But it is not at all clear that "sayings" are the same as a gospel. General agreement does exist among scholars that the Gospel of Matthew was not originally written in Hebrew but in Greek. So one can not be at all sure that Papias had our gospel in mind when he wrote. Nevertheless, that gospel may have been later ascribed to Matthew on the basis of Papias' words.

A very different and perhaps much earlier understanding of Matthew occurs in the *Gospel of Thomas*, logion 13. In response to Jesus' question about who he (Jesus) is like, Matthew answers: "A wise philosopher." This suggests that he is interested in and knowledgeable about philosophers. That interest places him outside, or beyond, those oriented solely to Jewish tradition and suggests a more cosmopolitan orientation. (Interestingly, it is Peter who gives the Judaistic answer, "a righteous angel or messenger," which is an obvious variation on Mark 8:29.)

As for Thomas and Bartholomew, neither is connected with the Judaistic interpretation of Christ in the post-resurrection period. The same is true of Mary. Although she accompanies Jesus during parts of his ministry (Luke 8:2; Mark 15:40–41; Matt 27:55–56) and witnesses the resurrection, the gospels give her little to say, and nothing that might imply a Judaistic interpretation of Jesus.

One further problem is why four male names were used rather than three. As has been noted, Bartholomew tends to be overlooked in gnostic tradition. Even in the Sophia of Jesus Christ he is only given one question, whereas Philip, Matthew, and Mary have two each, while Thomas has three. The most likely answer is that the writer was presenting a group that would not only replace in a sense the orthodox group (Peter, James, John, and Andrew) but would also mirror them as closely as possible (as far as the males were concerned). And since the orthodox group has a minor player, namely Andrew, the gnostic group should have one too, namely Bartholomew.[20]

This section has argued, then, that the reason for the choosing of Philip, Thomas, Matthew, Bartholomew, and Mary to be named in the Sophia of Jesus Christ is that the more obvious disciples, Peter, James, John, and Andrew, were already identified with a particular way of understanding Christ that the writer of the Sophia of Jesus Christ knew would have a negative impact upon his intended audience, presumably because it had negative overtones to him. Thus, these five were selected to be the gnostic disciples, not because of anything that was known about them, but precisely because little or nothing was known about them and hence they could easily be used in the presentation of gnostic Christianity. If the Sophia of Jesus Christ is to be dated as early as I have argued, and if these five disciples (the Philip circle) were indeed thought of as the special gnostic five in contrast to the orthodox four (the Peter circle), one would expect to find that distinction reflected in subsequent literature and traditions. It is to the examination of that material that we

---

[20] Twice Philip and Bartholomew are connected in gnostic tractates: in Pistis Sophia IV (Schmidt-MacDermot, Pistis Sophia, 353, lines 15–16) where they are paired, and 1 Jeu 41,11–12, where they are listed together in a grouping with James. These instances may simply be reflecting the pairing of Philip and Bartholomew in the synoptic lists (Mark 3:18 and par.).

now turn. We will be looking for indications that support the above position, as well as those that might disprove it.

III. Examination of Revelation Dialogues
Other than the Sophia of Jesus Christ

The texts to be examined are revelation dialogues involving Christ and his disciples in which disciples are named. I have divided them into four groups: first, clearly gnostic tractates in which members of the Philip circle either are named alone or seem dominant (*Thomas the Contender, Dialogue of the Savior,* the *Gospel of Mary, Pistis Sophia IV* and *I–III*); second, clearly gnostic tractates in which only a member of the Peter circle is named, or a member of that circle seems dominant (the *Apocryphon of John,* the *Apocalypse of Peter,* the *Letter of Peter to Philip*); third, the clearly orthodox tractates (*Epistula Apostolorum* and *The Questions of Bartholomew*); fourth, the probably orthodox, or at least non-gnostic, tractates (the *Apocryphon of James,* the *Acts of Peter and the Twelve* Apostles).

Group One: The Philip Circle Alone or Dominant

1. *Thomas the Contender.* Only Judas Thomas and Matthaias are present. Here Matthaias is the recorder, taking no part in the dialogue himself. Who is Matthaias? The spelling could be a variant for either Matthew, the original apostle, or Matthias, the replacement for Judas. That Matthew is the correct identification is supported by the presence of Thomas and Matthew together in the *Dialogue of the Savior* (see below) and the tradition that Matthew was one of the three recorders of revelation dialogues in *Pistis Sophia* I–III. Why should they be picked out from the Philip circle, assuming there was a recognition of the group? John Turner suggests that the tractate was composed in Syria, in part because of the prevalence of Thomas traditions there.[21] Matthew was also connected with Syria.[22] Thus it may be that Thomas and Matthew alone are referred to because of their identification with the place where the tractate was composed.

2. *The Dialogue of the Savior.* Twelve disciples are referred to (III,5:142,24), but only Matthew, Judas (presumably Thomas), and Mary are named. Regarding Matthew and Thomas, see the discussion under *Thomas the Contender.*

3. *The Gospel of Mary.* The number of male disciples is not extant

---

[21] Robinson, *NHLE,* 188.
[22] W. Bauer in Hennecke-Schneemelcher, *NT Apocrypha,* 2.60.

and may not have been given. Those named are Peter, Andrew, and Levi (presumably Matthew). Mary is present, and from the title of the tractate a reader would probably have assumed that she was the one who preserved the account. The interesting feature from the perspective of this paper is that Peter and Andrew question the veracity of Mary's account of the revelation she received from the savior; furthermore, Mary is defended by Levi (presumably Matthew), who sternly rebukes Peter (BG8502,1:17,7–18,21). Thus two disciples from the Peter circle are pitted against two from the Philip circle, and the latter two end the tractate in a morally superior position.

4. *Pistis Sophia IV*. Here the disciples as a group are designated, but no number is given. The only ones named are, of the males, Thomas, Andrew, James, Simon the Canaanite, Philip, Bartholomew, Peter, and John; and, of the females, Mary and Salome. Thus the list of males is a combination of all the Peter circle and three from the Philip circle. The fourth disciple from that group, Matthew, has been replaced by Simon the Canaanite. This is the only instance in the gnostic dialogues of the use of the name of a male disciple from the last four given in the synoptic list. It is noteworthy that Matthew is replaced by someone from the area with which he himself was identified.

In this tractate Mary predominates in the dialogue, while all the male disciples are given second place (and remain unnamed through the bulk of the dialogue). Although four crucial pages of the text are missing (Schmidt-MacDermot, *Pistis Sophia*, 374), little reason exists to doubt that Mary has played the lead, when we read Peter's complaining request, "My Lord, let the women cease to question that we may also question" (Schmidt-MacDermot, *Pistis Sophia*, 377,14–15). Philip, Thomas, and Bartholomew receive no special status in the dialogue, perhaps indicating that in this rather late tractate (first half of the third century)[23] the distinction among the males has been lost, under the influence of the (by the third century) standard orthodox emphasis on the totality of the (male) disciples.

5. *Pistis Sophia I–III*. The male disciples named are Peter, James, John, and Andrew, and three from the Philip circle, Philip, Thomas, and Matthew. There is no indication of a larger body of male disciples. As noted above, Philip, Thomas, and Matthew are afforded special status as the recorders of the dialogue and as the three witnesses to "everything of the kingdom of God" (71,18–72,20). Three female disciples are named: Mary (Magdalene), Martha, and Salome. Mary, the mother of Jesus, is also named. Mary Magdalene predominates throughout as the most

---

[23] Hennecke-Schneemelcher, *NT Apocrypha*, 1.250–51.

frequent and insistent questioner of Jesus. At one point she takes the lead and represents all the disciples to Jesus (Schmidt-MacDermot, Pistis Sophia, 218,10ff.). At another point the opposition between her and Peter is emphasized. There she states her fear of Peter, because he threatens her and hates "our race" (the gnostics? women?—Schmidt-MacDermot, Pistis Sophia, 162,16-18).

John also figures prominently and, in fact, is named along with Mary as surpassing the other disciples (Schmidt-MacDermot, Pistis Sophia, 233,1-2). This is explicable on the basis of the tradition, found in the Apocryphon of John (see next section), that John converted to Gnosticism. Here then he should probably be included among the gnostic disciples. Pistis Sophia I-III is generally dated in the second half of the third century.[24]

Summary of Group One. In these tractates Philip circle disciples, with, in one late case, the addition of John, appear by themselves or dominate. The Peter circle in the Dialogue of the Savior is simply submerged into "the twelve." When Peter appears (in the Gospel of Mary [with Andrew], and Pistis Sophia IV and I-III), he is portrayed as opposing the female (and gnostic) disciples, particularly Mary Magdalene. Significantly for our study, this attitude is found elsewhere in the Peter circle only in the case of Andrew (Gospel of Mary). It should also be noted here that evidence indicates that the distinction among the male disciples began to break down in the third century.[25]

Group Two: The Peter Circle, Alone or Dominant

1. The Apocryphon of John. Only one disciple, John, the son of Zebedee, appears. Although the grammatical third person is used in speaking of John at the very beginning and ending of the tractate, the first person is generally employed elsewhere. This suggests that the reader is expected to think of John himself as the author. The title "Apocryphon" may be intended to contrast with the Gospel; that is, we may be expected to think that the tractate contains the secret teachings communicated to John by Christ after the ascension (II,1:1,10-12), in

---

[24] Hennecke-Schneemelcher, NT Apocrypha, 1.250-51.
[25] Another tractate where the distinction among the males is lost is 1 Jeu. In it none of the apostles named actually enters into individual dialogue with Jesus. The emphasis is on the apostles speaking "with one voice" (40,3, passim) behind which one can see the influence of the orthodox emphasis on the totality of the apostolic witness. The writer is either somewhat confused, or the tractate is really a compilation of a number of sources that have not been fully reconciled, since in the beginning of it we are told that all the apostles are Matthew, John, Philip, Bartholomew, and James (41,1-12); but later we hear (once) about "the twelve" (92,23). That there are only five disciples may reflect the tradition found in Talmud, Sanhedrin, 43a.

contrast to the public ones in the Gospel, which were communicated prior to the ascension.

As in the *Sophia of Jesus Christ*, the issue here is Christ. The topic is initially broached by the question of the Pharisee Arimanius and it is continued by the questions John raises (II,1:1,21–24). In the revelation that follows, Christ is identified with the divine Autogenes (II,1:7,10–11, passim). Thus, as does the *Sophia of Jesus Christ*, the *Apocryphon of John* places Christ in a universal structure. Furthermore, he is never connected to the Jewish tradition.

Why was John, the Son of Zebedee, chosen to be the recipient of this revelation? Apparently a polemical situation lies in the background. John is initially depicted as closely attached to Judaism. We are given the impression that he regularly attends the worship at the temple (II,1:1,5–8). We observe him in conversation with a Pharisee, but the Pharisee attacks Christ. He has told lies and "turned you from the traditions of your fathers," Arimanius asserts. John does not respond, but he leaves the temple and goes to a desert place. This scene reveals the polemical situation. Arimanius' charges against Jesus emerge from a Jewish context. But they cannot be answered within that context. To deal with the doubts that Arimanius raised, John must leave the Jewish context (temple) and seek (in the desert) a different basis for his faith, and that basis is, as we have said, a revelation of the place of Christ within the universal scheme of things. Thus the polemical situation reflects the struggle between those who think that Christianity can keep its Jewish roots, and those who contend that *that* is not possible, but who opt, instead, for a clean break. John is portrayed in this tractate as moving from one side to the other. He who had been a devout traditional Christian is depicted here as becoming a gnostic Christian.[26]

2. *The Apocalypse of Peter.* Here only Peter is present. Presumably Peter wrote or dictated the account, since he speaks in the first person. The revelation is received while Peter is in a trance-like state (VII,3:84, 12–13), which accounts for the surrealism of portions of the account. Probably we are to envision the source of the account as the resurrected Jesus, and perhaps even the ascended Jesus, since a terrestrial Jesus (whether pre- or post-resurrection) could have spoken directly to Peter.[27]

---

[26] A tradition of the conversion of John to gnostic Christianity through a revelation from Christ may also be reflected in the revelation dialogue found in the *Acts of John* 97–102 (which might have been included here), having to do with the Cross of Light. Note its similarities to the *Apocryphon of John*. (See the discussion by Hornschuh in Hennecke-Schneemelcher, *NT Apocrypha*, 2.80–82.)

[27] Perkins takes the position that the revelation occurred before the resurrection (*Gnostic Dialogue*, 116), as does the Berlin *Arbeitskreis* (Tröger, *Gnosis*, 62); similarly, Brown-Griggs, "Apocalypse of Peter," 133. James Brashler (in Robinson, *NHLE*, 339–40)

The tractate is an anti-orthodox polemic in which ordinary church members (VII,3:73,23ff.) and church authorities (VII,3:79,22ff.) are attacked; worship of the crucified savior is derided (VII,3:74,13ff.), and the reality of Christ's crucifixion is denied (VII,3:81,12ff.). Moreover, Peter is supposedly the founder of the gnostic Christian community (VII,3:71,15–22). The tractate accepts the idea that Peter is generally regarded as the leader of the orthodox. The sons of this world, we are told, will slander Peter because of their ignorance (VII,3:73,16–21). This slander refers to the church's laying claim to Peter as the authority for its teaching, as Klaus Koschorke has correctly seen.[28] But, the writer claims, Peter will be praised "in knowledge" (VII,3:73,21–23); that is, those who have attained true understanding will know that Peter is really a Gnostic. One cannot be sure whether the writer is aware of traditions that connect Peter with Gnosticism or whether this is said for polemical reasons, i.e., to cast doubt on orthodox beliefs by casting doubt on the orthodox authority. In view of the polemical tone of the whole document, however, the latter is more likely the case.[29]

3. *The Letter of Peter to Philip.* "Apostles" are present, but no number is given. One can assume that all eleven or twelve are present from VIII,2:133,12–13 ("Then Peter gathered the rest"). No women are mentioned, only Peter and Philip are named, and Peter alone is named in the dialogue portion of the tractate.

The tractate begins with a letter from Peter to his "beloved brother and fellow apostle," Philip, and the brothers with him (VIII,2:132,13–15). The identity of these "brothers" is unclear. Perhaps they are simply other Christians, but they may possibly be other apostles. Peter states that Philip and his group have been separated from "us" (Peter and the apostles with him—VIII,2:133,1–2), and further that he (Philip) did not want to come back together "so that we might learn to limit ourselves (ⲧⲟⲱϣ-) in order to preach the gospel" (VIII,2:133,3–5). Peter, however, has orders from Jesus.

What is the separation about? Marvin Meyer suggests that it refers to the separation that occurred when all the Christians except the apostles left Jerusalem because of persecution (Acts 8:1–4). But the Philip involved in that separation was Philip the Evangelist, not Philip the Apostle (Acts 8:4–40). Meyer suggests that the two have been confused by the writer, and indeed there is some evidence of that having

is noncommital, but is said by Perkins to hold that the revelation takes place after the resurrection (*Gnostic Dialogue*, 116, n.6).

[28] *Polemik*, 32.

[29] For a similar view, cf. Perkins, *Gnostic Dialogue*, 122.

happened elsewhere.[30] However, no evidence in Acts indicates that Philip the Evangelist refused to return to Jerusalem. Meyer speculates that the writer of the *Letter of Peter to Philip* may have had access to traditions that would have clarified that point.[31]

There is, though, another way to interpret the text, which does not require the assumption of a confusion between Philip the Apostle and Philip the Evangelist, nor speculation about lost traditions. The writer may be thinking of Philip and Peter as representing different approaches to the preaching of the gospel. Their separation, then, would dramatize those differences, and the unwillingness to come back together for the purpose of somehow limiting themselves (geographically? in what they preach?) would become understandable.

Jacques É. Ménard thinks that Philip and Peter represent two different groups, although he considers the two to be gnostic.[32] However, the evidence from gnostic tractates, for Peter's having been considered a gnostic apostle is quite weak. Ménard refers to *Acts of Peter and the Twelve Apostles, Apocalypse of Peter* and the *Apocryphon of James.*[33] But of these only the *Apocalypse of Peter* can be considered gnostic with any assurance, and there Peter may be included not as a representative of some gnostic group but as part of the anti-orthodox polemic. Koschorke refers also to the Greek *Acts of Peter* in support of a gnostic Peter,[34] but Schneemelcher doubts the gnostic character of the work.[35] The passage cited by Koschorke (ch. 20) may be docetic, but it could also be taken as simply an affirmation of the paradox of the divine-human nature of Christ. Thus the result of the letter (Philip's rejoining Peter and the other apostles) does not necessarily point to a reconciliation of two gnostic groups, as Ménard suggests. Indeed, it does not appear to point to reconciliation at all, since at the end of the tractate we learn that the apostles separated (VIII,2:140,11) and "divided themselves into four words (ϣⲁϫⲉ—"messages"—Meyer) so they might preach" (VIII,2:140, 23-24). (The "four words" may mean four different approaches to preaching, and would therefore be reflective of the kind of self-limitation referred to in VIII,2:133,3-4.)[36] Neither does the result of the letter

---

[30] Meyer, *Peter to Philip,* 93–94; similarly Luttikhuizen, "Peter to Philip," 97.

[31] Meyer, *Peter to Philip,* 96.

[32] *Pierre à Philippe,* 7.

[33] *Pierre à Philippe,* 6–7. Cf. the discussion of these tractates later in this paper.

[34] *Polemik,* 33, n. 27.

[35] Hennecke-Schneemelcher, *NT Apocrypha,* 2.275.

[36] Ménard and Meyer, with different degrees of certainty, see here a reference to the fourfold gospel (*Pierre à Philippe,* 47; *Peter to Philip,* 160–61). But a literal rendering of the text makes that unlikely. The fourfold gospel meant to Irenaeus the same message expressed in four gospels, all of which (presumably) were bound together in his time (*Haer.* III.11.7–8). There was not a different message for different places, as seems to be

reflect the submission of Philip to Peter's authority, as Meyer proposes.[37] In truth, Philip submits not to the authority of Peter but the authority of Christ (VIII,2:133,7-8).

About all that can be said is that the letter sets the stage for the presence of both Philip and Peter at the revelation given by Christ (during which none of the disciples are named) and the subsequent dialogue, mostly among the disciples, in which Peter takes the lead (and only he is named). Peter and Philip then both receive a very gnostic revelation from Christ. In the subsequent discussion on suffering, Peter takes a gnostic position on the sufferings of Christ. He lists the things that happened to Jesus according to the traditional passion account in creedal fashion (VIII,2:139,15-21), and then he states that Jesus in fact did not experience suffering in all this (VIII,2:139,21-22). Suffering comes to those who are "in the transgression of the mother" (VIII,2:139, 22-23). What Jesus did when he was "among us" only resembled suffering (VIII,2:139,24-25).[38]

The exclusive focus on Peter in the last part of the tractate (after the revelation proper) implies that the writer was interested in associating him with the above gnostic position. His failure to mention Philip is difficult to explain. One attractive possibility is that a gnostic audience would have had no trouble knowing where he stood in regard to the suffering of Christ.

Summary of Group Two. These tractates challenge the thesis of this section. They are gnostic, but have Peter and John as their major figures. The question is whether these apostles are in fact being thought of as gnostic apostles. If so, that would call the thesis into question. However, in each case it is possible to understand their use as part of the gnostic

the case here. Perkins mistakes "words" for "worlds" and therefore misses the lack of unity (*Gnostic Dialogue,* 124). Bethge suggests emending the text to επιϥτοογ ñcλ, "four directions" ("Petrus an Philipus," col. 168-70, n. 58).

[37] *Peter to Philip,* 96-97.

[38] I take this passage to be essentially docetic and an elaboration of VIII,2:136,21-22. I assume, then, that VIII,2:138,18 ("He suffered on [our] account") should be read as having a hidden qualifier. Meyer contends that the tractate affirms the paradoxical position that Jesus both suffered and was a stranger to suffering (*Peter to Philip,* 154-56); similarly Bethge ("Petrus an Philipus," col. 164). But this position seems more contradictory than paradoxical. Ménard holds that what is being alluded to is the concept of the double identity of Jesus: the mortal form that suffered and the immortal being who only smiles at the suffering of his form (*Pierre à Philippe,* 46). But textual support is lacking. Luttikhuizen takes VIII,2:139,20-22 to mean "for Jesus this suffering is strange," suggesting that he did suffer, but that it was unusual for him to do so ("Peter to Philip," 101). But that changes the natural meaning of the text. The Coptic of lines 21-25 is ναcννϥ ογϣϻμο ϻπεϊχι ñκλ2 πε ιc· λλλλ λνον πετε λ[ν]χι ñκλ2 2ñ τπλρλβλcιc ñτμλλγ λγω ετβε πλϊ λϥειρε ñ2ωβ νιμ κλτλ ογεινε 2ρλϊ ñ2μτñ, which I translate: "My brothers, Jesus is a stranger to this suffering. But it is we who have suffered as a result of the transgression of the Mother. And therefore he did everything among us in a semblance."

anti-orthodox polemic. The *Apocalypse of Peter* offers the clearest instance of this, with its contrast between the common understanding of Peter, and the understanding available to the gnostic elite. But the same pattern can be detected in the *Letter of Peter to Philip* and the *Apocryphon of John*. These disciples whom "worldly" people consider the pillars of orthodoxy are secretly (it is claimed) Gnostics.

There is a difference, to be sure, between the way John and Peter are treated in these texts. John is depicted as a genuine convert to Gnosticism, a paradigm of the orthodox Christian who almost literally "sees the light." Peter, however, is set in the context of his leadership role in the church and among the disciples, so his public orthodoxy is more evident.

Group Three: The Orthodox

1. *The Epistula Apostolorum.* Eleven disciples are named: John, Thomas, Peter, Andrew, James, Philip, Bartholomew, Matthew, Nathanael, Judas Zelotes, and Cephas. The clear intention is to name all the disciples without exception or discrimination. The list contains both the Peter circle and the Philip circle, but it differs from the synoptic lists in the final group. The presence of Nathanael suggests that the writer may have used the Gospel of John, since only there is he listed among the disciples. (It may be significant in this regard that John and Thomas are given precedence over Peter in the list.) However, the last two names are found neither there nor in the synoptic lists. Their source, therefore, remains a mystery. The *Epistula Apostolorum* is dated in the first half of the second century.[39]

2. *The Questions of Bartholomew.* "All the apostles" are present (I.1), but only Bartholomew, Peter, Andrew, and John are named and participate in the dialogue (with the exception of the very first question). Mary, the mother of Jesus, is also present. Here one notes that apostles from the Peter circle (Peter, Andrew, and John) are with Bartholomew from the Philip circle, who is the principal questioner. Bartholomew appears to express conceptions that would have favored the orthodox side. For example, in II.3 he acknowledges the leadership of Peter among the apostles (an idea that is repeated elsewhere in the document), and in III.61–62 he affirms the reality of Jesus' crucifixion and suffering. In addition, Mary the mother may serve as a counterpoint to Mary Magdalene in the gnostic tractates. She, too, acknowledges the authority of Peter (II.7; IV.2) and, furthermore, she offers to defer to him because he is a male (II.7; IV.1–5). Research on the text has disclosed elements

---

[39] Duensing in Hennecke-Schneemelcher, *NT Apocrypha*, 1. 190–91.

coming from different periods, and so one must be hesitant about drawing conclusions that are too firm. The earliest portions of the document are dated in the third century.[40]

Summary of Group Three. These two tractates, the first early and the second late, show the emphasis often noted as characteristic of the orthodox approach, namely the totality of the apostolic witness. What has not so often been noted is that this is an exclusively male witness. The *Epistula Apostolorum* names all the male disciples (although the list is not completely in agreement with the synoptic lists), but no female disciples. The *Questions of Bartholomew* names only three of the Peter circle (Peter, Andrew, and John—is James considered martyred by the time of the tractate?) as well as Bartholomew. But again, no female disciples. Bartholomew apparently functions in a polemical way, just as Peter and John did in the gnostic tractates. Mary the mother of Jesus, possibly serves as a foil to Mary Magdalene.

Group Four: Probably Orthodox or Non-Gnostic.

1. *The Apocryphon of James.* Twelve disciples are present and initially all participate in the dialogue, but only two are named: James and Peter. These two alone receive the revelation, a revelation whose reception provides entrance into the kingdom of heaven (I,2:2,29–35). The one responsible for the preservation of the record is James (I,2:1,8–18). Here the Philip circle disciples are unnamed. Only two disciples, both from the Peter circle, are given the privilege of receiving the revelation.[41] How does one account for this if the Peter circle represents the orthodox side and if *Apocryphon of James* is gnostic? The answer may lie in the possibility that the *Apocryphon of James* is not a gnostic document at all. Nothing clearly renders it gnostic. Motifs are present that are found in gnostic literature, such as sleep, drunkenness, and sickness; and there is an emphasis on knowledge. But all of these can be

---

[40] Scheidweiler in Hennecke-Schneemelcher, *NT Apocrypha*, 1.488.

[41] There is a possibility that James in this tractate is the Lord's brother and not the son of Zebedee. That is the opinion of Puech, which he sets forth in his introduction to the *editio princeps* (Malinine-Puech, *Epistula Iacobi*, xxi–xxii; see also Hennecke-Schneemelcher, *NT Apocrypha*, 1.335). He argues that the role played by James in the tractate is like that which James the Just plays elsewhere. His position is followed by F. E. Williams in Robinson, *NHLE*, 29, and the Berlin *Arbeitskreis* (Tröger, *Gnosis*, 26). The opposite position is taken by W. C. van Unnik in "Origin," 149–56 (see also, Malinine-Puech, *Epistula Iacobi*, xx–xxi). Several things should be noted here: James the Just is apparently never placed among the twelve elsewhere, as he is here (I,2:2,7–16); nowhere in the tractate does Christ refer to a special relationship with James, as he does, e.g., in the *(First) Apocalypse of James*; finally, it is worth recalling that our knowledge of James the son of Zebedee is very limited—he may well have played an important role among the disciples before his martyrdom.

detected in non-gnostic literature. Furthermore, the very orthodox insistence on the reality of the suffering and crucifixion of Christ (I,2:5,9–21) and the necessity of believing in the cross to be saved (I,2:6,1–7) hardly favor a gnostic setting. Moreover, the crucifixion as atonement is affirmed (I,2:13,23–25).[42]

It is true that the presence of the *Apocryphon of James* in the Jung Codex creates a presumption that it is gnostic. But its presence could be an instance of a non-gnostic tractate attracting gnostics because of its motifs. If it is indeed orthodox, then the naming of James and Peter, only, would be understandable. What at first glance is less explicable is why the special revelation is granted only to them and not to the other disciples. This feature seems to violate the orthodox tradition that revelation is transmitted through *all* the apostles. That tradition, however, seems to be a late development within orthodoxy. Peter, James, John, and Andrew are all involved in special revelations during Jesus' earthly life according to the canonical Gospels, as noted earlier in this paper. Paul claims a special post-resurrection revelation concerning "his" gospel in Gal 1:12. The tradition of prophecy within the early church presumes special revelations, of which the last book of the New Testament is an example. All this suggests that the *Apocryphon of James* is a fairly early work, and it is not surprising, therefore, that the editors of the *editio princeps* date it in the second century (Malinine-Puech, *Epistula Iacobi*, xxx), and that van Unnik has suggested a date in the second quarter of the second century.[43]

2. *The Acts of Peter and the Twelve Apostles.* Eleven apostles are indicated, despite the title (see VI,1:9,21). Here Peter is the major figure among the apostles, and otherwise only John is named. The tractate is probably not gnostic; to be sure it has motifs that would have been attractive to Gnostics, as does the *Apocryphon of James*, but in fact it possesses no distinctive gnostic doctrines.[44] If it originated in orthodox circles, or at least non-gnostic circles, it is understandable why only Peter and John are named. The presence of motifs easily adapted by Gnostics would probably account for its being in NHC VI, which contains other non-gnostic tractates as well (the *Thunder: Perfect Mind* [probably], *Plato, Republic 588b–589b*, the *Discourse on the Eighth and Ninth, Prayer of Thanksgiving, Asclepius*).

[42] For the varieties of opinion among the editors of the *editio princeps* on the issue discussed in this paragraph, see Malinine-Puech, *Epistula Iacobi*, xx–xxv. Williams expresses the cautious judgment that the *Apocryphon of James* "may be a Gnostic document" (Robinson, *NHLE*, 29).

[43] See "Origin," 156.

[44] See Parrott, *Codices V and VI*, 202. Perkins takes the opposite view, but gives no specifics (*Gnostic Dialogue*, 127,n.35).

Summary of Section III

There is nothing in the evidence examined thus far that requires significant modification of the hypothesis that both gnostic and non-gnostic tractates recognize in appropriate ways a circle of gnostic disciples connected with Philip, and another group of orthodox, or at least non-gnostic, disciples connected with Peter. In the first group of tractates examined above we found that Peter, when present, was invariably seen as subordinate to and/or in opposition to one or more of the gnostic disciples. (One could assume that was the normal feeling among Gnostics about Peter and those associated with him, viz. Andrew in the *Gospel of Mary*.) In the second group, Peter and John were given center-stage in gnostic tractates. But that can be understood in each case as part of an anti-orthodox polemic. In groups three and four, in tractates that are definitely or probably orthodox, or at least non-gnostic, either all the disciples are listed as a group or only Peter circle disciples are listed (with the single exception of Bartholomew, as noted). Consequently we are justified in saying that in the gnostic tractates, Philip circle disciples are present routinely and Peter circle disciples appear only where there is some polemical reason. And the same situation, *mutatis mutandis*, prevails in the orthodox or non-gnostic tractates.

It is interesting to note in this connection that the female disciples (primarily Mary Magdalene) are present in all but one of the group one tractates, but they are absent in those that are orthodox or probably orthodox (groups three and four). In all likelihood their absence from group two tractates (gnostic) is because these tractates feature orthodox apostles. The gnostic authors may have considered it inappropriate to have women disciples appear in tractates in which those opposed to them played major roles. Also, the authors might have anticipated that their tractates would be used to influence orthodox Christians (almost certainly the case with the *Apocryphon of John*), who might have been negatively influenced by the presence of women disciples.

IV. Tradition Chains

But the revelation discourse was not the only way by which it was claimed that truth was conveyed from the source of revelation. The other way was through an oral tradition chain, originating with an apostle. We must now test the thesis against the reports about such chains. The questions to be addressed in this section are these: Who are the apostles from whom the Gnostics claim their tradition chains originated? Who are the apostles about whom the orthodox make the same claim? Do they support or challenge the two circles we have identified above? How are these claims to be assessed?

A distinction must be made here between public and secret tradition chains. The orthodox emphasized a tradition chain that was public—the chain of oral teaching that had been passed from the apostles to their successors, who were the leaders of the various churches, i.e., the bishops (Iren. *Haer.* III.3.1–2). And indeed Irenaeus, in the section just cited, argues that the public tradition is the complete tradition. The apostles would certainly, he says, have transmitted any secret teachings they had to those who would be most likely to assure their preservation, namely to those who followed them as leaders in their churches. That they did not suggests there was no such tradition.

But that does not prevent Clement of Alexandria, when he writes his *Stromata*, from claiming that he is transmitting secret traditions received from a chain of teachers that began with the apostles. He looks back not to all the apostles, however, as we might expect, but specifically to Peter, James, John, and Paul (1.11.3). The only ambiguity here has to do with the identity of James. Is he the son of Zebedee or the Lord's brother? According to Eusebius, Clement wrote in his *Hypotyposes*, Book 7, that after his resurrection Christ gave the gift of knowledge to James the Just, John, and Peter, and they delivered it to the rest of the apostles, who in turn passed it on to the seventy (*Eccl. Hist.* 2.1.4). This, at first glance, leads one to think that James the Just is meant in the *Stromata* reference. However, in *Hypotyposes*, Clement seems to be referring to a quite public tradition rather than the secret one he speaks of in the *Stromata*. A clearer light on the secret tradition occurs in Origen, Clement's younger contemporary in Alexandria. He writes in various places that he considers the only true Gnostics among the apostles to be Peter and the two sons of Zebedee (*Cels.* 2.64; 4.16; 6.77; *Comm. in Matt.* 12.36,41). Thus it seems likely that the James referred to by Clement in the *Stromata* is James the son of Zebedee.[45] It is unclear why Paul is included by Clement. Possibly he became attached to the tradition at some point because of 1 Cor 2:6–7: "Yet among the mature we do impart wisdom . . . a secret and hidden wisdom of God . . . ," and because of his claim to have had a revelation from Christ (Gal 1:12). His presence supports orthodox traditions from outside the original group of apostles. It seems, then, that the apostles involved in the secret orthodox tradition support the assumption of an orthodox Peter circle.[46]

---

[45] Hornschuh takes an ambivalent position on the question (Hennecke-Schneemelcher, *NT Apocrypha*, 2.82–83).

[46] For a discussion of what that secret tradition might have contained, see Hornschuh in Hennecke-Schneemelcher, *NT Apocrypha*, 2:80–85.

Now we must turn to the Gnostics. Just as Clement writes down the traditions he received, we might expect that the Gnostics would at some point have written down their traditions. We would expect loose collections of sayings and anecdotes. The obvious candidates in the Nag Hammadi collection are the Gospel of Thomas and the Gospel of Philip. In the first case, an introduction identifies the words as the secret sayings of Jesus, and states that Thomas is the writer. By that we are probably to understand that the words were preserved within the tradition that was thought to have originated with Thomas. As to the Gospel of Philip, it does not identify itself as the Gospel of Thomas does; the title is given only in a subscript. It is a miscellaneous collection, some of which is said to come from Jesus, but most of which one would have to ascribe (because of the subscript) to the Philip tradition itself. Thus two of the tradition collections of the Gnostics are attributed to apostles within the Philip circle.

Apparently at least one other such collection circulated in antiquity: The Traditions of Matthias, which may have been synonymous with The Gospel of Matthias.[47] Clement of Alexandria is probably referring to such a collection when he writes:

> Now regarding the sects, some are called by a personal name, as "The Sect of Valentinus" and "of Marcion" and "of Basilides," even if they boast that they bring forward the opinion of Matthias; for just as the teachings of all the apostles was one, so also was the tradition (Strom. 7.17.108).

The last clause makes clear that Clement is speaking of "tradition" (ἡ παράδοσις), and making a distinction between it and something more formal, which he calls "teachings" (διδασκαλία). That he has in mind, nonetheless, a literary document, is clear from references elsewhere to "The Traditions" in connection with Matthias (Strom. 2.9.45.4; 7.13.82.1). Hippolytus (Ref. 7.20.1) presumably alludes to this collection when he writes that Basilides and Isidore "say that Matthias told them secret teachings, which he heard from the savior in private instruction" (φησὶν εἰρηκέναι Ματθίαν αὐτοῖς λόγους ἀποκρύφους, οὓς ἤκουσε παρὰ τοῦ σωτῆρος κατ᾽ ἰδίαν διδαχθείς).

One might wonder why Matthias would have been chosen by the Gnostics. A certain answer is elusive, but it might have had something to do with his encratite views, as reported by Clement (Paed. 2.1.16). Also he seems to have been overlooked by the orthodox, as is suggested by his omission from the list of apostles in the Epistula Apostolorum.

In addition, according to Hippolytus, the Naassenes also claimed

---

[47] On the literature ascribed to Matthias, see Puech's discussion in Hennecke-Schneemelcher, NT Apocrypha, 1.308–13.

traditions originating with James, the Lord's brother, and transmitted through Mary (Ref. 5.7.1). In this case, someone was chosen who was not only not an original apostle but who never became an apostle. He was, of course, very prominent in the early community and was clearly identified with Jewish tradition (Acts 15:13-21 and Gal 2:12). But the Gnostics, as happened with John, developed traditions about James' becoming a Gnostic as a result of revelations from Christ—cf. (First) Apocalypse of James and (Second) Apocalypse of James. The transmission through Mary may have been a way of separating the "false" orthodox tradition from the "true" gnostic one, since presumably Mary would have been able to sort out the one from the other.[48] There is no suggestion in Hippolytus that these traditions existed in written form, although the existence of other written collections makes that a real possibility.

The traditions examined thus far support the concept of a gnostic circle of disciples. Those attributed to Thomas and Philip clearly do. Those connected with Matthias and James, the brother of the Lord, certainly do not challenge the idea, and can be thought of as lending additional support to traditions and teachings stemming from the circle.

There are two other reports that must now be examined that are much less secure than the above. These are the reports that have been taken to mean that the Basilidians had a tradition attributed to Peter, and the Valentinians had one attributed to Paul.[49] They are found in Clement of Alexandria's Stromata and are given in the context of Clement's argument that the establishment of the Christian-gnostic movement was later in time than the establishment of the church. He states (Strom. 7.17.106) that the Basilidians boast that Basilides "signed up for Glaucias as his teacher," and he was "the interpreter of Peter" (κἂν Γλαυκίαν ἐπιγράφηται διδάσκαλον, ὡς αὐχοῦσιν αὐτοί, τὸν Πέτρον ἑρμηνέα).[50] Likewise Clement says "they (the Valentinians) say that Valentinus heard Theodas (as a student)—but he was an acquaintance of Paul" (ὡσαύτως δὲ καὶ Οὐαλεντῖνον Θεοδᾶ διακηκοέναι φέρουσιν· γνώριμος δ᾽οὗτος γεγόνει

---

[48] It is an intriguing possibility that Hippolytus, when he refers to Mary, may be confusing her with the priest Mareim, who is identified in the (Second) Apocalypse of James as the writer of the tractate (V,4:44,13-17).

[49] See Hennecke-Schneemelcher, NT Apocrypha, 2.85-86; also Pagels, Gnostic Paul, 1-2.

[50] The Greek here is ambiguous and permits of the following translation by Hort-Mayor: "Basilides, in spite of his claiming to have been taught by Glaucias, whom they themselves boast to have been the interpreter of Peter" (Clement, 189). The structure of the next sentence, with φέρουσιν clearly referring to the preceding rather than the following, strongly suggests that αὐχοῦσιν also goes with the preceding. That is the way it is taken in the ANF translation.

Παύλου). Clement is implying that these claims for antiquity are ridiculous because of the time gap involved.

We, however, must ask who said what and who claimed what. Clearly the Basilidians said that Basilides was taught by Glaucias, and the Valentinians assert that Valentinus heard Theodas. But who claimed that these teachers were, respectively, "the interpreter of Peter" and "the acquaintance of Paul," suggesting thereby that they knew those apostles? It seems unlikely that either the gnostic leaders or their followers would have moved so far from reality as to have claimed that Basilides and Valentinus, who flourished in the middle third of the second century, could have been taught by those who would have been mature during the same period in the first century. It seems more likely that in this polemical context Clement himself adds the descriptions of these teachers, descriptions designed to make the Basilidians and the Valentinians appear foolish.

But it is nonetheless possible that there was some truth in what Clement says. Possibly Glaucias and Theodas, as teachers of Basilides and Valentinus respectively, taught about Peter and Paul—however, not in the first century, but in the second. And perhaps Clement felt that he was not stretching things too much to describe the one as an interpreter and the other, as an acquaintance; it is, after all, only in the context of his argument that one receives the clear impression that these two teachers were contemporaries of the apostles in question. Clement makes no mention of the transmission of secret teachings. Considering that, and the nature of these statements as we have examined them, one would have to say that Clement provides no real evidence for secret oral traditions among the Basilidians and the Valentinians purporting to stem from Peter and Paul respectively.

V. Conclusion

Before summarizing the argument of the paper, one question raised earlier remains: Why are the twelve and the seven referred to in the *Sophia of Jesus Christ*, when only four men and one woman are named? This problem is shared by the *Dialogue of the Savior* in regard to the twelve. One plausible response is that the term "the twelve" symbolizes the whole body of the apostles. Likewise, the "seven women" (in the *Sophia of Jesus Christ*) would be another way of saying that all the women disciples were there too (given the general understanding of seven as expressing fullness or completeness). So these terms mean that the totality of possible witnesses were present for the revelation, even though not all were named. It may have been necessary to make that point in order to deal with the orthodox emphasis on the totality of the apostolic witness, as in the *Epistula Apostolorum* (see also the *Didache*). But since the orthodox emphasis may have been a response to gnostic stress on special disciples, it might be that the twelve and the seven were later editorial additions in the gnostic tractates. Irenaeus suggests, in fact, that the Gnostics originally claimed only the named disciples, when he states that they held that Jesus "instructed a few of his disciples, whom he knew to be capable of understanding such great mysteries, in these things, and was then received into heaven" (*Haer.* I.30.14). Since the numbers only appear once in each tractate (at the very beginning of the *Sophia of Jesus Christ* and at *Dial. Sav.* III,5:142,24), it is easy to imagine their having been added after the original composition.

In summary, this study has sought to demonstrate that early in the Christian gnostic movement a circle of disciples of Jesus was chosen to be the bearers of the distinctive Christian-gnostic message, while at the same time another group was identified with the orthodox position. Further, an examination of tractates and collections of traditions has made it apparent that those choices had a significant influence subsequently; that is, the use of these names in later gnostic and orthodox revelation dialogues and in collections of traditions is consistent with the initial usage. Although the first use of the names was probably not polemical (e.g., the *Sophia of Jesus Christ*), but rather governed by the needs of early evangelism, their subsequent use tended to reflect the struggle between the Gnostics and their orthodox opponents. In the gnostic revelation dialogues, Peter, Andrew, James, and John, at one time or another, are seen as being secretly gnostic, in an inferior position in relation to the gnostic disciples, as opposed to the active role of the female (gnostic) disciples of Jesus, or as converting to Gnosticism. And the orthodox appear to have used at least one gnostic disciple in a similar fashion.

The polemical interest in the gnostic tractates focuses on Peter, though not to the exclusion of others. That is quite different from the sharing of the spotlight that occurs among the disciples of the Philip circle. All, with the exception of Bartholomew, have their day, and then step back to make room for someone else. This difference may reflect both the polemical and the sociological situation. On the one hand, Peter naturally had a prominent place, since he was perceived as in some sense the founder of orthodoxy and the authority for its teachings, and thus for the Gnostics, the chief representative of the opposition. On the gnostic side, on the other hand, no one disciple emerged to whom the Gnostics looked as their founder. Sociologically, the focus on Peter may reflect the increasingly monarchical situation within orthodoxy, while the lack of any corresponding focus upon any particular individual in the Philip circle reflects the rather fluid leadership situation within the gnostic movement.

One probable conclusion of this study is that there was probably no Petrine gnostic group, as has been suggested by some.[51] The use of the name Peter was apparently governed entirely by the needs of the struggle between the Gnostics and the orthodox. He is not adopted by any group of Gnostics. In this connection it is significant that we do not have a Gospel of Peter comparable to the Gospels of Thomas and Philip (i.e., a sayings collection, suggesting a period of oral transmission within a group).[52]

---

[51] For example, Perkins (*Gnostic Dialogue*, 115), Ménard (*Pierre à Philippe*, 5–7) and the Berlin *Arbeitskreis* (Tröger, *Gnosis*, 62).

[52] For a discussion of the extant *Gospel of Peter*, which is a passion-resurrection narrative, see Hennecke-Schneemelcher, *NT Apocrypha*, 1.179–87.

10

ORDERING THE COSMOS: IRENAEUS AND THE GNOSTICS

Pheme Perkins

Pheme Perkins is professor of Theology (New Testament) at Boston College where she has taught since 1972. She received her Ph.D. from Harvard University. Dr. Perkins is Vice-president (and President elect) of the Catholic Biblical Association and of the New England Region of the American Academy of Religion. She serves on the editorial boards of the *Journal of Biblical Literature, Catholic Biblical Quarterly, Horizons* and *College Teaching* and on the advisory councils for *Interpretation, Trinity Monograph Series* and *Biblical Research.*

She has written fourteen books, among them, *The Gnostic Dialogue* (1980), *Resurrection: New Testament Witness and Contemporary Reflection* (1984) and *Who is This Christ* with R. Fuller (1983), as well as numerous articles on gnosticism and New Testament. She lectures widely to both scholarly and lay groups in the U.S. and Canada. Current projects include studies of tradition history in gnostic cosmologies; work on Jesus as teacher, and a revision of her text *Reading the New Testament.*

Preface

This study is a limited analysis of Irenaeus' argument with the Gnostics; it will demonstrate that the objections in the cosmological section of his argument in *Adversus Haereses* form a pattern that derives its coherence from *topoi* of polemic between philosophical schools. The rhetorical genre of this section of *Adversus Haereses* is the demonstration of the opponent's self-contradictions and is itself a well-established pattern in the second-century philosophical schools. The investigation of the more striking philosophical *topoi* in *Adversus Haereses* reveals a pattern of anti-Platonist polemic that derives from an earlier attempt to compare the superior Christian account of creation, God, and providence with accounts that were common in philosophic circles. Because both the rhetoric of this section of *Adversus Haereses*

221

and the opposition to popular Platonism (a Platonism that appears, for example, in Albinus' *Didaskalikos*) are at home in Irenaeus' native Smyrna, it is possible that he learned this form of argument in Christian circles at Smyrna. He is able to turn it against the Gnostics because Platonic strains turned up in Gnostic writings. This explains why historians of Middle Platonism refer to the Valentinian system as "underworld Platonism." The genre which Irenaeus uses, however, has its limitations. Like Plutarch, who refutes Stoicism, Irenaeus is not compelled to represent the doctrine of his opponents accurately. It is even possible that Irenaeus has "over-Platonized" the Gnostic system. For Irenaeus is convinced that his Gnostic opponents are the sort of people who say anything that comes into their heads, a charge which Plutarch raises against Chrysippus.

I. Introduction

Studies of the Valentinian system reported in Irenaeus' *Haer.* I.1–8 have often pointed to the parallels between the cosmic structure of the Valentinian system and that of Middle Platonist speculation.[1] J. Dillon describes the Valentinian system as a parody of Plato's *Timaeus*; the Valentinian account of the ignorant demiurge creating the world makes it clear that there is no possibility for the Platonic salvation embodied in the upward movement of the soul.[2] What Dillon does not notice, however, is that Irenaeus brings that same objection against the Valentinian system: it makes salvation impossible (*Haer.* II.5.1–2).[3] And W. R. Schoedel's study of the topological argument in Gnostic texts has shown that Gnostic teachers responded to such philosophical criticism of their systems.[4]

---

[1] Dillon, *Middle Platonists*, 384–89. Dörrie, "Cosmologie," 400–405 sees the end of the Hellenistic period as one of dissatisfaction with previous cosmologies and of revolutionary philosophical changes. The elements of the second-century Gnostic systems, he argues, were germinating in the oral traditions of the first century; cf. Krämer, *Ursprung* 238–62. Daniélou (*Gospel*, 339) thinks that the vocabulary of negative theology in Gnosticism, and particularly in Valentinus, was borrowed from Middle Platonism.

[2] Dillon, *Middle Platonists*, 387–88.

[3] Irenaeus is aware that salvation and knowledge are philosophical issues. His collection of diverse philosophical sources for Gnostic opinions (*Haer.* II.14) includes the charge that either the earlier philosophers had the truth, in which case special revelation of gnosis is unnecessary; or they did not have the truth, in which case the Gnostic views based on them are untrue.

[4] Schoedel, "Theology," 88–108; Armstrong, ("Gnosis," 87–124) argues against any

This present study is not aimed at further investigation of the relationship between Gnostic and philosophical speculation. Instead, it un-
covers the philosophical substructure behind Irenaeus' refutation of the
Valentinian system in *Haer.* II. This presupposes W. C. van Unnik's
analysis of the topics appropriate to theological speculation in *Haer.*
I.10.3 which has pointed out that Irenaeus' refutation does not only
address the issues raised by the Gnostics, but that it moreover contains
other material not developed in that setting, though the appropriate
topics may have been part of the discussion with them.[5] Thus, one must
read Irenaeus with attention to the hints of the wider theological debates
of the 160s and 170s, the era that informed his argument. Van Unnik
observed that Irenaeus deliberately opposes this material to positions
held by "those teachers destitute of divine insight."[6] Though that objection might be thought to point to the heretical teachers, it is directed to a
school that emphasizes the contrast between the One God of Christianity and the plurality of divine ideas beyond the creator. That objection goes well beyond the Valentinians to whom it is applied in *Haer.* II;
it attacks a fundamental Platonic patterning of the world. Speculation
about the supreme God and the demiurge, and the location of ideas in
the divine mind are characteristic of second-century Platonism.[7] Van
Unnik observed also that in these contexts Irenaeus expands his typical
"creator of heaven and earth" motif with "things temporal and eternal,
visible and invisible."[8]

Irenaeus' stock arguments against the Valentinians have a parallel in
Philo's arguments against the Platonists. Philo's reconciliation of Genesis
with Platonic speculation providing for the divine creation of the intelligible world, concludes with a list of five points that characterize the
truth taught in Moses' story:

(1) The deity is and has been from eternity (against atheists).

(2) God is One (against polytheists who transfer the chaos of mob rule
from earth to heaven).

(3) The world came into being (against those who claim that it is
without beginning and eternal and thus deny the superiority of God).[9]

Gnostic influence on Middle Platonists like Plutarch and Atticus and he thinks that the
philosophical content of Gnostic systems is vastly overrated.

[5] van Unnik, "Document," 205; 225–26.

[6] van Unnik, "Document," 203–4.

[7] Dillon, *Middle Platonists*, 6–7, 113–14.

[8] *Haer.* I.4.5; 22.1; IV.5.1; see van Unnik, "Document," 211–12.

[9] Daniélou (*Gospel*, 324) traces the epithet *agenētos* "unoriginated" (cf. *Haer.* II.8.3) to
Hellenistic Jewish apologetic. Those apologists who adopt Middle Platonism use *agen-
nētos*, "ungenerated."

(4) The world, like God, is one and unique (against those who think that there may be a plurality or an infinite number of worlds).[10]

(5) God exercises providence over creation (against those who deny providence, for the laws of nature show that the maker cares for what has been made as the parent for children).[11]

To summarize, Philo's five points provide a "handbook" defense by which one can evaluate competing claims about the origin of the cosmos and its relationship to God. They do not embody, as he admits, the subtleties of the account of creation which were given earlier in the treatise. Such a pattern of stock argumentation also underlies Irenaeus' arguments. The anti-Platonic character of these arguments form part of a persistent theme in *Haer.* II.

It is possible that the anti-Platonic substructure of the argument Irenaeus employs against the Gnostics was learned in Christian circles in Smyrna. After all, the Smyrna of Irenaeus' youth was one of the three flourishing centers of the Sophistic movement in the second century and harbored two famous Platonist teachers, Albinus and Theon. Galen, the second-century physician and medical writer (C.E. 129–ca. 200), also studied with Albinus in Smyrna between C.E. 149 and 157.[12] Irenaeus' letter to Florinus, dissuading him from his attraction to the Gnosticism which he had apparently learned in lower Asia Minor (Smyrna?), documents this intellectual climate (Eusebius, *Eccl. Hist.* 5.20.1–6).

II. The Genre of *Adversus Haereses* II.1–19

Irenaeus learned more than doctrines from his teachers. He also learned the forms of argument which he employs.[13] In this section he promises to subvert the opinions of his opponents by first showing the improbability of Gnostic doctrines. It is followed by arguments against their misinterpretation of the "discourses of the Lord" (*Haer.* II. Preface; 11.2). The demonstration of the improbability of Gnostic doctrine is then divided into two subsections, each ending with a summary (at II.8.3 and II.19.9).

Both of these subsections of the first half of the argument demonstrate

[10] Both Stoics and Platonists rejected the Epicurean claims that there could be an infinite number of worlds (Cicero, *Nat. Deor.* I.20). The five solids of the *Timaeus* led Plutarch to an elaborate defense of the possibility of five rather than the commonly accepted one (*Def. Or.* 421F–425D).
[11] Philo, *Op. Mund.* 170–71. The Epicureans were regularly attacked for destroying divine providence. Philo extends the attack to all who deny that the world is "created."
[12] Cf. Dillon, *Middle Platonists*, 267 on the Middle Platonists in Smyrna. For the flourishing of these Asia Minor cities in the second century see Bowersock, *Greek Sophists*, 17–29 and Millar, *Empire*, 196–97 and 154 on the connection between Asia Minor and Gaul.
[13] On the rhetorical structure of *Haer.* I see Perkins, "Irenaeus and the Gnostics."

the contradictory character of Gnostic propositions, while the second half expands upon points already mentioned in the first half. Although arguments about Gnostic contradictions appear in the concluding section of the work as well, they are not its primary aim. In the conclusion, Irenaeus turns directly to scriptural demonstration of his points.[14]

The opening sections of *Haer.* II.1–19 fit a well-established genre in philosophical polemic flourishing in the period in which Irenaeus lived:[15] refutation of adversaries by demonstrating the contradictions in their system. Recognizing the genre of a treatise such as Irenaeus' *Haer.* II.1–19 is necessary for evaluating the accuracy of their evidence for doctrines held by opponents. Dillon describes the interschool polemic as typified by "a high degree of rhetorical unreasonableness."[16] H. Cherniss's detailed introduction to Plutarch's treatise *On Stoic Self-Contradictions* provides a warning both against those who would condemn the author of such a treatise for failing accurately to represent an opponent and against those who suppose that such treatises have no order at all. Such a work is neither intended to be an exegesis nor an aid to the opponent to reconcile his inconsistencies. An author's use of repetitious, ambiguous or careless formulations in arguing against his opponent does not prove that he was unfamiliar with the more sophisticated arguments of the opponent's philosophy.[17]

These catalogues seek to convict the opponent of as many inconsistencies as possible. For example, though he is using this genre, Plutarch does have a guiding theme in his refutation of Chrysippus. The opening collection of inconsistencies looks to prove that Chrysippus is "a person who says absolutely anything that may come into his head" (*Stoic. Repug.* 1047B). That summary of inconsistencies is followed in *Stoic. Repug.* 28–29 by a collection that appears to be random until one realizes that Plutarch has organized it around a theme: Chrysippus' disregard for evidence and authority, especially Plato and Aristotle.[18]

---

[14] These divisions might be intended to divide the book as a whole into the tripartite structure of the philosophical thesis; see the discussion of the thesis structure in Runia, "Philo," 118–19. *Haer.* I serves Irenaeus as the necessary doxographical compilation for such a thesis; on the doxographical compilation see Runia, "Philo," 124.

[15] The Epicurean school opens (*Nat. Deor.* I.8–15) with a condensed catalogue of paradoxes of other schools much like the summaries that Irenaeus uses in *Haer.* II. Plutarch's surviving writings on the self-contradictions of the Stoics represent only part of his own writings in this genre, since he also composed such works against the Epicureans.

[16] Any argument that comes to hand may be used in such a refutation. It need not reflect the author's own views or even those of his school. See Dillon, *Middle Platonists*, 248–49; Runia, "Philo," 130–31.

[17] Cherniss, *Moralia*, 402–404.

[18] Cherniss, *Moralia*, 387.

Irenaeus uses a similar logic: not only do the Gnostics show that they do not know what they are talking about, but they also have no regard for authority. The Gnostics have shown themselves to be as vacuous as the void in their cosmological systems (Haer. II.8.3). What is worse, their views about the creator contradict both the universal agreement of humanity and the explicit authority of Scripture (Haer. II.9.1). Such disregard for the sources of truth can only lead to ignorance (Haer. II.11.1–2).

This argument from "universal agreement of humanity" frequently appears in theological debate. Both the Stoic and Epicurean schools claimed that universally held "common notions," to use the Stoic term,[19] attested to the truth. Plutarch, who devoted a treatise to Stoic common notions, invokes the common notion of God to argue against Chrysippus. To add to the authority of the common notion of God, he quotes a definition of God from Antipater of Tarsus. He argued that though Jews, Syrians and poets do not agree that everyone considers God benign, no one believes that God is subject to the kind of generation and destruction suggested by the Stoics (Stoic. Repug. 1051E).

Plutarch is quite willing to use the Stoics' doctrine of common notions against their own system in the treatise on that topic. Not only do their "common notions" fall short of standards required of conceptions held by people generally, the Stoics even admit that only selected common notions are a natural guide to truth. Indeed, what is a common notion in one part of the system may contradict a common notion in another part (Com. Not. 1070DE; 1076CD).[20]

Though Irenaeus' own standard is finally the "rule of truth" which is universally believed (Haer. I.10.2; III.2.1),[21] he carefully includes the broader appeal in his use of the argument from consensus against his opponent's view of the creator (Haer. II.9.1). The pagans learn from nature, he argues, what all believers have learned from Scripture, namely, that the cosmos has been created and ordered by God.

Plutarch's treatment of the Stoic notion of "the whole of things" (to pan), i.e., the cosmos with the void (kenon apeiron), not only has parallels in Irenaeus, but it also suggests a rhetorical strategy which Irenaeus may have appropriated. Plutarch argues that the Stoic concept

[19] Both the Epicurean and Stoic representatives use this argument in Cicero, De Natura Deorum. The Platonist expresses skepticism, preferring to rely on the authority of the tradition handed down from the fathers (Nat. Deor. III.7). If the existence of God were indeed a universal notion, then discussion and argument about it could only produce doubt, he argues (Nat. Deor. III.8).

[20] Cherniss, Moralia, 627–30.

[21] For Irenaeus the content of the regula veritatis, or tradition, is identical with what is handed on in Scripture, so Daniélou, Gospel, 151–53.

actually coincides with the common notion that people have of the non-existent. He argues that when Stoics claim to apprehend the non-existent, they render their whole doctrine incoherent and unintelligible (*Com. Not.* 1073E–1074D).

Irenaeus also employs similar tactics against the Gnostics. He asserts that when they discern a god beyond the creator, they have, in effect, searched out the non-existent (*Haer.* II.1.3). Their account of the cosmos leaves the *plēroma* "Fullness" situated in an infinite abyss of *plēromata* and depths (*Haer.* II.1.4).[22] Indeed, he points out that there is no logically consistent account of the origins of the Gnostic void (*Haer.* II.4.1; 8.3). Thus, the arguments of the opponents are without substance, and they and their audience have become "empty" (*Haer.* II.8.3; 11.1). Because this pattern of argument resembles so closely Plutarch's treatment of the Stoic notions of "the All" and "the void," it would appear that Irenaeus has borrowed the argument and reapplied it to his debate with the Gnostics.

Irenaeus begins Book II with a catalogue of Gnostic self-contradictions. Such a catalogue gathers as many arguments as possible in order to prove that his opponents' views are irrational, self-contradictory and contrary to common opinion. This process of listing arguments often includes insights from different schools and need not reflect the account that an author would give in a non-polemical, philosophical analysis. One of the stock rhetorical ploys of the interschool rivalry between Platonists and Stoics equated the "indefinite void" of the Stoic cosmology with the "emptiness" of Stoic argument. Hence, the Gnostic description of the cosmos as *plēroma* and *kenōma* provided Irenaeus with a ready-made pattern of argument to use against his opponents.

III. Ideas and the Divine Mind

Irenaeus' mode of argument against the Gnostics reflects the polemic of Platonists against Stoic cosmology. Since Irenaeus is not the first Christian to adapt such argumentative *topoi* to a defense of the biblical cosmology, he has most likely learned this argument from the Christian polemic against philosophers. Further investigation of the content of Irenaeus' arguments suggests that they come from a tradition of Christian polemic less favorably disposed toward Platonism than, for example, the Alexandrian tradition.

The most striking examples of anti-Platonic argument occur in Ire-

---

[22] The argument against infinity in the world, or infinity of worlds, is a standard *topos* of anti-Epicurean polemic.

naeus' treatment of ideas and of the divine mind. Albinus' textbook summary of Platonism provides a guide to established Platonic concepts up to the mid-second century (Did.10–22). Since he taught at Smyrna, Albinus would have represented the Platonism known to Irenaeus and his teachers. Since according to Albinus Platonism distinguished the transcendent, self-intelligizing god from the active demiurgic one, it also separated the highest god from the world. Assimilation of the demiurge to the Stoic *logos* "World Soul" thus led to placing the ideas in the mind of the second or demiurgic god.[23] For Albinus, the World Soul is an irrational entity which must be awakened by the demiurge.[24] Once awakened, the World Soul creates order by looking upward toward the objects of intellection in the demiurge.

Dillon observes that the mythological strains in this account are more typical of the "underworld Platonism" in Valentinianism than of the strictly academic interpretations of Plato.[25] Similar mythic *topoi* in Plutarch's use of the Isis and Osiris myth, however, caution one against too sharp a division between academic and "underworld" Platonism.

The discovery of truth through the exegesis of "ancient traditions" appears to have been a preoccupation of Platonists in general. For example, Plutarch defends the introduction of a principle of disorder into cosmology with a stock catalogue of dualistic opinions from myth and philosophy (Is. Osir. 369E–370E). Having established by means of the catalogue the antiquity and universality of his view, Plutarch interprets Tim. 35A as a veiled account of a doctrine which Plato later put forward explicitly in Laws, 896DF, namely that there are two motions in the universe, the beneficent and the maleficent. Though the good always predominates, evil inheres inevitably in the body and soul of the cosmos (Laws, 370E–371B). Plutarch acknowledges the originality of this exegesis of the Timaeus. When God created the cosmos, Plutarch contends, he ordered the initially irrational soul by introducing into it intelligence and reason. Only at that point can it be spoken of as "World Soul" (Tim. 1014A–1015F: De animae procreatione).[26] The example of Plutarch shows that Platonist exegesis turns to the Timaeus to support the view that the world had a beginning, although as far as is known, Atticus is the only Platonist to agree that the world must have been created.[27]

[23] Dillon, Middle Platonists, 45–48. Albinus' teaching appears to have been particularly "mixed" in its use of Aristotelian and Stoic categories and arguments; so Merlan, "Plato to Plotinus," 64–65.
[24] Albinus, Did. 10,3; Dillon (Middle Platonists, 282–87) notes on p. 46 the comparison with Isis rejoicing at being impregnated by the divine logos (Plutarch, Is. Osir. 369ff.).
[25] Dillon, Middle Platonists, 286–87.
[26] Cherniss (Moralia, 136–37) emphasizes Plutarch's originality in this interpretation.
[27] See Cherniss, Moralia, 148, n. a; Dillon, Middle Platonists, 229 and 252–54.

These unusual views may have been the result of a wider development in Platonist circles that sought to interpret Plato in light of "ancient traditions." On this basis one can surmise that Plutarch possibly owes his interest in Zoroastrian theology to his teacher Ammonius.[28]

Irenaeus' arguments against the Gnostic account of the ignorant demiurge presuppose a cosmology in which the divine *logos* provides the ideas by which the demiurge/World Soul brings the world into being (*Haer.* III.7; 16.1). Irenaeus' objection to a creator of the world, who derives his plan from a conception outside himself, could apply to any formula that presupposed a series of "gods" involved in the creative process, since it would permit an infinite series of artificers (*Haer.* III.7.5). Irenaeus contrasts such a cosmology with the Christian view that there is one God, the Artificer who formed the world according to forms that he himself made.

This qualification fits the revision of Platonic theory in Philo, who rejects the passivity and transcendence of the God above the demiurge in favor of the activity of the creator. The paradigm, which the *Timaeus* holds to be independent of the demiurge, becomes God's creation. For Philo, on the other hand, the act of divine creation first provides the noetic world which is itself the necessary pattern for subsequent material creation (*Op. Mund.* 7-20). This double creation provides as many classes of being in the intelligible world as in the sensible one (*Op. Mund.* 16).[29] Hence, Philo rejects the view that the ideas exist somewhere outside of God, insisting that they are not in any "place" but constitute the divine *logos*. No other "place," he argues, could contain the divine powers; created being cannot do so. God is forced to limit his powers when he bestows divine goodness on creation (*Op. Mund.* 16–20). In sum, the central apologetic function of Philo's cosmology is to demonstrate the superiority of the Mosaic revelation of the single creator God to Platonic views.

Irenaeus' topological argument in *Haer.* II.3.1 to 4.3 also speaks of the overwhelming greatness of God, which is not limited to a particular place. He does not follow Philo's tradition of presenting the *logos* as the divine archetype. In fact, Irenaeus' tradition contrasted the Christian doctrine of creation to all systems of creation according to a divine paradigm. The argument against such a scheme contrasts the divine power and eternity to the changeable nature of the created world.

This argument against the view that created things are images of aeons in the *plērōma* raises the objection that, if the lower world was

[28] Dillon, *Middle Platonists*, 203.
[29] Dillon, *Middle Platonists*, 157–60.

created to honor the heavenly, it would have to continue eternally. Honor from a transitory creation is useless (*Haer*. II.7.1). Most Platonists understood "creation" in the *Timaeus* to be merely symbolic. Philo argued, for example, that the world was created because it was dependent upon divine power for its existence. Creation, however, could not mean a beginning in time, since time is created by the motion of the world (*Aet. Mund.* 13–19).[30]

Irenaeus does not have to argue with the Gnostics over the creation of the world. The argument about images appears to have begun from the fact of the corruptibility of the cosmos and to have been used to argue that the cosmos could not have been created according to heavenly archetypes. Had creation been based on heavenly archetypes, the world, like that of which it is an image, would be eternal. Such an argument cannot be addressed to Platonists, since they would agree that the cosmos is eternal. It presumes a dispute over the creation of the cosmos. Further challenges to the theory of "a world of ideas" might well apply to most Platonist accounts. Philo, perhaps dependent upon Eudorus,[31] held that there was an idea corresponding to each natural thing, although no ideas corresponded to an artificial thing—a view also held by Albinus.

Irenaeus, who frequently chides the Gnostics for thinking that thirty aeons would be sufficient to generate the multiplicity of beings in this world (*Haer*. II.7.3), grounds his argument in a theory of forms. He holds that the multiplicity of the animal creation cannot be represented as images of things in the heavenly world, since it includes wild, as well as tame, animals. This objection is based on a principle about spiritual being that Irenaeus uses throughout: spiritual being does not permit differentiation of quality in the sense that one spiritual entity could be defective, inferior or inharmonious with another. Beyond numerical speculations about the introduction of "difference" into the world of ideas, second-century Platonism gave little attention to the problems reflected in this objection. There was little concern over how to relate the diversity of the material world to the world of ideas.[32]

Irenaeus presses the argument. He argues that forms can only be the basis of the material world if one admits into the eternal realm the

[30] Dillon, *Middle Platonists*, 132f.; Runia, "Philo," 126.

[31] Dillon, *Middle Platonists*, 128.

[32] For Albinus' teaching as a summary of common Platonic *topoi*, see Dillon, *Middle Platonists*, 42; Xenocrates apparently attempted to combine the five solids with a material element in order to explain how the ideas could shape the material world (Dillon, *Middle Platonists*, 31).

limitations of space, figure, and corruptibility (*Haer.* II.7.6), but no one would make such an admission, as Philo's description of the relationship between the forms and the divine *logos* makes clear. This line of attack suggests that Irenaeus is not speaking from a tradition of Christian Platonism, for even his discussion of the divine mind diverges from such a tradition.[33] Clearly, any biblical interpretation of creation has to depart from the dual image of the passive, self-contemplating One and the active demiurge.

Philo describes the creative activity of God as the central facet of his divinity. He reminds the reader that one must think of God as doing all things simultaneously: there is no distinction between the thought behind what God does and the activity of commanding things into existence (*Op. Mund.* 13). Likewise Irenaeus draws upon the simultaneous character of divine operations to undermine the validity of the mind analogy. God, he contends, is all mind, all reason and active spirit (*Haer.* II.28.4–5). His opponents have misunderstood mental analogies because they think of separable activities such as humans experience. Irenaeus believes that the dual use of *logos* among the Greeks contributed to this mistake, because they used *logos* to represent both the principle of things and the instrument by which thought is expressed. Prior to making this argument, Irenaeus has attempted to ward off the objection that the ordered world would have to be co-eternal with the activity of the divine intellect, insisting that one cannot ask the question of what God was doing prior to the creation of the world (*Haer.* II.28.3).

Irenaeus is apparently using a tradition which had been formulated to dispute the Platonist teaching about the creation of the world. That tradition had rejected the distinction between a passive, transcendent God and an active demiurgic *logos* on the grounds that the activity of the divine creation was its highest mode of operation. Platonists, the tradition argued, were deceived in drawing too close an analogy between divine and human. This tradition further attacked the theory that the world was created according to eternal patterns, the forms. Since the forms are regularly situated in the divine mind, the two topics must be treated together. This world cannot be created according to unified, eternal patterns. Its diversity, its temporal limitations, and its spatial character see to that. Thus, Irenaeus presents the Christian doctrine of a single, active creator as superior to the Platonic view.

---

[33] The unity which is a fundamental characteristic of the spiritual world is later used as an argument against qualitative differences among the aeons. Sophia cannot, thus, have been "younger, weaker, separated from her consort" (*Haer.* II.12.2).

IV. Creation and the Pronoia of God

When Irenaeus rejects the creation of the cosmos according to eternal archetypes, he introduces the reader to another central theme in the interscholastic debates of the second century: *pronoia* "divine providence." Irenaeus holds that the Gnostics cannot account for the production of the world without a doctrine of divine foresight; yet, the doctrines of divine forms and of divine foresight conflict. If the forms are models for a creation that is arranged according to divine providence, then honor goes to what is actually arranged according to that providence, namely creation (*Haer.* II.15.3). The anti-Platonist cast of this argument becomes clear since Irenaeus goes on to describe the relationship between the model and creation. The model is like the clay model used to make a bronze or gold statue. It is nothing once the statue is made. This model analogy completely reverses analogies used in Platonic circles in which the form was likened to the ideal concept in the mind of the artist or the architect: matter is like wax which must receive the seal (Plutarch, *Is. Osir.* 373AB; Seneca, *Ep.* 65; Philo, *Op. Mund.* 20; Cicero, *Or.* 7–10).[34]

Both Stoics and Platonists of the period appealed to their vision of divine providence in arguments against the "chance" of Epicurean cosmologies. Seeking to avoid the determinism attached to the Stoic view of providence/necessity, Platonism had adapted elements of the Stoic *logos* to its account of *pronoia*.[35] Irenaeus' argument is clearly anti-Platonist when it proposes the doctrine of divine Pronoia as evidence that creation is superior to the transcendent world of forms. Although this argument might be a Stoic rather than a Platonist view of providence, the disparagement of forms (*Haer.* II.7.6) makes it clear that Irenaeus does not support the Stoic view, since the latter makes the divine immanent in the world.

Irenaeus' argument drives a wedge between the heavenly, divine world and this one, for it rejects the possibility of any *sympatheia* "harmony" between heaven and earth. For the Stoic, on the other hand, cosmic harmony proved the existence of divine control over the cosmos (Cicero, *Nat. Deor.* II.5.15). Philo likewise rejected the doctrine of *sympatheia* because he objected to a divinized cosmos (*Mig.* 178–84). Moses, he argues, corrected such doctrines by making it clear that the

---

[34] Cicero makes "eloquence" itself the reflection of an idea. The uniformity of ideas guarantees that they are the same for every intellect. See Dillon, *Middle Platonists*, 93–94.
[35] On the relationship between the *logos* and *pronoia*, see Dillon, *Middle Platonists*, 167–68.

creator of the world is entirely transcendent.[36] Plutarch challenges the Stoic claims for providence because their physics, in assigning all elements in the universe to their natural places, contradict, as far as Plutarch is concerned, their claims for divine providence. Their physics deprive God of the two fundamental activities of providential care: maintaining the cosmos in existence and unification of its diverse substances (*Stoic. Repug.* 1055D; also *De Fac. Lun.* 927AB).

Irenaeus' argument against cosmic *sympatheia* reflects the problem of unifying the diverse substances of the cosmos. Cosmic harmony between heaven and earth is not possible because the two are in fact contradictory: light over against darkness; fire over against water. Directed against the Stoics, this argument becomes a dispute about the character of the so-called four elements. Plutarch, for example, knows that for Stoic physics the elements air and fire are primary, while the elements earth and water are "mixed"—they can only maintain their unity through mixture with fire (*Com. Not.* 1085C-E). There does appear, then, to have been a tradition used by Irenaeus which protested the Stoic account of the elements as contradictory. Irenaeus' argument plays on that contradiction, rejecting Stoic doctrines of cosmic sympathy, as well as the Platonic tradition of creation through divine ideas.

The debate over *pronoia* serves primarily as testimony to the divine ordering of the cosmos, as in the Stoic defense of the existence of God (Cicero, *Nat. Deor.* II.30.75–77). Plutarch's unusual argument which supposes there to be a finite number of worlds created by the demiurge (one to correspond with each of the solid figures in the *Timaeus*) makes the additional claim that a finite plurality of worlds would not impinge upon divine providence or oversight, since there is neither less dignity nor more labor involved in administering several worlds rather than one. The basic premise of this argument is the distinction between the Platonic understanding of spiritual reality and Stoic materialism. With regard to the Stoics, Plutarch points out that a spiritual being is not tied to place or matter (*Def. Or.* 425E–426E).[37] That God cannot be tied to place or matter is a postulate of Irenaeus' argument for the unity of God in *Haer.* II.1.1, where God must contain all things (*Haer.* II.1.1–2). Irenaeus' anti-Platonist traditions pursued the argument for the unity of God within the context of debates about divine providence. For Albinus

---

[36] See Runia, "Philo," 132–33.

[37] Both Stoics and Platonists accused the Epicureans of denying providence. Plutarch admits preferring the Stoics to the Epicureans in that regard (*Stoic. Repug.* 1051E) but he insists that their physics of natural motion/place makes providence unnecessary.

(*Did.* 12,1) and Plutarch (*Plat. Qu.* 1007E; *De Fac. Lun.* 926), however, providence cannot be attributed to the highest god.[38]

A second feature in the conventional treatments of *pronoia* is easily adapted to the cosmological argument. As Cicero's Stoic comments (*Nat. Deor.* II.30.75–77), to deny divine providence is to claim that either the gods are ignorant of the most important things or they are powerless to bring them about. Divine knowledge and omnipotence are characteristic elements in Irenaeus' argument. Because, for example, the argument about divine place forces the opposition to admit that the creation cannot be "outside" God, it becomes impossible to claim that either ignorance or opposition to God could come to be within his domain. Consequently, the attempts of some to interpret the within/without of Gnostic myth as knowledge or ignorance are equally contradictory (*Haer.* II.7.1–2).

The argument for divine providence had also come to be linked with the argument for divine creation in some circles. Plutarch enunciates the basic principle of such views: whatever did not come into being has no need of a guardian (*Plat. Qu.* 1013EF).[39] Thus, providence supports Plutarch's unusual interpretation of the "created" in the *Timaeus* as a literal coming into being. Philo, who also knows that those who eliminate *pronoia* (like the Epicureans) eliminate true piety, couples this *topos* with his argument for the creation of the world. The maker naturally cares for what he has made as the father naturally cares for his offspring. Therefore, the doctrine of divine providence is most logically supported by the view that God himself created the universe (*Op. Mund.* 9–10).[40]

The creation-providence link also implies another activity of divine providence which is central to the Stoic and Platonic understanding of providence—the divine activity which keeps the world in existence.[41] Irenaeus' vision of providence includes the divine creation of the cosmos and the divine omnipotence in governing and maintaining it (*Haer.* II.11.1). He is even more uncompromising than Philo in rejecting the possibility that the creation of the world is mediated by an entity which

[38] Atticus' careful distinction is possibly another sign of his dependence upon Plutarch; for this theory, see Dillon, *Middle Platonists*, 252–53.

[39] Cherniss (*Moralia*, 148, n. a) points to Proclus *In Platonis Timaeum* as an indication that Atticus called *pronoia* the divine cause.

[40] Philo's critique of those who claim that the world is "forgetful" could be paralleled to Irenaeus' objections to ignorance in the aeons.

[41] Runia ("Philo" 126–27 and 133) argues that Philo goes beyond Platonism in holding that it is not the nature of God that is reflected in providence, but his mercy and his omnipotence. The quality of God's omnipotence is also central to Irenaeus' understanding of divine providence.

represents the active side of creation and governance. Irenaeus' *logos* never fills in for the demiurge of Platonic speculation, as it does for Philo. While this uncompromising refusal to allow any instrumentality in divine creation may have been sharpened by the conflict with the Gnostic picture of the demiurge, it originates in the traditional attack upon the cosmology of Platonism. Irenaeus makes it quite clear that God has no need of instruments to create (*Haer.* II.2.4–5).[42]

Irenaeus also connects providence and divine creation by arguing that the invisible, omnipotent creator is known through his providence (*Haer.* II.6.1). This knowledge of God makes the saving power of God available to all people outside the specific revelation in Christ (*Haer.* II.6.2). The basis for this knowledge of God is the "strong mental intuition" produced in all by the omnipotence of the creator. Although arguments for divine existence on the basis of providence are frequent, Irenaeus' claim that such knowledge of God is based on a "mental intuition" appears to revive a Stoic "common notion" in defense of divine existence. Later Stoics had to qualify those "common notions" which combined the certainty of truth with the specification "clarity" (Plutarch, *Com. Not.* 1074E).[43] Irenaeus claims that the power of the divine providence is part of the transcendence of God in his invisibility. This combination may also be part of the anti-Platonic tradition used by Irenaeus. Rejecting all mediators by which Platonist philosophers close the gap between the transcendent God and the world, Irenaeus finds a formulation of divine providence which will provide the necessary link. With respect to his Gnostic opponents, it now ensures the possibility of knowledge of God throughout creation.

V. Divine Omnipotence and the Creation of Matter

According to the Platonists, evil and disorder appear in the material world because material creation cannot realize the divine form. Although Irenaeus stands close to that tradition insofar as he rejects the doctrine of images and emphasizes the discordant transitory nature of the world, his understanding of providence and divine presence does

[42] The *logos* is not a replacement for the demiurge. Irenaeus is more radical than Philo on this point. He has gone out of his way to avoid any suggestion that there could be a mediator of creation. See the discussion of this phenomenon in Carr, *Angels and Principalities*, 159–60.

[43] Cherniss (*Moralia*, 629, n. b) argues that though *enargeia* "self-evident truth" does not appear in Stoic circles earlier than Antipater (Plutarch, *De Stoic. Repug.* 1017EF), the adjective *enargēs* (Plutarch, *Com. Not.* 1047C) was probably used to qualify conceptions as early as Chrysippus.

not include any weakening of divine power or presence in creation
(*Haer.* II.8.2). Irenaeus exploits the weakness and transitory character of
the world to destroy the doctrine of its creation according to the image of
eternal forms. He also attacks the common Platonist explanations of evil
and disorder (chaos) that can be attached to the Gnostic cosmologies.
These explanations include: (1) the necessity to which Plato refers in
Tim. 48; (2) the doctrine of a primordial, irrational motion that affects the
World Soul—a doctrine peculiar to Plutarch and Atticus in our sources;
(3) the account of matter as a pre-existent principle.

The cosmological necessity of *Tim.* 48 forced Platonists to distinguish
their view of the world from the necessity inherent in Stoic cosmologies.
Plutarch invokes an apparent Platonist slogan, "the better is always in
control of the necessary (*to katenagamenon*)" (*De Fac. Lun.* 928C).[44]
Platonists, who held that the world always existed, took the "chaos" in
the *Timaeus* to represent necessity, that element of the world which did
not come under divine control. For example, Plutarch argues that chaos
(=necessity) signifies the primordial disordered soul whose shaping by
the *logos* results in creation (*Is. Osir.* 370F).[45] He claims that a principle
of disorder is required because primordial matter is without any qualities. Consequently, the combination of the activity of the beneficent god
and a formless matter could not give rise to anything but good (*Tim.*
1014E–1015A: *De animae procreatione*). This account fits in with Plutarch's allegorization of the Isis and Osiris myth (*Is. Osir.* 369A–D).
Similar cosmological allegorization appealed to Irenaeus' opponents.[46]
Albinus, for his part, uses the existence of unformed matter as part of a
series of arguments by which he demonstrates the existence of ideas.[47]

Irenaeus rejects any attempt to place a principle between God and his
creation. He does not follow Justin in finding "unformed matter" in Gen
1:2 (1 *Apol.* 10,2; 59,1).[48] Philo likewise wavers between accepting such
an accommodation with the *Timaeus* (*Her.* 160) and asserting that God is
responsible for the creation of matter (*L.A.* 2,2; *Prob.* 18).[49] Hence,
Irenaeus' protest against the Gnostic stories of the origin of chaos,

---

[44] Cherniss-Helmbold, *Plutarch's Moralia*, 95.

[45] Cornford, *Cosmology*, 37.

[46] Plutarch never embraces the negative judgments of Gnosticism, but one must at
least allow that the necessity of giving such an account of evil in the cosmos and his
fascination with mythological exegesis would make Gnostic views palatable to some as
possibly legitimate philosophical reflection. He uses the image of the aging world (*Tim.*
1026EF: *De animae procreatione*) against the Stoic doctrine of *sympatheia*. See Dillon,
Middle Platonists, 201–206.

[47] Dillon, *Middle Platonists*, 281.

[48] Daniélou, *Gospel*, 115–16.

[49] Dillon (*Middle Platonists*, 158) thinks that the view that the supreme god is the
causal principle of all matter should be traced to Eudorus (p. 127).

matter, and the disorder of the lower world, draws upon all the objections to Platonism. He argues that it is not possible that something could exist through the agency of an intermediate being that is contrary to the good-will of the Father, because then the freedom of God becomes captive to necessity, and then necessity would come to rule the cosmos (Haer. II.5.2). Rejection of "necessity" as a cosmic principle is a stock topos of anti-Stoic polemic. For example, Plutarch wishes to avoid the implication that the necessity of the Timaeus might be equated with the Stoic concept of necessity so he insists that necessity cannot be taken as negative (Tim. 1014B: De animae procreatione). Even the irrational element in the World Soul is not evil, strictly speaking: it is merely the origin of motions from which evil results.[50] Thus do Irenaeus' objections to the view that matter has an origin outside God employ Platonic principles against the possibility of any external causes or principles beside the will of the creator.

The image of a "disordered soul" as one primal principle in Plutarch's account of Isis and in the Valentinian description of Sophia is invalidated by other philosophical principles. Irenaeus believes that it is impious to attribute to Sophia's desire the first cause of evil—a conclusion that Plutarch also attempted to avoid in his allegorizing of Isis.[51] In typical Platonist language Irenaeus challenges the Gnostic allegory: it is impossible to attribute disorder to a spiritual being (Haer. II.7.4). He uses a second principle of spiritual beings to counter the view that the lower world is a shadow of the heavenly one (Haer. II.8.1): spiritual bodies do not cast shadows.

This same principle helps Plutarch to refute the Stoic view that the moon is a fiery substance because of its location (De Fac. Lun. 921EF). Against the Stoic claim that matter and proper place are conjoined in the order of the cosmos, Plutarch holds that the variety of places in which elements are found—including the earthly moon in the heavens —testifies to providence's beneficent arrangement of the cosmos (De Fac. Lun. 927CD). Also Philo's exegesis of "Bezalel" (Exod 31:2) identifies the "shadow" of God with the logos, the paradigm by which all things were made (L.A. 3, 95–96). Irenaeus, however, rejects all mediation of creation. Therefore it is impossible to call something a "shadow" of the divine—least of all matter.[52]

---

[50] Dillon, Middle Platonists, 207–208.

[51] The possibilities of God's exercise of power in the sublunar realm are limited. Philo assigns God's regal power to that realm. But the demiurge of Middle Platonism is never the cause of evil; see Dillon, Middle Platonists, 169–70.

[52] Haer. II.8.2 also rejects the argument that the shadow could reflect distance from God, since divine power extends throughout his domain.

Irenaeus also denies that the "substance of matter" has an origin outside the will of God and his creative power. To claim the opposite is to attack the power of God.[53] Like the case of analogies to the divine mind, so the belief in primordial matter rests upon another false analogy between the human and the divine. Human inability to create without some prior material does not justify the assumption that God, who has the power to call into being the "substance of creation" (Haer. II.10.2–4), is similarly limited. The creation of matter ultimately demonstrates the superiority of the Christian vision of God, the creator, for it preserves the freedom and omnipotence of God against analogies falsely developed from the material world and from human modes of thought, feeling, and creation.

[53] Plutarch, Is. Osir. 372E. Isis' procreation in matter is described as the eikōn tēs ousias "image of being."

11

THE GOSPEL OF TRUTH
AS AN EXOTERIC TEXT*

Harold W. Attridge

Dr. Harold Attridge has studied at Cambridge University, the Hebrew University of Jerusalem and Harvard University, where he took a doctorate in 1975. After post-doctoral work at Harvard he joined the faculty of Perkins School of Theology, Southern Methodist University in Dallas, Texas. Since 1985 he has been a member of the Theology Faculty of the University of Notre Dame.

Dr. Attridge has made contributions to many aspects of the history of religion in Greco-Roman antiquity, particularly Hellenistic Judaism and Gnosticism. Among his publications are studies of first-century Cynicism and of the use of the Hebrew scriptures in the Jewish historian Josephus. For the Coptic Gnostic Library project he was the volume editor of Codex I of the Nag Hammadi collection and was responsible for the editions of the Gospel of Truth and the Tripartite Tractate.

Preface

T he problem of the relationship of the *Gospel of Truth* to the Valentinian tradition has troubled scholars since the discovery of the text. This paper suggests, through an analysis of the rhetorical techniques of the work, why that problem has been so acute. The text deliberately conceals whatever might be the particular theology of its author, although there are abundant hints that this theology is a developed form of Valentinian speculation. The presupposed theology is concealed so that the author may make an appeal to ordinary Christians, inviting

* The suggestions made about the *Gospel of Truth* in this paper reflect and elaborate elements in the introduction and notes to the text published in the critical edition (Attridge-MacRae, "Gospel of Truth"), edited by George W. MacRae and myself. In developing some of the ideas presented here, I have had the benefit of Fr. MacRae's reflections and criticisms. He, of course, bears no responsibility for the form in which these suggestions are now presented.

them to share the basic insights of Valentinianism. Thus the text should be considered more exoteric than esoteric.

I. Introduction

Since its initial publication in 1956,[1] the *Gospel of Truth* has been the object of considerable discussion in regard to its general theological affiliation and its literary techniques. Much of the earlier debate about the possible relationship of the text to Valentinianism was surveyed by R. McL. Wilson in his paper at the 1978 Yale Conference on Gnosticism[2] and it is not necessary to rehearse the details of that survey here. It will suffice simply to summarize the results of Wilson's critical essay by noting the spectrum of opinion which he traces. Some of the earliest attempts to relate the *Gospel of Truth* to Valentinianism argued that the text reflects a more primitive stage of Valentinian speculation than that represented, for example, in the Ptolemaic system on which Irenaeus reports.[3] Scholars holding to this option have frequently suggested that the text was an original composition of Valentinus from early in his career.[4] Another hypothesis on the subject held that the text rather presupposes, but does not fully articulate, a Valentinian system. Scholars of this opinion have tended to be agnostic on the question of the identity of the author.[5] Finally, some scholars have maintained that the text is not specifically Valentinian at all.[6]

Since Wilson's survey, the debate has continued and each of the three positions on the spectrum of opinion has found its adherents. Opting, for instance, for the association of the text with Valentinus himself is Benoit Standaert, in an article not treated by Wilson but mentioned at the Yale Conference in the discussion of Wilson's paper.[7] Standaert provides a literary analysis of the *Gospel of Truth* and compares it with the few fragments of Valentinus' own writings and suggests that commonalities of style indicate common authorship. In the same volume from the Yale

[1] Malinine, *Evangelium Veritatis* and id., *Evangelium Veritatis Supplementum.*
[2] Wilson, "Valentinianism."
[3] Iren. *Haer.* I.1–8.
[4] Cf., e.g., van Unnik, "Gospel of Truth," 98–99; Quispel, "Jung Codex," 50; Grobel, *Gospel of Truth,* 26.
[5] Cf., e.g., Jonas, "Review of Malinine"; id., "Evangelium Veritatis"; id., *Gnostic Religion,* 309–19; Nock, "Library"; Puech, "Gospel of Truth"; Ménard, *L'Évangile de Vérité,* 34–38.
[6] Cf., e.g., Haenchen, "Literatur"; Schenke, *Herkunft,* 20–25.
[7] Standaert, "L'Évangile de Vérité." See the comments on Wilson's paper in Layton, *Rediscovery,* 1.142.

Conference there is another important paper which represents a form of the second option. This paper, by William Schoedel,[8] maintains that the *Gospel of Truth* reflects a revisionist, monistic Valentinianism, also evidenced in Irenaeus, *Adversus Haereses* II. The text thus presupposes not only Valentinian theology as that developed in the school of Ptolemy, for example, but also orthodox criticism of that theology. As such it represents an attempt to accommodate some of the principles of that critique. Finally, Carsten Colpe presents a version of the third position on the spectrum in an essay which is part of an analysis of the Jewish, pagan, and Christian components in gnostic texts. Colpe argues that, while the author of the *Gospel of Truth* probably knew some Valentinian theology, he departs from it in important respects and "goes his own way."[9]

Later this paper will review some of the detailed arguments used to support these various positions, but first, one should note a second, less well-defined, set of issues which bear on the question of the Valentinian affiliations of the text. Much of the discussion of the literary character and techniques of the text has focused on the question of its genre. Most scholars agree with the original editors of the text that it is in some sense a homily,[10] although there have been various attempts to nuance that judgment. Scholars have suggested, for example, that the work is a meditative homily or even a "meditation," although what precisely is meant by that characterization remains unclear.[11] That the work is "esoteric" in some sense is often implied and frequently stated.[12] Presumably, those who use this category mean that the work is rich in allusion and, whatever its relationship to Valentinian or other traditions, it presupposes more than it explicitly states. This characterization assumes that the text utilizes this allusive quality in a distinctive, evocative way to recall in the minds of its enlightened readers the truths of the system to which it subscribes and which it presupposes.[13]

[8] Schoedel, "Monism."
[9] Colpe, "Überlieferung," especially 131–46. The comment cited here appears on pp. 144–45.
[10] Cf. Malinine, *Evangelium Veritatis*, xv. See also H.-M. Schenke, *Herkunft*, 10; Haardt, "Struktur"; Grobel, *Gospel of Truth*, 19–21; Ménard, *L'Évangile de Vérité*, 35.
[11] Cf., e.g., H.-M. Schenke, *Herkunft*, 11; Standaert, "L'Évangile de Vérité," 255. Note the discussion between Wilson and Joel Fineman on the issue in Layton, *Rediscovery*, 1.143–44.
[12] Cf. Malinine, *Evangelium Veritatis*, xiv. See, however, Ménard, *L'Évangile de Vérité*, 1: "A l'example de la *Lettre à Flora* de Ptolémée, l'*Évangile de Vérité* serait plus exotérique qu'ésotérique." Cf. also Fredouille, *Tertullien*, 1.34–39, a discussion brought to my attention by Paul-Hubert Poirier.
[13] Note, e.g., the remark of Wilson in the discussion of his paper at the Yale Conference (Layton, *Rediscovery*, 143): "It seems implausible that an author would write with the intention of provoking confusion. It is more likely that he wrote cryptically to those

This paper challenges both the characterization of the *Gospel of Truth* as an esoteric work as well as the presupposition about how it functions. It proposes a model for construing the text which has been largely ignored in the discussion of the *Gospel of Truth*. The *Gospel of Truth*, precisely because of the systematic ambiguity and polyvalence,[14] is an *exoteric* text, a text designed to be read and understood by people who do *not* share the fundamental theological presuppositions of its author. If correct, this proposal has implications for the question of the work's Valentinian affiliations.

An assessment of the theological aims and rhetorical techniques of the *Gospel of Truth* may usefully begin with a simple observation about the constant interplay between the familiar and the unfamiliar in the text. Among elements of the work which would, no doubt, be familiar to most Christians of the second and third centuries are the numerous allusions to early Christian literature, especially to those portions of it which eventually came to be canonized as the New Testament. Since catalogues of such allusions have frequently been made in the past,[15] it will be sufficient to note that on any evaluation of the data the author of the *Gospel of Truth* apparently knows and uses a large number of the writings of what came to be the canonical New Testament. These include the Synoptic Gospels,[16] Johannine literature,[17] and Pauline literature.[18] It needs to be recognized, of course, that in no case do we find an explicit citation of a New Testament text as scripture or even as an authoritative source.[19]

The author of the *Gospel of Truth* does not, however, confine himself to allusions to materials canonized as the New Testament in the second and subsequent centuries.[20] Some alleged allusions may, in fact, derive

who could, he knew, decipher it." The alternatives implicit here, a cryptic vs. a confusing writing, are hardly the only ones.

[14] The best analysis of these literary qualities of the text may be found in Standaert, "L'Évangile de Vérité," esp. 255–60.

[15] Cf. van Unnik, "Gospel of Truth," 115–21; Schelkle, "Zeugnis," 90–91; and Ménard, *L'Évangile de Vérité*, 3–9.

[16] E.g., Matt 5:48 at *Gos. Truth* I,3:27,24–25; Matt 11:25 at 19,25; Mark 14:24 at 20,15–16; Luke 2:46–49 at 19,19–20.

[17] E.g., John 3:19 at *Gos. Truth* I,3:25,35–36; John 10:3–4 at 21,33–34, 22,21–22; John 11:37 at 30,15–16; 1 John 1:1 at 30,27–31; and Rev 3:5, 5:2–4 at 19,35–36.

[18] E.g., Rom 8:30 and 1 Cor 8:2–3 at *Gos. Truth* I,3:19,32–34; 1 Cor 7:31 at 24,20–24; 1 Cor 8:6 at 18,34–35; 1 Cor 15:53–54 and 2 Cor 5:2–4 at 20,29; Phil 2:8 at 20,29; Phil 3:10 at 30,26; and the deutero-Pauline texts, Eph 3:3–4:9 at 18,15; Col 2:14 at 18,24; 1 Tim 2:4 at 19,12–17. Such lists could be considerably expanded and, while there might be debate about the possibility of specific allusions in individual cases, the examples listed above are all fairly clear references to New Testament texts.

[19] Contrast, e.g., the explicit citation of "the apostle" in *Treat. Res.* I,4:45,24–28.

[20] For discussion of the history of the canon, see, Campenhausen, *Bible* and Farmer, *Jesus*, 178–259.

from sources, written or oral, which were never canonized.[21] Furthermore, the author clearly draws on a corpus of early Christian literature
larger than that of the canonical New Testament. Evidence for this
appears particularly in connection with certain images and metaphors
which are not at home in New Testament works. Schenke, in particular,
has drawn attention to parallels between the *Gospel of Truth* and the
Odes of Solomon.[22] From such parallels he infers that the text is not to be
associated with Valentinianism. Although this inference is unwarranted,
Schenke's analysis rightly calls attention to the diversity of sources
which underlie the text's imagery. The flexibility in the author's use of
early Christian literature generally *may* have some implications for
dating the work. Because the *Gospel of Truth* does not seem to presuppose a fixed New Testament canon, it may well be dated in the
middle and late second century, a period when figures such as Clement
of Alexandria regularly draw upon a broad range of early Christian
sources without strict regard for their canonical status, a situation which
changes significantly by the middle of the third century. Caution,
however, is required in this area, first, because the *Gospel of Truth* itself
renders no explicit judgment on the authoritative status of the works to
which it seemingly alludes and, second, because the development of a
strictly limited canon did not take place at the same pace and with the
same rigor throughout the Christian world.

Alongside the elements of the text which with the proper qualifi-
cations one can judge to be familiar, common, early Christian property,
there are in the *Gospel of Truth* a number of distinctive elements more
closely associated with gnostic, and particularly Valentinian, traditions.
These include the basic soteriological principle, repeatedly enunciated
in the text, that the fundamental problem of the human condition is
ignorance, which is eliminated by the coming of *gnōsis*, "Knowledge,"[23]
and such specific details as the technical terms "the Totalities,"[24] "those
of the middle,"[25] "the spaces,"[26] and "emanations."[27]

---

[21] Cf. Ménard, *L'Évangile de Vérité*, 8 and Koester, "Gnostic Writings."
[22] Cf. H.-M. Schenke, *Herkunft*, 26–29. Note, e.g., the image of the Holy Spirit as the Father's breast in *Gos. Truth* I,3:24,9–11 and the similar imagery in *Odes Sol.* 19:2–4; or the image of truth as the Father's mouth in *Gos. Truth* I,3:26,34–35 and *Odes Sol.* 12:3.
[23] Jonas ("Review of Malinine," 330), in particular, has called attention to this formula (*Gos. Truth* I,3:18,10–11; 24,30–32) and to its significance for understanding the Valentinian association of the text.
[24] *Gos. Truth* I,3:17,5, and frequently.
[25] *Gos. Truth* I,3:17,35.
[26] *Gos. Truth* I,3:20,22.
[27] *Gos. Truth* I,3:21,37.

II. The "Familiar" Features

Even more significant perhaps than the juxtaposition of "familiar" and "unfamiliar" features in the text is the way in which each feature is treated. Throughout the work there is an attempt to render the familiar unfamiliar and vice versa. The process begins in the opening paragraph where the topic of the discourse is said to be the gospel.[28] All that is said about the gospel in the first lines of the text would hardly surprise the ordinary Christian reader or listener; yet, the note that the gospel, "a proclamation of hope," is also the "discovery for those who search for him (sc. the Father),"[29] introduces, in a muted and ambiguous way, what is distinctive in the text. Here it is not so much that the familiar is made unfamiliar, but that a specific twist is given to the familiar, "the gospel," which introduces the gnostic perspective.

After describing the human condition in terms of *Planē* ("Error"), the text enunciates its soteriology in traditional and broadly acceptable language. Jesus, the Christ,[30] came to enlighten those in darkness and show them a way, which is the truth.[31] In the process, he was persecuted by cosmic powers and "nailed to a tree."[32] While both the language and the conceptuality would be familiar to most early Christians, the text continues and throws a new and surprising light upon the historical event of Christ's passion. By being "nailed to the tree," Christ becomes "a fruit of knowledge of the Father." This trope suggests a further allusion to the tree of knowledge in the garden of Eden, for Christ, as the fruit of knowledge, "did not become destructive."[33] Through the symbolic reinterpretation of the death of Christ effected here, the general soteriological principle of the text[34] once again emerges. While the

---

[28] For discussion about the titulary significance of the incipit, see especially Standaert, "Titre," 138–50.

[29] *Gos. Truth* I,3:17,2–4. The description of the Gospel as a proclamation possibly contains a play in Greek on εὐαγγελία and ἀναγγελία, or something similar.

[30] Note that this title appears in the text only here (18,16) and at 36,14.

[31] Note the strikingly Johannine language. Cf. John 1:5, and 14:6. This is but one of the numerous allusions to Johannine images and themes. The contention of Ménard (*L'Évangile de Vérité*, 8) that the author "ne cite pas davantage le quatrième Évangile," is surprising. While in all cases of the author's use of early Christian literature there is more allusion than citation, the evidence for allusions to Johannine traditions is quite as abundant as is evidence for use of other New Testament texts.

[32] *Gos. Truth* I,3:18,22–24. Cf. 1 Cor 2:8; Acts 5:30; 10:39.

[33] *Gos. Truth* I,3:18,26. The language here is ambiguous and the verb could be translated intransitively, "become destroyed," as suggested by Till ("Bemerkungen," 272). The transitive rendering, with its allusion to Genesis is, however, more likely. Cf. Ménard, *L'Évangile de Vérité*, 89.

[34] Cf. n. 23 above.

Gospel of Truth does not, in a strictly docetic fashion,[35] deny the reality of the physical death of Jesus, it does "correct" the familiar interpretation of that death as an atoning sacrifice.[36]

The movement from a more familiar or "orthodox" to a more "heterodox" or gnostic Christology has been noted before,[37] although the precise nature of the movement has not been correctly perceived. It is hardly the case, for example, that the text as a whole moves from a more "orthodox" to a more "heterodox" position. Instead, at all points where the "familiar" descriptions of Christ's person and work are given (and they appear subsequent to the passage under discussion)[38] that familiar presentation is reinterpreted with unfamiliar metaphors.

A further example of the process underway throughout the work appears in the discussion of the "living book," a particularly varied symbol whose development is Protean and complex. The theme is enunciated at 19,35–36, where the "little children"[39] are said to have had revealed in their hearts the "living book of the living."[40] Already, in the initial deployment of the image, the familiar and the unfamiliar unite. For, while the notion of the heavenly book into which the names of the righteous are inscribed is familiar from Jewish and early Christian apocalyptic sources,[41] it is striking that the "book" is within the heart of the "children" and that it is, at the same time, "the one written in the thought and the mind [of the] Father."[42] The intimate connection of the subject, object, and agent of the revealing *gnōsis* is thus symbolically suggested.[43]

---

[35] On the question of whether the text maintains a docetic Christology, cf. Arai, *Christologie* and Shibata, "Character." For recent discussion of the divergences within the Valentinian tradition on the nature of Christ's flesh, cf. Kaestli, "Valentinianisme." For a clear Valentinian affirmation of the reality of the Incarnation in NHC I, see *Tri. Trac.* I,5:114,31–35.

[36] The *Gospel of Truth* thus continues the sort of reinterpretation of the significance of Christ's passion found in the Gospel of John where the primary meaning of the event is seen to be revelatory.

[37] Cf., e.g., Fecht, "Der erste 'Teil,'" 387; Ménard, *L'Évangile de Vérité*, 10, 15; and Colpe, "Überlieferung," 138, 143.

[38] Cf., e.g., *Gos. Truth* I,3:20,4–14 and 30,32–31,12.

[39] There is here a possible allusion to such texts as Matt 11:25 and Luke 10:21.

[40] It has been suggested that this and similar phrases are evidence of a Syriac original. Cf. Nagel, "Herkunft," but this hypothesis is highly unlikely. Cf. Böhlig, "Ursprache," and Ménard, "Structure."

[41] For a thorough survey of the motif, cf. Koep, *Buch.*

[42] *Gos. Truth* I,3:19,36–20,1.

[43] The connection of the subject and object is explicitly affirmed at 18,30–31: "he (*sc.* the Father) discovered them in himself, and they discovered him in themselves." The connection of subject and agent of the revelation is affirmed in various ways, but particularly in the dialectic on the "name" at 38,7–40,22.

Developing the image of the "book," the text reverts to the familiar, in what is clearly an allusion to Rev 5:9: "the (book) which no one was able to take since it is reserved for the one who will take it to be slain."[44] The suggestion is made that the book is the mode of revelation, for on it depends the "belief in salvation."[45] Although the author may still be moving in the realm of relatively traditional symbolism, the revelatory function of the book must be understood in the light of its "interiority" which has already been described, and, to this extent, the imagery has already received a new dimension.

The surprising novelty in the image rapidly increases in the next segment of the text where the book, in rapid succession, becomes a specific type of document and, metaphorically, that which surrounds or embodies the revealer. The next phase of the exposition begins with a simple analogy, comparing the revelation of "the all" to the opening of a will. As a will when opened reveals the material substance (ousia) of the testator, so the book when opened by the death of Christ reveals the spiritual substance (ousia)[46] of the Father, the source of the totality. The image of the testament, already used in several New Testament texts, is familiar although the pun on ousia develops it in a new and specifically gnostic way. The familiar becomes even more unfamiliar as the metaphorical language changes. For Jesus takes, and implicitly opens, the revelatory book by "putting it on."[47] Without explaining this arresting image, the author reverts to familiar language: Jesus was "nailed to the tree," and thereby, "published the edict."[48] One may suspect an allusion to Col 2:14, although the author takes the image of the book in another direction and, once again, a familiar image is reinterpreted. The edict, unlike the bill of accusation in the deutero-Pauline text, is not negative, but positive. At the same time, the "donning" of the book receives a fuller explanation, for at his death on the cross Christ "puts on" imperishability, and rectifies the condition of "naked" oblivion.[49] In other words, the death of Jesus is once again seen to be a revelatory act. For Jesus himself, the significance of his death is that it is the point of entry to "imperishability." For all others, that death taught a lesson about the transcendent Father, a lesson which reverses the human condition created by the work of Error. Because the passion is primarily construed

---

[44] Gos. Truth I,3:20,3–6. The syntax of the Coptic here is somewhat problematic. The translation follows the suggestion of Till ("Bemerkungen," 273), who construes the feminine subject in ескн as impersonal and the conjunctive ñсеглгшлq as complementary.

[45] Gos. Truth I,3:20,15–17.

[46] For the two senses of οὐσία used here, cf. LSJ 1274b.

[47] Gos. Truth I,3:20,24.

[48] Gos. Truth I,3:20,25–26.

[49] Gos. Truth I,3:20,37–38.

as a revelatory event, it may be imagined as the opening of a book, and because, at the same time, it reverses the human condition symbolized both by the "nakedness" of fallen humanity and its clothing in "perishable rags," it may be depicted with the image of stripping and clothing.[50]

After this complex metaphorical development, the author returns to a simpler and more familiar image of the book. Those who receive the teaching (about the Father, conveyed by Jesus) are inscribed in the book of the living.[51] At this point, the focus of the metaphor shifts from the nature of the book and the process of its "opening" to the preconditions and results of that revelatory process, symbolized by the act of inscription. Those written in the book of life are not, as in Rev 20:12–15, the martyrs who have borne testimony to Jesus, but those whom the Father "knew in advance"[52] and who have thus heard the Father's call.[53]

The image of the book surfaces once again after an exploration of the interrelated themes of naming and calling.[54] In a final application of the image[55] the focus shifts once again to the topic with which the whole symbolic development began, namely, the content of the "book." The revelation provided by the "book" contains a "knowledge in which all the emanations concur"[56] and the letters written in the book are the agents of this knowledge. In an unfamiliar and surprising way the author affirms that the contents are not expressed in simple "vowels or consonants,"[57] but in "true letters," each of which "is a complete thought."[58] The image of the book now provides a vehicle for commenting on the nature of the "gospel" as conceived in the text, as it affirms that the whole is in each of its parts equally. While the message

---

[50] The clothing imagery here was, of course, traditional in baptismal contexts. Cf. Smith, "Garments." There have been several discussions of sacramental allusions in the *Gospel of Truth*. Cf. especially, Segelberg, "Confirmation Homily," and Jansen, "Spuren." While the author clearly utilizes images and themes widespread in early Christian ritual practice, the fact that such themes are well-known and widely used in early Christian literature precludes any simple inference about a liturgical setting for the work. The following chart illustrates the symbolic oppositions of nakedness and being clothed. The reception of the revelation provided by Christ reverses the process inaugurated by Oblivion. There is an ellipse in the presentation of the symbolic opposition, since the clothing of humanity in "perishable rags" is only implicit.

Humanity:	"made naked by oblivion" (20,37–38)	:	clothed in perishable rags (Cf. Gen 3:6–7)
Christ:	"strips off perishable rags" (20,30–31)	:	"clothed in the book and in imperishability" (20,32)

[51] *Gos. Truth* I,3:21,3–5.
[52] *Gos. Truth* I,3:21,26.
[53] *Gos. Truth* I,3:21,27–31.
[54] *Gos. Truth* I,3:21,6–22,37.
[55] *Gos. Truth* I,3:22,38–23,18.
[56] *Gos. Truth* I,3:22,36–37.
[57] *Gos. Truth* I,3:23,3–5.
[58] *Gos. Truth* I,3:23,11.

may appear complex, it is ultimately simple and the formal unity of the message mirrors its material unity; it is a message about the unity of the Father and the beings dependent on him.[59]

The enunciation of the theme of unity, followed by a hymnic section on the Wisdom and Word of the Father,[60] concludes the first major segment of the text.[61] Thereupon, the image of the book is abandoned, but the author's literary method of making the ordinary unusual continues.

The image of the shepherd[62] offers a second example of the same technique. The passage is rich in allusions to gospel material, particularly to the synoptic parable of the shepherd.[63] These allusions, however, develop into the famous numerological symbolism explaining the significance of 99 and 100. While the details of the symbolism are hardly transparent,[64] the basic point of the allegory is clear. Jesus is the shepherd who provides perfection to the lost sheep which he draws up from the pit. This act provides "interior knowledge,"[65] enabling its recipients to speak from the "day from above, which has no night" and "from the light which does not sink."[66] Here, a group of traditions and widespread images are combined to provide a new application of the basic pastoral image.

---

[59] Cf. especially Gos. Truth I,3:24,9–25,19.

[60] Gos. Truth I,3:23,18–24,9.

[61] There have been many attempts to analyze the structure of the work. Cf. Grobel, Gospel of Truth; Story, Truth; H.-M. Schenke, Herkunft; and Ménard, L'Évangile de Vérité, who largely follows Schenke. The most elaborate analysis of the work's structure has been proposed by Fecht ("Der erste 'Teil'") although his detailed analysis only extends through 22,20. Colpe, "Überlieferung," builds upon Fecht's work.

While all the proposed structural analyses offer some insight into the complexities of the work, none is entirely satisfactory, for the Gospel of Truth defies a single simple structural explanation. Standaert's description of the author's technique is apt, "La pensée evolue telle une abeille qui butine de fleur en fleur, a-t-on même écrit très joliment . . ." ("L'Évangile de Vérité," 245).

Any analysis of the structure needs to recognize the function of two discrete sections of the text, the hymnic material of 23,18–24,9 and the exhortation of 32,31–33,32, which mark major divisions in the text.

[62] Gos. Truth I,3:31,35–32,30.

[63] Matt 18:12–14; Luke 15:4–7; cf. also John 10.

[64] For discussion of the symbolism, see the remarks of Grobel, Gospel of Truth, 129–31; Ménard, L'Évangile de Vérité, 150–51; Marrou, "Diffusion"; and Poirier, "L'Évangile de Vérité." The imagery can be interpreted in several ways. Basically it seems to provide a model of the process of redemption which follows the reception of revealing gnosis. That process involves a movement from the inferior (material, left) to the superior (spiritual, right). The process also involves the attainment of unity, just as it is the number 1 which is involved in the shift from 99, counted on the left hand, and 100, counted on the right.

[65] Gos. Truth I,3:32,38. Note that lines 38 and 39 on this page were meant to follow line 23. They were accidentally omitted by the scribe, who wrote them at the bottom of the page with sigla indicating their proper placement.

[66] Gos. Truth I,3:32,26–31.

The passage on the shepherd is followed by another highly structured segment of the text which apparently concludes the second major portion of the argument. Here the literary technique of the work is particularly evident. The passage[67] consists of a series of exhortations, remarkable, initially at least, for their attention to ordinary physical needs ("make firm the foot of those who have stumbled . . . feed those who are hungry . . . give repose to those who are weary"); yet, the familiar soon becomes unfamiliar. In the exhortations to "raise up those who wish to rise and awaken those who are asleep,"[68] the metaphorical quality of the injunctions becomes clear, and one may detect a metaphorical significance even within the opening hortatory salvo. The exhortations become less usual as the section proceeds and the author urges his audience to "be concerned with yourselves,"[69] and finally grounds his imperatives in the indicative dictated by his fundamental theology, "do the will of the Father, for you are from him."[70]

One could construe these injunctions as esoteric, metaphorical invitations to spread the gnostic gospel, and they may indeed have been perceived as such by members of the author's audience who shared his basic perspective. They could, however, just as easily be construed as operating in a way similar to expository sections of the text, namely, by trading on what was familiar in the general Christian tradition, and gradually transforming it into a new mode.

One final example of the author's literary procedure may be cited. In the final segment of the text one finds the much discussed passage on the Son as the name of the Father.[71] Since the roots of the language and conceptuality of this pericope have frequently been explored, it is sufficient to note that the basic categories with which our author operates derive from a variety of sources familiar to second-century Christians, such as the inherited Jewish speculations on the divine name; New Testament passages such as John 17 or Philippians 2, which may reflect such speculations and which describe the divine name as being borne or revealed by Jesus; and second-century Christological reflections on Christ as the Word.

What the author does with the theme of the name bears some relationship to these various speculative strands; although his development of it is not simply a reproduction of any one of them. At the risk of

---

[67] Gos. Truth I,3:32,32–33,32.

[68] Gos. Truth I,3:33,6–8.

[69] Gos. Truth I,3:33,1–30.

[70] Gos. Truth I,3:33,31–32.

[71] Cf., e.g., Orbe, Procesión del Verbo, 68–97; Ménard, "Élucubrations"; Dubois, "Contexte"; and Fineman, "Piety."

oversimplifying the complex dialectic on the Father's name, one may note that it basically makes two affirmations. The first asserts that the Son bears the name of the Father.[72] The second, and more important, asserts that the Son functions as the name of the Father, indicating the reality of the object named.[73] The first affirmation is in some ways a "familiar" element, reflecting especially the New Testament's remarks about Jesus and the divine name. It should be noted, however, that the precise name which Jesus bears is not specified, an observation which bears on the meaning of the term "name" itself, to which we shall return presently. The second affirmation, that Jesus reveals the Father, is also, to a degree, familiar; yet, here Jesus reveals the Father in virtue of the fact that he is the Father's name.[74] At this point, the familiar becomes strangely unfamiliar.

The passage on the Son as name owes its subtlety and obscurity, in part, to the fluidity of the term "name" itself, a fluidity or polyvalence similar to the development of the image of the "book." The significance of the term "name" fluctuates, in fact, between two poles. On the one hand, the name is external to the thing named. Hence, the Son, as name, is distinct from the Father whom he names.[75] On the other hand, the name is the essence of the thing named and is thus identical with it.[76] Hence, the Son, as name, is identical with the Father.[77] The relationship between these two, apparently contradictory, notions about the name becomes more transparent when one realizes that in this superficially epistemological discussion important ontological principles are being affirmed. In this complex interplay of traditional language about language with a particular metaphysics and theology, the unfamiliarity of the text is most obvious. The two contrary affirmations about the status or function of the Son as name are simply ways of speaking about the intimate relation of Father and Son. The Son is the name of the Father in the second sense (i.e., is the essence of the Father), because that

---

[72] Gos. Truth I,3:38,11–12: "He gave him his name which belonged to him," and 40,26: "he gave the name to him."

[73] Gos. Truth I,3:30,25–28.

[74] Contrast the complexity of the treatment of the name in the Gospel of Truth with the much simpler and more logical treatment of the name "Son" in the Tri. Trac. I,5:51, 14–15.

[75] E.g., the Son, as "name," "comes forth from the Father," Gos. Truth I,3:28,9.

[76] E.g., "the name is invisible because it alone is the mystery of the invisible" (Gos. Truth I,3:38,17–19). The epistemological and semantic roots of the theory expressed here may be found in the Greek philosophical tradition. Cf. especially the theory of natural names in Plato, Cra. 383A and Aristotle's discussion of the meaning of οὐσία in Metaph. Z, where it is seen to be primarily the τὸ τί ἦν εἶναι or "essence," which is expressed in a definition: ὥστε τὸ τί ἦν εἶναι ἐστιν ὅσων ὁ λόγος ἐστιν ὁρισμός (1030a6). Cf. also 1030b4–6, 1031a12–14, 1032b1–2.

[77] Gos. Truth I,3:38,9.

which comes forth from the Father is the Father himself.[78] In the language of later Christological dogma, the Son is *homoousios* (i.e., one in being) with the Father.[79] The Son is the name of the Father in the first sense (i.e., the visible pointer to the invisible reality of the Father) because he does indeed "come forth."

Consequently, the familiar first and second-century Christological speculation and early creedal affirmations are here transformed. The text does so not simply in order to wrestle with a fundamental Christological problem, the like of which troubled theologians from the second to the fourth centuries and beyond, but primarily in order to convey the same sort of insight suggested by the earlier intricate metaphorical developments of the image of the "book." The subject of this whole work, the revelation provided by the gospel, is—obliquely to be sure[80]— conveyed in this passage. The gospel proclaimed by Jesus provides insight for its recipients into their essential identity with the transcendent source of all reality. The agent of the revelation is capable of awakening that insight because, in a primary sense,[81] he is identical with that reality. He and his revelation provide not only extrinsic information about, but effective unity with,[82] that transcendent reality. When those on whom the name (Son = essence of Father) rests "utter the name" along with both Father and Son,[83] this unity is expressed and experienced.

III. The "Unfamiliar" Features

The phenomenon which we have been exploring has focused on one type of material in the *Gospel of Truth*, which, for convenience, has been labeled the "familiar," that is, images, motifs, and terminology which appear to be widespread in early Christianity and closely related to texts that eventually came to be associated with orthodoxy. The literary dynamics of the text can also be illuminated by an examination of the less familiar, more typically gnostic, elements of the work. Here

---

[78] Gos. Truth I,3:38,9.

[79] For a similar affirmation of the consubstantiality of the Father and Son, cf. *Tri. Trac.* I,5:56,1–58,18 and the comments ad loc. in the notes to the text in Attridge-Pagels, "Tripartite Tractate."

[80] This discussion of the passage on the Son as name has necessarily overlooked a number of exegetical difficulties which contribute to the obscurity of the text at this point. For a fuller treatment, see the notes in Attridge-MacRae, "Gospel of Truth."

[81] The Son "did not receive the name on loan" (40,9–10), but it is the proper name (κύριον ὄνομα). For similar language about the divine names, cf. *Tri. Trac.* I,5:51,8–52,6.

[82] Cf. Gos. Truth I,3:25,3–24; 26,33–27,4.

[83] Gos. Truth I,3:38,25–32.

the inverse procedure seems to obtain: the unfamiliar is, to some extent, domesticated.

Nowhere is this more clear than in the discussion of Error or *Planē* at 17,5–19,23. The discussion of the Valentinian affiliations of the work has often centered on this pericope and on the cosmogonic myth which the text may presuppose.[84] That some such myth is presupposed is suggested in particular by the remark that "for this reason, Error became powerful. It set about creating, with (all its) might preparing, in beauty, a substitute for the truth."[85] Error also emerges as a quasi-personal force or power in the remark that she (or it) grew angry at the revealer and persecuted him.[86] The second personification, however, already makes difficult the attempt to identify the sources of the image. While the cosmogonic function of Error parallels that of Sophia, Error in persecuting Jesus belies that identification, since Sophia "Wisdom" nowhere is said to act in that way.

If there is a cosmogonic myth of the Sophia variety behind our text, it is well concealed. There are two important dimensions to that process of concealment, the first and most important of which is the studied ambiguity in the use of the motif of Error. The second is a similarity in the motif's deployment to Pauline language.

One difficulty in assessing the provenance and affiliation of Error is that the use of the term fluctuates between personification of a cosmic force and a psychological category. Such fluctuation, while not unusual in gnostic and other early Christian literature, is particularly striking here. On the one hand, there are passages (already cited) which suggest that Error is a potent objective force.[87] On the other hand, there are passages where such cosmic dimensions are lacking.[88] Because similar ambiguity affects other related central terms such as "oblivion"[89] and "deficiency,"[90] it would appear that the fluidity and polyvalence of the terminology constitute a deliberate and systematic attempt to prohibit a single, simple application of any of the key terms to cosmic or personal psychological spheres.[91]

The author of the text may have found a particular model for his use

---

[84] Cf., e.g., Jonas, *Gnostic Religion*, 309–19; Haardt, "Struktur"; Ménard, *"Plane"*; Finnestad, "Fall"; and Heldermann, "Isis."

[85] *Gos. Truth* I,3:17,14–20.

[86] *Gos. Truth* I,3:18,21–23.

[87] *Gos. Truth* I,3:17,14–20; 18,21–23; 26,19–20.

[88] *Gos. Truth* I,3:17,28; 22,21–24; 31,25; 32,37.

[89] *Gos. Truth* I,3:17,33; 18,1; 18,10; 18,18; 20,38; 21,36.

[90] *Gos. Truth* I,3:24,21; 25,1; 35,8–9; 35,33–36,13.

[91] On the intentional ambiguity of the author's language, cf. Standaert, "L'Évangile de Vérité," 258–60.

of language in such Pauline texts as Rom 5:12–6:14, where Sin and
Death appear as personified cosmic powers, although it is clear that Paul
understands these terms as pertaining primarily to the personal, human
sphere.[92] While the categories of the Gospel of Truth reflect the particular, gnostic orientation of the author, their deployment is, when
compared to such early Christian texts as Romans, hardly unfamiliar.

Another "unfamiliar," distinctively gnostic, or even Valentinian element, in the text is a suggested partition of humanity into several
classes.[93] The presence of such an anthropological theory has, in fact,
been disputed,[94] and it must be admitted that the evidence is weak.
There is certainly no explicit distinction between pneumatics, psychics
and hylics. Indeed, the text seems to treat all offspring of the Father as
members of a single group. Nonetheless, there are a few indications that
a more complex theory is presupposed in the text. Some passages divide
humanity into at least two groups, those who ultimately accept and those
who ultimately reject the saving revelation of the Gospel of Truth. The
former are "those who will receive teaching,"[95] whose names are
"inscribed in the book of the living,"[96] whose "names have been
called,"[97] who "are from above."[98] One passage developing the imagery
of the jars contrasts the two groups as full vessels to empty ones.[99] The
text once identifies the second group in recognizable and common
Valentinian terms: "the material ones are strangers."[100]

These references to two contrasting types of human beings, together
with the various remarks made about them in the text, suggest the
spirituals and hylics of gnostic anthropology. Particularly problematic,
however, for those who see the text as Valentinian is the lack of any
explicit reference to psychics.

The one passage where there may be an allusion to the third, intermediate class of human beings appears toward the end of the text. After
a lengthy discussion of the soteriology proper to the first class[101] (which

---

[92] Cf. esp. Rom 4:12; 6:1; 6:15.

[93] The significance of the Valentinian anthropological theory continues to be a matter
of dispute. Cf. Schottroff, "Animae"; Mühlenberg, "Erlösungen"; Aland, "Herakleon";
Pagels, "Valentinian Eschatology" and McCue, "Valentinianism."

[94] See, e.g., H.-M. Schenke, Herkunft, 22.

[95] Gos. Truth I,3:21,2.

[96] Gos. Truth I,3:21,4–5.

[97] Gos. Truth I,3:21,25–34.

[98] Gos. Truth I,3:22,3–4.

[99] Gos. Truth I,3:26,10–15. The text may here echo Pauline language; cf. Rom 9:22–23; 2
Cor 4:7. At the same time there may be here a further development of the image of Error
working on matter (17,14–20).

[100] Gos. Truth I,3:31,1.

[101] Gos. Truth I,3:41,14–42,39.

for convenience we may call the pneumatics, though the term is absent from the text), the author affirms that "for the rest, may they know in their places, that it is not fitting for me . . . to speak of anything else."[102] This remark hardly pertains to the "material ones," because the author has commented frequently on this group. It would seem, then, that the people in view here are members of neither class to which reference has been made, but constitute a third group.

The language of the allusive comment supports the suggestion, for such people are invited to know something, implying that they are not totally beyond the pale of revelation. Furthermore, they are said to be "in their places." This comment would be insignificant were it not for the technical sense of the term "place" in the preceding discussion. There, the pneumatics[103] are said to ascend in thought to that place which is their root.[104] They thus, in other words, anticipate through the reception of gnōsis an eschatological return "to the source of their being." This eschatological or proleptic reintegration into one's proper place is apparently not possible for the hylics, who have neither root nor fruit[105] and who do not intellectually "ascend" to the Father because of their mistaken belief in their own autonomous existence.[106] Thus, the expressions "the rest" and "in their places"[107] presuppose a third group distinct from both pneumatics and hylics.

There is one further argument to support the hypothesis that the author of the Gospel of Truth has in mind a tripartite division of humanity. In a section already mentioned where the text describes the soteriology of the pneumatics, there is an allusion to their understanding of the Father. They think of him not as "small," "harsh," or "wrathful," but as "a being without evil, imperturbable, gentle, knowing all spaces before they come into existence."[108] This description of the understanding of the nature of God resembles what is characterized elsewhere in gnostic literature generally, and Valentinian literature in particular, as the inadequate theology of psychics.[109] While this does not conclusively demonstrate that the author works with a tripartite anthropology, it does suggest that this section of the text owes its description of pneumatic beings to a distinction between pneumatics and psychics.

One final detail is relevant to this topic. On several occasions the text

---

[102] Gos. Truth I,3:42,39–43,2.
[103] Or emanations or pleromas, cf. Gos. Truth I,3:41,15–16.
[104] Gos. Truth I,3:41,24–26.
[105] Gos. Truth I,3:28,16–17.
[106] Gos. Truth I,3:28,20–24.
[107] Gos. Truth I,3:42,39–40.
[108] Gos. Truth I,3:42,5–9.
[109] Cf. Ptolemy's Letter to Flora, in Epiph. Pan. 33.3.2–7. Cf. also Tri. Trac. I,5:110,22–113,1.

refers rather obscurely to the revealer "coming into the midst."[110] This language has biblical parallels,[111] but they do not fully account for the unusual usage of the phrase in the text. At best, they illustrate once again the interplay between familiar and unfamiliar in the work. The absolute use of the term "midst" or "middle" may well reflect a cosmological scheme, apparent in many other gnostic works, where the realm dominated by psychic forces is the stage on which the drama of redemption is played out.[112]

The anthropology of the Gospel of Truth illustrates clearly that the author does not offer anything like a systematic account either of the whole soteriological process or of the division among humankind effected by the Savior's appearance.[113] There are enough hints, however, to indicate that some such systematic account is presupposed. The author's reticence on this score is easy enough to understand if the text is designed primarily as an exoteric work. The Valentinian doctrines of the three classes of humanity were among the more offensive elements of the school's teaching, to judge from the severe criticism of these doctrines by opponents of the school.

IV. Conclusion

If our reading of the literary dynamics of the Gospel of Truth is correct, then the discussion of Error and the allusions to the recipients of gnōsis represent the obverse of the coin presented by the biblical imagery of the work, and the text becomes a carefully constructed attempt to domesticate the unusual and to minimize the potentially problematic. At the same time, through a careful manipulation of traditional imagery, the text inculcates and reinforces a fundamental theological perspective that stands in some tension with important elements of that traditional material.

This analysis explains why there has been so much debate about the Valentinian affiliation of the Gospel of Truth: the text conceals major elements of the system which it presupposes. While one consequence of this position is that a firm determination of the affiliations of the work is probably impossible, it still remains highly likely that the work is based on some form, and possibly a highly developed form, of Valentinian theology. The work itself simply does not provide enough information to decide the question of where that form fits in the development of Valentinian theory.

---

[110] Cf. ei ⲁⲧⲙⲏⲧⲉ, similarly at 19,19; 20,9–10; 26,4–5; 26,27–28.
[111] Cf. Luke 24:36; John 20:19, 26.
[112] Cf. Iren. Haer. I.7.5 and Pistis Sophia, passim.
[113] Contrast Tri. Trac. I,5:118,14–124,25.

12

EXEGESIS AND EXPOSITION
OF THE GENESIS CREATION ACCOUNTS
IN SELECTED TEXTS FROM NAG HAMMADI

Elaine H. Pagels

Princeton University welcomed Elaine Pagels as Harrison Spear Paine Professor
of Religion in 1982. Professor Pagels distinguished herself early in her career
through her first two books (*The Johannine Gospel in Gnostic Exegesis*, 1973;
The Gnostic Paul: Gnostic Exegesis of the Pauline Letters, 1975) as well as
numerous articles appearing in the *Journal of Biblical Literature*, *Harvard
Theological Review*, *Interpreter's Dictionary of the Bible*, and many other
journals. She participates in numerous professional societies including the
American Academy of Religion and the Society of Biblical Literature, where she
chaired the section on Nag Hammadi for six years.

Professor Pagels' current responsibilities as a member of the Coptic Gnostic
Library Project of the Institute for Antiquity and Christianity include co-
authorship (with Harold Attridge, Helmut Koester, and John Turner) of introductions and textual notes for four of the Nag Hammadi texts.

Professor Pagels is best known outside of academic circles for her third book,
The Gnostic Gospels, 1979, which won the National Book Award and the
National Book Critic's Circle Award, and has been translated into fourteen
languages. Each chapter of *The Gnostic Gospels* first appeared in scholarly form
in the above mentioned journals.

Preface

D rawing upon a selection of Nag Hammadi texts, this paper investigates a wide range of gnostic exegeses of Genesis 1-3. Comparison of such texts as the *Testimony of Truth*, *Apocryphon of John*,
Exegesis on the Soul, and *Hypostasis of the Archons* suggests that their
authors concern themselves not only with "cosmological speculation," as
scholars too often have assumed, but equally with practical issues—

specifically, issues concerning sexual behavior: marriage, procreation, celibacy.

A comparison of the *Testimony of Truth* and the *Apocryphon of John* shows, for example, how different gnostic authors can use contrasting hermeneutical methods to validate the same practical conclusion: namely, that sexuality is directly—but antithetically—related to spirituality.

The *Hypostasis of the Archons*, finally, as scholars have recognized, draws upon a wide range of sources, and uses a common gnostic scheme (cf. *On the Origin of the World*) in order to present an elaborate mythical exegesis of Genesis 1–3. This paper demonstrates, however, that the *Hypostasis of the Archons* draws upon another body of sources its author values as much as the Genesis accounts themselves: the letters of Paul (or, alternatively, written sources upon which Paul himself drew). Comparison of Greek and Coptic parallel passages shows that the author of the *Hypostasis of the Archons*, interpreting Genesis 1–3, closely follows, in dramatic sequence and in terminology, Paul's own exegesis of Genesis 2, which he gives in 1 Cor 15:43ff. Then, turning from the theme of creation to revelation, the author draws especially upon such passages as 1 Corinthians 2, to show how the archons, "being psychic, could not grasp the things that are spiritual" (cf. 1 Cor 2:14; *Hyp. Arch.* II,4:87,17–18). So, confusing spiritual with sexual knowledge, they failed to grasp the hidden power of Wisdom, "whom none of the archons of this age knew" (cf. 1 Cor 2:7–8). The *Hypostasis of the Archons*, far from being superficially "Christianized," draws its specific structure and much of its terminology from the only authority the author actually cites—the "spirit-inspired apostle," Paul.

Diverse as their hermeneutical methods are, these gnostic authors agree on the same practical conclusions, requiring celibacy of all truly "gnostic" Christians.

I. Introduction

Gnostic authors, fascinated by the creation accounts of Genesis 1–3, often incorporated these into their theological and mythological constructions. But what is it about the creation accounts that so fascinates the gnostics? What do they hope to understand or "explain" from their own diverse exegeses?

What Clement, Irenaeus, and Hippolytus told us long ago—that gnostics abused the scriptures to construct their own "bizarre inventions"—appears confirmed by recently discovered texts. Contemporary scholars, however, attempting to answer the same questions, usually attribute such exegesis to gnostic "interest in cosmological and theological speculation." This observation, so far as it goes, states the obvious. Such texts as the *Apocryphon of John, Hypostasis of the Archons,* and *On the Origin of the World,* elaborating dazzling images of the heavenly hierarchies and narrating complex interplay between celestial and demonic forces, certainly do evince their authors' concern with issues of cosmology, theodicy, and anthropology. But closer investigation of specific elements in such texts—in particular, their exegesis of such passages as Gen 1:28 and 2:24-25—suggests another perspective. What motivates these authors, as much as any interest in cosmological speculation, is common concern with urgent *practical* matters, especially sexual desire, intercourse, marriage, and procreation.

Clement of Alexandria, attacking "heretics" whose teaching deprecates the God of creation, directly connects such doctrines, above all, with implications for sexual practices. Clement challenges those who claim that marriage is "an invention of the law" to make their practices consistent: "Why do you not oppose all the commandments? For (the Lord) said, 'Increase and multiply' (Gen 1:28). You who are opposed to the creator ought to abstain from sexual relations altogether."[1] Some heretics, Clement admits, agreed with him, explicitly linking doctrine with practice. But their continence itself, he charges, serves only "to blaspheme . . . both the creator and the creation," since they teach "that one must reject marriage and procreation."[2]

Their orthodoxy notwithstanding, Clement and his colleagues wrestled with the same problems that engaged their opponents. How might Christians, in the light of Christ's revelations, obey the divine order established, in Jesus' words, "from the beginning" (cf. Mark 10:6, par.)? Those passages traditionally read as divine commands instituting procreation and marriage—Gen 1:28 and 2:23-24—presented particularly thorny problems. Throughout the early centuries of Christian history the exegesis of the Genesis creation accounts—and their practical implications—formed a storm center of controversy.

Concern with the sexual ethos of Genesis 1-3, was, of course, shared by Christians with the majority of their Jewish predecessors and contemporaries. As early as the second century B.C.E., Jewish teachers often introduced passages from the creation accounts into discussions of sexual practices. The author of *Jubilees,* for example, cites passages from

---

[1] Clem. Alex., *Strom.* 3.37 (Oulton-Chadwick, *Alexandrian Christianity*), 56.
[2] Clem. Alex., *Strom.* 3.45 (Oulton-Chadwick, *Alexandrian Christianity*), 61.

the creation accounts to promote strict observance of the laws on sexual purity and nakedness;[3] the author of the *Apocalypse of Moses* reads into Genesis his own deprecating view of sexual intercourse;[4] the author of *Testament of the Twelve Patriarchs* sees there warnings against sexual pleasure;[5] and Ben Sira agrees with many others that Genesis 2-3 offers reasons for avoiding women.[6] Philo simultaneously builds into his various exegeses warnings against sexual pleasure, women, and sexual acts not conducive to procreation.[7] Rabbinic literature echoes and amplifies, of course, many of the same themes.[8] Jesus himself, according to synoptic tradition, mentions the Paradise story only once, citing Gen 1:27 and 2:24 to answer a practical question concerning the grounds for divorce.[9] Paul invokes the latter passage to warn against intercourse with prostitutes;[10] he knows from Genesis 2 that Christian women, like their Jewish contemporaries, must accept subordination to men in worship as well as in the social order.[11] This use of the creation accounts does not surprise us, for anthropological studies have shown how, in various cultures, creation accounts establish as if "in the nature of things" the generally accepted values of a given society.[12]

Jesus' and Paul's pronouncements raised, however, more problems than they solved. Controversies concerning the correct interpretation of Genesis 1-3 split second-century Christian groups into hostile factions, driving a wedge between radically ascetic Christians, who insisted that "the gospel" abolished procreation and marriage, and the Valentinians, who took an equally radical but opposite position, namely, that Christ sanctified marriage, at least for gnostic Christians. Furthermore, such controversy divided both ascetics and Valentinians, in turn, from groups represented by such teachers as Clement who claimed that Genesis, read through the teachings of Jesus and Paul, both affirms and trans-forms Christian sexual practice.[13] The aim of this paper is to explore the *Testimony of Truth, Apocryphon of John, Exegesis on the Soul,* and *Hypostasis of the Archons* to see how these authors, equally obsessed with the Genesis creation accounts, interpret their theological—and practical—meaning.

---

[3] On purity laws, cf. *Jub.* 3:4–12; on nakedness, esp. 3:26–32 (Charles, *APOT*).

[4] Cf., for example, *Apoc. Mos.* 19:3–21:6 (von Tischendorf, *Apocalypses Apocryphae*; or *Revelation of Moses, ANF*, 8.565–70).

[5] *T. Reub.* 2:1–9; 4. Cf. Genesis 6 to *T. Reub.* 5:1–7 (Charles, *APOT*).

[6] *Sir* 25:24–26 (Charles, *APOT*); for discussion, cf. Trenchard, *Ben Sira*.

[7] Cf., for some examples, Wegner, "Image of Woman."

[8] For only a few examples, cf. *Midr. Gen. Rab.* 17.8; 18.2; 20.11; 22.2.

[9] Cf. Mark 10:2–9, 10–12, par.

[10] 1 Cor 6:16.

[11] 1 Cor 11:2–11.

[12] Cf. Douglas, *Symbols*, 77–92.

[13] Pagels, "Controversies concerning Marriage."

II. The Testimony of Truth

The author of the Testimony of Truth, while affirming teaching that Clement condemns (that marriage is "an invention of the law"), avoids the inconsistency with which Clement charges other "heretics." Referring indirectly to Gen 1:28 and 2:24–25, the author of the Testimony of Truth sees the law's "defilement" manifested especially in the commands to "take a husband or a wife, and to beget, and to multiply."[14] Whoever fulfills the law by engaging in sexual intercourse (or, worse, by taking pleasure in it) thereby enslaves himself to the "archon of [darkness],"[15] the "archon of the womb."[16] Sayings like Luke 16:16 ("The law and the prophets were until John") and Luke 7:28 ("among those born of women none is greater than John; yet he who is least in the Kingdom of God is greater than he") seem to underlie the author's symbolic exegesis of John's baptism:

> The Jordan river is the power of the body, that is, the senses of pleasures. The water of the Jordan is the desire for sexual intercourse. John is the ruler of the womb.[17]

John's own birth, initiated through sexual intercourse, stands in direct antithesis to the birth of Jesus.[18] The Spirit's descent, effecting his virgin birth and signalling his baptism, ends "the domination of carnal procreation"[19] initiated, apparently, through Adam and Eve. Christ himself, appearing in the form of the serpent, taught the primordial parents the folly of obeying the creator, opening "the eyes of (their) mind."[20] Receiving gnōsis "knowledge," they responded immediately by covering their genitals.

What the exegesis of the Genesis story here only suggests, the author elsewhere states explicitly. The author intends to lay aside "loquacity and disputations"[21] to concern himself or herself above all with "deeds" which alone distinguish true followers of Christ from their imitators: "[Those that are] from the seed [of Adam] are manifested by their [deeds] which are their work."[22] Even professed Christians, the author says, fail-

---

[14] Testim. Truth IX,3:29,26–30,4. Translation from Pearson, Codices IX and X, 122–203. For a discussion of this specific point, cf. p. 103.

[15] Testim. Truth IX,3:30,16.

[16] Testim. Truth IX,3:31,4–5.

[17] Testim. Truth IX,3:30,30–31,5.

[18] Testim. Truth IX,3:45,6–18.

[19] Testim. Truth IX,3:30,30.

[20] Testim. Truth IX,3:46,7, cf. Pearson, "Haggadic Traditions"; van Unnik, "Neid" and Nagel, "Auslegung."

[21] Testim. Truth IX,3:44,8–9.

[22] Testim. Truth IX,3:67,9–11.

ing to understand Christ spiritually,[23] "follow the law and obey it,"[24] including the commands to marry and procreate; and "not only that": for sake of pleasure alone "they have intercourse while they are giving suck."[25]

Apparently on the same basis—a concern for practice, not doctrine—this author censures certain gnostic teachers: Isidore and Basilides, who accept the validity of marriage;[26] the Simonians, who "take [wives] (and) beget children";[27] and certain Valentinians who allow (or even advocate) marital intercourse among allegedly gnostic Christians.[28]

Accompanied by such "deeds," profession of faith means nothing. No less than Clement, this author insists upon direct correlation between doctrine and practice, and censures an immature concern with the body both in faith and in corresponding action. Professing faith in Jesus' incarnation and bodily resurrection, for example, they advocate and practice martyrdom.[29] But if the "sons of Adam" manifest their affiliation with their prototype through their deeds, those who belong to Christ manifest theirs through opposite action: "he who is able to renounce (money and sexual intercourse) shows [that] he is [from] the generation of the [son of man], and has the power to accuse them."[30] The law joins male and female; the word of the cross, on the other hand, divides "the males from the females" and "separates us from the error of the angels."[31]

The author of the Testimony of Truth bases this antithesis between marriage (ordained by the law) and celibate renunciation (initiated through Christ's word) upon a literal—and negative—reading of Gen 1:28 and 2:24–25. Other ascetically inclined exegetes often understood the description in Gen 2:18 of the divine intention to send Adam a feminine "helper" as the end of Adam's pure and solitary communion with God—in Philo's words, "the beginning of all evils."[32] Yet others,

---

[23] Testim. Truth IX,3:50,1–2.

[24] Testim. Truth IX,3:50,8–9.

[25] Testim. Truth IX,3:67,30–31.

[26] Testim. Truth IX,3:57,6, cf. Clem. Alex., Strom. 3.1.

[27] Testim. Truth IX,3:58,2–4.

[28] Testim. Truth IX,3:56,1–7. Pearson (Codices IX and X, 116), noting doctrinal parallels between the author of the Testimony of Truth and Valentinian gnosticism, comments, "Yet, as we have seen, our gnostic author regards the Valentinian Gnostics as foremost among the 'heretics' and 'schismatics'!" The apparent paradox may be resolved if the basis of our author's opposition concerns not doctrine so much as the practice they advocate: cf. Clem. Alex., Strom. 3.1; Iren. Haer. I.6.1; cf. Pagels, "Controversies concerning Marriage."

[29] Testim. Truth IX,3:34,1–37,9.

[30] Testim. Truth IX,3:68,8–12.

[31] Testim. Truth IX,3:40,25; 41,4.

[32] Philo, Op. Mund., 152.

while agreeing with the author of the *Testimony of Truth's* negative view of sexual differentiation, procreation, and marriage, adopted opposite hermeneutical patterns. Some, reading "spiritually," that is, symbolically, both the injunction to "be fruitful and multiply" (Gen 1:28) as well as the accounts of Eve's creation (Gen 2:18) and Adam's recognition of her (2:24-25), claimed to find in these very passages inspiration for sexual renunciation.

III. The Apocryphon of John

The author of the *Apocryphon of John*, for example, reads in Gen 2:24 a "spiritual" meaning. He explains that Adam's divinely sent helper, far from being a mere human partner, manifests the luminous *epinoia* "intelligence" called Zōē, who "helps the whole creation" as she teaches Adam in order to restore him to his *plērōma* "fulness."[33] Genesis 2:24-25, read "spiritually," then, initiates not his degrading involvement with carnal marriage, but rather his restoration to primordial union with his spiritual *syzygos* "counterpart."

When Adam first sees beside himself the woman formed by the creator, the luminous *epinoia* appears simultaneously, so that he recognizes in her his "counterimage,"[34] the spiritual power of Sophia. Adam expresses this act of spiritual recognition in an amplified version of Gen 2:24-25:[35]

> "This is indeed bone from my bones, and flesh of my flesh." Therefore the man will "leave his father and his mother and he will cleave to his wife, and they will both be one flesh, for they will send him his consort, and he will leave his father and his mother . . . <'His mother' is> our sister Sophia, she who came down in innocence, in order to rectify her deficiency. Therefore she was called Life, which is, "the mother of the living" (cf. Gen 3:20).

Adam's experience prefigures that of the gnostic Christian, who, while imprisoned within the body, is awakened, like Adam, and raised from the "deep sleep" of ignorance, when the *pronoia* "forethought" of the pure light, the "thought of the virginal spirit" appears to him.[36]

Whence, then, the fierce resistance to spiritual revelation that human

---

[33] *Ap. John* BG8502,2:68:19; translation here from Giversen, *Apocryphon*. While awaiting the forthcoming volume of Codex II from the *Nag Hammadi Studies* series, I have referred to Giversen for his reconstruction of the Coptic text, checking this with Wisse's translation published in the *NHLE*, 98-116. Further citations follow Wisse's numeration and translation, except where indicated.

[34] *Ap. John* II,1:23,9.

[35] *Ap. John* II,1:23,10-24.

[36] *Ap. John* II,1:30,32-31,22.

beings experience, the internal opposition that hinders humanity from recognizing its spiritual "fulfillment"? To answer this question, among others, the author of the *Apocryphon of John* narrates a complex drama, played out in three stages: theological, cosmological, and anthropological. Underlying the whole drama is an assumption shared by many others that sexuality and spirituality are essentially—but antithetically— related energies: the first is the insidious, dark side of the second.

Without entering into the intricacies of the dramatic plot, let us note that this theme dominates the whole narrative. The author of the *Apocryphon of John* shares with other gnostics an ontological perspective in which all being, apart from the original Monad, is drawn by divine inspiration not toward solitude but toward communion.[37] Since each element of spiritual being is essentially interdependent, each strives toward union with its appropriate counterpart. But after one aeon— Sophia—fails to achieve harmonious union with the spirit, her masculine syzygos,[38] the cosmic drama expands in a series of broken symmetries. Yaldabaoth, born from Sophia's isolated energy, himself joins in a series of degrading unions, first with his *aponoia* "madness," a union that engenders the authorities.[39] Uniting himself with them in turn,[40] his deficient creative energies bring forth the cosmos and then the psychic form of Adam, each of which suffers from the same deficiencies.

The introduction of sexuality into human experience involves, at every stage, a series of hostile acts in the archontic powers' attempt to capture and enslave the human race for themselves. The chief archon, after joining with his powers to commit adultery with Sophia, sends his angels to the daughters of men to "raise offspring for their enjoyment" (cf. Genesis 6). Failing at first to accomplish this, "they created a despicable spirit who resembled the spirit who had descended, so as to pollute the souls through it," leading them into desires for material things, seducing them with "many deceits," and finally luring them into sexual union and procreation.[41]

As the *Apocryphon of John* describes it, the battle for control of Adam also proceeds in several stages. First the powers construct a psychic and material body that engenders in Adam the demonic impulses expressed in pleasure, desire, grief, and fear.[42] Because Adam received afterwards

---

[37] For discussion of the *schēma*, which the author of the *Apocryphon of John* shares, for example, with the Valentinians, cf. Pagels, "Controversies concerning Marriage."

[38] *Ap. John* II,1:9,25–35.

[39] *Ap. John* II,1:10,26–28.

[40] *Ap. John* II,1:12,10–12.

[41] *Ap. John* II,1:29,16–30,11.

[42] *Ap. John* II,1:15,13–19,15.

the luminous *epinoia*, the powers cast him in "earth and water and fire and the *pneuma* 'air' all of which originate in matter (the ignorance of darkness and desire) and in their opposing spirit (the tomb of the newly formed body)."[43] Finally, the powers place in Paradise the "tree of their life," whose "fruit is death, and desire is its seed."[44] After the serpent "taught (the man and the woman) to eat from wickedness, procreation, lust, and destruction,"[45] the man and woman found themselves bound in traditional marriage: the man dominates his wife, and she prepares herself for intercourse with him.[46] But the chief archon intervenes, himself seducing the woman. Through this act, which temporarily deprives her of spiritual life, "he planted sexual desire in her who belonged to Adam. And he produced through intercourse the copies of the bodies, and he inspired them with his opposing spirit."[47] As a result of these successive acts of violence, seduction, and betrayal, "sexual intercourse continued to the present day."[48]

Redemption occurs only for those in whom spiritual power overcomes the "despicable spirit," men and women, who, recognizing the presence of *pronoia* within themselves, renounce that hostile spirit and all its works. *Apocryphon of John* implies that they too, like Adam, by rejecting carnal marriage and procreation, receive restoration to that primordial spiritual marriage in union with the divine spirit.

IV. The Hypostasis of the Archons

The author of *Hypostasis of the Archons* shares with many other gnostic teachers the conviction that sexuality bears a direct but antithetical relation to spirituality. Like *Testimony of Truth*, *Hypostasis of the Archons* depicts the commands to marry and procreate as deceptions that lesser spiritual powers have invented to enslave humanity. And like *Apocryphon of John*, *Hypostasis of the Archons* uses the literary genre of *pesher* to comment on the Genesis creation accounts.[49] Birger Pearson characterizes the account of human creation in the *Hypostasis of the Archons* as "an epexegetical commentary on Gen 2.7 (and other passages), i.e., on how man derives his spiritual nature."[50] Here, Pearson observes, however, "traditional exegesis of Gen 2.7 has been overlaid

[43] Ap. John II,1:20,28–21,13.
[44] Ap. John II,1:21,34–35.
[45] Ap. John II,1:22,10–15.
[46] Ap. John II,1:23,37–24,3.
[47] Ap. John II,1:24,28–31.
[48] Ap. John II,1:24,26–27.
[49] Tardieu, Mythes, 23; Pearson, Terminology, 61.
[50] Pearson, Terminology, 73.

with new interpretations peculiar to this discussion."[51] What sources have contributed to such "new interpretations"? In his brief discussion, Pearson does not name them, but his analysis here and elsewhere agrees with other commentators that they are to be found in Jewish apocryphal sources as well as in such philosophical sources as Plato's *Timaeus*.[52] Bentley Layton concurs:[53]

> The plundering of Genesis 1–4, despite characteristic inversion of Scriptural categories, shows deep dependence upon Jewish sacred texts. The author, or his sources, also draws from a reservoir of apocryphal or parabiblical tradition.

Layton adds that the author of the *Hypostasis of the Archons* draws, however, upon another body of sources which is second in importance only to Genesis (or perhaps even equal to Genesis, being essential for his exegetical understanding): the letters of Paul.[54] As Layton points out, "the whole story is explicitly an elaboration of St. Paul's reference to the Christian struggle with malevolent rules and authorities of heaven."[55] The opening lines of the texts cite two passages attributed to "the great apostle, who is inspired by the spirit of the Father of truth," and signal the intention to read Genesis through Paul's eyes.

Although some commentators treat these lines either as a superficial attempt to "Christianize" the author's sources or as a gloss tacked on to non-catholic material by an hypothetical redactor,[56] our analysis suggests the opposite view. The author of the *Hypostasis of the Archons*, intending to read Genesis 1–3 "spiritually," closely follows and then mythically elaborates Paul's own exegesis of the creation account given in 1 Corinthians 15. Second, when the author turns from the theme of creation to revelation, he or she tends to read this process through passages such as 1 Corinthians 2 and Ephesians 3–5.

In saying this, I do not intend to deny, of course, that the author made use—often extensive use—of non-Christian images and sources as did the *Testimony of Truth* and the *Apocryphon of John*; nor do I intend to deny that the *Hypostasis of the Archons* draws on philosophical and mythical traditions and above all upon Jewish traditions concerning Adam's creation. This raises the following question: how has he or she (and other gnostic authors) incorporated and adapted such traditions into this specific exegesis of the creation accounts? Like many other

---

[51] Pearson, *Terminology*, 73.
[52] Pearson, *Terminology*, 51–81; cf. also id. "Haggadic Traditions."
[53] Layton, "Hypostasis." I follow Layton's text and translation here unless otherwise indicated. This is a point well-illustrated, as Layton notes, by Fallon's *Enthronement*.
[54] Layton, "Hypostasis," 373.
[55] Layton, "Hypostasis," 364.
[56] For the most recent example, cf. Barc, *L'Hypostase*; Roberge, *Norea*.

"spiritually minded" Christians, this author intends, while interweaving diverse materials into this exegesis, to read Genesis through the framework offered by the "spirit-inspired" apostle. I will return to this text below.

V. The Exegesis on the Soul

The *Exegesis on the Soul* offers a limited parallel. This text expresses the same antithesis found in *Testimony of Truth* and the *Apocryphon of John* between carnal marriage and procreation and their spiritual counterparts. Setting aside for the present the obvious differences between the texts, one may note a few basic similarities. Like the *Apocryphon of John*, *Exegesis on the Soul* describes the soul in isolation as essentially unstable. Drawn in two opposite directions, the soul must join either with the "opposing spirit" or with the holy spirit. Having fallen into the body and come into the "hands of many robbers,"[57] the soul suffers rape, or, at best, seduction.[58] What can release her from her spiritual and physical[59] prostitution?

Like the author of the *Apocryphon of John*, the author of the *Exegesis on the Soul* sees in Gen 2:24 not the problem but the beginning of its resolution. Citing the passage explicitly, this author (like the author of the *Apocryphon of John*) rejects the literal interpretation that refers it only to "the first man and woman," and to the institution of "carnal marriage."[60] Read "prophetically"[61] or symbolically, with the help of specific Pauline passages, Gen 2:24–25 signals the soul's restoration to her primordial spiritual union with her "true love, her real master."[62]

Having cited 1 Cor 5:9 and Eph 6:12 to show how the soul's prostitution leads to actual sexual immorality (in the author's understanding, to "prostitution of the body as well"),[63] the author can claim Paul's support for his exclusively symbolic reading of Gen 2:24, even invoking for this purpose passages generally read in reference to actual marriage.[64] Rejecting the literal meaning of Gen 1:28 and 2:24–25 and the practice they advocate, the author says, permits the soul to fulfill spiritually the prophetic significance of the Genesis commands. Freed from the bondage of "carnal marriage," burdened nonetheless "with the annoyance

---

[57] *Exeg. Soul* II,6:127,25–27; cf. *Ap. John* II,1:21,10–12.
[58] *Exeg. Soul* II,6:127,29–32.
[59] *Exeg. Soul* II,6:130,28–131,8.
[60] *Exeg. Soul* II,6:132,27–35.
[61] *Exeg. Soul* II,6:133,1.
[62] *Exeg. Soul* II,6:133,1–11.
[63] *Exeg. Soul* II,6:130,28–131,13.
[64] For example, Eph 5:23.

of physical desire,"[65] the soul joins in spiritual union with her heavenly
bridegroom, receiving from him "the seed that is the lifegiving spirit," to
fulfill "the great, perfect marvel of birth."[66]

VI. The Hypostasis of the Archons

Returning to the *Hypostasis of the Archons*, we recall again that our
author begins by invoking the authority of the "great apostle, inspired by
the spirit of God,"[67] to explain the nature of spiritual struggle. If quoting
from Col 1:13, the author may have in mind Paul's prayer that the
hearers be "filled with knowledge (ἐπίγνωσιν) of (the Father's) will, in all
wisdom and spiritual understanding (ἐν πάσῃ σοφίᾳ καὶ συνέσει πνευματικῇ, Col 1:9–10), for he or she interprets the Father's will[68] as it is
revealed through Eleleth (ⲦⲘⲚⲦⲢⲘⲚ̄Ϩ ⲏⲦ), which Layton takes as the
Coptic translation of σύνεσις[69] and Sophia (94,5). Σύνεσις and σοφία
become, in this account, hypostasized figures who reveal the spiritual
meaning of the primordial drama. As Col 1:15 describes the revelation of
the "image of the invisible God," so *Hypostasis of the Archons*, having
explained that "starting from the invisible world the visible world is
created,"[70] determines that although the "image of God" first appeared to
the authorities in the waters,[71] they failed to grasp that spiritual image:
"for psychics cannot grasp the things that are spiritual" (cf. 1 Cor 2:14).[72]

These opening passages already indicate the interplay of hermeneutics and theme that the rest of the text clearly demonstrates. Like
Basilides and the Valentinians, this author intends to take Pauline words
and phrases as veiled allusions to mythical acts, drawing out, as it were,
"the story behind the story." What Paul states either abstractly (cf. Col
1:9) or in principle (cf. 1 Cor 2:14) becomes in *Hypostasis of the Archons*
clues to each act of the primordial drama.

Some scholars, noting the peculiar character of "Pauline" passages

---

[65] *Exeg. Soul* II,6:132,27–133,15.
[66] *Exeg. Soul* II,6:133,31–134,5. Although striking, such exegetical practice is far from
unique. Tatian, Julius Cassianus, and the authors of the apocryphal Acts agree with this
author in reading the Corpus Paulinum (especially Ephesians) as advocates of total
renunciation of marriage and procreation in favor of the spiritual counterparts.
[67] *Hyp. Arch.* II,4:86,20–21.
[68] *Hyp. Arch.* II,4:87,20.
[69] *Hyp. Arch.* II,4:93,19; Layton, "Hypostasis," p. 67, n. 130: "We can conclude that in
our text . . . tmntrmnhet ("understanding") corresponds to σύνεσις."
[70] *Hyp. Arch.* II,4:87,11–12.
[71] *Hyp. Arch.* II,4:87,32; 87,14; cf. Layton, "Hypostasis," p. 49, n. 22.
[72] *Hyp. Arch.* II,4:87,17–18; for Coptic and Greek citations of this and other parallels,
cf. Table I.

most often cited in the *Tripartite Tractate*, suggest, alternatively, that the author, rather than using Paul's own letters, used sources upon which Paul himself drew. This possibility cannot be excluded and deserves exploration. For the purpose of the present study, however, it is important to note that the author of the *Tripartite Tractate* consciously intends to evoke Paul's authority for this exegesis.

The contrast between psychic and pneumatic perception, first drawn in the archons' futile attempt to grasp the image, recurs thematically throughout a drama in which each act intensifies the conflict. After failing to "grasp" the image appearing in the waters, the archons hope to seize upon it by means of its modeled form.[73] Foiled, they attempt to seize and rape the woman who manifests it,[74] and, failing that, to capture her progeny.[75]

As the scene changes from the archons' experience to the story of Adam and Eve, the thematic contrast between psychic and pneumatic perception expresses itself in the antithesis between "carnal knowledge" and "spiritual knowledge." The assertion that "our contest is not against flesh and blood, but against authorities of the universe and spirits of wickedness"[76] bears anthropological as well as cosmological implications. Read in the context of the concern shown by the *Hypostasis of the Archons* with sexuality, this passage suggests that opposition to the spirit derives not merely from physical and emotional impulses arising from our bodily nature, but from sinister spiritual forces that, having created these impulses, surface in them.

While the archons create a man (ογρωμε) out of "soil from the earth," (ογχογc εβολ ?μ πκα?; cf. Gen 2:7), they nonetheless mold their creature as one entirely "made of earth," a term that, as Layton notes, Paul uses in his own exegesis of Gen 2:7 (1 Cor 15:47).[77] Despite the creation of man's psychic body, the archons, because they do not understand the power of God (τΔγναμιc μπνογτε), find themselves too weak to raise him from the earth: "They could not make him (the psychic man) arise because of their weakness." Only the spirit possesses power to raise their psychic creation; when the spirit descends, "man became a living soul" (Gen 2:7).[78]

Scholars have noted in such exegesis the influence of both the Genesis creation epic and apocryphal and other Jewish legends.[79] To

---

[73] Hyp. Arch. II,4:87,34–88,2.
[74] Hyp. Arch. II,4:89,19–24.
[75] Hyp. Arch. II,4:91,9–12 (passim).
[76] Hyp. Arch. II,4:86,24–25; Eph 6:11–12.
[77] Layton, "Hypostasis," p. 49, n. 31.
[78] Hyp. Arch. II,4:88,12–15.
[79] Cf., for example, Böhlig-Labib, *Schrift ohne Titel*, 19–35; H.-M. Schenke, *Gott*

this, one may add that the author of *Hypostasis of the Archons* owes this version of Adam's creation to Paul, specifically and appropriately to Paul's own exegesis of the creation account of Genesis 2 in 1 Corinthians 15. In short, terminology and action in *Hypostasis of the Archons* offer a dramatized version of Genesis 2 read through 1 Cor 15:43b–48:

> Sown in weakness, it is raised in power (σπείρεται ἐν ἀσθενείᾳ, ἐγείρεται ἐν δυνάμει). What is sown a psychic body is raised a pneumatic body (σπείρεται σῶμα ψυχικόν, ἐγείρεται σῶμα πνευματικόν). If there is a psychic body, there is also a pneumatic body (Εἰ ἔστιν σῶμα ψυχικόν, ἔστιν καὶ πνευματικόν). Thus it is written, "The first man Adam became a living soul"; the last Adam became a life-giving spirit. But it is not the pneumatic which is first, but the psychic, and then the pneumatic (ἀλλ᾽ οὐ πρῶτον τὸ πνευματικὸν ἀλλὰ τὸ ψυχικόν, ἔπειτα τὸ πνευματικόν). The first man was made of earth, choic; the second is from heaven (ὁ πρῶτος ἄνθρωπος ἐκ γῆς χοϊκός, ὁ δεύτερος ἄνθρωπος ἐξ οὐρανοῦ). Like the choic, so are those who are choic; and like the heavenly, so are those who are heavenly.

As *Hypostasis of the Archons* tells it, the archons, sensing in their weakness (ἀσθενείᾳ, ⲧⲟⲩⲙⲛ̄ⲧⲁⲧϭⲟⲙ)[80] that their hold over Adam is threatened by the spirit's plot to lull him back to ignorance, attempt to lay hold of the divine image within Adam by opening his side. The spirit departs, and "Adam became wholly psychic."[81] But the spirit (here personified as the pneumatic woman) returns to that "psychic body," and bids it: "Arise, Adam."[82] Here again, I suggest, the author is translating Paul's statements into dramatic action: "sown in weakness," the psychic body is "raised in power" at the spirit's descent.

Although the *Apocryphon of John* and *Exegesis on the Soul* interpret Gen 2:24–25 "spiritually," allowing Adam to recognize his pneumatic "co-likeness," *Hypostasis of the Archons*, on the contrary, avoids the passage—deliberately, one supposes, because of its association with marriage and sexual union. To emphasize that Adam here awakens to spiritual and not carnal knowledge, the author chooses Gen 3:20 ("It is you who have given me life; you will be called 'Mother of the living'"[83]) to express the awakening of Adam's spiritual knowledge. Likewise she whom Adam recognizes is not the "carnal woman" whom the text later calls "his wife"; instead, she is Adam's pneumatic "female counterpart, Eve," who manifests Wisdom, his spiritual mother.

From this point in the drama, the thematic contrast between psychic and pneumatic modes of perception (cf. 1 Cor 2:14) turns on the paradox

---

"Mensch," 61–154; Bullard, *Hypostasis of the Archons*, 42–114; Fallon, *Enthronement*, 25–88; Barc, *L'Hypostase*, 74–130; and relevant remarks in Layton, "Hypostasis," 372–73, and Pearson, "Haggadic Traditions."

[80] Hyp. Arch. II,4:86,6; 87,15; 88,3.
[81] ψυχικος τηρϥ: Hyp. Arch. II,4:87,16; 88,3; 88,6.
[82] Hyp. Arch. II,4:89,14.
[83] Hyp. Arch. II,4:89,14–17; cf. Iren. Haer. I.30.2.

of Eve's identity. Adam, himself raised from psychic to pneumatic perception, recognizes Eve spiritually. The archons, however, aroused instead to passion, attempt to "know" her sexually. As the revelation section of *Hypostasis of the Archons* suggests even more clearly, the author alludes to the description of wisdom's (σοφία) hidden identity in 1 Cor 2:6-8, whom "none of the archons of this age knew (ἣν οὐδεὶς τῶν ἀρχόντων τοῦ αἰῶνος τούτου ἔγνωκεν). When their third attempt to "grasp what is spiritual" ends, like the others, in failure, Eve laughs at their foolish (ⲧⲟⲩⲙⲛ̄ⲧⲁⲧⲉ̄ⲏⲧ ⲙⲛ̄ ⲧⲟⲩⲙⲛ̄ⲧⲃⲁ̄ⲗⲉ)[84] confusion of sexual with spiritual knowledge. Their foolishness and consequent condemnation recalls not only 1 Cor 2:14a that the author of *Hypostasis of the Archons* previously paraphrased but also the verses that directly follow:

> The psychic . . . does not receive the things of the spirit of God: for they are foolishness to him (μωρία γὰρ αὐτῷ ἐστιν), nor can he know them (καὶ οὐ δύναται γνῶναι) because they are spiritually discerned (ὅτι πνευματικῶς ἀνακρίνεται). But the pneumatic judges all things, but himself is judged by no one (ὁ δὲ πνευματικὸς ἀνακρίνει μὲν πάντα, αὐτὸς δὲ ὑπ᾽ οὐδενὸς ἀνακρίνεται).

Escaping rape at their hands, "she became a tree." "In the original exegesis implied by this metamorphosis," as Layton notes, "undoubtedly (she became) the 'Tree of Life' (Gen 2:9), since the Aramaic ḥayyayā, 'life,' gives another pun on the name Ḥawwāh, 'Eve.'"[85] The pun probably extends, as Layton and Pearson agree, to her next metamorphosis as the Instructor manifested in the form of the serpent.[86] Yet the author's familiarity with the verbal connection between Eve, Life, Instructor, and Beast, as well as his or her later identification of Eve with Wisdom,[87] suggest a more direct scriptural source of inspiration: the Wisdom passages of Proverbs 1-4. Prov 3:18 specifically identifies Wisdom as a "tree of life": "She is a tree of life to those who lay hold upon her; those who hold her fast are happy." Prov 4:13 not only combines the image of "holding on" to wisdom with the term for Instruction (παιδεία) but again identifies her with life (Eve): "Keep hold of Instruction; do not let her go; guard her, for she is your life."[88]

According to Hippolytus, Basilides juxtaposes passages from Proverbs with those from the Pauline letters, reading both, like the author of

---

[84] *Hyp. Arch.* II,4:89,25.

[85] Layton, "Hypostasis," 57.

[86] *Hyp. Arch.* II,4:89,33; Layton, "Hypostasis," 55; Pearson, "Haggadic Traditions." Pearson ("Tree") recently has added to his previous research an example of a Pompean mosaic that illustrates a similar transformation.

[87] *Hyp. Arch.* II,4:94,4f.

[88] We note too that Prov 1:11f. warns "fools" who attempt to "get gain by violence" that their own violence deprives them of "life"; cf. 1:19. Like the Eve of *Hypostasis of the Archons*, Wisdom herself laughs "at their calamity" and eludes their pursuit.

Hypostasis of the Archons, as references to specific acts in the primordial drama. Basilides explains, for example, that Prov 1:7 ("The fear of the Lord is the beginning of wisdom") refers to the Great Archon's terror at discovering the power of Wisdom above him. Repenting for his arrogant ignorance, he receives oral instruction concerning the "wisdom of God spoken in a mystery" (cf. 1 Cor 2:7), wisdom "not revealed to previous generations" (cf. Eph 3:4b–5a).[89] One need not assume, of course, that the author of *Hypostasis of the Archons* knows the work of Basilides, Valentinus, and other exegetes. What the parallels do suggest is an acquaintance with widespread hermeneutical methods and practices.

In the *Hypostasis of the Archons* Eve's escape, separating her spiritual being from its bodily form, focuses the dramatic tension on the paradox of her identity. The pneumatic feminine principle (ⲧⲡⲛⲉⲩⲙⲁⲧⲓⲕⲏ), appearing as Instructor (fem. ⲧⲣⲉϥⲧⲁⲙⲟ), now engages in dialogue with her sarkic counterpart (ⲧⲥϩⲓⲙⲉ ⲛ̄ⲥⲁⲣⲕⲓⲕⲏ) who, after receiving spiritual instruction partakes of the tree of knowledge and persuades her husband, so that "these psychic beings ate."[90] Recognizing their spiritual nakedness, they respond by covering their sexual organs. Here again the narrative uses Genesis to emphasize the antithesis between sexual and spiritual knowledge.

The arrogant archon, discovering their transgression, "cursed the woman."[91] But *which* woman? The obvious answer is that he cursed the sarkic woman along with the snake. But the narrator, having previously used ⲧⲥϩⲓⲙⲉ to designate both pneumatic and sarkic manifestations, here leaves the term ⲧⲥϩⲓⲙⲉ ambiguous, implying that the archon's cursing of the woman and the snake unwittingly (and blasphemously) includes their instructor, the *spiritual* woman, as well.

The sarkic woman answers the archon's charge, accusing the serpent of seducing her. Nonetheless the sarkic man and woman suffer exile from Paradise. The archons then attempt to bring humanity into "great distraction (ⲡⲉⲣⲓⲥⲡⲁⲥⲙⲟⲥ) and into a life of toil" to prevent them "from devoting themselves to the holy spirit."[92] The author may have in mind

---

[89] According to Rensberger ("Apostle," 134–40) Hippolytus knows that Basilides cites Prov 1:7 to describe the Great Archon's terror at discovering the powers above him (*Ref.* 7.26.2): receiving oral instruction through Christ, he learns the "wisdom spoken in a mystery," cf. 1 Cor 2:7; "not in words taught by human wisdom, but in those taught by the spirit," 1 Cor 2:13; wisdom "not known to previous generations," Eph 3:4b–5a (*Ref.* 7.25.3). Cf. also Luke 8:10 and 10:21.

[90] *Hyp. Arch.* II,4:90,15. This translation clarifies the text for me more than Layton's version of the line.

[91] *Hyp. Arch.* II,4:90,30.

[92] *Hyp. Arch.* II,4:91,9–12.

not only Paul's warning that marriage involves both husband and wife in concern for τὰ τοῦ κόσμου, but also the apostle's antidote: Let those who remain unmarried devote themselves to the Lord ἀπερισπάστως "without distraction" (1 Cor 7:32-36).[93]

Expelled from paradise, the woman, now impregnated by the archons, bears "their son" Cain.[94] Then "he knew his wife," and she bears Abel.[95] Clarifying the antecedents to the text's ambiguous pronouns, Layton identifies Cain and Abel's mother as Eve, and Abel's father as *Adam*.[96] Yet the author's ambiguity is both intentional and significant. The proprietary archons, who regard their creature (*plasma*) as "their Adam,"[97] regard his female companion as Eve, because she is formed, like him, in their image.[98] But this, as the author sees it, is their fatal mistake. The archons' *plasma*, "their man," remains nameless, allowing the spirit to name Adam, a name that, according to *Hypostasis of the Archons*, attests his spiritual vitality.[99] In a second descent the spirit speaks his name and raises him to gnōsis: "Arise, Adam."[100] Recognizing his spiritual mother, Adam calls her, in turn, by *her* true name, "Mother of the Living," Eve.[101] That *Hypostasis of the Archons* attributes this name to the spiritual mother—and withholds it, in turn, from the woman who, raped by the archons and "known" sexually by her husband, bore Cain and Abel—is, as Barc recognizes, no accident.[102] Following the birth of Cain and Abel, "Adam knew his feminine counterpart, Eve," and the naming of the two partners indicates that this sentence narrates *not* an act of "carnal knowledge" as Layton infers[103] but a reawakening

---

[93] Shortly before, in fact, Paul even quotes from Gen 2:24, a passage *Hypostasis of the Archons* avoids. Using a rather shocking exegesis of the Genesis passage, Paul grounds his condemnation of *porneia* "fornication" in the sense of intercourse with a prostitute in this text contrasting *porneia* with the believer's spiritual union with Christ (1 Cor 6:16-20). Ascetic and gnostic Christian exegetes made widespread use of these passages. For examples, cf. Pagels, "Controversies concerning Marriage."

[94] *Hyp. Arch.* II,4:91,13; cf. Layton, "Hypostasis," p. 60, n. 4. Barc, *L'Hypostase*, 104-107.

[95] *Hyp. Arch.* II,4:91,14: Layton infers Adam ("Hypostasis," p. 61, n. 85); Barc infers Sabaoth (*L'Hypostase*, 104-107).

[96] In agreement with Barc (*L'Hypostase*, 104-107); yet I do not find his more complex theory of Abel's paternity conclusive.

[97] *Hyp. Arch.* II,4:89,19; 91,4; cf. also 89,5; 90,5.

[98] Cf. especially *Hyp. Arch.* II,4:92,20-21.

[99] *Hyp. Arch.* II,4:88,16-17; for discussion, cf. Barc, *L'Hypostase*, 82.

[100] *Hyp. Arch.* II,4:89,13.

[101] *Hyp. Arch.* II,4:89,14-17; cf. Layton, "Hypostasis," p. 57, n. 57.

[102] As Barc perceptively observes (*L'Hypostase*, 93-94): "Dans Gn., 3,20 l'exégèse du nom d'Ève est 'Mère de tous les vivants.' La suppression du mot 'tous' est certainement intentionnelle et veut exprimer qu'à la différence de *Genèse* Ève n'est pas la femme charnelle, mère de tous les hommes, mais la Femme spirituelle, mère des seuls vivants véritables, les spirituels."

[103] *Hyp. Arch.* II,4:91,32; Layton, "Hypostasis," p. 61, n. 92. I agree here with Barc, who

of the *spiritual* knowledge initiated in their first encounter. The mutual act of spiritual "knowing" produces Seth, born "through God" (cf. Gen 4:25).[104] Just as the spirit previously gave "birth" to Adam and put him in the place of the archons' psychic "man," so now she replaces the psychic Abel with Seth, born of the spirit. Finally, the spiritual mother, like her sarkic predecessor, receives a second child, now fully "born of the spirit": Norea. *Hypostasis of the Archons* explains that Norea's birth *spiritually* fulfills[105] the command of Gen 1:28 ("be fruitful and multiply").

The archons, aroused at this new subversion, decide to obliterate the whole creation. Opposed by their ruler, who attempts to sabotage their plan, they encounter Norea's outright defiance. The drama reaches its first climax when the riddle of the mother's identity explodes into open confrontation.

The archons, responding with their characteristic error, go to meet Norea in order to seduce her. Their ruler declares to Norea "your mother Eve came to us"—sexually.[106] But Norea challenges them all, for, in her view, it is a case of mistaken maternity. She attacks them where they are most vulnerable; again they are confusing sexual with spiritual knowledge: "You did not *know* my mother: instead, it was your female counterpart that you *knew*."[107] Having raped the female *plasma*, they imagined that they had "known" Eve. Norea declares, however, that they never "knew" her since she is "known" only spiritually. Norea sets them straight: having mistaken her mother's identity, they mistake hers as well. Norea knows that she is not born from the female *plasma*, wife of "their Adam"; she is born rather from "his feminine counterpart, Eve," the spirit: "I am not your descendant; rather, it is from the world above that I come."[108] And, as Norea soon learns from Eleleth, Eve's *own* mother is wisdom,[109] "whom none of the archons of this age knew" (cf. 1 Cor 2:8).

But the arrogant archon, rejecting the revelation of Eve's true identity—and, consequently, Norea's—persists in his error, demanding that Norea submit sexually to him and his archons, "as did also your

---

comments (*L'Hypostase*, 108) that "Ève, la mère de Seth et de Noréa, est donc la Femme spirituelle, celle qui est venue d'en haut pour s'unir à Adam. Seth est le fruit d'une union opérée dans le monde céleste entre Adam le spirituel et la Femme spirituelle."

[104] *Hyp. Arch.* II,4:91,33–34.
[105] *Hyp. Arch.* II,4:92,4–5.
[106] *Hyp. Arch.* II,4:92,19–21; cf. Layton, "Hypostasis," p. 68, n. 103.
[107] *Hyp. Arch.* II,4:92,24–25.
[108] *Hyp. Arch.* II,4:92,25–31.
[109] Cf. *Hyp. Arch.* II,4:95,7f.

mother Eve."[110] Norea, recognizing her need for spiritual understanding, cries out for help to "the God of the Entirety," pleading for help from the holy spirit.

Does the author of the *Hypostasis of the Archons* have in mind Paul's quotation from Isa 40:13 at 1 Cor 2:16: "who has known the mind of the Lord? Who can teach him?" Possibly; for, as Paul explains in 1 Cor 2:10, only the spirit reveals "the deep things of God"; thus, only those taught by the spirit, the pneumatics, understand "the gifts bestowed on us by God" because they receive gnōsis through oral instruction. The apostle discloses, too, the content of that teaching: it is the "wisdom hidden in a mystery, whom none of the archons of this age knew" (a passage that our author reads, apparently, in terms of a double meaning of "knowing" suggested in Genesis 1–4). Paul's prayer in Col 1:9 that *Hypostasis of the Archons* alludes to at the beginning of his exposition is fulfilled in Eleleth's appearance to Norea. Personifying spiritual understanding (συνέσει πνευματικῇ cf. Col 1:9), Eleleth reveals to Norea "all wisdom" (cf. Col 1:10). Specifically, he reveals the mystery concerning σοφία previously unknown to the archons (cf. 1 Cor 2:8, Ephesians 3); that mystery fills the spiritual one with "knowledge of (the Father's) will" (cf. Col 1:9). Describing wisdom's creative work without any hint of deprecation or blame, Eleleth explains that whatever evil later derived from such work came into being "through the will of the Father of the whole" (ⲡⲟⲩⲱϣ ⲙ̄ⲡⲉⲓⲱⲧ ⲙ̄ⲡⲧⲏⲣϥ).[111]

Norea's second question to Eleleth barely conceals her own anxiety concerning her mother's identity. Although her defiance had once concealed her anxiety from the archons, she now asks, "Sir, am I also from their matter (hylē)?"[112] Having already heard that she and her generation are from "the place where the virgin spirit dwells,"[113] Norea now learns her paternal identity as well: she and her offspring are from the primordial Father.[114] She and her "seed" (ⲥⲡⲉⲣⲙⲁ) receive spiritual life "in the midst of mortal humanity," but that "seed" will not be manifested until after three generations.[115]

To what source does *Hypostasis of the Archons* owe this specific conjunction of images? The contrast among those who have come to know "the way" and are immortal (and are freed from the mortality otherwise common to all humanity), "the seed" that awaits future

[110] *Hyp. Arch.* II.4:92,30–31.
[111] *Hyp. Arch.* II,4:96,13; cf. 87,21–23.
[112] *Hyp. Arch.* II,4:96,18–19.
[113] *Hyp. Arch.* II,4:93,30.
[114] *Hyp. Arch.* II,4:96,20–22.
[115] *Hyp. Arch.* II,4:96,25–27.

manifestation, and the three generations that must come into being before that "seed" comes to be known occur commonly in gnostic literature. There is, however, one Pauline passage already used by the author of *Hypostasis of the Archons* to interpret Genesis 2 that contains and links all three images together: 1 Cor 15:35–50. If Plato introduces the *sperma* terminology into the *Timaeus* account of human creation,[116] so does Paul. Paul, however, goes on (as Plato does not) to connect the image of the *sperma* not only with the theme of mortality, but also with the origin and destiny of three distinct *genē* "generations": pneumatic, psychic, and choic. And in this respect he stands close to *Hypostasis of the Archons*.

We note that the author of *Hypostasis of the Archons* reads Paul's account in terms of a concern with the primordial process of creation apparently taking the clue from 1 Cor 15:45, where Paul quotes Gen 2:7, and he reads this text as a reference to creation and to eschatological transformation.

Rebuking those who "have no knowledge of God (ἀγνωσίαν γὰρ θεοῦ τινες ἔχουσιν), Paul explains that what is "sown," and spiritually raised is not "the body which is to come into being" but the "bare kernel" of *seed*:

For God gives to each body, as he wills, and to each of the seeds (καὶ ἐκάστῳ τῶν σπερμάτων) its own body. Not all flesh is the same flesh . . . there are heavenly bodies, and earthly bodies (καὶ σώματα ἐπουράνια, καὶ σώματα ἐπίγεια).

Paul says additionally that "what is sown in corruption is raised in incorruption; sown in weakness, it is raised in power; sown a psychic body, it is raised a pneumatic body." The author of *Hypostasis of the Archons* reads Paul's reference to three *genē* in 1 Cor 15:42–48, especially in 1 Cor 15:47, as an anticipation of the eschatological result of the interplay of archontic and spiritual powers in human creation:

The first man is from earth, choic (cf. *Hyp. Arch.* II,4:87,26); The second man is from heaven (ὁ δεύτερος ἄνθρωπος ἐξ οὐρανοῦ). Like the choic, so are those who are choic; like the heavenly, so are those who are heavenly.

How long must one await the manifestation of that spiritual seed, the heavenly race? The author gives Norea's question a Pauline answer: one must wait until that "heavenly man" (cf. 1 Cor 15:48), the "true man," appears in human form to reveal it.

---

[116] Pearson (*Terminology*, 79–81), seeking a source for the introduction of the σπέρμα/σπείρω terminology in Valentinian exegesis of Gen 2:7 (cf. Iren. *Haer.* I.5.6), rightly notes that "one must look outside the book of Genesis for its origin." While acknowledging that the Valentinians themselves attribute their terminology to Paul, Pearson argues, surprisingly, that "the Valentinians themselves probably forgot the ultimate source of their terminology," and proceeds to trace it instead to the influence of Plato's *Timaeus!*

At the revelation of the second, spiritual Adam, those who belong to his generation, freed from bondage to the archons

will trample under foot death (ᴄᴇɴᴀϥᴋᴀᴛᴀᴨᴀᴛᴇɪ ᴍᴨᴍᴏʏ), which is from the powers (ɴᴇϫᴏʏᴄɪᴀ), and will ascend into the eternal light, where this seed belongs.

Here again our author owes the inspiration to Paul (specifically 1 Cor 15:24-29):

Then comes the end, when (Christ) will give the kingdom to God the Father, when he shall destroy every rule and every authority and every power (πᾶσαν ἀρχὴν καὶ πᾶσαν ἐξουσίαν καὶ δύναμιν) for it is necessary that he shall reign until he puts all his enemies under his feet (ἄχρι οὗ θῇ πάντας τοὺς ἐχθροὺς ὑπὸ τοὺς πόδας αὐτοῦ). The last enemy that shall be destroyed is death (ὁ θάνατος). For God has placed all things under his feet (ὑπὸ τοὺς πόδας αὐτοῦ). And when all are subjected to him, then the Savior himself will be subjected to him who has subjected all things under him, that God may be all in all.

Scholars have noted (and usually attributed to a redactor) increased scriptural references in the closing lines of *Hypostasis of the Archons*.[117] Michel Tardieu, for example, finds several allusions to Ephesians. *Hyp. Arch.* II,4:97,14, for example, reporting that "all the children of the light will truly know the truth," alludes, he suggests, to Eph 5:8 ("once you were darkness, but now you are light . . . walk as children of light; cf. also 1 Thess 5:5). Reference to the ᴨᴇɪⲱᴛ ᴍᴨᴛʜᴩϥ refers, Tardieu suggests, to such passages as Eph 4:6 (εἷς θεὸς καὶ πατὴρ πάντων). The image of the son, who "presides over all" (Coptic ᴩɪᴛ̄ɴ "is over"; *Hyp. Arch.* II,4:97,19) recalls Eph 4:6. The concluding phrases of 97,20-21 may refer to such passages as Rom 16:27 and Eph 3:21.[118]

Hypostasis of the Archons derives the content and action of its drama, then, as Böhlig, Schenke, Fallon, Barc, and others have indicated, primarily from a wide range of Jewish traditions and shares the common schema with, for example, the authors of the *Apocryphon of John* and *On the Origin of the World*.[119] But the author of *Hypostasis of the Archons* casts the sources into Pauline form, and narrates that common scheme in specifically Pauline terminology. If, as Barc notes, this author "chooses to conserve the vocabulary of Genesis, wherever possible,"[120] he or she chooses as well to conserve the technical vocabulary found in Paul.

---

[117] Cf. Bullard, *Hypostasis of the Archons*, 114-15: "The editor of the document was a Christian Gnostic, and is responsible for what Christian influence can be seen in the writing." Bullard acknowledges, however, that "This is evident not only in the beginning and closing, but in parenthetical statements throughout." Barc presents a complex theory involving two redactors (*L'Hypostase*, passim) which Pearson ("Review") criticizes. To me Eph 4:6 recalls 1 Cor 15:28 as well.

[118] Tardieu, *Mythes*; cf. especially textual notes on 295.

[119] For Barc's analysis of this scheme, see *L'Hypostase*, 1-48.

[120] Barc, *L'Hypostase*, 83.

VII. Conclusion

This investigation, then, takes up the research agenda Schenke suggested.[121] The starting point was obvious since *Hypostasis of the Archons* names only one authority, the "great apostle," and the work begins with explicit citations from Paul and ends with multiple Pauline allusions. We can hardly be surprised, then, that its exegesis of Genesis 2 reflects the influence of Paul's own exegesis of the same chapter (and of other passages in which the apostle refers to spiritual conflict with hostile cosmic powers; cf. 1 Corinthians 2; Colossians 1; Ephesians 5–6). The exegetical techniques *Hypostasis of the Archons* adopts have parallels in the work of the Naassenes, of Basilides, and of the Valentinians. It shares, too, with many of its contemporaries, a radically ascetic reading of Paul's meaning.[122] But comparing *Hypostasis of the Archons'* reading of the primordial drama with that of related texts, one finds its approach quite unique. The author of *On the Origin of the World*, for example, envisioning a *triple* manifestation of Adam (deriving, apparently, from Gen 1:3, 1:26, and 2:7), shows no interest in following the type of Pauline scheme that 1 Corinthians 15 suggests to the author of *Hypostasis of the Archons*.

The gnostic texts surveyed here diverge widely in their hermeneutical approaches to Genesis; yet, their authors demonstrate remarkable agreement when they interpret the *practical* implications of the creation accounts. *Testimony of Truth, Exegesis on the Soul, Apocryphon of John, Hypostasis of the Archons,* and *On the Origin of the World* all agree (against the range of views expressed, for example, by Basilides, Isidore, the Valentinians, and by "orthodox" Christians) that marriage and procreation, instigated by archontic powers who foisted them upon the human race as "divine commands" (Gen 1:28 and 2:24–25) have no place in the Christian life. "Carnal marriage" stands in radical antithesis to spiritual union. Sexual intercourse and procreation, so closely related with spiritual "increase" that they form its demonic "imitation," remain anathema to those regenerated through the spirit. While avoiding the hortatory form so popular among their orthodox opponents, these authors leave no doubt about the practical implications of such Genesis exegesis. As they see it, the ontological structure of being itself as well as the historical structure of divine revelation impose the demand of celibate renunciation upon all genuinely "gnostic" Christians.

---

[121] H.-M. Schenke, *Gott "Mensch,"* 156.

[122] Among recent studies, see Rensberger, "Apostle" and Pagels, "Controversies concerning Marriage."

APPENDIX

PASSAGES PARALLEL TO *HYPOSTASIS OF THE ARCHONS* IN THE PAULINE CORPUS AND PROVERBS

Introduction:

The author, invoking the authority of "the great apostle, inspired by the spirit of the Father of truth," promises to explain the reality of the rule exercised by "powers of darkness" (Col 1:13)

86,22 [87,14]

ⲛⲉϫⲟⲩⲥⲓⲁ ⲙ̅ⲡⲕⲁⲕⲉ.

Col 1:13

ὃς ἐρρύσατο ἡμᾶς ἐκ τῆς ἐξουσίας τοῦ σκότους.

and the nature of the spiritual struggle in which we are engaged (Eph 6:11–12).

86,23–25

ⲡⲛ̅ϣⲱϫⲉ ϣⲟⲟⲡ ⲁⲛ ⲟⲩⲃⲉ ⲥⲁⲣϫ ϩⲓ [ⲥⲛⲟϥ], ⲁⲗⲗⲁ ⲉϥⲟⲩⲃⲉ ⲛⲉϫⲟⲩⲥⲓⲁ ⲙ̅ⲡⲕⲟⲥ[ⲙⲟⲥ] ⲙ̅ⲛ̅ ⲙ̅ⲡⲛⲉⲩⲙⲁⲧⲓⲕⲟⲛ ⲛ̅ⲧⲡⲟⲛⲏⲣⲓⲁ.

Eph 6:11–12

ὅτι οὐκ ἔστιν ἡμῖν ἡ πάλη πρὸς αἷμα καὶ σάρκα, ἀλλὰ πρὸς τὰς ἀρχάς, πρὸς τὰς ἐξουσίας, πρὸς τοὺς κοσμοκράτορας τοῦ σκότους τούτου, πρὸς τὰ πνευματικὰ τῆς πονηρίας ἐν τοῖς ἐπουρανίοις.

Part I: The Drama of Creation

A. The "image of God" appears in the waters; from that "image of the invisible God" (cf. Col 1:15) all things come into being, including "all things visible and invisible, thrones, dominions, rules and powers" (Col 1:17).

87,32

ⲡⲓⲙⲉ] ⲙ̅ⲡⲛⲟⲩⲧⲉ.

87,14

ⲁⲡⲉⲥⲓⲛⲉ ⲟⲩⲱⲛϩ ⲉⲃⲟⲗ ϩⲛ̅ⲛ ⲙ̅ⲙⲟⲟⲩ.

Cf. 87,11–12

ϫⲉ ⲉⲃⲟⲗ ϩⲛ̅ ⲛⲉⲑⲏⲡ ⲁⲩϩⲉ ⲁⲛⲉⲧⲟⲩⲟⲛϩ ⲉⲃⲟⲗ.

Col 1:15–17

ὅς ἐστιν εἰκὼν τοῦ θεοῦ τοῦ ἀοράτου, πρωτότοκος πάσης κτίσεως, ὅτι ἐν αὐτῷ ἐκτίσθη τὰ πάντα ἐν τοῖς οὐρανοῖς καὶ ἐπὶ τῆς γῆς, τὰ ὁρατὰ καὶ τὰ ἀόρατα, εἴτε θρόνοι εἴτε κυριότητες εἴτε ἀρχαὶ εἴτε ἐξουσίαι.

B. The "powers of darkness" (87,15; Col 1:13) cannot grasp that image, "since those that are psychic cannot grasp the things that are spiritual" (cf. 1 Cor 2:14).

87,17–18
ϫⲉ ⲙ̅ⲯⲩⲭⲓⲕⲟⲥ ⲛⲁⲱ ⲧⲉ2ⲉ
ⲙ̅ⲡⲛⲉⲩⲙⲁⲧⲓⲕⲟⲥ ⲁⲛ.

1 Cor 2:14
ψυχικὸς δὲ ἄνθρωπος οὐ δέχεται τὰ τοῦ
πνεύματος τοῦ θεοῦ.

C. For the authorities are from below; the "image of God" from above (cf. Col 3:2).

87,19–20
ϫⲉ 2ⲛ̅ⲛⲁⲃⲟⲗ ⲛⲉ ⲙ̅ⲡⲥⲁ ⲙ̅ⲡⲓⲧⲛ, ⲛ̅ⲧⲟϥ
ⲁⲉ ⲟⲩⲉⲃⲟⲗ ⲡⲉ ⲙ̅ⲡⲥⲁ ⲛⲧⲡⲉ.

Col 3:2
τὰ ἄνω φρονεῖτε, μὴ τὰ ἐπὶ τῆς γῆς.

D. The author claims to convey knowledge of "the will of the Father" (cf. Col 1:9).

87,22
ⲡⲟⲩⲱⲱ ⲙ̅ⲡⲉⲓⲱⲧ.[123]

Col 1:9
ἵνα πληρωθῆτε τὴν ἐπίγνωσιν τοῦ θελή-
ματος αὐτοῦ ἐν πάσῃ σοφίᾳ καὶ συνέσει
πνευματικῇ.

E. The archons plan to create a man (cf. Gen 1:26) who will be "dust from the earth" (Gen 2:7): they mold him wholly "from the earth, choic" (cf. 1 Cor 15:47).

87,24–26
ⲁⲛⲁⲣⲭⲱⲛ ... ⲡⲉϫⲁⲩ ϫⲉ "ⲁⲙⲏⲉⲓⲧⲛ̅
ⲛⲧⲛ̅ⲧⲁⲙⲓⲟ ⲛ̅ⲟⲩⲣⲱⲙⲉ ⲛ̅ⲛⲟⲩⲭⲟⲩⲥ
ⲉⲃⲟⲗ ⲡⲕⲁ2." ⲁⲩⲣ̅ ⲡⲗⲁⲥⲥⲉ
ⲙ̅ⲡⲟⲩⲧⲁ[ⲙⲓⲟ] ⲉⲩⲣⲙⲛ̅ⲕⲁ2 ⲧⲏⲣϥ ⲡⲉ.

1 Cor 15:47
ὁ πρῶτος ἄνθρωπος ἐκ γῆς χοϊκός.

F. The archons, "because of their weakness" (ⲧⲟⲩⲙⲛ̅ⲧ6ⲱⲃ; ἀσθενεία 88,3) do not understand "the power (ⲧⲁⲩⲛⲁⲙⲓⲥ) of God"; further-more, "because of their weakness" (86,6) they cannot raise the psychic man from the earth (1 Cor 15:43b–44a). Previously, "because of their weakness," (87,15) they could not grasp "the things which are spiritual" (87,15; cf. 1 Cor 2:14).

88,3–7
ⲉⲩⲣ̅ ⲛⲟ[ⲉ]ⲓ ⲁⲛ ⲛ̅ⲧⲁⲩⲛⲁⲙⲓⲥ ⲙ̅ⲡⲛⲟⲩⲧⲉ
ⲉⲃⲟⲗ 2ⲛ̅ ⲧⲟⲩⲙⲛ̅ⲧⲁⲧⲃⲟⲙ. ⲁⲩⲱ ⲁϥⲛⲓϥⲉ
ⲉ2ⲟⲩⲛ 2ⲙ̅ ⲡⲉϥ2ⲟ (Gen 2:7a) ⲁⲩⲱ
ⲁⲡⲣⲱⲙⲉ ⲱⲱⲡⲉ ⲙ̅ⲯⲩⲭⲓⲕⲟⲥ 2ⲓϫⲙ̅
ⲡⲕⲁ2 ⲛ̅2ⲁ2 ... ⲙ̅ⲡⲟⲩⲱ 6ⲛ̅ 6ⲟⲙ 6ⲉ
ⲛ̅ⲧⲟⲩⲛ̅ⲟⲥϥ ⲉⲧⲃⲉ ⲧⲟⲩⲙⲛ̅ⲧⲁⲧⲃⲟⲙ.

1 Cor 15:43b–44
σπείρεται ἐν ἀσθενείᾳ, ἐγείρεται ἐν δυνά-
μει· σπείρεται σῶμα ψυχικόν, ἐγείρεται
σῶμα πνευματικόν.

---

[123] On the role of σύνεσις and σοφία, cf. pp. 268 and 275 above.

G. The power of God descends in the spirit to dwell within the psychic man, "and the man became a living soul" (Gen 2:7b; compare 1 Cor 15:44b–47).

88,1–16

ⲘⲘⲚⲚⲤⲀ ⲚⲀⲈⲒ Ⲁ<Ⲡ>ⲠⲚⲀ ⲚⲀⲨ ⲀⲠⲢⲰⲘⲈ ⲚⲮⲨⲭⲒⲔⲞⲤ ϨⲒⲬⲘ ⲠⲔⲀϨ. ⲀⲨⲱ ⲀⲠⲠⲚⲀ ⲈⲒ ⲈⲂⲞⲖ ϨⲘ ⲠⲔⲀϨ . . . ⲀϤⲈⲒ ⲈⲠⲒⲦⲚ̄. ⲀϤⲞⲨⲰϨ Ⲛ̄ϨⲎⲦϤ. ⲀⲠⲢⲰⲘⲈ ⲈⲦⲘⲘⲀⲨ ϢⲰⲠⲈ ⲀⲨⲮⲨⲬⲎ ⲈⲤⲞⲚϨ (Gen 2:7b).

1 Cor 15:44b–47

εἰ ἔστιν σῶμα ψυχικόν, ἔστιν καὶ πνευματικόν. οὕτως καὶ γέγραπται· ἐγένετο ὁ πρῶτος ἄνθρωπος ᾿Αδὰμ εἰς ψυχὴν ζῶσαν· ὁ ἔσχατος ᾿Αδὰμ εἰς πνεῦμα ζῳοποιοῦν. ἀλλ᾿ οὐ πρῶτον τὸ πνευματικὸν ἀλλὰ τὸ ψυχικόν, ἔπειτα τὸ πνευματικόν. ὁ πρῶτος ἄνθρωπος ἐκ γῆς χοϊκός, ὁ δεύτερος ἄνθρωπος ἐξ οὐρανοῦ (Gen 2:7b).

H. The archons throw humanity into "great distraction" (ⲠⲈⲢⲒⲤⲠⲀⲘⲞⲤ) and into the toils of earthly life, so that they will be occupied with worldly affairs and not be able to devote themselves to the holy spirit. Compare 1 Cor 7:32–35, where Paul warns against marriage, which involves concern for τὰ τοῦ κόσμου, hindering one's devotion to the Lord.

91,8–12

ⲀⲨⲚⲞⲨϪ Ⲣ̄ⲢⲰⲘⲈ ⲆⲈ ⲈϨⲢⲀⲒ ⲀϨⲚⲚⲞϬ ⲘⲠⲠⲈⲢⲒⲤⲠⲀⲤⲘⲞⲤ ⲘⲚ ϨⲚ ⲘⲔⲀϨ Ⲛ̄ⲦⲈ ⲠⲂⲒⲞⲤ, ϢⲒⲚⲀ ⲈⲚⲞⲨⲢⲰⲘⲈ ⲚⲀϢⲰⲠⲈ Ⲛ̄ⲂⲒⲰⲦⲒⲔⲞⲤ Ⲛ̄ⲤⲈⲦⲘ̄Ⲣ̄ ⲤⲬⲞⲖⲀⲌⲈ Ⲁ Ⲣ̄ⲠⲢⲞⲤⲔⲀⲢⲦⲈⲢⲈⲤ ⲈⲠⲠⲚⲀ ⲈⲦⲞⲨⲀⲀⲂ.

1 Cor 7:32–35

Θέλω δὲ ὑμᾶς ἀμερίμνους εἶναι. ὁ ἄγαμος μεριμνᾷ τὰ τοῦ κυρίου, πῶς ἀρέσῃ τῷ κυρίῳ· ὁ δὲ γαμήσας μεριμνᾷ τὰ τοῦ κόσμου, πῶς ἀρέσῃ τῇ γυναικί, καὶ μεμέρισται. καὶ ἡ γυνὴ ἡ ἄγαμος καὶ ἡ παρθένος μεριμνᾷ τὰ τοῦ κυρίου, ἵνα ᾖ ἁγία καὶ τῷ σώματι καὶ τῷ πνεύματι· ἡ δὲ γαμήσασα μεριμνᾷ τὰ τοῦ κόσμου, πῶς ἀρέσῃ τῷ ἀνδρί. τοῦτο δὲ πρὸς τὸ ὑμῶν αὐτῶν σύμφορον λέγω, οὐχ ἵνα βρόχον ὑμῖν ἐπιβάλω, ἀλλὰ πρὸς τὸ εὔσχημον καὶ εὐπάρεδρον τῷ κυρίῳ ἀπερισπάστως.

Part II: The Drama of Revelation

A. Norea identifies those who claim to have "known" her mother Eve (and so wisdom) sexually as "rulers of darkness" (cf. related phrase in Col 1:12). She declares that "you did not know my mother" (Eve, nor her mother, Sophia), accusing them of confusing sexual with spiritual "knowledge." In so doing, they mistake "their female *plasma*" for the spiritual woman (and her mother, Sophia), who, as this author reads Paul's words, "none of the archons of this age knew" (cf. 1 Cor 2:6–15).

92,23 [Norea speaks]

Ⲛ̄ⲦⲰⲦⲚ̄ ⲚⲈ ⲚⲀⲢⲬⲰⲚ Ⲙ̄ⲠⲔⲀⲔⲈ . . .
ⲞⲨⲦⲈ ⲘⲠⲈⲦⲚⲤⲞⲨⲰⲚ ⲦⲀⲘⲀⲀⲨ ⲀⲖⲖⲀ
Ⲛ̄ⲦⲀⲦⲈⲦⲚ̄ⲤⲞⲨⲰⲚ ⲦⲈⲦⲚ̄ϢⲂ̄ⲢⲈⲒⲚⲈ.

1 Cor 2:6–8

Σοφίαν δὲ λαλοῦμεν ἐν τοῖς τελείοις,
σοφίαν δὲ <u>οὐ τοῦ αἰῶνος τούτου οὐδὲ τῶν
ἀρχόντων τοῦ αἰῶνος τούτου τῶν καταρ-
γουμένων</u>· ἀλλὰ λαλοῦμεν θεοῦ σοφίαν
ἐν μυστηρίῳ, τὴν ἀποκεκρυμμένην, ἣν
προώρισεν ὁ θεὸς πρὸ τῶν αἰώνων εἰς
δόξαν ἡμῶν· <u>ἣν οὐδεὶς τῶν ἀρχόντων τοῦ
αἰῶνος τούτου ἔγνωκεν·</u>

Cf. 89,24–25

The spiritual woman laughed at the folly ⲦⲞⲨⲘⲚ̄ⲦⲀⲦⲐⲎⲦ of those who, being psychic, cannot "grasp what is spiritual" (87,17–18/1 Cor 2:14) and so fail to "know" the spiritual woman.

1 Cor 2:14

ψυχικὸς δὲ ἄνθρωπος οὐ δέχεται τὰ τοῦ
πνεύματος τοῦ θεοῦ· μωρία γὰρ αὐτῷ
ἐστιν, καὶ οὐ δύναται γνῶναι, ὅτι πνευ-
ματικῶς ἀνακρίνεται.

89,25–26

ⲀⲚⲞⲔ ⲞⲨⲈⲂⲞⲖ ⲄⲀⲢ ⲀⲚ ⲍ̄Ⲛ ⲦⲎⲚⲈ, ⲀⲖⲖⲀ
Ⲛ̄ⲦⲀⲈⲒ<ⲈⲒ> ⲈⲂⲞⲖ ⲍ̄Ⲛ ⲚⲀ ⲠⲤⲀ ⲚⲦⲠⲈ.

Col 3:1–2

τὰ ἄνω φρονεῖτε, μὴ τὰ ἐπὶ τῆς γῆς.

1 Cor 15:47

ὁ πρῶτος ἄνθρωπος ἐκ γῆς χοϊκός,
ὁ δεύτερος ἄνθρωπος ἐξ οὐρανοῦ.

B. The archons, attempting to reduce Adam to his former ignorance, bring upon him a "deep sleep" (cf. Gen 2:21) and open his side; the Spirit departs from him, and he becomes "wholly psychic" until the Spirit comes to raise him, the *second* Adam, as a pneumatic man (cf. 1 Cor 15:43–44,46). As the first Adam was psychic, a "living soul," the second is pneumatic, receiving spiritual life from above (cf. 1 Cor 15:45–47).

89,11–13

ⲁⲩⲱ ⲁⲇⲁⲙ ϣⲱⲡⲉ ⲙ̄ⲯⲩⲭⲓⲕⲟⲥ ⲧⲏⲣϥ.
ⲁⲩⲱ ⲧⲥ̅ϩⲓⲙⲉ ⲙ̄ⲡⲛⲉⲩⲙⲁⲧⲓⲕⲏ ⲁⲥⲓ
ϣⲁⲣⲟϥ. ⲁⲥϣⲁϫⲉ ⲛⲙ̄ⲙⲁϥ, ⲡⲉϫⲁⲥ ϫⲉ
"ⲧⲱⲟⲩⲛ ⲁⲇⲁⲙ."

1 Cor 15:43b–48

σπείρεται ἐν ἀσθενείᾳ, ἐγείρεται ἐν δυνά-
μει· σπείρεται σῶμα ψυχικόν, ἐγείρεται
σῶμα πνευματικόν. Εἰ ἔστιν σῶμα ψυχικόν, ἔστιν καὶ πνευματικόν. οὕτως καὶ
γέγραπται· ἐγένετο ὁ πρῶτος ἄνθρωπος
Ἀδὰμ εἰς ψυχὴν ζῶσαν· ὁ ἔσχατος
Ἀδὰμ εἰς πνεῦμα ζῳοποιοῦν· ἀλλ' οὐ
πρῶτον τὸ πνευματικὸν ἀλλὰ τὸ ψυχικόν, ἔπειτα τὸ πνευματικόν. ὁ πρῶτος
ἄνθρωπος ἐκ γῆς χοϊκός, ὁ δεύτερος ἄνθρωπος ἐξ οὐρανοῦ.

C. The archons pursue Eve, "daughter of wisdom" (95,7f.), and she, laughing at them for their folly, eludes them as she "became a tree" (89,25), the Tree of Life (cf. Gen 2:7). This episode reflects specific wisdom sayings of Proverbs 1–4, which declare, of wisdom, "she is a tree of life to those who lay hold upon her" (Prov 3:18), and identify her with "instruction," adding that "she is your life" (Ζωή, Eve). Passages here quoted from LXX: cf. Hebrew text.

Prov 1:22b–26

οἱ δὲ ἄφρονες τῆς ὕβρεως ὄντες ἐπιθυ-
μηταί. Τοιγαροῦν κἀγὼ (i.e., σοφία) τῇ
ὑμετέρᾳ ἀπωλείᾳ ἐπιγελάσομαι.

Prov 1:29

Ἐμίσησαν γὰρ σοφίαν.

Praise of wisdom:

89,24–25

ⲁⲩⲱ ⲁⲥⲥⲱⲃⲉ ⲛ̄ⲥⲱⲟⲩ ⲉⲃⲟⲗ ϩ̄ⲛ
ⲧⲟⲩⲙⲛ̄ⲧⲁⲧⲑⲏⲧ ⲙⲛ̄ ⲧⲟⲩⲙⲛ̄ⲧⲃⲁⲗⲉ.
ⲁⲩⲱ ⲁⲉⲣ̄ ⲟⲩϣⲏⲛ.

Prov 3:18

Ξύλον ζωῆς ἐστι πᾶσι τοῖς ἀντεχομένοις
αὐτῆς, καὶ τοῖς ἐπερειδομένοις ἐπ' αὐτὴν
ὡς ἐπὶ Κύριον ἀσφαλής.

Prov 3:19

Ὁ Θεὸς τῇ σοφίᾳ ἐθεμελίωσε τὴν γῆν.

Prov 4:13

Ἐπιλαβοῦ ἐμῆς παιδείας, μὴ ἀφῆς, ἀλλὰ
φύλαξον αὐτὴν σεαυτῷ εἰς ζωήν σου.

D. Eleleth proceeds to reveal to Norea what this author apparently considers the "mystery of wisdom" (1 Cor 2:7) hidden from "the archons of this age" (1 Cor 7:8). Norea learns that she and her generation are from the Father, from above, from the "imperishable light," and so are saved from the "power of darkness" (cf. Col 1:12–13).

96,20–22 [Eleleth speaks]

ν̄το μ̄ν νογϣηρε, ερεηπ ⲁπειωτ
ετϣοοπ ϫιν ν̄ϣορπ, ν̄ⲧⲁⲛⲟⲩψⲩⲭⲏ
ει <ε>ⲃⲟⲗ ϩ̄ⲙ πⲥⲁ ν̄ⲧⲡⲉ ⲉⲃⲟⲗ ϩ̄ⲙ
ⲡⲟⲩⲟⲉⲓⲛ ν̄ⲛⲁⲧⲧⲉⲕⲟ. ⲇⲓⲁ ⲧⲟⲩⲧⲟ
ν̄ⲉϫⲟⲩⲥⲓⲁ ⲛⲁϣ ⲧϩⲛⲟ ⲁⲛ ⲉϩⲟⲩⲛ
ⲉⲣⲟⲟⲩ.

Col 1:12–13

εὐχαριστοῦντες τῷ πατρὶ τῷ ἱκανώσαντι ἡμᾶς εἰς τὴν μερίδα τοῦ κλήρου τῶν ἁγίων ἐν τῷ φωτί· ὃς ἐρρύσατο ἡμᾶς ἐκ τῆς ἐξουσίας τοῦ σκότους.

Cf. 86,23; 87,14; 92,23

where Norea curses the archons, saying

"ν̄ⲧⲱⲧⲛ̄ ⲛⲉ ⲛⲁⲣⲭⲱⲛ ν̄ⲡⲕⲁⲕⲉ."

E. Norea learns that she and those who belong to her are "immortal in the midst of mortal humanity"; they are the seed (ⲥⲡⲉⲣⲙⲁ) that shall be manifested only after three generations (cf. 1 Cor 15:35–49).

96,25–29

ⲟⲩⲟⲛ ⲇⲉ ⲛⲓⲙ ν̄ⲧⲁϩⲥⲟⲩⲱⲛ ⲧⲉⲓϩⲟⲇⲟⲥ
ⲛⲁⲉⲓ ⲥⲉϣⲟⲟⲡ ν̄ⲁθⲁⲛⲁⲧⲟⲥ ϩ ⲧⲙⲏⲧⲉ
ν̄ⲣ̄ⲣⲱⲙⲉ ⲉϣⲁⲩⲙⲟⲩ. ⲁⲗⲗⲁ
ⲡⲉⲥⲡⲉⲣⲙⲁ ⲉⲧⲙ̄ⲙⲁⲩ ⲛⲁⲟⲩⲱⲛϩ ⲁⲛ
ⲉⲃⲟⲗ ⲧⲉⲛⲟⲩ. ⲁⲗⲗⲁ ⲙⲛ̄ⲛ̄ⲥⲁ ϣⲟⲙⲧⲉ
ν̄ⲅⲉⲛⲉⲁ ⲁⲩⲛⲁⲟⲩⲱⲛϩ.

Norea asks how long she must await the manifestation of that "seed"; and learns that she must await the revelation of the πⲣⲱⲙⲉ ν̄ⲁⲗⲏθⲓ(ⲛⲟⲥ) 96,32–35.

1 Cor 15:35–39

Ἀλλὰ ἐρεῖ τις· πῶς ἐγείρονται οἱ νεκροί; ποίῳ δὲ σώματι ἔρχονται; ἄφρων, σὺ ὃ σπείρεις, οὐ ζωοποιεῖται ἐὰν μὴ ἀποθάνῃ· καὶ ὃ σπείρεις, οὐ τὸ σῶμα τὸ γενησόμενον σπείρεις, ἀλλὰ γυμνὸν κόκκον εἰ τύχοι σίτου ἤ τινος τῶν λοιπῶν· ὁ δὲ θεὸς δίδωσιν αὐτῷ σῶμα καθὼς ἠθέλησεν, καὶ ἑκάστῳ τῶν σπερμάτων ἴδιον σῶμα. οὐ πᾶσα σὰρξ ἡ αὐτὴ σάρξ, ἀλλὰ ἄλλη μὲν ἀνθρώπων, ἄλλη δὲ σὰρξ κτηνῶν, ἄλλη δὲ σὰρξ πτηνῶν, ἄλλη δὲ ἰχθύων. καὶ σώματα ἐπουράνια, καὶ σώματα ἐπίγεια.

Paul goes on to describe the three γενή: pneumatic, psychic, and choic, concluding with the words:

ὁ πρῶτος ἄνθρωπος ἐκ γῆς χοϊκός, ὁ δεύτερος ἄνθρωπος ἐξ οὐρανοῦ. οἷος ὁ χοϊκός, τοιοῦτοι καὶ οἱ χοϊκοί, καὶ οἷος ὁ ἐπουράνιος, τοιοῦτοι καὶ οἱ ἐπουράνιοι· καὶ καθὼς ἐφορέσαμεν τὴν εἰκόνα τοῦ χοϊκοῦ, φορέσομεν καὶ τὴν εἰκόνα τοῦ ἐπουρανίου (1 Cor 15:47–49).

F. Those belonging to the "seed" of the coming "true man" (96,34), being freed from bondage to the deception of the authorities (96,30) and freed from spiritual blindness (97,6), shall "trample under foot death, which is of the authorities" (97,7–8). The authorities shall relinquish their power (97,11) to the Son (cf. 1 Cor 15:24–28).

96,30

ⲛϥⲛⲟⲩϫⲉ ⲉⲃⲟⲗ ⲙ̄ⲙⲟⲟⲩ ⲛ̄ⲧⲙ̄ⲣ̄ⲣⲉ
ⲛ̄ⲧⲡⲗⲁⲛⲏ ⲛ̄<ⲛ>ⲉϫⲟⲩⲥⲓⲁ.

97,6

ⲧⲟⲧⲉ ⲥⲉⲛⲁⲛⲟⲩϫⲉ ⲉⲃⲟⲗ ⲙ̄ⲙⲟⲟⲩ
ⲙ̄ⲡⲙⲉⲉⲩⲉ ⲃⲃⲗ̄ⲗⲉ.

97,7–8

ⲁⲩⲱ ⲥⲉⲛⲁⲣ̄ⲕⲁⲧⲁⲡⲁⲧⲉⲓ ⲙ̄ⲡⲙⲟⲩ
ⲛ̄ⲛⲉϫⲟⲩⲥⲓⲁ.

97,11

ⲧⲟⲧⲉ ⲛⲉϫⲟⲩⲥⲓⲁ ⲥⲉⲛⲁⲕⲱ ⲛ̄ⲥⲱⲟⲩ
ⲛ̄ⲛⲟⲩⲕⲁⲓⲣⲟⲥ.

97,18–19

ⲁⲩⲱ ⲡϣⲏⲣⲉ ϩⲓϫⲛ̄ ⲡⲧⲏⲣϥ̄.

97,15

ⲡⲉⲓⲱⲧ ⲙ̄ⲡⲧⲏⲣϥ.

1 Cor 15:24–28

εἶτα τὸ τέλος, ὅταν παραδιδοῖ τὴν βασι-
λείαν τῷ θεῷ καὶ πατρί, ὅταν καταργήσῃ
πᾶσαν ἀρχὴν καὶ πᾶσαν ἐξουσίαν καὶ
δύναμιν.
δεῖ γὰρ αὐτὸν βασιλεύειν ἄχρι οὗ θῇ
πάντας τοὺς ἐχθροὺς

ὑπὸ τοὺς πόδας αὐτοῦ. ἔσχατος ἐχθρὸς
καταργεῖται ὁ θάνατος

πάντα γὰρ ὑπέταξεν ὑπὸ τοὺς πόδας
αὐτοῦ . . .
ὅταν δὲ ὑποταγῇ αὐτῷ τὰ πάντα, τότε
καὶ αὐτὸς ὁ υἱὸς ὑποταγήσεται . . .

ἵνα ᾖ ὁ θεὸς πάντα ἐν πᾶσιν.
Eph 4:6
εἷς θεὸς καὶ πατὴρ πάντων, ὁ ἐπὶ πάντων
καὶ διὰ πάντων καὶ ἐν πᾶσιν.

G. The author concludes with a scene of all the children of light unanimously giving glory to God, through the trisagion, and pronouncing amen (cf. Eph 3:21 and Rom 16:27).

Cf. Col 1:12; cf. above, 96,20–22.

97,14

ⲧⲟⲧⲉ ⲛ̄ϣⲏⲣⲉ ⲧⲏⲣⲟⲩ ⲙ̄ⲡⲟⲩⲟⲉⲓⲛ
ⲥⲉⲛⲁⲥⲟⲩⲱⲛ . . . ⲡⲉⲓⲱⲧ ⲙ̄ⲡⲧⲏⲣϥ ⲙⲛ̄
<ⲡ>ⲡ̄ⲛ̄ⲁ ⲉⲧⲟⲩⲁⲁⲃ.

97,20

ⲁⲩⲱ ⲉⲃⲟⲗ ϩⲓⲧⲛ̄ ⲟⲩⲟⲛ ⲛⲓⲙ ϣⲁ ⲛⲓⲉⲛⲉϩ
ⲛ̄ⲉⲛⲉϩ. ϩⲁⲅⲓⲟⲥ ϩⲁⲅⲓⲟⲥ ϩⲁⲅⲓⲟⲥ
ϩⲁⲙⲏⲛ.'

Eph 5:8
ὡς τέκνα φωτὸς περιπατεῖτε.

Rom 16:27
μόνῳ σοφῷ θεῷ, διὰ Ἰησοῦ Χριστοῦ ᾧ ἡ
δόξα εἰς τοὺς αἰῶνας τῶν αἰώνων· ἀμήν.
Eph 3:21
αὐτῷ ἡ δόξα ἐν τῇ ἐκκλησίᾳ καὶ ἐν
Χριστῷ Ἰησοῦ εἰς πάσας τὰς γενεὰς τοῦ
αἰῶνος τῶν αἰώνων· ἀμήν.

13

WITH WALTER BAUER ON THE TIGRIS: ENCRATITE ORTHODOXY AND LIBERTINE HERESY IN SYRO-MESOPOTAMIAN CHRISTIANITY

Stephen Gero

The University of Tübingen welcomed Dr. Stephen Gero to its faculty in 1980, as Professor of Oriental Studies. His areas of specialization are the history and philology of the Christian Orient, including Byzantium; he has written two monographs on Byzantine iconoclasm and one more recently on Syriac church history.

After an undergraduate education at McGill University, Dr. Gero received his Ph.D. from Harvard University. He held several fellowships including the prestigious Arthur Darby Nock Fellowship at Harvard (1971–72). He was Assistant Professor of Religious Studies at Brown University from 1973 to 1980.

Dr. Gero has a specific research interest in Gnostic studies and has written numerous articles for such periodicals as *Novum Testamentum, Harvard Theological Review*, and the *Journal of Jewish Studies*. His breadth of language competency, which includes Armenian, Georgian, Syriac, Arabic, and Coptic, has permitted him to participate in a variety of academic forums from a discussion of medieval Hebrew texts to an investigation of textual problems in oriental versions of early Christian apocrypha.

Preface

T he self-definition and development of Christianity in the East proceeded in certain respects in a manner quite different from that in the West. In particular, due to an array of special political and cultural conditions, a number of heterodox groups survived or maintained a dominant role in the general area of eastern Syria and Mesopotamia well into late antiquity and the early Middle Ages. The discovery of the

Nag Hammadi texts, several of which have demonstrable affinities to
the Syrian cultural milieu, has reawakened scholarly interest in the
special features of Syrian Christianity, building upon the pioneering
insights of the German church historian and exegete Walter Bauer. But
the generally ascetic ethical stance of the new texts has *prima facie*
reinforced the hitherto prevalent opinion that Syrian Christianity,
whether orthodox or heretical theologically, was uniformly encratite in
temper, and that libertine, non-ascetic gnosticism is but an invention of
the hostile orthodox heresiographers and apologists.

In the present paper the contention is made that this blanket characterization of Syro-Mesopotamian Christianity needs to be modified; a
dossier of texts, from Greek, Latin, Syriac, Armenian, Coptic, Arabic,
and Mandaean sources, pertaining to the history of one such libertine
gnostic group (called "Borborites") known only from reports of its
opponents, is presented and analyzed as a test case. Even after all due
allowance has been made for tendentious and distorted representation,
it will appear that there is an element of factuality, a historical core in
these reports. The Borborites survived tenaciously in Mesopotamia and
elsewhere in the Christian East. As the widely scattered material from
various independent sources demonstrates, they were not just a fiction
of the prurient imagination of celibate ecclesiastical heresy-hunters.
This group reacted to the—admittedly prevailing—ascetic ethos of fasting and sexual abstinence. In its stead they preached (and acted upon)
the view that salvation from the evil powers which rule the world can
only be obtained through a deliberate and full exercise of human sexual
potentialities, specifically in a ritual form wherein the various sexual
emissions, male and female, played a central, sacramental role, and in a
manner which was aimed at the prevention of conception and birth.

This widespread, yet clandestine movement should be strictly distinguished from other non-ascetic gnostic sects of a more "nihilistic" kind.
The possibility furthermore exists that the Borborites (whose separate
existence cannot be traced earlier than to the third century) derive from
the still older Nicolaitan sect, which is already noted with disappro-
bation in the canonical book of Revelation. This and other connections
of the various Eastern non-encratite sects with what one can call
"libertine" phenomena in earliest Christianity deserve to be investigated
further. The study of the material does show the fascinating ethical
diversity within the gnostic movement itself, and more generally in
Eastern Christianity, in the context of which the gnostic movement as a
historical phenomenon is to be placed.

I. Introduction

Walter Bauer found one of the most impressive pieces of evidence for his revolutionary thesis of the priority of "heresy" to "orthodoxy" in a rather exotic hagiographical source, the Syriac biography of Mar Aba, a sixth-century patriarch of the Christian community in the Persian Empire.[1] Only some of the details of the episode in question, the fateful encounter of Mar Aba with a Christian ascetic, as he was about to cross the Tigris river swollen by spring rains, directly concern us now;[2] the important statement is that Mar Aba, at the time still a Zoroastrian, mistook the monk[3] for a Jew or a *kristyānā*—i.e., "Christian," the current local designation for the Marcionites, according to the hagiographer.[4] The traveler, not just a simple monk but in fact a learned scholar from the famous Nestorian ecclesiastical academy of Nisibis,[5] claims the name *mšihāyā*, "Messianist," for himself, hastening, however, to explain its etymological equivalence to *kristyānā*.[6] An intriguing text indeed! Though the material he presents can be expanded and placed more solidly in a historical context, Bauer was surely on the right track in directing his attention first of all to Syria and Mesopotamia and the native Syriac sources.

The precise import of the various eastern Syriac designations for "Christian" is still not quite clear; but it is likely that the loanword *kristyānā* was introduced by Greek-speaking immigrants from the Byzantine provinces, at a relatively early date,[7] and this later became the most common self-designation.[8] The Marcionites' possession of the

---

[1] *Rechtgläubigkeit*, 28; text edited by Bedjan, *Histoire*, 206ff.; the translation is not always accurate: Braun, *Märtyrer*, 188ff.

[2] Cf. Peeters, "Observations," 122.

[3] Bedjan, *Histoire*, 213, lines 8–9.

[4] Bedjan, *Histoire*, 213, lines 2–3 from the bottom.

[5] *'eskolāyā had malpānā* (Bedjan, *Histoire*, 211, line 9). Braun's translation of *'eskolāyā* as "Student" (*Märtyrer*, 189–90) is misleading. Cf. Peeters, "Observations," 122. Bauer merely calls him "a Christian ascetic."

[6] Bedjan, *Histoire*, 214, lines 6–7. The Syriac words in question, correctly given in Syriac script in the German edition, are not quite accurately transcribed in the English translation of Bauer's book (*Orthodoxy*, 23).

[7] This is attested by the occurrence of the (persecuted) group of the *klstyd'n* (read *kristidān*) in two third-century Middle Persian inscriptions of the *res gestae* of the Zoroastrian priest Kartīr (Chaumont, "L'inscription," 343, line 10; 347; Gignoux, "L'inscription," 395). In a third inscription the word in question has been read by the editor as *kristiyān* (Hinz, "Inschrift," 258 [translation 261]. The precise significance of the various groups mentioned, in particular that of the *n'cl'y* (Nazarenes ?) is still *sub judice*. See below, n. 9.

[8] Brock, "Greek Words in Syriac," 91ff. This very plausible explanation does not, to my mind, exclude the possibility that in certain areas these "Greek" immigrants were in fact Marcionite refugees. Marcionism, unlike Manicheeism, was not of native Mesopotamian

name "Christian," according to this text, points to their predominance among rival Christian groups,[9] and relatively late, in eastern Mesopotamia. In fact there is other evidence which indicates that the peak of Marcionite presence and influence in Persian territory should be dated to the fifth and sixth centuries;[10] the immediate reason for this may have been the increasingly effective drive by the Byzantine state authorities to impose ecclesiastical uniformity, which in turn occasioned the flight of non-conforming groups of various sorts to Persian territory.[11]

In contrast to the situation in Byzantium, "orthodox" Christianity in Persia came to be centrally organized only at a late date,[12] was but a politically suspect minority religion[13] and, except on rare occasions, did not have the secular arm at its disposal in its struggle against dissidents. Admittedly the late flourishing of Marcionite Christianity in Persian Mesopotamia presupposes an earlier strong presence in the eastern Roman provinces. Bauer, however, seems to overtax the evidence of the Mar Aba text when, returning to his original focus of interest, he

growth. Incidentally in one ninth-century hagiographical text, recounting a missionary enterprise already in the Islamic period, the Marcionites and the Manichees are still the only identifiable groups among the pagan masses in an outlying region of Persia (Budge, Book of Governors, 1.261, line 14).

[9] The juxtaposition of mšiḥāyā with the (supposedly "secret") confession of Judaism by the monk who bears the very Hebraic name of "Joseph who was called Moses" (Bedjan, Histoire, 211, lines 11–12) should be noted. Bauer makes no comment on it, being interested in the "Marcionite" aspect of the text. Another early Syriac designation for Christians (not discussed by Bauer at all) was naṣrāyā, which in the Syriac NT uniformly translates both Nazōraios and Nazarēnos. The word has been linked with the n'cl'y (read nazarai ?) of the Kartīr inscriptions (Chaumont, "L'inscription," 343). Cf. further Brock, "Greek Words in Syriac," 92. In a Coptic Manichaean Text Mani is represented as debating with a Nazoreus (variant, Nazoraios) who denies that God can be legitimately described as a judge, kritēs, because that would ipso facto make him responsible for objectively evil, violent acts (Polotsky, Kephalaia, 222). Rather than identifying the Nazoreus as a Mandaean, naṣuraya, as do, for example, Rudolph (Mandäer, 1.44, n.1) and Böhlig ("Manichäismus," 189, 193), it is to my mind more likely that the text (generally admitted to go back through a Greek intermediate stage to an Aramaic Vorlage) in fact presents the typical objection of a Marcionite, who bears the still current Syriac designation for Christians, namely "Nazarene." H.-Ch. Puech has earlier, in a book review, suggested the identification of the Nazoreus as a Marcionite, but gave no reasons for it ("Review of Drower," 64,n.1).

[10] Fiey, "Marcionites," 183ff., expanding the documentation collected in Vööbus, Asceticism, 1.45ff. Much of the evidence about Marcionites in Persia comes from the Chronicle of Se'ert, an eleventh-century ecclesiastical chronicle in Arabic, which, however, depends on earlier sources. Bauer, in a somewhat summary fashion dismisses this text, to which he only alludes apropos an apocryphal story of Ephrem and Bardaiṣan as "eine nestorianische Sammlung von Erzählungen" (Rechtgläubigkeit, 35, n.1).

[11] The coming of Manichees and Marcionites to Persian territory, along with other heretics, because of expulsion from Byzantium is explicitly noted in a creedal statement, dated 612 C.E., presented by Christian bishops to the Sasanian emperor Ḥosrou II (Chabot, Synodicon, 567, lines 20ff.; translation 585).

[12] Cf. Gero, "See of Peter" and "Kirche."

[13] Cf. Brock, "Christians."

disarmingly claims that the situation must have been similar with respect to the beginnings of Christianity in Edessa;[14] unfortunately the evidence directly pertaining to Edessa cited by him is not nearly as cogent.[15] He is either not quite aware of, or fails to inform the reader of, dissimilar features in the historical development of Christianity in Byzantine Syria on the one hand and in Persian Mesopotamia on the other.[16] In particular, the previously noted, very specific reasons which seem to have led to the upsurge of Marcionite influence militate against linking the Persian evidence to the thesis of the Marcionite origin of Edessene Christianity.

The study of the intellectual and religious situation in Mesopotamia in late antiquity has made much progress since the first publication of Bauer's book, and has led to a modification of his all too rigid distinction between "orthodoxy" and "heresy."[17] Concretely, the very priority of the Marcionite presence in Edessa as claimed by Bauer has been challenged, in part because of the possible (though not undisputed) relevance of "Thomas" material from Nag Hammadi.[18] Is there any other relation between groups or sects identifiably connected with the Nag Hammadi texts and those in Walter Bauer's Edessa? Bauer does briefly mention the Edessene Valentinians;[19] their presence cannot be traced past the late fourth century in Mesopotamia.[20] The special case of the "worldly" Bardaiṣan (supposedly influenced by Valentinianism) is not directly relevant to the Nag Hammadi corpus and will be left aside here, as will be the sect of the Quqites.[21] What about the other gnostic groups? The appearance of the Syrian "Thomas" tradition in the Nag Hammadi

[14] In Bauer's own words: "Liegt es da nicht nahe, Ähnliches für die Anfänge des Christentums in Edessa zu behaupten" (Rechtgläubigkeit, 29).

[15] Bauer, Rechtgläubigkeit, 41, n. 1, with a precarious argument from silence.

[16] It is, to my mind, telling that Bauer is apparently unaware of the (still standard) history of Persian Christianity by Labourt (Christianisme). See now also Fiey, Jalons.

[17] In particular through the work of Drijvers; cf. e.g., his articles "Edessa," "Rechtgläubigkeit," "Christentum" and "Syriac-Speaking Christianity."

[18] Cf. Koester's seminal article, "Gnomai."

[19] E.g., Rechtgläubigkeit, 29.

[20] On the famous incident, known from Ambrose's letters, of the Valentinian meeting house, Valentinianorum conventiculum in Callinicum in the Osrrhoene cf. Koschorke "Patristische Materialien," 124, 133. We are of course talking about concrete, identifiable, "institutional" presence; the mere survival or influence of certain gnostic ideas (e.g., Vööbus, Asceticism, 1.55, n. 120: Liber graduum and Valentinianism) is beyond our purview here. The appearance of Valentinianism in lists of exotic Christian heresies presented by Muslim authors who lived in Mesopotamia is seemingly only literary antiquarianism (cf. e.g., al-Nadim, Fihrist, 2. 815, s.v. Walānashīyah [sic]; al-Akbar, Häresiographie, 82 [Arabic], lines 1–2, s.v. Walinṭinīyā; cf. comment, 81).

[21] Cf. Drijvers, "Bardaiṣan, Repräsentant des syrischen Synkretismus," evaluating critical reactions to his monograph, Bardaiṣan. On the case of the Quqites, where the sources in part coincide with those here investigated; cf. the same author's "Quq."

texts has made scholars even more acutely aware of the predominantly
ascetic character of early Syrian Christianity, whether gnostic or not.
More generally, the evidence of the Nag Hammadi corpus as a whole
has increasingly led to the interpretation of gnosticism, at last seen
through its own texts, as a uniformly ascetic, encratite movement.[22] But
one abiding lesson of Bauer's pioneering work is that one should
patiently look for evidences of variety before opting for uniformity.

Our specific goal here is to explore the possibility of still more variety,
specifically of a non-encratite type within the movement broadly characterized as Syro-Mesopotamian Christian gnosticism. Our study will
furthermore concentrate on material pertaining only to one group, that
of the Borborites, and will attempt to trace the "trajectory," on the basis
of, in part, very scattered and fragmentary evidence.

II. The Borborites in the Fourth Century and Later

Though we intend to deal with Syro-Mesopotamian gnosticism, paradoxically the key evidence comes from Epiphanius' well-known, supposedly firsthand description of the practices of the sect of the Borborites in Egypt.[23] We take Epiphanius' evidence[24] as defining at a
particular time and place the character of the group, in a sense fixing a
small portion of its trajectory. We shall first attempt to project this
forward, tracing its presence elsewhere in the fourth century and later,
and then backward, to its origins in the early Christian centuries. The
occurrence of the epithet "Borborite" or "Borborian,"[25] though not a self-
designation,[26] and occasionally perhaps quite inaccurately used, will
serve as a first diagnostic feature in sifting the material.

[22] Cf. the programmatic statements of Wisse, "Die Sextus-Sprüche."
[23] For orientation and a partial listing of the sources, cf. Fendt, "Borborianer" and
Bardy, "Borboriens."
[24] Epiph. Pan. 26 (Holl, Epiphanius, 1.275ff.).
[25] Borboritai (Holl, Epiphanius, 1.268, line 21); Borborianoi (279, line 7); so also
Philostorgius. In Syriac the form bārboryānē (Ephrem, Vita of Rabbula, catalogue of
Maruta) seems to be the earlier, and corresponds to Borborianoi; the form bārboryānu
(Letter to Cosmas, Theodore of Mopsuestia, Testament of Pseudo-Ephrem, Michael
Syrus, Bar Hebraeus, Theodor bar Koni) is later, with the Grecizing plural-suffix ū (cf.
Nöldeke, Grammatik, 59). The Armenian plural form Borboritonkʻ (Moses Khorenaçi)
reflects Borboritai; the other Armenian form, Borborianoskʻ (Koriwn), corresponds to
"Borborians." Priscillian, Augustine, Jerome, and Gennadius attest the Latin form
Borborita, whereas Filastrius has Borborianus. The imperial legislation attests both
Borborita and Borborianus. In the subsequent discussion we shall, merely as a matter of
convenience, stay with the uniform designation "Borborite."
[26] That "Borborite" is originally a deformation of some name connected with Barbelo
(e.g., cf. Epiphanius' Barbelita; Holl, Epiphanius, 1.279, line 26) though sometimes
asserted (e.g., Quispel, "Borborianer") is not imperative. In any case, the immediate
derivation from borboros "slime" (the metaphorical use of which as "moral filth" is early

Epiphanius' account of the Borborites has been repeatedly the object of close scrutiny;[27] only a few salient features will be registered here. Epiphanius completed the Panarion sometime in the 370s;[28] since he refers to experiences of his youth in the text in question, we are probably dealing with the Borborites around 340. Epiphanius presents the sect as being already widespread in his time, and seemingly well organized. Its adherents were known under several names,[29] though, as was the case with several other groups, their preferred self-designation was that of Gnōstikoi.[30] Epiphanius does not claim that the sect is of recent vintage, and he does not link it with an individual founder. It is described as being closely connected with the sect of the Nicolaitans, but the two groups are not regarded by him as identical.[31]

The central, distinguishing feature of the sect, its devotion to the so-called sperma cult, described by him in vivid detail, can hardly be dismissed as a prurient invention. In the simplest of terms it involved the extraction, collection, and solemn, sacramental consecration and

and well attested) is fairly clear. It should perhaps be noted that in one Armenian text the rare adjective borboriton is employed in a context not connected with the Borborites, describing the amours of Semiramis in the sense of "lascivious" (Moses Khorenaçi, Book I, ch. 15 (Tiflis edition, 48, line 15; cf. Thomson, Moses, 96, n. 1 and Hübschmann, Grammatik, 344). B. Pearson suggested in the course of the discussion of the paper that nevertheless the pejorative epithet may have eventually been adopted as a self-designation, much like "Cynic."

[27] Benko, "Phibionites"; Fendt, Mysterien, 3ff.; Leisegang, Gnosis, 186–95. For a complete translation and a commentary cf. Tardieu, "Épiphane contre les gnostiques." I owe this reference to the kindness of P.-H. Poirier. Koschorke's sweeping denial of any reliability to the patristic material about libertine gnosticism (Polemik, 123-4) is unfortunately not based on an analysis as detailed and careful as his close investigation of the Nag Hammadi texts; it is marred by an unargued dismissal of Epiphanius' testimony and a regrettable refusal to enter into dialogue with scholarship which has been willing to take the patristic evidence into serious consideration. It is to be hoped that Wisse's announced monograph on the ethics of gnosticism (cf. "Die Sextus-Sprüche," 123, n. 23) will put the entire matter in a more balanced perspective.

[28] Quasten, Patrology, 3. 388.

[29] For a listing cf. Holl, Anakephalaiosis, 1.235, lines 17–22 (a post-Epiphanian?) compendium of the Panarion). Stratiotikoi, Phibionitai, Sekundianoi are, according to Epiphanius, Egyptian designations; elsewhere they are known as Sokratitai, Zakchaoi, Koddianoi, and Borboritai. Not mentioned here are the exclusively homosexual Levitai (a self-designation), supposedly regarded as the elite of the sect (Holl, Epiphanius, 1.292, lines 9ff.).

[30] E.g., Holl, Epiphanius, 1.274, line 18. Cf. below, n. 106.

[31] E.g., the deluded Gnōstikoi derive from Nikolaos (Holl, Epiphanius, 1.275, line 1). One should not obliterate too readily the distinction between the Borborites and other groups, though affinities surely existed (cf. below, n. 114). Thus M. Tardieu's interpretation of a passing remark of Epiphanius about a detail of "Sethian" mythology, shared by several groups (Pan. 40; Holl, Epiphanius, 2.88, lines 10–12) as implying that "Sethiens, Archontiques et Gnostiques [i.e., Borborites] ne constituent pas trois groupes distincts, mais une seule et même ideologie" ("Les livres de Seth," 206, n. 11) unjustifiably neglects Epiphanius' very precise data about the origins of the Archontics.

consumption of bodily fluids, male and female,[32] which contributed to the further propagation of the human race, and thus to the continued entrapment of divine substance by the evil archons. In these fluids is concentrated the spiritual element, found scattered in the world, in particular in food-stuffs (including meat!), of which the initiates can and should partake.[33] The mythology proper is a version of the Barbelo-gnostic myth, as known from Irenaeus and the *Apocryphon of John*.[34]

Epiphanius reports the sectarians' use of biblical texts, and gives samples of their allegorical exegesis; more interestingly he cites at some length from a number of apocryphal works. In particular the "Questions of Mary" give a taste of the kind of "libertine" gnostic literature which is conspicuously missing from the Nag Hammadi Library, and their "Birth of Mary" gives a violently anti-Jewish version of the murder of Zacharias.[35] The Gospel of Philip used by the Borborite "Levites" gives a liturgical formula for the ascent of the soul through the archontic spheres; perhaps from the same source comes the story of the ascetic prophet Elijah's inability to ascend to heaven, because of his having begotten children with a female demon through involuntary *pollutio nocturna*.[36] None of this material is found in the Nag Hammadi *Gospel of Philip*.

No extracts are given by Epiphanius from the Borborites' *Apocalypse of Adam*, so one cannot say whether a relation to the Nag Hammadi text by this name exists.[37] A stronger connection is found, however, between their book *Noria* and the Nag Hammadi *Hypostasis of the Archons*; as one investigation suggests, the Borborite text may be a liturgical adaptation of a common source.[38] The quotation from the Borborite "Gospel of

---

[32] The menstrual discharge was popularly regarded as actively contributing to generation; hence the Borborite preoccupation with it and its designation as *haima tou Christou* (Holl, *Epiphanius*, 281, lines 16–17).

[33] Holl, *Epiphanius*, 1.285, line 25–286, line 4. The same pantheistic notion is of course operative in the (ascetic) eating habits of the Manichaean elect (cf. e.g., Böhlig, *Gnosis*, 37). What is here missing is the Manichaean sense of guilt connected with the concomitant wounding of nature.

[34] Cf. Schmidt, "Irenaeus," 334 and "Borborianer (Borboriten)," and Fallon, *Enthronement*, 81ff.

[35] On these fragments cf. Hennecke-Schneemelcher, *NT Apocrypha*, 1. 338, 344.

[36] Holl, *Epiphanius*, 1.293, lines 1ff. It should be noted that according to Epiphanius, the members of the pseudo-monastic sect of the "First Origenists" (*Pan.* 62), who in their ethical aberrations were related to the *Gnōstikoi*, imitated Onan, son of Judah and carefully stamped their sexual emissions into the soil, lest the demons get hold of them (Holl, *Epiphanius*, 2.399, lines 21–23). One wonders what the Acts of Andrew used by this group (399, lines 25–26) were like, and their relation, if any, to the extant encratite Acts of Andrew!

[37] Böhlig-Labib is cautiously optimistic about a possible connection (*Apocalypsen*, 86).

[38] Dümmer, "Angaben," 205–7; slightly expanded in the same author's "Sprachkenntnisse," 429–30.

Eve," concerned with the mystical "ingathering" theme has now been tentatively linked to the intriguing Nag Hammadi tract called *Thunder*, and to a large cluster of other "Sethian" texts.[39]

Supposedly as a result of Epiphanius' denunciation, the Borborite clique he personally knew was exposed and expelled from the city (Alexandria?).[40] At any rate the Borborite trail in Egypt comes to an end here. In the Latin West the Borborites existed for the most part only in the late learned "Epiphanian" heresiological tradition.[41] What was the situation in Syria and adjacent areas? One could surmise that Epiphanius already hints at the existence of a Syrian branch by giving an Aramaic etymology for *Koddianoi*,[42] one of the many names of the sect; however, this may well be just part of his pedantic exhibition of a much-praised, but in fact rather limited multilingualism.[43] It has been suggested, on rather general history-of-religions grounds, that the sect originated in Syria;[44] we shall discuss this matter later. But there is other, more solid literary evidence, of an abundant and varied sort, for the continued presence of the Borborites in the Levant, including the region of Edessa. This material, though understandably overshadowed by Epiphanius' detailed and very sensational report, deserves further scrutiny.

On the western flank of the Syrian region, there is evidence for the presence of Borborites, specifically in Cilicia in southern Asia Minor,

[39] Cf. above Layton, "Riddle," pp. 37–54.

[40] Holl, *Epiphanius*, 1.298, lines 14ff. The plural "to the bishops (*episkopois*) in that place" is curious—Alexandria surely had only one bishop. Is Epiphanius referring to secular authorities?

[41] Cf. Filastrius of Brescia, *Haer.* (written between 385 and 391; see Altaner-Stuiber, *Patrologie*, 369), ch. 83, 247–48 for a curious reference to the Borborites as *membra sua deformantes* (248, line 1); Augustine, *De haeresibus* (written ca. 428, dependent on Filastrius [Altaner-Stuiber, 425]), ch. 6, 292–93. Priscillian writing earlier (ca. 380) makes a perhaps independent passing mention of the *Borborita* heresy in a list of anathematized sects (*Tractatus* I, Schepps edition, 23, line 16).

[42] Epiphanius derives the name from *kodda* which, he says, in the *syriake dialektos* means "dish" (*paropsis, tryblion*); he would relate the designation to their enforced solitary eating habits—no one would have table fellowship with such polluted folk! (Holl, *Epiphanius*, 1.279, lines 18 ff.). Is there anything trustworthy here? *Kaddā* in Jewish Aramaic in fact refers to a narrow-necked jug for water or grain; the corresponding Syriac word is *kadānā* (See Brockelmann, *Lexicon*, 318). Could perhaps the name rather allude to the practice of abortion and be connected with Syriac *kudā* "placenta" or "afterbirth," admittedly a rare medical term (Brockelmann, *Lexicon*, 320)?

[43] See Dümmer, "Sprachkenntnisse," 396ff. The Aramaic and Hebrew etymologies for the name of the prophet Barkabbas, whose writings circulated among the Borborites (Holl, *Epiphanius*, 1.277, lines 3ff.), have no evidential value.

[44] "Unzweifelhaft hat die Sekte ihren Ursprung in Syrien gehabt; der ganze orgiastische Kult mit seinen Obszönitäten erinnert nur zu sehr an die berühmten Schilderungen von Herodot über den phönikischen Astarte-Kult" (Schmidt, *Schriften*, 575, n. 2). The crucial difference of course is that the Astarte rites were part of a fertility cult—though it is precisely the gnostics who can be expected to reverse the original purpose!

approximately at the same time as Epiphanius encountered them in Egypt. A fifth-century source[45] preserves a very curious story, hardly a heresiological commonplace: the Arian Aetius was roundly defeated in disputation by a Borborite; his despondency was only cured by his subsequent rhetorical victory over a Manichaean notable.[46] Epiphanius himself mentions that (this ?) Aetius unmasked the Palestinian ascetic Peter, founder of the sect of the Archontics, as belonging to the Gnōstikoi (a term which for Epiphanius is, of course, synonymous with "Borborites").[47] Aetius of Antioch was, as it is well known, the founder of the extreme Arian party of the Anomoeans.[48] Against the background of his antignostic and anti-Manichaean activities and the generally rationalistic tendency of his adherents, one can understand the apparent negative reference to the Anomoeans in the Nag Hammadi tractate Concept of Our Great Power (VI,4),[49] as indeed a concrete allusion to the Arians, reflecting perhaps original contact in a Palestinian or Syrian milieu,[50] and not merely as the gnostics' adoption of orthodox heresiological cliches.[51]

[45] The ecclesiastical chronicle of the Arian Philostorgius, preserved for the most part only in a Byzantine epitome. Cf. Quasten, Patrology, 3.530–32.

[46] Bidez, Philostorgius, 46, lines 15ff. The episode took place during the early part of the reign of Constantius II, ca. 340, when Aetius was forced to go into one of his several exiles (cf. Venables, "Aetius," 52). Unfortunately the contents of neither disputation are indicated.

[47] Haer. 40; Holl, Epiphanius, 2.81, lines 12ff. Admittedly the Aetius in question is usually identified with another, local Palestinian bishop (cf. Venables, "Aetius," 53 and Puech, "Archontiker," cols. 634–5). But, despite some minor chronological difficulties, there is no cogent reason against taking this Aetius to be the Arian controversialist, who was ordained bishop without see in the early 360s. The Borborite component of the Archontic system may well explain the split of the sect into an ascetic and an antinomian group (Holl, Epiphanius, 2.82, lines 20ff.). This very specific anchoring of a gnostic group in monasticism should be welcome support to recent attempts to situate the Nag Hammadi Library in a Pachomian milieu (e.g., Wisse, "Monasticism in Egypt," 430ff.; Orlandi, "Catechesis," 85ff.; Hedrick, "Gnostic Proclivities").

[48] This is explicitly asserted e.g., by Epiphanius (Haer. 76; Holl, Epiphanius, 3.414, lines 15ff.). Cf. further Abramowski, "Eunomios," cols. 936ff.

[49] "Hand out the word and water of life. Cease from the evil lusts and desires and (the teachings of) the Anomoeans (ni-anhomoion)" (NHC VI, 4:40,5–7; translation by Wisse in Parrott, Codices V and VI, 304). It should be noted, however, that Krause renders the crucial phrase as just "ungleiche Dinge" (Codex II und Codex VI, 155); Chérix translates it as "ces (énergies) disparates" (Le Concept, 14) and argues rather cautiously against Wisse's interpretation (Le Concept, 27 n. 56. A recently published word-list gives as equivalent "was (dem Gnostiker) nicht entspricht" (Siegert, Register, 213). The matter clearly demands further investigation.

[50] It should be noted that Ephrem mentions the Arians and the Aetians ('a'eṭyānē) in the same listing of Edessene heresies as that in which the Borborites also appear (Contra haereses, Beck edition, 79, line 11; 84, line 29). Cf. below, p. 298. The Arian persecution of the Valentinians in Edessa is attested in a letter of the emperor Julian (Wright, Julian, 3.126).

[51] So Wisse, "Heresiologists," 208; Koschorke, Polemik, 8, n. 15.

At any rate, the Asia Minor Borborites lived on; Jerome, who resided for a long time in the East, in his commentary on Galatians (composed around 387–89)[52] mentions the Borborites among the heretics who posed a danger to the see of Ancyra in Galatia.[53] The famous dyophysite theologian, Theodore, bishop of Mopsuestia (in Cilicia!), in his commentary on the Gospel of John, written in the early fifth century, and extant in its entirety only in Syriac translation,[54] refers to the Borborites, ostensibly in a historical context, but one which seems to indicate his acquaintance with the sect either from his earlier years in Antioch or through his episcopal experience in the Asia Minor milieu. In the course of commenting on John 16:2, Theodore identifies the crypto-Christian followers of Simon Magus with the Borborites[55] and makes the nefarious deeds of the sectarians responsible for the second-century persecution of Christians in Gaul, during the reign of the Emperor Verus, as reported by Eusebius of Caesarea.[56]

Turning now to Syria proper, we find the earliest mention of the Borborites there in a poetical work of Ephrem the Syrian, the hymns *Contra haereses*, written probably in the late 360s, after his migration from Nisibis to Edessa.[57] The "Borborites who defiled themselves"[58] are

---

[52] Altaner-Stuiber, *Patrologie*, 400.

[53] *PL*, 26 (1884), col. 383 BC.

[54] Altaner-Stuiber, *Patrologie*, 321; Geerard, *Clavis* 2.350–51.

[55] "They are called Borborites (*bārboryānu*) by many and are with difficulty distinguished from the faithful" (Vosté, *Theodori Mopsuestensi*, 289, line 29–290, line 1).

[56] Vosté, *Theodori Mopsuestensi*, 290, lines 11ff. A sixth-century author, Barḥadbešabbā of Halwan, in reworking this passage misinterpreted the name of the emperor as Pērōz, the Sasanian ruler of Persia in the late fifth-century (Nau, *La Lettre à Cosme*, 190). The resulting picture of a persecution of Christians in fifth-century Iran occasioned by the misdeeds of the Borborites, so presented in this writer's earlier discussion of the matter (Gero, *Barṣauma*, 18), should be modified accordingly.

[57] The date of Ephrem's coming to Edessa is not known; probably it was 363 C.E. the year of Jovian's surrender of Nisibis to the Persians, or slightly later. Ephrem died in 373 (Guidi, *Chronica*, 5, lines 6ff.). The Edessene origin of the hymns *Contra haereses*, apparently assumed as a matter of course by Bauer (*Rechtgläubigkeit*, 26), is not an undisputed datum. Beck, the foremost expert on Ephrem and indefatigable editor of his works, regards the *Contra haereses* as ideologically an early work, on the same level as the Paradise hymns ("Ephraem," cols. 521–22), but he has not spelled out his views in detail. El-Khoury (*Interpretation*, 155), following Beck's hint, explicitly sets the *Contra haereses* in the Nisibine period (306–363). R. Murray would date the work to the early Nisibine period, because supposedly the Arians do not yet appear among the opponents ("Ephraem," 755); this is simply not correct, since Arians and Aetians are mentioned in *madrāšā* 22 (see above, n. 50). That these hymns against heresies were written in Edessa rather than in Nisibis seems, to my mind, indicated by the fact that Ephrem identified himself with the local "Paluṭ" tradition, and that the spectrum of heresies is much broader than what can be extracted from the Nisibine works. The whole question, however, deserves further study.

[58] *Contra haereses*, Beck edition, 79, line 15.

mentioned in a list of heresies, though no detailed description of their practices is provided.[59] Despite the activities of the bishop Qunē, of whom Bauer makes so much,[60] one can assume that the subsequent weakening of episcopal authority in Edessa, in the latter half of the fourth century, in the wake of the Arian controversy, contributed to the survival of various heterodox groups there.[61] But then Rabbula, the powerful bishop of Edessa in the early fifth century (412–436),[62] according to his *Vita*, drove out the Borborites entirely from his diocese;[63] unfortunately the biographer was so outraged at their conduct and tenets that he refuses to describe the same![64] A like reticence about the "shameful folly" of the Borborites is found in the Christological homily of Narsai, which ranges them among the docetists.[65]

Energetic inquisitorial action against the Borborites is recorded as having been undertaken in the Byzantine-controlled section of Armenia by no less a person that Maštoç (Mesrop), the inventor of the Armenian alphabet, the father of Armenian literature—and longtime friend of Rabbula! According to his *Vita*,[66] Maštoç had little success in converting

[59] The pseudonymous *Testament* of Ephrem also mentions the Borborites (Ps.-Ephrem, *Testament*, 58, line 505); this is probably based on the passage just noted from the *Contra haereses*. The *Testament*, according to the latest investigations, is in its entirety post-Ephremic; it dates perhaps from the fifth century, at any rate from before 502 (cf. Outtier, "Ephrèm," 24–25).

[60] *Rechtgläubigkeit*, 38ff.

[61] Theodoret mentions the presence of Messalians in Edessa in the 380s (*Hist. eccl.* IV.10; Parmentier, *Theodoret*, 230, lines 10ff.). It is telling that it is not by the bishop of Edessa that they are exposed, but by the bishop of Antioch, Flavian, who sends a contingent of monks to Edessa to apprehend them!

[62] Cf. Blum, *Rabbula*, 7, 39 on the chronology of Rabbula's episcopate.

[63] Overbeck, *Ephraemi*, 194, lines 2ff. Bauer paraphrases at some length this portion of the Rabbula biography (*Rechtgläubigkeit*, 30ff.); but singles out only the mention of the Marcionites and Manichees.

[64] It should be noted that the Borborites, in contrast to the 'Audāyē and Zaduqāyē are not said to possess ecclesiastical buildings which could be confiscated. The Borborites further are regarded as totally incorrigible; by contrast Marcionites, Manichees, and Messalians are but erring sheep, who could be easily integrated into the orthodox community (Overbeck, *Ephraemi*, 194, lines 9ff.). G. Hoffmann's attempt to identify the Zaduqāyē mentioned in the Syriac *Vita* of Sābā, missionary in the fifth century in Persian Kurdistan (Bedjan, *Acta*, 2.67), with these Edessene victims of Rabbula's zeal is already very doubtful; but clearly untenable is his further linking of the Kurdistan sect with the "Levite" section of the Borborites, merely because the Kurdish Zaduqāyē are said to have been like the Sodomites! (*Auszüge*, 124). Their worship of a boar's head (probably the boar incarnation of the Persian divinity Vᵉrᵉtragna) is hardly to be connected with the Borborites' Sabaoth archon, who had the head of an ass or a boar (Holl, *Epiphanius*, 1.287, lines 15ff.). Harnack unfortunately accepts Hoffmann's tentative identifications and asserts accordingly that the Borborites of the patristic sources worshipped a boar's head and were to be found in Kurdistan (*Ketzer-Katalog*, 10, n. 7).

[65] *bedyā daškirutā* (Martin, "Homélie," 471, line 17). Narsai was active in Edessa and Nisibis in the late fifth century; cf. Gero, *Barṣauma*, 60ff.

[66] Written by his disciple Koriwn: Cf. Akinian, *Koriwn*, 40, lines 55ff. For a partial

the Borborites; thereupon, with the active aid of the Byzantine authorities,[67] he turned to the harsher methods of imprisonment and even
torture. Since the Borborites, despite these steps, remained recalcitrant,
they were all branded (a common punishment for heresy),[68] smeared
black, then painted various colors,[69] and finally expelled from the land.
Rather significantly, no similar measures are reported in the Persian-
controlled part of Armenia.

The presence of the Borborites is attested not only in these provincial
areas; a fifth-century Syriac source explains why, at the time of his
coming to Constantinople, Nestorius had to resort to energetic, and in
part unpopular, measures: ecclesiastical discipline was in such disarray
that the Arians were openly building a church for themselves, normally
cloistered monks were sauntering in public places, and "the Borborites
went freely into the churches together with the Christians."[70] The sixth-

translation based on the critical edition cf. Inglisian, "Leben," 123ff.

[67] The later writer Moses Khorenaçi (ninth century?) claims to reproduce the text of a
letter from the emperor Theodosius II and the patriarch Atticus to Maštoç and his
superior, the *catholicos* Sahak, authorizing them either to convert or to expel the
Borborites (III.58, Tiflis edition, 334–35; translation by Thomson, *Moses*, 330). Moses
further implies that Maštoç or his agents had recourse to capital punishment (Tiflis
edition, 337). This is not corroborated by Koriwn; he only mentions in more general terms
an imperial rescript which authorized, *inter alia*, that steps be taken against "the
pestilential sect of the *Borborianos*" (Akinian, *Koriwn*, 36, line 36). Moses gives the
spelling *Borboriton* for the name of the sect (Tiflis edition, 337, line 19).

[68] The council of Šahapiwan, legislating against adherents of the sect of the Mclnē
(literally "filthy," which would well correspond to "Borborite"; but probably Messalians
or even Paulicians are meant), decreed, *inter alia*, branding in the face with "the sign of
a fox" (*aluesdrošm*) (Akinian, *Kanones*, 93, line 444); for a translation cf. Garsoian,
Heresy, 83.

[69] Obviously some ancient Armenian equivalent of tarring and feathering! Inglisian
supposes this to have been the punishment for the Borborites' smearing themselves with
semen in their sacramental rites ("Leben," 183, n. 22).

[70] The whole episode is approximately dated by the patriarchate of Atticus (406–425);
in fact one can arrive at a closer date of 422 for the visit of Maštoç to the Byzantine
capital (Peeters, "Pour l'histoire," 180–81). I suspect, though, that we may be dealing with
a tendentious substitution, and Maštoç's patron was in fact the patriarch Nestorius!
Though Atticus did urge Amphilocius of Iconium to deal sternly with the Messalians, he
was not, it seems, a heresy-hunter by inclination; he is in fact remembered for his
conciliatory attitude to the Novatians and the diehard followers of John Chrysostom (cf.
Disdier, "Atticus"). In contrast to Nestorius he was not a controversial figure and for
patriotic Armenian historiography, moreover, had the great advantage of being a native
of Sebasteia in Lesser Armenia (Socrates, *Hist. eccl.* VI.20; Hussey, *Socrates*, 718, lines
5ff.). But it was Nestorius who was from the outset a *malleus haereticorum* (Socrates,
VII.29; Hussey, *Socrates*, 799); his contact with Borborites in the capital and the imperial
law of 428 against heretics by name would also have provided a more natural setting for
the launching of a campaign against Borborites in the eastern provinces. But for the
hagiographer Koriwn (or a later reviser?), of course, it would have been highly compro-
mising to make his hero the agent of the future archheretic Nestorius; hence the possible
doctoring of the chronology and of the name of one of the principals in the episode in
question.

century chronicle of Barḥadbešabbā elaborates the account, claiming that Nestorius had to oppose hidden Borborites and Manichees among the clergy of the capital.[71]

It is hardly a surprise to find an imperial law, in the name of Theodosius II and Valentinian III, dated a few months after Nestorius' accession (and promulgated at his instigation?) in which for the first time the Borborites are mentioned along with a number of other heretical groups, in part very actual (Arians, Macedonians, Eunomians, Manichees); they are forbidden to build churches and to hold religious services.[72] The validity of the enactment was reiterated in a *novella* "decree" of the same emperors some ten years later.[73]

In the following century a summary of the original enactment is again found, in the Justinianic codex.[74] The Borborites are then further mentioned in an independent *novella* of Justinian, concerned with preventing heretics from giving binding legal testimony.[75] The persecuting pressure indicated by these surviving pieces of legislation may have had some effect: the so-called pseudo-Nicene canons, probably composed in Syria in the late fifth century,[76] mention the Borborites among those sects whose converted adherents should be rebaptized.[77] Gennadius of Marseilles also notes the Borborites in a similar connection, among heretics whose baptism is invalid because they do not employ the trinitarian formula.[78]

That Borborites in the post-Justinianic period were not merely a curiosity of the law books is made plausible by the account preserved in the twelfth-century monophysite chronicle of Michael the Syrian, which goes back to good, earlier sources. According to this text, during the reign of Justinian's successor, Emperor Justin II (565–78),[79] the Borborites

---

[71] Nau, *Barḥadbešabbā*, 530, lines 9ff.

[72] Mommsen, *Theodosiani*, 1. pt. 2. 878 (Book XVI, 5, 65, dated May 30, 428).

[73] Meyer-Mommsen, *Leges*, 10 (*novella* 3, dated January 31, 438).

[74] Krüger, *Corpus*, 59.

[75] Krüger, *Corpus*, 59 (I, 5, 21, dated 531 C.E.).

[76] See Graf, *Geschichte*, 1.587–88.

[77] Vööbus, *Canons*, 57, line 19; translation is found in CSCO volume 440 (1982), 52 and Braun, *Nicaena*, 62.

[78] The name of the *Borboritae* is already in the list of the genuine, short recension of the text (ch. 22; *PL*, 42, 1217), composed in the 470s, and is also kept in the sixth-century long recension (ch. 52; *PL*, 83, 1238 D; *PL*, 58, 993 D; Oehler, *Corporis haereseologici*, 1.348). On the two recensions of the work cf. Hamman, *Patrologiae*, 3.722.

[79] The text has "*Justinian* the Second," but the context makes it clear that the events take place in the sixth century. Hence the emperor in question cannot be Justinian II, who reigned at the end of the seventh and in the early eighth century. "Justin" and "Justinian" are easily confused in Syriac script. Doresse's statement about the Borborites (*Livres secrets*, 1.354) should accordingly be rectified.

"who are called *mlywn'* in our language"[80] supposedly affected by anti-Manichaean persecution,[81] left Persian territory, went first to Armenia and then to Syria. They disguised themselves there as monks and occupied monasteries abandoned by the monophysites, fleeing Chalcedonian oppression. Michael further attributes ritual child murder, magical practices, and promiscuous behavior to these pseudo-monastic sectarians.[82] The thirteenth-century chronicle of Bar Hebraeus copies Michael's account, and additionally claims that the immoral feasts in question are also attested in one particular Muslim source.[83]

The foregoing material, though frankly of unequal value, already illustrates the widespread and persistent presence of the Borborites in the Orient, and should give a pause to those inclined to dismiss the statements of the early heresiographers; but it provides relatively little concrete information about the Borborites tenets. It should be admitted that no other source gives information as detailed as that found in Epiphanius, and some later notices in fact are merely the literary echoes of Epiphanius' work.[84]

A number of authors (out of genuine indignation or merely to shield their ignorance?) refuse to recount particulars. Thus the (fifth-century?) heresy catalogue, attributed to Maruta of Mayperkat (Martyropolis)[85] only says: "Because of their obscenity and their defilement, great lasciviousness and abominable deeds and foul works and (because) they pour out the blood of babes for sorcery, I am excused from their story, from writing anything about them."[86] The work of Barḥadbešabbā,

---

[80] To be vocalized *malyonē*? The Syriac designation is a *hapax legomenon* and has no obvious explanation. Bar Hebraeus gives the form *mlywny* (vocalized *malyonāyē*?); Brockelmann merely glosses the word as "*borborianoi secta*" (*Lexicon*, 391), following Smith (*Thesaurus*, col. 2138).

[81] Probably the Zoroastrian sect of the Mazdakites are meant, heavily persecuted by the Persian emperor Ḫosrou I. The chronicler's additional connecting of these Borborites with the Marcionites is either a simple *lapsus*, or the result of a confusion with the sect of the Markianites, a Messalian group in Byzantium at this time.

[82] Chabot, *Chronique*, 4.312, inner column, top; for translation cf. vol. 2, pp. 248–9.

[83] Abbeloos-Lamy, *Chronicon*, 1. cols. 219–21. The eleventh-century Muslim scholar al-Bīrūnī, to whom Bar Hebraeus explicitly refers, does not associate any sexual excesses with the Nestorian feast al-Mašuš (for translation cf. Sachau, *Chronology*, 309); but promiscuous sexuality is mentioned in this context by the tenth-century writer al-Šabusti (Sachau, *Klosterbuch*, 11).

[84] E.g., Theodore bar Koni (eighth century?): Scher, *Theodorus bar Koni*, 300, lines 9–12; John of Damascus (eighth century), *Liber de haeresibus*, ch. 26: Kotter, *Schriften*, 4.27. The appearance of the Borborites in an extremely long, learned list of heresies in the seventh-century *Epistula synodica* of Sophronius of Jerusalem (*PG* 87.3, 3189 C) is seemingly also merely due to the literary influence of Epiphanius' *Panarion*.

[85] Bauer mentions the preamble of this text (*Rechtgläubigkeit*, 33), but takes too literally, it seems, the rhetorical expressions about the prevalence of heresy in the writer's milieu (Byzantine Armenia?).

[86] Vööbus, *Canons*, 25, lines 11–16.

already noted,[87] expands this entry; it singles out the Borborite belief that the world was created by angels, and claims that the central rite consisted of the ritual defilement of ten virgins in the sanctuary. If one of these conceived, the foetus was extracted and sacramentally consumed. Interesting is the additional detail that the woman in question was thereupon worshipped "in the place of Mary."[88]

It is this last trait of eccentric Mariolatry which is seemingly taken up in the tenth-century Arabic chronicle of the patriarch Eutychius of Alexandria. He makes the Barbarāniyyah into tritheists, who associated Christ and Mary as gods alongside the supreme divinity, and dates the sect back to the time of Constantine and the council of Nicaea.[89] The fourteenth-century compendium of Abu'l-Barakāt reproduces bodily the accounts of both Maruta and of Eutychius.[90]

Potentially more important than these late literary echoes are what appear to be concrete allusions to Borborites in the ninth book of the Mandaean Right Ginza.[91] The work mentions specifically a sect (literally "gate") of the mnunayya, characterized by immorality and magical practices;[92] one of the epithets specifically seems to correspond to the designation "Borborite."[93] From the viewpoint of the puritanical Mandaean family ethic the text further execrates, in "Borborite" terms, Christian ascetics, male as well as female.[94] It connects the Christian sacramental practices of baptism and communion with infanticide and

---

[87] Cf. above, pp. 297, n. 56 and p. 300.

[88] Nau, Barhadbešabbā, 190.

[89] Eutychius, Annales, Cheikho ed., 126, lines 1–4. On the author cf. Graf, Geschichte, 2.32ff.

[90] Abu al-Barakât, Lampe des ténèbres, 689, 694–95. On the author, cf. Graf, Geschichte, 2.438ff.

[91] Petermann, Thesaurus, volume 1; translation is found in Lidzbarski, Ginza.

[92] Petermann, Thesaurus, 1.225, lines 10ff.; translation and commentary in Lidzbarski, Ginza, 226. As Lidzbarski points out (226, n. 4), though the designation is similar to that of the Manichees (in Syriac manināyē), these cannot be meant, since the Manichees, devotees of Mar-Mani, are later separately described. Lidzbarski further already suggests a possible connection with malyonāyē, the alternative designation for Borborites in Bar Hebraeus (cf. above, n. 80).

[93] Namely kita mšakna, "a slimy clod" (Petermann, Thesaurus, 1.225, line 15). The adjective mšakna is derived from šikna "mud" or "filth" (see Lidzbarski, Ginza, 226, n. 5). As the Syriac škānā, it could also specifically refer to "faeces"; so translated in Drower-Macuch, Mandaic Dictionary, 279. The epithet paradoxically coupled with this, sada d-gubria gabaria, "block of mighty men" (Petermann, Thesaurus, 1.225), could à la rigueur reflect the Syriac zakāyē "victorious ones" underlying Zakchaioi (Holl, Epiphanius, 1. 279, line 25), an alternative designation for the Borborites.

[94] The semen of the former runs down their legs, the latter destroy the foetus in the womb! All this is regarded as part of a mysterious qudsa d-atana d-arba ligria "sacrament of the she-ass with four legs" (Petermann, Thesaurus, 1.226, lines 11ff.). Cf. Lidzbarski, Ginza, 27.

the consumption of sexual excretions;[95] like charges are made against the Manichees.[96] The virulence and specificity of this battery of charges leads one to surmise that perhaps the Borborites were in fact relatively strong and numerous in the seventh and eighth centuries[97] in the marshes of southern Mesopotamia, where, like the Mandaeans themselves earlier, they found, in Persian territory, a haven from persecution.

III. The Borborites Before the Fourth Century

Now we turn to the second part of the investigation: can one trace the history of the Borborites further back than Epiphanius and Ephrem, the fixed points of fourth-century heresiology? The violence of the late Mandaean polemic last noted is in fact paralleled by the well-known statements in the *Pistis Sophia* and the *Second Book of Jeu*, works commonly dated, on rather general grounds to be sure, to the third century.[98] These gnostic texts, without mentioning the Borborites by name, polemize against those reprobates who make the consumption of semen and menstrual fluids a sacramental action.[99] The statements give the impression that the people involved are nevertheless regarded as part of a gnostic sub-culture, so to speak.[100] To proceed even further back, one can explore the implications of Epiphanius' claim that the

[95] Specifically, the wine of the eucharistic cup is mixed with the menstrual discharge of an adulterous nun (Petermann, *Thesaurus*, 1.226, lines 11ff.). On the historical context of this very crude polemic cf. Rudolph, *Mandäer*, 1.47ff. and in more detail the same author's "Christentum," 656. Cf. also Brandt's useful study, *Mandäische Religion*, 140ff.

[96] Called *zandiqia* and *mardmania* (Petermann, *Thesaurus*, 1.228, line 10). The first epithet is the standard Arabo-Persian designation for dualist heretics; Drower-Macuch suggest that the second is a corruption of *d-mar mania*, "of the Lord Mari" (*Mandaic Dictionary*, 253). These Manichees are accused of mixing semen obtained through *coitus interruptus* with (sacramental?) wine. In an eastern Syriac source from approximately this period, Manichees of a particular village in the southern Euphrates region are accused of several "Borborite" practices; Guidi, *Chronica*, 33, lines 14ff.; cf. further Nöldeke, "Chronik," 36–37.

[97] The prophet Mohammed and Muslim (civil?) wars are mentioned in the text. On the dating question see Lidzbarski, *Ginza*, 221.

[98] Schmidt-Till, *Schriften*, XXIV, XXXII; Rudolph, *Gnosis: Wesen und Geschichte*, 32. At least as far as the *Pistis Sophia* is concerned, the dating would have to be revised if Drijvers's arguments for the presence of anti-Manichaean polemic in the *Odes of Solomon* (several of which are incorporated and commented on in the *Pistis Sophia*) have any cogency ("Odes," 117ff.).

[99] *Pistis Sophia* IV,147: Schmidt-MacDermot, *Pistis Sophia*, 381; *Second Book of Jeu*, ch. 43: Schmidt-MacDermot, *Bruce Codex*, 100–101.

[100] See Schmidt-MacDermot, *Bruce Codex*, 100–101; the *Second Book of Jeu* claims to know that these serve "the eight powers of the great archon" and that their true god is the "third power of the great archon," the lion- and pig-faced Taricheas! The recipients of the revelations are explicitly warned against sharing the secrets with them. By contrast, in the *Pistis Sophia* the culprits are described in more general terms, almost as hearsay.

Borborites formed an offshoot of the older sect of the Nicolaitans;[101] this is a specific statement, which to my mind deserves *prima facie* some credence (in contrast to Theodoret's improbable derivation of the Borborites from the Valentinians).[102] Rather significantly, Epiphanius says that one group among the Nicolaitans proclaimed the general imperative of gathering the scattered seed of Prunikos from bodies, that is to say, from sexual excretions.[103] This is not the place to review the whole dossier pertaining to the Nicolaitans. It is pertinent to our problem that several sources from the late second and early third centuries talk about the Nicolaitans' luxurious and dissolute mode of living,[104] and some attribute to them a dualistic cosmological system;[105] there is no cogent reason to dismiss out of hand all of this evidence as mere invention. Furthermore it is possible that this sect, as it appears at the end of the second century, possesses a historical continuity with the group of the Nicolaitans in Asia Minor, perhaps a hundred years earlier, as described, in summary terms, in the canonical book of Revelation.[106]

This, of course, has to be kept strictly separate from the problematic claim (of the sectarians themselves or of the orthodox heresiologists?) that the shadowy deacon Nicolaos of Acts was their founding father.[107] That the Borborites originate from within a loosely knit Nicolaitan movement of the second century, and specifically developed from the above-mentioned splinter group, perhaps at the end of the second or early third century, is entirely feasible; the actual splitting off was marked by an adoption of Barbelo-gnostic cosmology coupled with the establishment of the ingathering of the pneumatic seed, through a variety of sexual acts, as the central, constitutive ritual.

This tentative chronology is supported by the fact that the self-

---

[101] Cf. above, p. 293.

[102] PG, 83, 361C. In fact inversely Valentinianism may be tributary to the Barbelo-gnosticism of the *Apocryphon of John* (Quispel, "Valentinian Gnosis," 118ff.).

[103] Holl, *Epiphanius*, 1.270, lines 1–2. By contrast Epiphanius' imputation of specific sexual "ingathering" rites to the Simonian gnostics (Holl, *Epiphanius*, 242, lines 20ff.) is, to my mind, not credible, and seems to be simply an elaboration of Irenaeus' remarks on the licentious living and erotic sorceries of the Simonians (*Haer.* I.23.4; Rousseau-Doutreleau, *Haereses*, 318).

[104] E.g., Iren. *Haer.* I.26.3 (Rousseau-Doutreleau, *Haereses*, 348); Clem. Alex. *Strom.* 3.25 (Stählin-Früchtel, *Clem. Alex., Stromata*, 207).

[105] In particular cf. Ps.-Tertullian, *Haer.*, ch. 5 (reflecting Hippolytus' lost *Syntagma*?), 1401. Cf. Harnack, "Nicolaitans," 415–6.

[106] To my mind, this is still the valid result of the first portion of Harnack's basic study (cf. preceding note), confirmed by the recent investigation of Prigent ("L'hérésie asiate," 17ff.). I do not share Wisse's total scepticism vis-à-vis the veracity of the patristic material concerning the Nicolaitans ("Die Sextus-Sprüche," 65ff.).

[107] See Brox, "Nikolaos und Nikolaiten." This is not the place to go into this exegetical problem, but it is probably safest to conclude as Haenchen does (*Acts*, 264) that the connection with the obscure deacon of Acts is a later fiction, based on the name only.

designation of the group was *Gnōstikoi*, a self-designation they shared with a number of other *non-ascetic* second-century groups,[108] though *not* with the Nicolaitan mother body.[109] Though the Nicolaitans first appear in the cities of western Asia Minor, it would be hazardous thereupon to claim this area as the place of origin of the derivative Borborite movement; admittedly the orgiastic cults, associated with various mother goddesses in Asia Minor and Syria that survive into the Roman period, provide a more plausible background than Egypt.[110] At any rate, the spread of the movement from Syria to Egypt by the third century would be consonant with what is known about some other groups.[111]

IV. Conclusion

It would be an error to attribute too great an antiquity to this Christian sect, the Borborites;[112] it seems to represent already a fairly developed stage of libertine thinking. In particular a direct link with scattered traces of what is generally designated as antinomianism and libertinism in the writings of the early Christian communities[113] cannot be found. The preoccupation with frustrating the process of generation is hardly compatible with an eschatological fervor. The roots of Borborite ide-

---

[108] In particular the followers of Prodicus and the Carpocratians but also the Ophites and Naassenes. (On *Gnōstikoi* as a heretical subdivision cf. Hilgenfeld, *Ketzergeschichte*, 230ff.) It is telling that Epiphanius specifically refuses to grant the label "gnostic" to the (half-mythical?) group of the Valesians, who supposedly systematically practiced castration (Holl, *Epiphanius*, 2.358, lines 8–9). Specifically on Prodicus see Smith, "Gnostikos," 802–4. Quispel suggests that the Alexandrian Gnostics of Prodicus' party may have reached Carthage before the arrival of Tertullian-type orthodoxy ("Valentinian Gnosis," 119). In this connection it is noteworthy that neither *gnōstikos* nor any Coptic equivalent thereof is found as a self-designation in the Nag Hammadi writings (see Siegert, "Selbstbezeichnungen," 129, n. 1). Did the "ascetic gnostics" feel that the term had acquired undesirable "libertine" connotations?

[109] Particularly intriguing is the unnamed heresiarch (known to Clement) who claimed to be a gnostic, and proclaimed that one combats *hēdonē* through the use of *hēdonē* (Clem. Alex., *Strom.* 2.20.117,5: Stählin-Früchtel, *Clem. Alex., Stromata*, 176). Clement compares this view to those of the Nicolaitans, but does not say that the individual belonged to them (*contra* Schoeps, *Zeit*, 260).

[110] Cf. Hörig, *Dea Syria*.

[111] In his youth Origen had to share the hospitality provided by a patroness in Alexandria with a famous Antiochene heretic (a Gnostic?) called Paulus (Eusebius, *Eccl. Hist.* 6.13). The Manichees in Egypt would be another example (cf. Grant, "Manichees and Christians," 431–2).

[112] This view is usually combined with the assumption that the Borborites were a pagan sect subsequently Christianized; so Fendt, *Mysterien*, 13–14 and de Faye, *Gnostiques*, 128. Speyer's argument ("Vorwürfe," 133) that the charges of immorality and cannibalism recorded in the early apologists imply the existence of all the libertine sects described by Epiphanius already in the second century needs refinement.

[113] For a convenient collection of such texts cf. Smith, *Secret Gospel of Mark*, 258ff.

ology are to be sought elsewhere. The theoretical advocacy and actual practice of sexual and dietary encratism is well attested in the second and third Christian centuries. Despite the carefully balanced attitude of intellectuals like Clement and Origen, it often resulted in what can be called a demonization of sexuality.[114]

Particularly interesting, however, is that the uncompromising solution that celibacy is a requirement for full membership in the Christian community was only put into effect in Syria-Mesopotamia, under circumstances and for a length of time which are not entirely clear.[115] The attachment to asceticism, in fact, cut across party lines, so to speak, and the encratite zeal of Mesopotamian Valentinians and Marcionites, for instance, rivalled that of the orthodox.

The evidence of several texts from Nag Hammadi which reflect encratite Syrian traditions reinforces this picture. The Borborite option was simply the other facet of the preoccupation with fasting and sexuality, and is best understood as having initially taken shape in this particular Mesopotamian religious environment. The Borborites knew and rejected the encratite alternative as deceptive and ineffective,[116] and were, it seems, also dissatisfied with the general libertine notion of regarding the free exercise of sexual appetites as simply a symbolic expression of moral indifference or ethical nihilism.[117] They maintained the encratite emphasis on sexuality, but claimed to be able to master it, to neutralize its venom, through a purposeful, systematic exercise thereof.

The Borborites constituted for the most part a secret society that led a clandestine existence within other Christian groups (lay or monastic) in contrast to, for instance, the well-defined Valentinian church in Mesopotamia. Thus it is perhaps safer to talk in terms of a metamorphosis rather than of an extinction of the movement, even when the evidence seems to disappear.[118] The movement drew its sustenance from, and

---

[114] See Chadwick, "Enkrateia," cols. 349ff.

[115] Vööbus, Celibacy; for updating and critique see Murray, "Exhortation," 59–80.

[116] The polemical thrust is made particularly clear by the story of the (attempted!) ascension of Elijah (cf. above, p. 294). By contrast, according to Ephrem, Elijah could ascend to heaven before the eyes of admiring angels because of his virginity (De paradiso, VI.24: Beck, 25, lines 1–2).

[117] This seems to have been the case in particular with the Carpocratians. See Liboron, Gnosis, 28ff. Possible specific connections between the Borborites and the Carpocratians deserve to be investigated in more detail. But one should avoid constructing a synthetized picture of libertine gnosticism, where the real differences of the various groups are disregarded (as unfortunately Jonas [Gnosis, 1.233ff.] does).

[118] In particular the possibility of a late fusion with Messalianism deserves to be looked at, although this is to some extent explaining obscurum per obscurius. One also should note the astonishing similarity of the details of the sexual practices of the Frankist

owed its astonishing persistence to, the same religious and psychological factors which led so many Christians from early on to regard the restraining, or entire suppression, of sexual appetites as absolutely central to salvation. As such, it deserves the attention of historians of religion, in particular of those who, following the insights of Walter Bauer, attempt, in specific historical contexts, to do justice to all of the rich diversity within early Christianity.

sect (the final stage [eighteenth-nineteenth century] of the Jewish Messianic movement launched by Sabbatai Zvi) to those of the Borborites, reported again by opponents, to be sure (see Schoeps, Zeit, 269–70).

ANCIENT TEXTS

Acts, cont.

13:1–3	139
15:13	145
15:19	189
15:13–21	216
21:11	173
21:18	145
General	6, 173, 178, 180, 182, 198, 208, 304

Rom

1:2–5	6
3:8	189
4:12	253
5:12–6:14	253
6:1	253
6:15	253
8:30	242
9:22–23	253
16:27	277, 285

1 Cor

1–4	9, 147, 148, 156
1:11–17	146
1:12–13	284
2	258, 266, 278
2:6–7	147, 214
2:6–8	271, 282
2:6–15	282
2:7	272, 284
2:7–8	258
2:8	244, 274, 275
2:9	143, 146, 147
2:10	275
2:13	272
2:14	258, 268, 270, 271, 279, 280, 282
2:14–3:1	5
2:16	275
5:9	267
6:16	260
6:16–20	273
7:8	284
7:25–40	141
7:31	242
7:32–35	281
7:32–36	273, 281
8:2–3	242
8:6	242
9:5	141
11:2–11	260
15	266, 270, 278
15:3–5	6
15:22	277
15:24–28	285

15:24–29	277
15:28	277
15:35–39	284
15:35–50	276
15:42–48	276
15:43ff.	258
15:43–44	280, 282
15:43–48	270, 283
15:44–47	281
15:45	276
15:45–47	282
15:46	282
15:47	269, 276, 280, 282
15:47–49	284
15:48	276
15:53–54	242
General	141, 143

2 Cor

4:7	253
5:2–4	242

Gal

1:12	212, 214
1:18	145, 201
1:19	145
2:3	188
2:7–9	145
2:9	145, 201
2:12	145, 214, 216
3:23	189
3:26–28	134
General	178, 186, 189, 297

Eph

3	275
3–5	266
3:3–4:9	242
3:4–5	272
3:21	277, 285
4:6	277, 285
5–6	278
5:8	277, 285
5:14	62
5:23	267
6:11–12	269, 279
6:12	267
General	2, 6, 277

Phil

2	249
2:5–11	6, 69
2:8	242
3:10	242

C. NT Apocrypha

D. OT Apocrypha, Pseudepigrapha, Qumran, Mishna, Targumic Material

INDEX

G. Nag Hammadi Codices; Other Gnostic and Related Literature

MODERN AUTHORS

329

332 INDEX